MOVIES
a language
in light

RICHARD L. STROMGREN
MARTIN F. NORDEN
University of Massachusetts at Amherst

PRENTICE–HALL, INC., ENGLEWOOD CLIFFS, NEW JERSEY 07632

Library of Congress Cataloging in Publication Data

Stromgren, Richard L., (date)
  Movies, a language in light.

  Bibliography: p.
  Includes index.
  1. Moving-pictures. 2. Cinematography. I. Norden,
Martin F., (date). II. Title.
PN1994.S85 1984   791.43'024   83-26922
ISBN 0-13-604307-0

Editorial/production supervision:
    Virginia L. McCarthy
Cover design: Photo Plus Art
Manufacturing buyer: Ronald Chapman

Printed in the United States of America

10 9 8 7 6 5 4 3 2 1

ISBN 0-13-604307-0

Prentice-Hall International, Inc., *London*
Prentice-Hall of Australia Pty. Limited, *Sydney*
Editora Prentice-Hall do Brasil, Ltda., *Rio de Janeiro*
Prentice-Hall of Canada Inc., *Toronto*
Prentice-Hall of India Private Limited, *New Delhi*
Prentice-Hall of Japan, Inc., *Tokyo*
Prentice-Hall of Southeast Asia Pte. Ltd., *Singapore*
Whitehall Books Limited, *Wellington, New Zealand*

CONTENTS

PREFACE

‶

Movies have been a part of our lives for as long as most of us can remember, yet we're often at pains to describe what it is about these works that we find entertaining, educating, or enlightening. As "film consumers" living in an unprecedented age of visual communication, we have a particular obligation to ourselves to learn more about the structured images that bombard us daily and the directorial intent behind those images. Filmmakers themselves have long been concerned with understanding the particular manipulative powers of film, as evidenced in this 1926 statement by Russian film pioneer Vsevolod I. Pudovkin: "In order to write a scenario suitable for filming, one must know the methods by which the spectator can be influenced from the screen."[1] This concern has continued through the present day, as indicated in this rather stark statement by contemporary filmmaker Roman Polanski: "I feel pure film exists independently of moral judgments and has no purpose except to manipulate an audience."[2] Since we frequently find ourselves at the "receiving end" of movies, we are obliged to understand their nature more fully, if only to increase our ability to separate the cherries from the pits, so to speak. As Stanley J. Solomon has asserted, "All artists manipulate their material and

[1] V. I. Pudovkin, *Film Technique and Film Acting* (London: Vision Press, 1957), p. 29.
[2] Cited in *Swank Cinématheque* (St. Louis: Swank Motion Pictures, 1975), p. 68.

thereby, to an extent, their audiences—not to mislead them, but to emphasize areas of importance. But audiences have a responsibility to themselves of intellectual awareness, a need to evaluate not only the effects of the art experience but the procedures and techniques that the artist uses to achieve his purpose."[3]

Fully appreciating this point of view, we have provided here a basic introduction to the nature and several functions of film, including an examination of narrative and nonnarrative approaches to film communication. The identification, definition, and basic analysis of film form and function are the keys to the focus and scope of this work. We have looked at the broader spectrum of styles than the term "cinema" or "movies" usually connotates and have also examined the links between filmic style and function as well as those between film and other narrative forms.

Chapter 1 introduces the historical underpinnings of the realist and formalist traditions in film, along with an overview of various film styles and functions. The chapter also briefly examines the influences of technology, industrial considerations, and socio-political climate on the medium.

Chapters 2 through 4 are what we call the "nuts and bolts" chapters, in that they deal primarily with film's basic element of form. Chapter 2 focuses specifically on aspects related to the camera, including visual composition and the various types of movement in front of the camera and by the camera. Apparent movement caused by editing is also briefly considered. The major topics of Chapter 3—editing and sound—are united by the fact that they represent major "post-production" considerations for filmmakers. Chapter 4 concentrates on the subjects the camera records: the setting and the actor.

The remaining chapters explore the medium's functions, or the various ways it may be employed. Chapter 5 studies the ways that filmmakers have used their medium to tell stories, while Chapter 6 examines the growth of particularly durable genres and narrative patterns. Chapters 7 through 9 compare film with other narrative media and also examine the problems of translating a work from one medium to other. In particular, Chapter 7 focuses on the relationship between film and literature, Chapter 8 on film and theatre, and Chapter 9 on film and television.

Chapters 10 and 11 examine the variety of nonnarrative roles of film. The former chapter studies the emergence and characteristics of the documentary film, while the latter focuses on similar issues regarding the avant-garde or experimental film. Finally, Chapter 12 examines the growth and development of film theories and methods of film criticism.

We would be the first to admit that these chapters are not definitive treatments of their topics. At best, they are points of departure. We hope the book will leave the reader with a basic understanding of what film is all about and will also inspire said reader to continue probing critically into this medium that has mesmerized audiences for generations.

ACKNOWLEDGMENTS

We would like to thank Steve Dalphin at Prentice-Hall for his encouragement and unflagging dedication to this project and Seymour Rudin, whose suggestions greatly

[3] Stanley J. Solomon, *The Film Idea* (New York: Harcourt Brace Jovanovich, Inc., 1972), p. 5.

aided us in the preparation of the manuscript. We also wish to thank Mary Corliss of the Museum of Modern Art Film Stills Archive and Paula Klaw of Movie Star News for their assistance in obtaining the majority of the photographs for this book. Other stills were gathered from the Library of Congress and the authors' personal collections.

A final word of appreciation goes to Pip and Kim for their endless patience, sustenance, and moral support.

Richard L. Stromgren
Martin F. Norden
Amherst, Mass.

PHOTO ACKNOWLEDGMENTS

The authors would like to thank the following for making photographic stills available:

Courtesy Library of Congress— 1-1, 1-4a, 2-15, 2-17.

Courtesy Movie Star News— 1-3, 1-4b, 2-1, 2-4, 2-9, 2-11, 2-16, 2-21, 2-22, 2-25, 2-26, 3-1, 3-2a, 3-2b, 3-5, 3-6, 3-7, 4-6, 4-8, 4-9, 4-10, 4-11, 4-12, 5-3, 6-2b, 6-3a, 6-3b, 6-4, 6-6, 6-7, 6-8, 7-1, 7-4, 9-1, 12-2.

Courtesy Museum of Modern Art/Film Stills Archive— 1-5, 2-3, 2-5, 2-6, 2-8, 2-13a, 2-13b, 2-14, 2-18, 2-19, 2-20, 2-24, 3-3, 3-8, 3-9, 4-1, 4-2a, 4-2b, 4-3, 4-4, 4-5, 4-7, 4-15, 5-2, 5-5a, 5-5b, 5-7, 6-2a, 6-9, 6-10, 7-2, 7-5, 8-3, 9-2, 12-3, 12-5.

Courtesy National Film Archive/Stills Library (British Film Institute)— 5-1, 6-1, 6-5.

Courtesy University of Massachusetts Film Archive— 1-2, 2-2, 2-7, 2-10, 2-12, 2-23, 3-4, 4-13, 4-14, 5-4, 5-6, 7-3, 8-1, 8-2, 8-4a, 8-4b, 8-4c, 10-1, 10-2a, 10-2b, 10-3, 10-4, 10-5, 10-6, 11-1, 11-2, 11-3, 12-4.

1

AN EVOLUTION
IN FILM FORM
AND FUNCTION

EARLY TRENDS:
THE REALIST AND FORMALIST TRADITIONS

Even as the first films flickered across Parisian and New York screens in the 1890s, the film medium began revealing a considerable range of styles and uses. Some filmmakers quickly discovered that certain qualities of film allowed them to use their cameras as more than straight recording devices. They learned they could use the medium to interpret and comment on the world surrounding them or to create a world of their own through the magic of camera composition, special effects, and editing. Motion pictures quickly became a means of instruction, documentation, diversion, and self-expression

Though the emerging cinematic styles extended over a broad range, most early filmmakers tended to embrace one of two philosophies: the belief that film should be a mirror held up to nature, a view that emphasized the recording and revealing properties of film; or the belief that the medium's special creative potential should be exploited to render imaginative worlds or fanciful versions of the real one. The former tendency, frequently labeled *realism*, stressed the *content* of film, while the latter tendency, *formalism*, emphasized the *form* of the medium. In very basic terms, we may say that it was a conflict of "the what" versus "the

1

how." The differences of these two approaches, which eventually served as the foundations for the first two schools of film theory, were reflected in some of the first films ever produced. We need look no further than to the works of a handful of pioneers to see one tendency or the other.

Recordings of Life

Auguste and Louis Lumière, two brothers who manufactured photographic equipment and supplies in southern France, quickly became associated with the rudiments of newsreel-like cinema. Their brief films, made near the turn of the century and running less than a minute each, provided a collage of real-world happenings in and around the region in which they lived. Among the events they recorded on film were boats leaving a harbor, military maneuvers, a train pulling into a railway station, activities at a Marseilles fish market, Auguste Lumière having breakfast with his family, and, in what may be the earliest of all films, the Lumière workers leaving the factory for their lunch break. With their brevity and lack of story lines, these films very much resembled today's home movies.

American studios of the day, such as the Edison and Biograph companies, were also busy recording events on film, many of which were momentous and newsworthy. Personalities in the news and natural disasters were particular favorites. Among the topics preserved on film were Queen Victoria's Diamond Jubilee (and, a few years later, her state funeral), Pope Leo XIII in his carriage in Rome, the visit of Prince Henry of Prussia, and the 1901 inaugural parade of President William McKinley and, later that same year, his funeral. Also recorded were the Galveston flood of 1900, the great Baltimore fire of 1904, and the San Francisco earthquake of 1906. Perhaps less arresting but still popular were the human-interest films of people at work, at play, and on tour, including countless fire department and military drills. Among the "travelogues," themselves both exotic and pedestrian, was a clip showing the arrival of immigrants at New York's Ellis Island.

The Reconstruction

Whenever time or distance prevented the recording of a newsworthy event on film, many of the early studies frequently reconstructed the events before their cameras. Though today we may find such actions questionable, the studios demonstrated undeniable imagination and ingenuity in the creation of such works. In addition to such historical recreations as Thomas Edison's *Execution of Mary Queen of Scots* (1895), contemporary events—such as the Russo-Japanese, Boer, and Spanish-American wars—were staged on studio battlefields, or, in the case of sea battles, in studio watertanks with miniature gunboats. The 1901 electrocution of President McKinley's assassin was staged at Edison's studio that year, while a popular boxing match of the time (the 1903 McGovern-Corbett fight) was recreated by the fighters themselves at the Biograph Studio, which used a painted backdrop of an audience-filled arena. And when major natural phenomena could not be recorded, they too were recreated (as Biograph did in 1906 with the eruption of Mt. Vesuvius) through miniatures and other wonders of early special-effects cinematography.

Recorded Stage Business

The reconstruction of news events illustrates that the division between the realistic and formalistic traditions was not as clear-cut as it might appear at first. A good deal of artistic inspiration and studio wizardry clearly went into many of these recreations of real-life events. By the same token, the earlist nondocumentary footage came close to fulfilling a straight recording function: not of news events but of bits of staged business. Much of it was little more than the docu-

Figure 1-1 Many turn-of-the-century films consisted of slightly risque presentations, such as this serpentine dance performed in an 1896 Biograph film by the exotic dancer "Annabelle."

menting of stage routines: brief vignettes of business that had their roots in vaudeville and the variety theater. Edison's *Pie Eating Contest* (1897) and Biograph's
Flag Dance (1903), in which a girl in a costume resembling Old Glory performs a
flag-waving dance, are fairly typical, but the routines were so diverse as to make
categorizing difficult. One significant trend, however, was toward the presentation
of mildly erotic dances and skits. Edison's *Dance of Fatima* (1897) was followed by
Biograph's *The Summer Girl* (1903), in which a woman removes her shoes and
stockings and wades across a stream, and *As Seen on the Curtain* (1904), which
depicts a woman dressing behind a window shade in silhouette. Voyeuristic appeal
was further demonstrated in a 1906 series of Biograph films that went beyond the
limits of burlesque and vaudeville entertainment by focusing on such questionable
or illegal "sports" as dog fighting (*Police Raid on a Dog Fight*), cock fighting (*A
Raid on a Cock Fight*), and rat killing (*Scene in a Rat Pit*).[1]

The practices of reconstructing news events and recording staged bits of
business help illustrate this basic observation on the nature of cinema: that virtually every film consists of a tension or balance between the formalistic and realistic tendencies. The reconstruction, while replicating to some degree the
authenticity of the straight cinematographic record, owed its success largely to the
ingenuity of the filmmaker and the tricks of the camera. The recorded bit of staged
business, on the other hand, usually consisted of a creative routine that had little
in common with the content of the newsreel, but their forms were nearly identical;
they both involved little cinematic invention and usually remained straight recordings of what was in front of the camera.

Storytelling

Almost as soon as filmmakers began using film to record and recreate action from life and from the stage, they also started using it for storytelling purposes.
Many of our earliest films revealed that storytelling could consist of a linkage of
realistic events or could provide fanciful excursions into imagined worlds. By 1900,
French magician-turned-filmmaker Georges Méliès was experimenting with the
rudiments of narrative by joining together a series of highly inventive (if rather
stagy-looking) tableaux which he himself called "artificially arranged scenes." With
wit and humor, Méliès recreated such fairy tales as *Cinderella* (1899), and even
brought his audiences to another world in his best-remembered film, *A Trip to the
Moon* (1902). Many of the special moments in Méliès' films were created through
careful staging and editing. In *The Terrible Turkish Executioner* (1903), for example,
four men beheaded by the title character manage (via editing) to "pull themselves
together" before taking their revenge on the executioner by cutting him in two
at the waist. Again through the magic of editing, the executioner attaches his lower
half, as if it were a pair of pants, before running after his former victims (see Fig.
1–2).

While some audiences were losing themselves in the contrived settings of
Méliès, others were finding equal pleasure recognizing the very lifelike situations
into which they found themselves projected. The Lumière brothers' brief comic
routine *Teasing the Gardener* (1895) involves a boy stepping on the hose of an
unsuspecting gardener and then releasing it when the gardener holds the nozzle
to his face for inspection. Film historians have frequently heralded it as the first
film to contain the rudiments of storytelling, and it clearly went beyond cinematic

Figure 1-2   *The Terrible Turkish Executioner* (1903—French). Georges Méliès was the most prominent early filmmaker to explore the magical side of the medium. He frequently wove fanciful if not downright bizarre stories and relied heavily on artificial surroundings. His films tend to look very theatrical with one notable difference: he frequently employed editing to create trick effects that would be impossible to accomplish on the stage. *The Terrible Turkish Executioner,* which features beheaded men regaining their heads through the artifice of editing, is one of countless examples of Méliès' editing ingenuity.

reporting and into the realm of staged events. Despite its contrived nature, the film drew praise for its realistic quality. Russian author Maxim Gorki, for example, responded to *Teasing the Gardener* by exclaiming, "You think the spray is going to hit you, too, and instinctively shrink back."[2]

The realist and formalist traditions continued to manifest themselves in the narrative works of such major pioneer filmmakers as Méliès, Edwin S. Porter, D. W. Griffith, Thomas Ince, and Mack Sennett, as well as in the works of their protégés and imitators, who were legion. Méliès' highly imaginative fantasies, the French trick films that combined chases with a variety of special effects, and the post-World War I German films depicting mythological stories and visions of disturbed minds were all elements of the formalistic tradition. Porter's *The Life of an American Fireman* (1903), which combines a rudimentary narrative with documentary footage of firemen on the job, was an early model of screen realism, as was his celebrated *The Great Train Robbery,* a 1903 "eastern Western" filmed in New Jersey, particularly in its rendering of the pursuit of the bandits. Other films striving for a sense of realism were Ince's westerns and social dramas and Griffith's period dramas, both large and small. In Griffith's *The Birth of a Nation* (1915), for example, the director took great pride in creating "historical facsimiles" of such events as Lee's surrender at Appomattox and the Lincoln assassination. As shown in Fig. 1–3, Mack Sennett's Keystone Kops movies struck an interesting balance

Figure 1-3 This publicity photo suggests the anarchy and, in particular, the hair-raising stunts that became the Keystone Kops' trademark. Automobiles, streetcars, and other vehicles came ever so close to colliding during the high-speed chases that marked virtually every Keystone Kops movie.

of formalistic and realistic qualities by featuring highly improbable stories and situations (primarily crazy chases offered in endless variations) presented in highly realistic, even death-defying, ways.

Messages

Several early directors also demonstrated an interest and ability to go beyond recording or recreating elements of the real world to reflect, interpret, and comment on what they depicted. They gave an added dimension to the realist tradition by moving beyond mere surface detail to embrace *ideas about* the real world. Edwin S. Porter was one of the first filmmakers to explore social problems. In *The Ex-Convict* (1904), he portrayed a poverty-stricken young man released from prison only to find himself at the mercy of an affluent industrialist. The following year, Porter directed *The Kleptomaniac*, which focuses on the unequal treatment of a penniless young mother accused of stealing a loaf of bread and the rich and influential title character when both are brought to trial. Following Porter's lead,

Thomas Ince sought to reflect social injustice in many of his films. A fine exam.. ....
is a feature-length work entitled *The Italian* (1915), in which an immigrant gon-
dolier and his family become the victims of both poverty and the judicial system
in the land of opportunity.

Filmmakers also exhibited an early awareness of the medium's ability to
sell goods and services as well as to explore and promote ideas. Even before Porter
and Ince were producing their "persuasive" works, the film medium was being
enlisted as a means of commercial advertising. In 1897, just a year after the first
public showing of films in the United States, the Edison company was helping to
sell cigarettes in a short film that shows Uncle Sam, a clergyman, an Indian, and
a businessman sitting in front of a backdrop bearing the words "Admiral Cigarettes." An ashcan-size box breaks apart and a girl, attired in a striking costume,
moves across the stage toward the seated men and hands them cigarettes. She
then unfurls a banner that reads, "We All Smoke." The strangeness of this early
"commercial" was matched by Edison's *Romance of the Rails* (1903), which featured the rewards of travel on the Lackawanna Railroad, including clean air, instant romance, and on-board marriage ceremonies.

DEVELOPING RANGE IN STYLES
AND FUNCTIONS

The wide range of styles and functions that emerged since the medium's salad
days reflects the ways in which film has stimulated the imagination, sparked the
curiosity, and finally met the needs of artists, entertainers, historians, social activ-
ists, educators, and business people. Tremendously diverse patterns and styles have
evolved from the initial images of the real and fictional worlds. In particular, the
ten- and twenty-minute slapstick comedies and melodramas that filled the screens
of the earliest makeshift theaters have given way to an almost endless proliferation
of story categories. These include: the horror, gangster, western, war, adventure,
costume spectacle, musical comedy, science fiction, social realist, and comic fantasy genres. Over the years, the integration of two or more of these generic forms
has produced such hybrids as western comedies, musical comedy adventures, and
western musical comedy spectacles.

The documentary and experimental films have likewise evolved into a
range of frequently overlapping styles and functions. Films that draw from both
the documentary and experimental traditions may be traced to the poetic naturalism of Robert Flaherty's documentaries, made in the 1920s, and the expressive
"city symphony" films produced in European capitals during the same decade.
Experimental approaches to storytelling, and narrative films that follow stylistic
approaches usually associated with documentaries, have tended to obscure the
divisions between these major forms. Just as Shakespeare mixed historical, tragical,
comical, and pastoral elements into seemingly limitless combinations, we have today such generic entities as the experimental narrative, the creative documentary,
and documentary narrative. In addition, the perspective, philosophy, or humor
may also be varied, as Ivor Montagu has pointed out in his discussion of range:

Cynically sentimental . . . scathing and unsentimental . . . philosophically pessimistic . . . philosophically optimistic . . . philosophically satirical . . . philosophical-poetical . . . or plain lyrical-poetical.[3]

Commentary by the artists, educators, theorists, and business people who have worked in film helps illustrate the range of motion-picture forms and functions. Sergei Eisenstein, the leading filmmaker and theorist of the Soviet silent cinema, called film "an international meeting place for living ideas." Iris Barry, founder of the New York Museum of Modern Art Film Library, described the function of film as a vehicle "to reflect contemporary history as it flows." Contemporary experimentalist Ed Emshwiller sees the mission of film as something "to share and expand awareness," while Greek director Michael Cacoyannis says it is "to attack people's minds via their emotions."

Stan Brakhage, another prime mover in the American experimental film movement, sees a dichotomy of functions—"on the one hand: Provision—that is, the maintenance of 'ritual' in the society (Hollywood/TV, etc.); on the other: Vision—the extension of human perceptibility (works of Art)." Brakhage's focus on human perceptibility is in itself an echo of D. W. Griffith's incantation of some sixty years before—"The thing I am trying to do, above all else, is to make you see."[4]

Ivor Montagu best summarizes the range of possibilities:

Films are as complex as living beings, their ultimate possibilities as unpredictable. With the power of graphic representation of movement, with the power of narrative that temporal succession of appearances brings, with enhancement by association of sound, with precise control of all these elements, the range and depth of expression, the vividness and impressiveness of communication by film become virtually unbounded.[5]

Thus, the styles and functions of film have evolved according to the ways that its variously motivated practitioners have perceived and explored its potential. This evolution is also affected by changes in technology, methods of production, and the conditioning and resulting changes in audiences as well.

EFFECTS OF TECHNOLOGY, INDUSTRY, AND AUDIENCE DISPOSITION

We are in a better position to understand and appreciate the development of film's diverse styles and purposes if we examine some of the key factors affecting the medium's growth. These include its technical aspects, the nature of the film industry, and the constantly changing film audience.

The evolution of motion pictures has always been closely tied to technology. The combination of several inventions designed to record and exhibit images directly influenced the directions the new medium would take. The integration of photography and projection produced the *projected, moving, photographic picture* that we know today as movies or film.

A means of projecting the hand-drawn image had been developed as early as the seventeenth-century with the invention of the magic lantern. With it came the slide show, which could take the form of illustrated lectures and stories for the enlightenment and amusement of audiences. The photographic image—a child of mechanics, optics, and chemistry—made its appearance in the 1840s, and besides its influence on theater, journalism, and graphic arts, it eventually replaced the hand-drawn slides exhibited in theatres and salons. The photographic image allowed the slide show to become a setting for photojournalism (that is, the depiction of real persons, places, and events). It also provided a new dimension of realism to those slide shows that attempted to tell stories. The final ingredient—motion—was added with the invention of the motion-picture camera and projector in the 1880s. The medium now was the new picture gallery, the new illustrated story-book, and the new photographic journal, all rolled into one.

Technology has continued to be a key to stylistic development and to the expansion and refinement of the ways in which film can be utilized. For example, the coming of sound profoundly affected the nature of screen comedy, allowing it to expand from slapstick, mime, and visual byplay to include witty repartee, double entendre, and wisecrack. The introduction of a whole new film genre—the musical—was likewise the result of the screen finding its voice. More recent technological refinements have resulted in the creation of highly light-sensitive lenses and film stocks, which in turn have provided more flexibility in composition and the use of available light sources. The ever-expanding capabilities of studio and laboratory technicians have contributed to new explorations of styles and functions, while increasingly versatile camera, projection, and sound-recording equipment have extended the range of the medium to an extent not even fathomed by the film pioneers. Some innovations, such as "Sensurround" (huge bass speakers which send low-tone vibrations through auditoriums and audiences alike), have played very limited roles, while others, such as the wide-screen processes, which use special lenses to stretch images to about twice their normal widths, have become basic to the industry and to the art.

The organization of the international film industries and the methods of production have also influenced the styles and functions of film. The inauguration of longer narrative films, brought about by both the inclination of progressive studios and audience acceptance, allowed for refinements and further definition within the story form. These include not only more intricate plotting but also fuller character developments and detail in setting and decor. Another important influence has centered on the varying degrees of involvement of individual directors in the various stages of film production, from original script to final cut. Under the old Hollywood studio system, the division of responsibility among several studio departments for the creation of a film had decentralized creative contributions and placed the director in the position of *metteur-en-scène*, or the person who stages the action and is barely a step removed from the cinematographer. Only the most assertive and creative filmmakers have earned the reputation of *auteur,* or key creator of a film.

Along with the refinements in motion-picture technology and the development of the three-tiered film industry (namely, production, distribution, and exhibition), an audience for the new medium was receiving its training. Human conditioning and training in visual communication had their beginnings long before the production of the first motion picture, of course. Film historians have paid particular attention to the trends in late nineteenth-century theater as a sig-

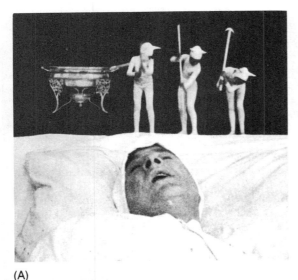

(A)

(B)

Figure 1-4 (A & B)   *Dreams of a Rarebit Fiend*
(1906—American) / *Raiders of the Lost Ark* (1981—
American). The range in cinematic style and treatment
of the fantasy/adventure film can be seen by
comparing the early short by Edwin S. Porter, *Dreams
of a Rarebit Fiend,* with Steven Spielberg's more
recent *Raiders of the Lost Ark.* Although the length
and complexity of narrative and production values put
the films light years apart, they both make effective
use of special effects cinematography and have
proven popular with large numbers of moviegoers.

nificant prelude to screen drama. They have pointed out that a strong tendency
toward naturalistic detail in both setting and the way the action progressed created
an appropriate climate for the naturalistic storytelling and reportage that were to
follow on the screen. Turn-of-the-century theater whetted audiences' appetites for
realistic visual detail, and the new medium of cinema more than satisfied them.

A tendency toward detailed visual description in literature that foreshadowed cinematic means of composition and storytelling probably had a conditioning effect on film audiences as well. Charles Dickens is the most prominent of
several nineteenth-century authors credited with providing strong senses of visual
perception, shot composition, iconography, and other cinematic-like characteristics in their literary works. Dickens' descriptions of what young Pip encounters

when he enters the home of Miss Haversham in *Great Expectations* and of Ebenezer Scrooge's visitation by the Ghost of Christmas Present in *A Christmas Carol* are only two of many examples of a "cinematic" quality in Dickens' writings.

More pervasive factors that primed audiences for the coming of cinema were the developments in photoengraving, which made possible the mass dissemination of photographs through both journalistic and pulp-fiction outlets. Such illustrations became easily accessible to mass audiences at low cost and began playing central roles in everyday communication. Following their exposure to such developments in theater and mass media, audiences met the arrival of moving photographic images with enthusiasm and fascination.

Audience conditioning, which modifies expectations and behavior, also helps determine the directions in style and content of the films themselves. Repeated viewing sharpens analytical and interpretive skills, and it also reinforces our notions concerning the nature of film styles and techniques according to what we have experienced in past viewing situations. For example, the use of the hand-held camera suggests an impromptu, unrehearsed view of life to us because of the associations we have already established between spontaneous events and their casual or unplanned capture by the camera. Conditioning also involves the social climate or mood at the time of viewing. For instance, the temperament of audiences of the late forties and early fifties set the stage for a new era of screen realism, while the bitter experience of the Vietnam War left a void as far as dramatic treatment of that experience is concerned. John Wayne's *The Green Berets* (1968) was one of the few major films produced with a Vietnam setting while the war was still being fought (see Fig. 1–5). The void was filled by escapist delights

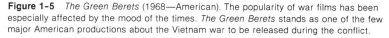

Figure 1-5 *The Green Berets* (1968—American). The popularity of war films has been especially affected by the mood of the times. *The Green Berets* stands as one of the few major American productions about the Vietnam war to be released during the conflict.

of nostalgic reverie, flirtations with the occult, and science fiction—unique blendings of the formalist and realist traditions. Since 1975, the Vietnam War has been accepted, however tentatively, as a suitable subject for screen storytelling. But the fanciful exploits featured in the *Superman* and *Star Wars* movies and in fantasy films by superstar director Steven Spielberg, such as *Close Encounters of the Third Kind* (1977), *Raiders of the Lost Ark* (1981), and *E. T.* (1982), have proven far more popular with modern audiences than films focusing on the grim realities of the war and various social ills. There seems little question that the ways viewers comprehend, accept, and use the information on a movie screen depend a great deal on prevailing social attitudes and on the ways they as individuals have adapted to them.

Viewers' perceptions and uses of film-mediated information also depend on the extent to which the viewers have absorbed and understood the techniques and styles of filmmaking that have evolved over the years. Today's moviegoers readily understand such devices as the jump cut (an editing technique that creates a momentary rupture in a film's continuity) and the flashforward (a brief glimpse at a future development in a film's story edited into the film's present situation). However, their counterparts of yesteryear would have been perplexed after viewing these techniques. Audiences today have experienced a wide range of film and television communication in substantial doses, and this exposure has changed both their abilities and perspectives in relating to the medium. They are able, even eager, to cope with such elements of the recent "schooling" in screen language, as elliptical narrative films bearing complex messages, the unmanipulated and spontaneous experiences of modern documentaries, and the often indescribable beauty of the abstract mosaics-in-motion created by experimental filmmakers through computers. The education and conditioning of film audiences continue to affect both viewer perceptions and filmmaker judgments today.

Technology, industry, and the sociopolitical climate have also contributed to the evolution of the nonnarrative film as well as to the inspiration of filmmakers. The documentary film, long a subject of experimentation during the medium's silent era, became, by the 1930s, a firmly established genre serving a variety of functions. It was further revolutionized by the development of lightweight film-making equipment, and highly light-sensitive lenses and film stocks (making it relatively easy to film under uncontrolled low-lighting situations) during the late 1950s and early 1960s. And television continues to influence the styles and functions of documentaries on both the large and small screens.

The experimental film has by definition been about the business of exploring new approaches to film form and function. From its origins in the silent era and through successive waves, it has continued to examine both real and imagined worlds through untried and unfamiliar applications of film's capabilities and resources. Of the major film forms, it has been the least inhibited by industrial and audience demands and expectations, and it has the greatest potential for leading the way in discovering the developing new filmic possibilities. The yet unrealized uses and forms of film will only serve to expand the range of the medium, which to date is already tremendous. As Ivor Montagu has suggested, "The range and depth of expression, the vividness and impressiveness of communication by film become virtually unbounded. . . ."[6]

NOTES

[1]Kemp R. Niver, *Motion Pictures from the Library of Congress Paper Print Collection, 1894–1912* (Berkeley: University of California Press, 1967), p. 3.

[2]Cited in Siegfried Kracauer, *Theory of Film: The Redemption of Physical Reality* (New York: Oxford University Press, 1960), p. 31.

[3]Ivor Montagu, *Film World: A Guide to Cinema* (Baltimore: Penguin, 1964), p. 301.

[4]A number of these views were expressed in "Film Directors on Film: A Symposium," *Arts in Society*, 4, no. 1 (Winter 1966–67), pp. 60–103.

[5]Montagu, *Film World*, p. 305.

[6]Ibid.

2

FILM PROPERTIES
AND FUNDAMENTALS
OF TECHNIQUE:
COMPOSITION AND
MOVEMENT

THE FILM EXPERIENCE

Before we begin our initial discussions of the nature of film and the basic compositional techniques that filmmakers employ, we find it important to examine, however briefly, the nature of the film experience. Whether a filmgoer is absorbing a story, a news event, or visual poetry, the film experience is a marvelously varied and complex process and is determined by a combination of technological processes and human traits, both psychological and physiological. The technological aspects involve the photographing and subsequent projection of a series of still images that have been recorded by a camera. The process, like straight photography, permits the recording of images on a light-sensitive emulsion that, when developed, provides a permanent record of the photographed scene. The basic difference between photography and cinematography is that the latter process records images repeatedly and in rapid succession, usually at the rate of 24 frames (that is, 24 individual photographs) per second. If neither the camera nor its subject moves, the differences between the resulting succession of cinematic images and the single photographic image are negligible. However, with the introduction of movement by either the movie camera or its subject or both, the cinematic images become a series of phase photographs with each frame recording a step or phase of the action. In a sense, the term *motion picture* is a misnomer, as no motion ever actually occurs within any single frame.

Yet the film experience depends on more than technology. The physiological phenomenon known as *persistence of vision* contributes to the experience a great deal by creating an illusion of motion when the series of still images are run through a projector and reflected on a screen at the rate of 24 frames per second. This characteristic of the human eye permits the retention of the image on the retina for a fraction of a second after the image on the screen has disappeared. The eye then blends this "after-image" with the next cinematographic image to appear a split-second later. This process repeats many times a second during the film-viewing experience and makes the succeeding images within a shot appear as one continuous image evolving over time. The "moving" photograph, the recording of actuality with action preserved, fascinated early audiences and allowed such early cinema subjects as breaking surf, hurtling trains, and countless street parades to win enthusiastic followings.

Persistence of vision is only part of the story, however; it takes psychological motivation and conditioning to make the *experience* of film complete. Viewing a film activates not only the optic nerve but also the powers of imagination, which are considerable.[1] For example, our imagination is capable of extending an image beyond the borders of the frame. If we are viewing a close-up of a person's face, we do not find ourselves asking, "What happened to the rest of that person?" Instead, we accept that person's total presence because our minds have compensated for the lack of information. This extension of "seeing" also allows us to assume that the setting continues indefinitely even though our view may be restricted by the limits of the camera lens. Our imagination is also capable of compensating for the lack of color in black-and-white films, since we seldom ask ourselves, during the course of a film, "Why is that man's face off-white?" or "Why is the apple that woman is eating not red but gray?" Our mind automatically fills in the gaps in this information, just as it helps us bridge the gap between two shots; it enables us to make the necessary links between seemingly unrelated shots and to accept them as details of the same action.

The film experience thus goes beyond the physical characteristics of the medium and the qualities of human vision to include the ways that viewers absorb and interpret the images thrust before them. The interpretation of images is in turn shaped to some degree by the controls exercised by the filmmaker over specific properties of the medium and their employment in the general design of the film.

FILM PROPERTIES AND AREAS OF CONTROL

With the aid of viewers' imaginations, filmmakers communicate thoughts, interpret the world around them, and give visual expression to mental images through the employment of specific attributes of film. Some are almost exclusively "filmic" (though they extend considerably into the realm of television) and are the most readily recognizable elements of what we might call *film language*. These include the qualities of the two-dimensional moving image and various characteristics of the editing process. Film shares other characteristics, such as line, color, mass, tempo, and sound, with many other art forms and media.

Whether they are unique to the medium or shared, the properties of film form the basis for cinematic expression and style. In addition, a number of film's *limitations* have also become important elements of style. Although a handful of early filmmakers experimented with variously shaped frames (most notably, D. W. Griffith, Sergei Eisenstein, and Abel Gance), most filmmakers of the time worked within the fixed proportions of the frame. Moreover, most of these same directors had to give vent to their expressions through a two-dimensional medium that lacked naturalistic color and sound, and subtleties of lighting. Even in the wake of the technical advances that eliminated or drastically curtailed these limitations, many still remain and have become significant factors in the nature of film communication and aesthetics.

Whether they are dealing with simple film records or elaborate visions of the world, filmmakers have essentially six major elements or controls with which to work. They stand as reasonably distinct elements that provide a logical framework for the study of the characteristics, limitations, and implications for the more creative and efficient use of film. Offered here are brief summaries of these elements, with in-depth discussions to follow.

Composition, the first of these elements, embraces factors identical with photography. These include matters of perspective, framing, lighting, apparent distance between the camera and the objects it records, and reduction of the subject matter to a two-dimensional image: in general, the organization of space and objects within the frame. A number of these factors obviously have links with theater, painting, sculpture, and the other graphic and dramatic arts.

Movement, the second of the elements, is shared to some degree with theater and dance but only implied in photography and painting. It may be conveniently categorized and examined according to the three ways it may be created. *Primary movement* refers to the movement of objects within the frame. The images of leaves blowing in the wind, a horse trotting along a country road, or two lovers running to embrace one another are all examples of primary movement (provided the camera itself is stationary). *Secondary movement* suggests movement by the camera while it records the scene. Instances of secondary movement occur when the camera appears to be following someone or something within the frame, for example, or when the size of stationary objects appears to increase or decrease during the course of a shot. *Tertiary movement* refers to apparent movement created or suggested through the editing process; that is, by the shifting perspective of the camera between shots. Any or all of the three methods of movement may be combined, as in this example from the British film *Great Expectations* (1947), directed by David Lean. In the opening scene, young Pip crosses the moors to a churchyard cemetery. Lean "choreographed" the scene by combining the primary movements of the boy walking along the bleak path into the churchyard with branches of nearby trees swaying in the wind. He then added to this a secondary movement involving the exploration of the graveyard by a moving camera that provides a nervous look at the surroundings, much as the boy would have seen them. Shortly thereafter, a shocking confrontation for Pip (and for the audience) occurs when the convict, Magwitch, looms suddenly over the headstones. This frightening moment is created by a cut from the boy kneeling at his parents' grave to a close-up of the convict's face. This technique is, of course, part of the editing process, and it represents an example of tertiary movement. Through this combination of movements, Lean has quickly and effectively provided both basic exposition and dramatic intensity within the opening moments of the film.

Editing, the third element, covers the larger range of functions served by the selection and arrangement of film pieces. Filmmakers follow numerous criteria for determining choice, length, and sequence of individual shots in their films. The editing styles that have emerged from these criteria include the basic forms of linkage that provide continuity for both narrative and nonnarrative construction. They also include the constructive or creative editing styles through which filmmakers build scenes or metaphors from individual shots. If a shot of a fox followed that of a politician, for example, the symbolic or metaphoric meaning of such a juxtaposition would be clear. They further include rhythmic editing that creates and controls a film's tempo and the passage of time.[2]

Sound constitutes the fourth element of control in film construction. Natural and artificial sound effects and the human voice brought a new dimension to all cinematic forms with the arrival of "the talkies" in the late 1920s. Music, though not then recorded in synchronization with the images on film, had been a conspicuous part of early film exhibition by way of piano accompanists and theatrical orchestras, and it has remained a critical ingredient. Both sound and silence frequently play more than incidental roles in the creation of mood, as witnessed in the graveyard scene from *Great Expectations,* for example. Visual elements provide much of the dramatic force in this opening scene, but they are greatly enhanced by whistling wind, the clacking of tree branches, and, finally, the unnerving absence of human sounds.

Setting and decor, the fifth area of control, is often linked with composition and combined with several other factors that make up the total atmosphere of the scene. At its most basic, it gives the action of the scene a physical presence or location; in its more refined form, it provides the film with its total environment replete with a wealth of visual detail. Again, the graveyard scene from *Great Expectations* works well as a case in point, with its trees, headstones, and moors contributing to a general atmosphere or ambience rich in mysterious and foreboding qualities.

Acting, the final element, has a strong affinity with theater, yet critical differences remain. The celluloid medium usually requires far subtler and more naturalistic performances because of its greater intimacy created through close-ups. In addition, film directors often give priority to actors' physical appearances over their actual acting abilities, which in some cases may be minimal. Theater actors must give performances sustained over a period of minutes or even hours, but film actors are usually called upon to emote for periods of only a few seconds at a time. What appears to be a sustained acting performance in film is actually built from short bursts of acting recorded on celluloid by the director and arranged by the editor. In the final analysis, theater is the actor's medium but film is the director's medium.

Filmmakers thus exercise their techniques and artistry through the selection and control of these six broad areas. Whether they are recording life on the run, recreating history, creating spectacle, or telling a simple story, screenwriters, producers, directors, actors, composers, scenic designers, and the other artists and technicians involved in designing and constructing films must either consciously or unconsciously make creative decisions involving these areas. Recognizing their importance, we have devoted the remainder of this chapter and the entire next two chapters to a thorough exploration of the range of choices within these six categories.

COMPOSITION AND PERSPECTIVE

> *To show something as everyone sees it is to have accomplished nothing.*
> —V. I. Pudovkin, *On Film Technique*

The Shot

Film scholars continue to wrangle over the most basic unit or means of expression in film. "The image" and "the frame" have their proponents, but we prefer *the shot*, the unit of construction that begins and ends with a single running of the camera. In a completed film, it eventually gives way to another shot providing some change in angle, perspective, location, time, subject, or any combination thereof (unless of course the shot is the last one in the film). This is perhaps as close as we can come to an immutable law in filmic construction.

A shot usually runs between three and twenty seconds, but numerous filmmakers have worked with shots running much shorter or longer. At the former extreme, experimentalists such as Charles Braverman and Robert Breer have included shots as brief as one and two frames in their films—shots only fractions of a second long. For example, Braverman's aptly titled *American Time Capsule* (1968), a film that condenses nearly 200 years of American history into three minutes through approximately 1,300 paintings and photographs, contains a single-frame shot of the event that signaled the official end of World War II: the Japanese surrender aboard the battleship *Missouri*. The shot is not identifiable at normal running speed, yet a two-frame shot of Mickey Mouse, inserted at another point in the film, is easily recognizable. The extent to which such shots can be seen and recognized depends on the complexity of their designs and the familiarity of their images, if indeed the images have representational qualities at all. Robert Breer's *Blazes* (1961), for instance, consists of 100 different splashes of pure color repeated 40 times, each shot lasting one frame. The "viewability" of very brief shots depends not only on their familiarity and clarity but also on the length of the shots with which they are juxtaposed. Most viewers could probably identify a single-frame image of the Coca-Cola trademark inserted in the midst of a 20-second shot but not a single-frame shot of a nondescript landscape edited together with other equally brief shots.

At the other end of the shot-length spectrum are films that consist solely of one shot each and that run for a seemingly interminable amount of time. Controversial artist Andy Warhol is responsible for most of these rarities, including *Sleep* (1963–64), a six-hour shot of a person sleeping, and *Empire* (1964), an eight-hour shot of the Empire State Building. Both films feature a near-total lack of movement of any kind and they demonstrate, if nothing else, the intolerability of real time on the screen. A number of narrative films have also manifested an interest in the use of long-running shots, though not nearly on the scale of the Warhol epics. These include Miklós Jancsó's *Red Psalm* (1971), an 88-minute film that depicts a peasant revolt in nineteenth-century Hungary through the use of less than 20 carefully rehearsed and choreographed shots. Also included is Alfred Hitchcock's *Rope* (1948), a feature-length murder mystery that appears to consist of a single run of a highly mobile camera but is actually made up of ten-minute shots edited together to form a relatively seamless movie (see Fig. 2–1).

For the sake of clarity, we will initially set aside the element of motion in our examination of shot composition and perspective. These variables, which are also basic to photography, include the relationship of various elements within the shot to one another, relationships of the camera to elements within the shot (that is, camera angle, perspective, and apparent distance between the camera and the objects it has recorded), framing or scope of the shot, and the quality of the filmed objects as they are affected by focus, lighting, color, and the employment of other technical properties.

Composing Within the Frame

The creative choices of painters, photographers, and cinematographers center around the arrangement of objects within space, or composing materials within the fixed proportions of the frame. A cinematographer's major decision focuses on the apparent distance between the camera and the subject. This distance comes in infinite gradations, and a particular shot will be identified according to the relative distances of the other shots that make up a scene. Three basic shots, however, are generally recognized as standard to film composition: the *long shot*, the *medium shot*, and the *close-up*.

The *long shot* provides an orientation or setting for the subject and puts it in its proper context and relationship with its surroundings. Filmmakers have often used it as the opening for a scene (and often in its extended form, the *extreme*

Figure 2-1 *Rope* (1948—American). In addition to confining this film's action to a single penthouse apartment setting, Alfred Hitchcock edited together ten-minute shots to form a relatively seamless movie presented in "real time" (i.e., the running time of the film is identical to the time period covered by the film's story). One of the results is a feeling of growing entrapment as the murderers' guest, a philosophy professor played by James Stewart, becomes aware of their crime.

long shot) to put the characters and action within a larger context or environment. They have also traditionally used it to present the background over which are superimposed the film's opening title and credits. The extreme long shot enhances the scope and grandeur of film settings, as illustrated by the panoramic vistas in a number of David Lean's films. These include the lonely moors through which Pip crosses in *Great Expectations*, the limitless desert expanses in *Lawrence of Arabia* (1962), and the sweeping Russian countryside in *Dr. Zhivago* (1965). Other, more recent films featuring the use of panoramic views include works as otherwise disparate as Francis Ford Coppola's *Apocalypse Now* (1979) and Woody Allen's *Manhattan* (1979), which incorporate breathtaking views of Vietnamese jungles and Manhattan skylines, respectively.

The *medium shot* is one that takes in all or most of the subject or action and pays relatively equal attention to it and the surrounding setting. In other words, it is the intermediary shot between the long shot and the close-up. Occasionally called a "two shot," it is frequently used to frame two people interacting within the scene. The depiction of two British teachers (Alan Bates and Richard O'Callaghan) from Harold Pinter's comedy *Butley* (1974), shown in Fig. 2–2, is only one of countless examples of the medium shot.

The *close-up* moves the viewers in for an intimate study of the subject or action and permits them to examine the subject's major details. Despite the chiding of some of his contemporaries that he could not present only half an actor, D. W. Griffith was willing to bring the camera toward his subject to reveal such details as a pair of eyes nervously looking back and forth or hands wringing in melodramatic fashion. In this way, he learned to use the close-up as a unique and indispensable tool for drawing audience attention to specific details usually reflecting points of dramatic interest. Theorists and filmmakers have long recognized the power of close-ups of the human face in particular to communicate thoughts,

Figure 2-2 *Butley* (1974—British). As with the long shot, the medium shot preserves the space between actors and makes the contributions of the setting more apparent. Yet, like the close-up, it allows the director to present relatively minute detail, such as facial expressions and fleeting gestures.

moods, feelings. Film theorist Béla Balázs suggested that such close-ups "are often the dramatic revelations of what is really happening under the surface of appearances."[3] In *Great Expectations*, close-ups of both the convict Magwitch and the frightened boy are essential to the dramatic intensity of the film's opening scene. More striking examples of the dramatic potential of close-ups may be found in Carl Dreyer's *The Passion of Joan of Arc* (1928). This film has been heralded since its release as a memorable collection of close-ups, mostly of the anguished facial expressions of the title character. Dreyer clearly understood the potential impact of these supremely effective techniques for exploring and revealing human emotions (see Fig. 2–3).

A considerable part of the power of the close-up resides with the fact that it provides a strong sense of intimacy between the performers and the audience, which is one of the greatest differences between cinema and live theater. Actor James Stewart has described the difference in these terms: "On the screen, actors seem very close to the audience—much more so than on the stage, where the spoken word is very important. You get very close to the actor on the screen, and even a gesture or silence can speak volumes."[4] Of course, filmmakers have also integrated close-ups into their films to promote the careers of their stars, but when they use close-ups to explore and reveal detail rather than promote personalities and satisfy egos, close-ups—especially those of faces—become indispensable to film communication (see Fig. 2–4).

The people following the formalist tradition quickly embraced close-ups, but the cinema realists also found them invaluable tools for scrutinizing physical detail and for magnifying and revealing what Siegfried Kracauer called "things normally unseen." Balázs suggested that close-ups "not only revealed new things, but shown up meaning of the old." He also suggested that they help give "star

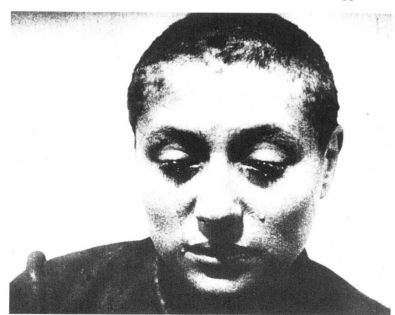

Figure 2-3 *The Passion of Joan of Arc* (1928—French). No filmmaker understood the power of the close-up better than Carl Dreyer, the Danish director who worked with an international cast and crew to create *The Passion of Joan of Arc*. Dreyer and his Polish cameraman Rudolph Maté frequently photographed Joan (played by the Italian actress Marie Falconetti) in tight close-ups, allowing her marvelously expressive face to suggest the agony, determination, and spirituality of the doomed French maid. It remains an extraordinarily moving performance.

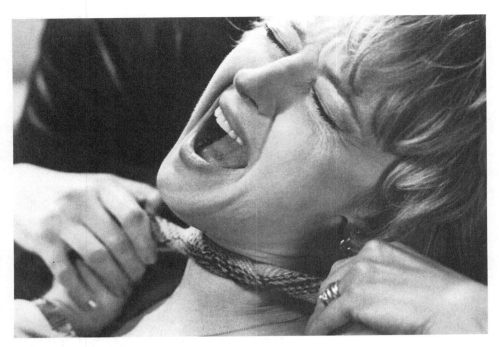

Figure 2-4 *Frenzy* (1972—British). The close-up, which became an indispensable part of filmic composition during the latter years of the silent-film era, has remained an important means of exploring human expression. For example, directors have often punctuated a grisly act of murder with an extreme close-up of the victim's face, as Alfred Hitchcock did in *Frenzy*.

status" to inanimate objects.[5] Close-ups carry the viewer *into* the scene, isolate details of the setting from its background and surroundings, and uncover that which is indistinguishable in the longer view of things. We need look no further for a memorable example than to the penetration of the camera into the mouth of a furnace at the conclusion of Orson Welles' *Citizen Kane* (1941) or to the close-ups of photographs in Michelangelo Antonioni's *Blow-Up* (1966), which suggest evidence of a murder in a bucolic London park.

In addition to the three basic shot types, there are limitless intermediary shots between long shot, medium shot, and close-up, as well as extensions of the long shot and close-up to their extremes. As the terms themselves imply, the *extreme long shot* and the *extreme close-up* extend the scope and penetration within the scene and allow for further sweep or scrutiny. Alfred Hitchcock managed to include examples of both extremes within a single run of the camera in his *Notorious* (1946), a suspenseful World War II drama of espionage and romance set in Rio de Janeiro. What begins as an extreme long shot of a fancy formal party eventually becomes a tight close-up of a key clasped in Ingrid Bergman's hand, which Hitchcock accomplished by moving a platform-mounted camera down and in from the studio set's ceiling. The shot is not only critical to the story exposition but also to a heightened tension: discovery of the missing key will put her in mortal danger.

Lenses

Filmmakers largely define the elements within the frame by selecting appropriate lenses and camera placements. *Focal length*—the length of the lens from its outer side to the surface of the film—comes in infinite gradations but, like shot type, is usually identified in terms of three basic lenses: normal, wide-angle, and telephoto.

The *normal lens* has a focal length that provides the minimal distortion in size, shape, and perspective from the way things appear to the human eye. In a sense, it offers the perfect perspective for the realist filmmaker who wishes to provide as objective a view of the scene as possible. In switching from the standard normal lens to lenses of longer or shorter focal lengths, the filmmaker will find significant variations in depth of focus (that is, the area in acceptably sharp focus within the frame), the apparent distance of objects from one another and from the camera, and the apparent speed of the objects if they are in motion.

The *wide-angle lens* provides a function similar to the long shot in that it affords a wider range to the camera's "vision." The *telephoto lens*, on the other hand, will bring distant objects closer to the viewer by magnifying them in a fashion similar to telescopes and binoculars. Filmmakers often use telephoto lenses (occasionally called *long lenses*) to create close-ups when it is not feasible to move the camera close to the subject, particularly in wildlife studies, anthropological films, and other "candid camera" situations where the presence of the camera would be distracting or inhibiting to the subject.

Lens choice affects not only the size and apparent distance of the camera to the objects within the frame but also the viewer's perception of depth and the relationship of objects within the scene. As lenses become longer, the apparent distance between objects becomes foreshortened and the image appears flatter than normal, reducing the sense of depth that the image might suggest. In the 1939 documentary *The City*, directors Ralph Steiner and Willard Van Dyke underscored the problems of urban traffic congestion by installing a telephoto lens on their camera and then placing the camera in front of a line of oncoming vehicles on a busy highway. The lens accentuated the congestion through depth reduction; as illustrated in Fig. 2–5, it squeezed the space taken up by the cars and the space between the cars to such an extent that the vehicles seem virtually piled on top of one another.

The short focal-length lens—in other words, the wide-angle lens—has the opposite effect. It accentuates or stretches out the space of and between objects, and it also imparts more of a three-dimensional quality to the scene. Filmmakers wishing to suggest a character's feeling of loneliness and isolation will frequently use a wide-angle lens to exaggerate the sense of distance. In *Citizen Kane*, for example, director Orson Welles and cinematographer Gregg Toland used a wide-angle lens to give additional depth to the cavernous recesses of Xanadu, newspaper magnate Charles Foster Kane's pleasure palace. At the same time that the increased sense of space reinforces the isolation of Kane from the outside world, it also emphasizes the growing estrangement between Kane and his wife, Susan. They are yards apart from one another, lost in their own private worlds (see Fig. 2–6).

The filmmaker's choice of lenses will also affect the depth of field, or area

Figure 2-5 *The City* (1939—American). The telephoto shot frequently suggests the compression or flattening of objects and of the space between objects, as it does here in this view from Ralph Steiner and Willard Van Dyke's *The City*.

of focus, within the frame. The telephoto lens creates a shallow depth of field in which foreground and background objects become fuzzy and blurred. The wide-angle lens, however, brings objects both close and distant into acceptably sharp focus and makes their spatial relationship a significant part of the composition. The combined effect of extending space and providing sharpness of focus within that space is known as "deep-focus photography"; it became a hallmark of many Hollywood features of the 1940s.

The filmmaker can vary the focal length within a single shot by using a *zoom lens*. The zoom lens was originally designed for use *between* shots because its variable focal length allowed it to replace a full complement of fixed focal-length lenses. For example, a filmmaker might shoot one scene with the zoom lens set on a wide-angle setting and then, after the shot is over, adjust the lens to a tele-photo setting for the next shot. In addition, the filmmaker is able to change the focal length of this cost-saving and versatile lens *during* shots. By using the zoom lens in this manner, the filmmaker can alter the apparent size of objects, the depth of the scene, and the sharpness of focus within a single shot, and can give a sense

Figure 2-6 *Citizen Kane* (1941—American). This publicity photo suggests the way Orson Welles and his cinematographer Gregg Toland used a wide angle lens in *Citizen Kane* to stretch out the physical space between Charles Foster Kane and Susan Kane. Charles looms large in the foreground while Susan is a distant figure near the ridiculously large fireplace, where she works on a jigsaw puzzle out of sheer boredom.

of motion to static objects—all without having to move the camera. The effect of the zoom lens differs primarily from that of moving the camera toward or away from the photographed objects in this regard: The spatial relationships of the objects (both between themselves and to the camera) do not change within the frame during the zooming process, only the degree of magnification. During a *zoom-in* on a single object, for example, the zoom lens only enlarges while it simultaneously eliminates the object's surrounding detail from the frame; the act of moving the camera toward the same object, on the other hand, imparts a more three-dimensional quality to the shot since the perspectives of the camera change as it moves through the area it is photographing.

Another variable produced by changes in focal length (whether accomplished through manipulating a zoom lens or changing fixed focal-length lenses) is an apparent alteration in the speed at which objects move toward or away from the camera. Shorter focal lengths create the greater apparent speeds while longer focal lengths produce slower speeds. If a filmmaker uses a telephoto lens to photograph someone running toward the camera, the resulting effect suggests a lack of progress or achievement. In fact, the character may even appear to be running in place, an effect director Mike Nichols achieved near the conclusion of his 1967 film *The Graduate* when Benjamin Braddock (Dustin Hoffman) races to the church where the woman he loves is about to be married to someone else. By shooting this scene with an extremely long telephoto lens, Nichols has imparted a strong sense of desperation to Ben's mission; indeed, the character appears to be covering very little ground even though he is running very hard. This technique has proven popular with filmmakers attempting to create dream-states, particularly the premise of a character running but seldom getting anywhere. For example, Robert Enrico used this dream-imagery technique effectively in the final moments of his famous short film *An Occurrence at Owl Creek Bridge* (1961), in which Payton Farquar runs toward the outstretched arms of his wife.

The other extreme in focal-length lenses—the extreme wide-angle or "fish-eye" lens—will produce not only elongations of time but also considerable linear distortions of the object it photographs. Filmmakers usually reserve the fish-eye lens for sequences depicting a character's subjective experience, particularly when that character is undergoing an "altered state of consciousness" such as a dream state, drunkenness, a drug trip, and so on. F. W. Murnau's use of an image-splitting lens in *The Last Laugh* (1924) achieved a similar effect (see Fig. 2–7).

Camera Angle and Perspective

Anyone composing a shot in either still or motion-picture photography must go beyond the basic decisions of focal length and distance of camera from subject. Pictorial composition involves *perspective*, or point of view, which in turn involves choices for focusing the attention of viewers. By controlling perspective, the filmmaker can suggest relationships of objects or elements within the scene, reveal something that may normally go unnoticed, or provide fresh insights into things observed many times before. By controlling perspective, the filmmaker can place the viewers in a variety of positions: involved participant in an unfolding drama, neutral observer, even an omniscient overseer looking down from on high, to name several.

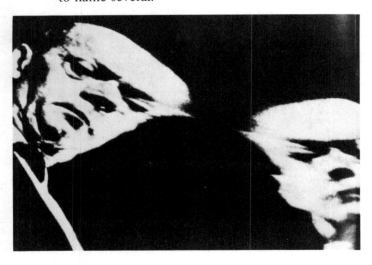

Figure 2-7 *Überfall* (1928—German). Lens distortion allows the viewer to see the world through the eyes of a man just robbed and beaten by a gang of thugs in Ernö Metzner's *Überfall.*

The director's choice of *camera angle* for observing a scene is essential to perspective and represents a way for the director to inflect the photographed objects. The filmmaker may photograph the subject at or near eye level, a camera angle favored by those in the realist tradition since it does not call attention to itself and represents the way we normally view the everyday world. Virtually all films consist of a preponderance of eye-level shots, but filmmakers have a wide range of camera positions both above and below eye level from which to choose. The more extreme the camera angle, the more it calls attention to itself; for this reason, directors in the formalist tradition often favor extreme high-angle shots and extreme low-angle shots. The former shots present a "bird's-eye view" of whatever is photographed, while the latter shots offer a "worm's-eye view" or, as the noted cinematographer Rudolph Maté has suggested, a "frog perspective."

Directors usually reserve these extremes in perspective for special dramatic effect, as they are the farthest removed from our normal way of seeing things and tend to be disorienting. Formalist directors have used such shots effectively in a broad range of situations. For example, German director Leni Riefenstahl photographed Nuremberg through the clouds with an extreme high-angle shot at the beginning of her *Triumph of the Will* (1935) when Adolf Hitler descends by plane to receive the enthusiastic welcome of the people of that city. Alfred Hitchcock used a less dramatic but still effective high-angle shot in his final film, *Family Plot* (1976), when he presented an overhead shot of the film's protagonist (Bruce Dern) quietly pursuing a woman along the maze-like paths of a cemetery.

Instead of the more obvious and extreme camera placements from bird's-eye or worm-like perspectives that suggest lofty or lowly vantage points, filmmakers may create subtle shifts in perspective to enhance the psychological quality of a scene. A camera angle slightly above eye level, in which the camera looks down on the subject, imparts a sense of inferiority to the subject and superiority—even, in some cases, omniscience—to the viewers. This angle is a favorite of directors when portraying children, poor people, and others of lesser power and status. An angle somewhat below eye level, in which the camera looks up at the subject, lends a sense of power, authority, and occasional menace to the subject. It also places the viewers in a subordinate position with regard to the subject. The courtroom scene from *Great Expectations* provides a conventional example of this technique (see Fig. 2–9).

Stanley Kubrick used a low-angle shot to great ironic effect in *Dr. Strangelove*, a 1964 satire on cold war relations between the United States and the Soviet Union. In one scene, a cigar-chomping general named Jack D. Ripper (Sterling Hayden) discusses his version of the Communist threat to America with Colonel Mandrake (Peter Sellers). Kubrick presented Ripper in a harshly lit, tight close-up, the camera tilted up at him. Through these techniques, and with cigar smoke swirling about his head, Ripper creates an imposing figure. His words ring with absolute authority until he utters the phrase that reveals him to be a psychotic kook.

F. W. Murnau used a combination of views slightly below and above eye level in his film *The Last Laugh* to suggest the change in status of the film's protagonist, a proud doorman (Emil Jannings) of a posh German hotel. In early scenes photographed slightly below eye level, the doorman seems to dominate his environment as he struts and bustles from street to lobby. After he has been demoted

Figure 2-8 *Triumph of the Will* (1935—German). This distant view of Adolf Hitler and two henchmen walking in dramatic isolation along a pathway lined with hundreds of thousands of the Nazi Party faithful in Nuremberg is one of several high-angle shots employed by Leni Riefenstahl in her monumental *Triumph of the Will*.

to the lowly position of washroom attendant, his humiliation and withdrawal are likewise accentuated by a shift in camera angle to slightly above eye level.

Filmmakers can shift camera angles not only vertically but also horizontally, allowing the viewer to move from in front of the subject to the side of it or behind it. Such a shift in perspective can be used for dramatic effect by moving the viewer into the action, behind the scene, and even to the perspective of a character within the film. In *Citizen Kane*, for instance, the sequence consisting of Susan Alexander Kane's opera–debut flashback contains a shot from behind the stage looking out at the audience. Though not strictly from her point of view, this shot allows the viewer to share her anxiety as the curtain rises. During Jed Leland's visualized reminiscences of the same event presented earlier in the film, we saw the same scene from his viewpoint in the audience.

Though we have focused our attention thus far on the pyschological aspects of camera angles, filmmakers frequently decide perspective on a very practical basis: the best position for observing the scene most advantageously. Even

Figure 2-9 *Great Expectations* (1947—British). The low angle shot can enhance the stature of a character or object, or make it appear more menacing. In the courtroom scene from *Great Expectations*, the solemn and life-threatening mood of the action is reinforced by this low-angle perspective.

the realist directors wishing to record physical reality in as neutral a fashion as possible look for the perspective that will render the scene most completely, unobstructedly, and revealingly in terms of detail and relationship among various components of the scene.

Occasionally directors use camera angles to withhold details of scenes, an approach that serves a variety of purposes. It is frequently pressed into service for mysteries and thrillers, wherein filmmakers often wish to keep the villain's identity a secret from the audience for as long as possible. A good example is the British thriller *See No Evil* (1971), in which director Richard Fleischer photographed the villain exclusively from the waist down until the last few minutes of the film, thereby obscuring his identity while at the same time ascribing a malevolent quality to the most conspicuous elements of his attire—his cowboy boots. Alfred Hitchcock has used the device in many of his suspense thrillers to raise our anxiety level by obstructing our view during key moments. In *Frenzy* (1972), for instance, he presented a secretary entering the building where she works, unaware that moments before her employer had been raped and murdered in the office several flights up. Instead of following the secretary up the stairs, Hitchcock elected to

Figure 2-10   *Macbeth* (1971—British). The high-angle shot can provide an overview of an extended scene or action. In Roman Polanski's *Macbeth,* the camera surveys the invading hordes as Birnam Wood begins its move on the castle of the murderous monarch.

keep the camera outside the building. Suspense mounts as the camera holds on the building while we wait for the now-unseen secretary to discover the body. After what seems an interminable duration (the shot of the building actually runs about 30 seconds), we finally hear the secretary's off-screen scream.

Directors may withhold information from the audience for other reasons. Charlie Chaplin achieved one of many comic effects in his 1917 film *The Immigrant* by positioning the camera behind his Tramp character, who is bending over a ship's railing and whose heaving shoulders suggest seasickness. This camera position masks what is really going on: the Tramp happily fishing. Other directors have used the device to suggest sexual intimacies without actually showing them. Countless movies have featured the camera discreetly moving away from a couple's passionate embrace, in what may be the most obvious example of cinematic *information interruptus.*

Framing

Revealing and withholding detail are functions of framing as well as of camera angle. Aware of the fixed proportions of the frame, the filmmaker will determine what will be included within—as well as excluded from—the frame, through distance, angle, and the focal length of the lens. The dimensions of the rectangle within which the filmmaker must work are in a sense restrictive. In other graphic arts, the limits of the frame are adjustable according to the content; for example, a painter would probably select a canvas much greater in width than in height for purposes of depicting a panoramic desert scene or seascape but would choose a canvas of completely different proportions to reproduce a skyscraper or giant sequoia. Filmmakers have lacked such freedom to choose the shape of their frames, though a handful of early directors experimented with different proportions. Sergei Eisenstein, for example, proposed a system of film exhibition that incorporated movable panels for purposes of adjusting the ratio of the frame and thus could more easily accommodate the vertical or horizontal thrust of the scene. D. W. Griffith partially solved the problem through an internal device; he masked off the top and bottom or sides of a scene by applying a matte device in front of the camera lens. French director Abel Gance developed a screen format wider than normal that he termed "Polyvision." Among the films in which he implemented it was his epic masterpiece *Napoleon* (1927), which featured imagery from three synchronized projectors running side-by-side during the last 18 minutes of the film. Filmmakers who have worked with Polyvision's wide-screen progeny such as CinemaScope, VistaVision, and Cinerama (all of which were initially developed during the 1950s) have been able to offer broader, more panoramic views of their subjects. Yet such horizontally oriented formats have a number of drawbacks; wide-screen filmmakers have difficulty editing their films, focusing audience attention, and keeping relatively tall subjects within the frame, among other shortcomings. Hence, all fixed frames have potential problems.

Yet every fixed frame, regardless of its width to height ratio, has advantages and creative possibilities as well as limitations. Filmmakers can help focus viewer attention on key details of the scene through framing while eliminating unnecessary and irrelevant detail. Framing functions as the basis for composition and as a reference by which filmmakers organize the content of the shot. They can convey varying degrees of balance by the extent to which they align the frame with the horizontal and vertical dimensions of the objects within the shot. While filmmakers have often composed their pictures so that such dimensions perfectly parallel the sides of the frame, resulting in a natural and unobtrusive perspective, they occasionally turn the camera at an oblique angle to impart a sense of imbalance, dynamism, or uncertainty to the surroundings, and thereby to the story itself. Eisenstein tilted his camera to underscore the energy and confusion of the street riots in his film *Strike* (1924), which dealt with factory-worker brutalization and murder. Director Carol Reed frequently turned his camera at unsettling angles to give an aura of uneasiness and uncertainty to the postwar Vienna setting of his 1949 film *The Third Man* (see Fig. 2–11).

Realist filmmakers, interested in suggesting the larger world beyond the frame, tend to emphasize arbitrary compositions. They often suggest casual or even accidental perspectives rather than predetermined ones. Formalist directors are more likely to use the fixed frame to create balance and tension, develop visual symbols, and control viewer attention and accessibility to certain details. They may, for example, fill the frame with only a small segment of some larger object, thereby producing a visual synecdoche in which the part represents the whole.

Figure 2-11 *The Third Man* (1949—British). Sir Carol Reed often tilted his camera at odd angles in *The Third Man,* as he did for this shot from the famous chase through the Vienna sewers which occurs near the end of the film. The tilted camera shots impart a sense of unease to the events and surroundings of the film. Reed stated in an interview that "the angle of vision was just to suggest that something crooked was going on." Cited in Charles Thomas Samuels, *Encountering Directors.*

Eisenstein used this very device in *The Battleship Potemkin* (1925) by focusing on the *pince-nez* of the battleship's doctor whenever that character appeared on screen. These old-fashioned eyeglasses were all that remained of the unfortunate physician later in the film after mutinous sailors had pitched him overboard. Dangling from a string, the *pince-nez* act as a reminder of both the doctor's frailty and that of the class he represented (see Fig. 2–12).

Filmmakers may also control framing to keep a part of the scene from the audience. Inextricably linked with a similar function of camera-angle selection mentioned earlier, this technique helps build suspense, surprise, or general viewer interest. Hitchcock has used the device numerous times; during the opening shots of *The 39 Steps* (1935) and *Strangers on a Train* (1951), for instance, he presented only the lower legs and feet of several main charcters as they walk respectively into a London music hall and a Washington railroad station. Another example may be found in François Truffaut's tribute to Hitchcock entitled *The Bride Wore Black* (1967), in which Jeanne Moreau's final act of vengeance in prison takes place just out of the range of the camera. As for an example of a comic surprise effect resulting from this technique, we need look no further than René Clair's playfully anarchic *Entr'acte* (1924). In this short experimental film, Clair periodically cut away to a slow-motion shot of a ballerina, filmed from such an extremely low, "worm's-eye" perspective that all we see of her are her legs and billowing skirt. (Clair obtained the shot by having the ballerina dance on a sheet of glass while he filmed from below.) Later in the film, Clair brought his camera up to a higher level

Figure 2-12 *The Battleship Potemkin* (1925—Russian). The *pince-nez* which Sergei Eisenstein used to characterize the *Potemkin's* czarist doctor during the early portions of the film are all that is left of the physician after rebellious sailors have jettisoned him overboard during the film's "Drama on the Quarterdeck" sequence.

to reveal that the ballerina was not a "she" but a "he": a bearded male dancer in a tutu (see Fig. 2–13).

Composing with Light

The uses of light and shadow are also compositional elements at the film-maker's disposal, and they serve a broad range of expository and dramatic functions. The very term *photography* comes from the Greek *photos* and *graphos* and means *writing with light*. Like the photographer, the cinematographer composes with light; because of movement of camera or objects within the scene, however, the cinematographer's use of light is more complex. Factors affected by lighting include the color, shape, and surface texture of scenic detail, as well as movement within the shot and the depth of field. Such factors help determine the placement and intensity of the light source.

The pioneer filmmakers' original concern with lighting was simply to have enough available to obtain a discernible image on film. Thomas Edison constructed his first studio—the "Black Maria"—on a turntable with moveable panels in the roof so that the sun's rays could be captured and directed to the filming area below at any hour of the day. Many early directors shot their films on make-shift stages located on the rooftops of tall buildings. They would shoot exterior as well as interior scenes after simply constructing settings without ceilings and then making use of available sunlight. Except for the vagaries of weather, this early use of solar power was an effective and inexpensive means of general illumination. With the development and adoption of giant mirror-like reflective panels, film-makers could contol to a considerable degree both the intensity and direction of natural light.

Along with technological refinements resulting in the increased light-sensitivity of lenses and film stocks and more versatile lighting instruments came greater possibilities for using light beyond the purpose of general illumination. Cinematographers such as Billy Bitzer (D. W. Griffith's longtime cameraman) and Rudolph Maté in the teens and twenties, and Gregg Toland and James Wong

(A)

Figure 2-13 (A & B)   *Entr'acte* (1924—French). René Clair employed
several unusual low-angle shots of a ballerina in his famous Dadaist film,
Entr'acte. The viewer learns later that Clair used the angle to disguise the
sex of the dancer and fool the audience.

(B)

Figure 2-14 Since the earliest film stocks were comparatively insensitive to light, the pioneers of film production often had to develop ingenious ways of drenching their studios with as much sunlight as possible. One solution was the rooftop studio, such as this early Biograph construction. The rail system allowed the filmmakers to maneuver both the corrugated-metal "camera car" and the set-wall framework to take maximum advantage of the sunlight.

Howe in the thirties and forties, explored these potentials. They gradually discovered a full range of creative functions for lighting that made it a central and indispensable filmmaking tool for both realist and formalist pursuits (see Fig. 2–15).

The eventual development of color film brought with it limitations and setbacks to what had become a fine art of black-and-white cinematography. It imposed severe curtailments on the range of shading with light that had been developed with black-and-white cinematography. *Rembrandt lighting*, a term coined by Cecil B. DeMille to label the use of lighting from the side in the dramatic manner of Rembrandt's paintings, quickly became a lost art in the hands of early cinematographers working with color film. Recently, however, such cinematographers as Laszlo Kovacs, Haskell Wexler, Nestor Almendros, and Vilmos Zsigmond have adapted the concept of "painting with light" to the color medium and have recaptured some of its preeminence as a means of composition. For example, Almendros frequently photographed the itinerant wheat harvesters of Terrence Malick's loosely structured *Days of Heaven* (1978) at either sunrise or sunset. This decision led to several dramatic lighting effects in the film, since the throw of the sunlight at these times of day is virtually horizontal, creating long, stark shadows, and the light itself is quite reddish in hue. By exploiting this latter quality of the lighting in particular, Almendros helped romanticize the otherwise harsh working conditions depicted in the film; indeed, the workers and the rippling wheat fields practically glow in the sunlight's rosy warmth (see. Fig. 2–16).

When filmmakers compose with light, they must make basic choices concerning its intensity and concentration, the degree of its diffusion, and its direction or source. By controlling these variables, filmmakers are able to establish particular patterns or designs in light which may lead to one or more effects. These effects range from the imitation of natural light, the accenting of forms and textures, and the control of viewer attention to creating and enhancing mood, suggesting subjective experiences, and providing some symbolic detail. Through the control of lighting, filmmakers can either rediscover and draw attention to the real world or design, embellish, and create the atmosphere for the world of their own fancies.

Figure 2-15 *A Comedy in Black and White* (1908—American). This early short suggests an interest by pioneering filmmakers in using lighting for more than general illumination of a scene. Improvement in both film stock and lighting equipment soon expanded the range of uses for film lighting to include a variety of dramatic functions.

Realist and formalist filmmakers share an interest in using light to direct audience attention and enhance objects detected by the camera. They have discovered they can make objects or components of the scene stand out by controlling lighting intensity and direction. They have also learned to use lighting variations to lead the eye from one part of the shot to another, thus giving prominence to objects or details that might otherwise escape attention. In addition, filmmakers can use lighting to establish the borders of the image within the often arbitrary limits of the frame. In other words, filmmakers can employ shadows as framing devices by concentrating the lighting on the main subject of the shot while leaving the background in relative darkness. What D. W. Griffith accomplished through a variety of iris and masking devices can be handled in a less artificial and obtrusive way with light and shadow (see Fig. 2–17).

Besides using lighting effects to control space and direct attention, filmmakers have employed them to help enhance the *mise-en-scène* (the arrangement and movement of objects within the frame, and the ambience arising therefrom) and establish mood. At one end of the range of possibilities is the highly stylized use of light by the German expressionists during the late teens and twenties. Their

Figure 2-16 *Days of Heaven* (1978—American). Terrence Malick counterbalanced the slim storyline of his *Days of Heaven* with numerous lingering and breathtaking shots of the Texas countryside. Malick shot much of the film at times when the sun was low on the horizon, creating many striking lighting effects.

films, including *The Golem* (1920), *Siegfried* (1924), and *Metropolis* (1927), are replete with bold, angular shafts of light dramatically contrasting with heavily shadowed areas (see Fig. 2–20). At the other end of the spectrum are the natural lighting effects achieved by the Italian neorealists of the forties and fifties and many modern documentary filmmakers. Both of these latter filmmaking groups have worked primarily with available lighting, which underscores a sense of life caught "on the run" in their films. The feeling of genuineness and spontaneity in *Bicycle Thieves* (1948), an exemplary film of the Italian neorealist movement, and *Harlan County, U.S.A.* (1977), a documentary focusing on the effects of a Kentucky coal miners' strike on the lives of local people, is due in part to the unobtrusive, natural ways that their scenes are lit (see Fig. 2–18).

Lighting a scene can be more than a matter of pictorial composition and atmospheric effects. It can also take on special dramatic functions, such as offering a symbolic reference, suggesting a subjective experience, or even providing a plot-triggering device. For instance, Carl Dreyer had shadows of leaves fall on a young woman's face in his 1943 Danish film *Day of Wrath* to symbolize the idea that she had become a witch. Further examples may be found in Swedish director Ingmar Bergman's black-and-white films of the 1950s, which provide a veritable catalogue of symbolic lighting functions. In *The Seventh Seal* (1956), the contrast between life and death imagery depends heavily on lighting, especially during those moments when scenes of the "Holy Family" (Jof, Mia, and child) are set against those of the cloaked figure of Death (see Fig. 2–19). In a similar fashion, Bergman's *Wild Strawberries* (1957) features a vivid contrast between elderly professor Isak Borg's nightmare visions, laden with heavy, menacing shadows, and his pleasant dreams of childhood, drenched in sunlight.

Figure 2-17   The iris was an early means of focusing audience attention, as in this shot from the 1907 film, *The Trainer's Daughter, or A Race for Love.*

Filmmakers may reserve lighting effects for key dramatic moments or may use them as parts of the film's overall visual style. An instance of the former usage may be found in Mervyn LeRoy's *I Am a Fugitive from a Chain Gang* (1932), in which Paul Muni becomes enshrouded by darkness as he retreats into the life suggested in the film's title. It is a singular image that has haunted several generations of moviegoers. Jean-Luc Godard's *Alphaville* (1965), in its entirety, provides an example of the latter usage. In this film, Godard presented detective Lemmy Caution (Eddie Constantine) exploring a futuristic city controlled by a totalitarian omniscience. Godard greatly enhanced the city's mysterious and forbidding qualities by turning the film into a continuous and cryptic light show consisting of very harsh fluorescent lighting, flashing neon signs, and other stylized lighting effects set off against murky and shadowy backgrounds.

Filmmakers occasionally use lighting in concert with other cinematic elements to suggest the inner experiences of one or more characters. Robert Wiene

Figure 2-18 *Bicycle Thieves* (1948—Italian). Vittorio de Sica's use of natural sunlight enhances the realistic qualities of his classic film, *Bicycle Thieves*. In this scene, Ricci (Lamberto Maggiorani) fends off angry townspeople who want to bring him to justice after his unsuccessful attempt to filch a bicycle.

and his scenic designers effectively demonstrated this general principle in the famous German expressionist film *The Cabinet of Dr. Caligari* (1919), in which the audience views the world through the eyes of a madman (see Fig. 2–20). Stark, angular light streaks and shadows zigzagging through both interior and exterior settings help characterize the bizarre subjective experience. Wiene and his associates created many of the lighting effects by painting light and dark areas directly on the walls and floors of the studio sets. Film historian and theorist Siegfried Kracauer has suggested this decision was part of an economy move by the studio to save electricity, yet the painted light-and-shadow patterns effectively complement the film's costuming, settings, and even the makeup and movement of the actors to create an overall expressionistic style.

Lighting is also important to narrative progression. In Hitchcock's *Strangers on a Train*, for example, a slight tilt of the head brings the villain Bruno out of the shadows and into the view of park attendants, triggering the final terrifying chase in that film. Lean's *Great Expectations* uses shadows to heighten the impact of the lawyer's arrival at the forge, as demonstrated in Fig. 2–21. As a part of a film's

Figure 2-19 *The Seventh Seal* (1956—Swedish). Soft, dappled sunlight played on Jof, Mia, and the bucolic forest setting stands in contrast with the scenes in which Antonious Block tries to outwit Death in Bergman's *The Seventh Seal*. The director made careful use of the natural lighting of his exterior locations in northern Sweden.

narrative progression, lighting—like framing—can be used to withhold detail and keep the viewers at least temporarily in the dark. By extinguishing matches and unplugging sources of light, Susy Hendrix (Audrey Hepburn), the blind protagonist of Terence Young's *Wait Until Dark* (1967), saves herself from an attacker by intermittently plunging him, herself, and the audience into total darkness. Another example may be drawn from Lawrence Kasdan's thriller *Body Heat* (1981). During a late-night scene, the film's *femme fatale*, Matty Walker (Kathleen Turner), turns away from her lover, Ned Racine (William Hurt), and heads for a building to retrieve an incriminating piece of evidence. Both Ned and the audience know the building is rigged to blow up, which it indeed does moments after Matty disappears into the inky darkness. We later learn that the darkness veiled the fact that Matty had not entered the building but set up the scene to appear as if she had.

Several filmmakers have employed lighting for shock value or surprise effects, though such uses are infrequent. Perhaps the most famous example occurs near the conclusion of Hitchcock's *Psycho* (1960) when a wildly swinging bare light

Figure 2-20 *The Cabinet of Dr. Caligari* (1919—German). The scenic designers of this German classic horror tale wanted to suggest the distorted view of the world as the film's central character would see it. To do this, they have a highly stylized and angular look to the settings, costumes, make-up, and even the lighting. They produced the desired lighting effects by painting the illuminated areas and shadows directly on the walls and floors of the sets.

bulb (accidently but conveniently struck by a surprised Vera Miles) brings to life the eye sockets of Norman Bates' mother.

Color

Because color is a part of both our everyday life experiences and the worlds we create in the interpretation of life, it becomes a natural and useful means of visual communication. Photographers and other graphic artists have long demonstrated the important contributions of color to images of real or imagined settings or actions. In a similar fashion, many filmmakers have employed color cinematography to add an essential dimension of realism to their works or to contribute to dramatic expression.

Interest in color cinematography dates back to the earliest days of the medium. As with other technological developments, such as sound, the wide screen, and stereoscopy, color has gone—and continues to go—through several

Figure 2-21 *Great Expectations* (1947—British). David Lean's use of shadows in the forge scene from *Great Expectations* contributes to the dramatic impact of the moment when the lawyer Jaggers (Francis L. Sullivan) arrives. The intrusion of the lawyer between the two shadowy figures of Joe Gargery and Pip also carries symbolic meaning, as the information he brings will eventually split up the twosome.

stages of development. The first stage involves the *anticipation* of the new form before technological know-how permits its artistically controlled use. With color, this period of anticipation began with some of the earliest films produced in the United States, France, and Great Britain. The people working on a number of early films meticulously painted parts or all of the individual frames by hand, a painstaking process indeed. Other filmmakers employed a coloring technique not nearly as tedious as hand-painting called *toning*, in which they bathed selected film segments in a color dye. A number of prominent silent-era directors used one method or the other to color various segments of the original copies of their films. For example, many of Georges Méliès' fantasies, including the original *A Trip to the Moon*, had hand-painted segments, as did such other brief films of the time as Ferdinand Zecca's *The Pearl Fisherman* (circa 1900) and Edwin Porter's *The Great Train Robbery*. Interested in the psychological effects of color but doubtlessly aware of the unsuitability of the hand-tinting process to feature-length films, D. W. Griffith toned various film segments in several of his works. According to one report, the original print of his *Intolerance* (1916) was toned in blue for the Judean story, sepia for the French, gray-green for the Babylonian, and amber for the modern. In addition, Griffith dyed night scenes blue and battle scenes red.

The second stage of color development involved the *experimentation* with various methods of color processing, which led to the refinements of a two-color Technicolor process in the 1920s and a three-color process in the 1930s. Rouben Mamoulian's adaptation of Thackeray's *Vanity Fair* entitled *Becky Sharp* (1935) marked the end of the second stage of development; as the first feature film made in the full three-color Technicolor process, it illustrated the fact that color technology had sufficiently matured to permit its regular and sustained use. Writing on "The Future of Color" for *The New York Times* at the time of *Becky Sharp*'s release, André Sennwald anticipated the next stage of development, *exploitation*. He wrote: "The major hazard is that this precious new element may fall into the hands of the unlettered and cause such a rape of the laws of harmony and contrast, such a blare of outrageous pigmentations, that only the color-blind will consider it safe to venture inside a motion picture theatre."[6]

Though color cinematography has at times indeed been exploited, history has antiquated Sennwald's fears. He did, however, have the foresight to perceive the next stage of color development when, in the same article, he suggested that the next step "must be to repress color deliberately to the needs of our modern literature and to recite films in grays and pastels and the subdued coloring of the life which we live in these 1930s."[7] Sennwald's observations reflect both the fears and the aspirations for the use of natural color in film at the time of its inauguration, and the problems and advantages that have since been realized.

In addition to the possible "blare of outrageous pigmentations" voiced by Sennwald, color film manifested other problems and limitations that gradually became evident to both its detractors and those who approached its use with cautious optimism. Filmmakers quickly discovered the difficulty of maintaining harmony between shots while working in the color medium, which in turn diminished the flexibility of the film-editing process. Another pitfall was the fact that many filmmakers decided not to explore the more creative uses of color; instead, they devoted themselves to the slavish imitation of nature. In their quest to reproduce faithfully the hues of the natural world, they readily abandoned formalistic, impressionistic, and other forms of stylized visual conception. One can only imagine the ways that the expressionistic extremes of *The Cabinet of Dr. Caligari* might have been extended had the Technicolor processes been around at that time.

Caligari is only one of many films that proves that black-and-white cinematography had become an art with a considerable range of expression by the early 1900s. Aided by improvements in incandescent lighting and improved film stocks, cinematographers could more easily control tone and brightness variables, and emphasize qualities of mass, contrast, and texture. With the arrival of Technicolor, however, many cinematographers soon realized that the range of some of these variables, especially that of contrast and texture, was limited.

Yet some filmmakers found ways of using color as a new dimension in human expression not necessarily tied to the imitation of nature. By controlling film stock, lighting, lens filters, set design, costuming, and laboratory processing, filmmakers learned to extend the use of color beyond the simple recording of surface reality to suggest mood, atmosphere, or symbolic meanings. Filmmakers accomplished such possibilities by emphasizing the psychological and associative values of color, as Griffith had done years before. Sergei Eisenstein recognized the psychological impact of color even though he only used color in one brief segment of his *Ivan the Terrible*, part two (1946). Writing on "Color and Meaning" in his theoretical treatise *The Film Sense*, Eisenstein begins by stating his belief that "specific colors exert specific influences on the spectator"[8] and he then proceeds to examine a range of associative values of various hues.

While generally avoiding the danger of making too direct an association between colors and specific emotions, directors today often use the general emotional tone of certain colors to create a sense of time and place (basically an expository function), to establish or reinforce mood, to enhance atmosphere, and to complete the sense of *mise-en-scéne*. Directors Robert Altman and George Roy Hill, each charged with the task of making a turn-of-the-century Western, helped create a feeling for that period through differing uses of colors. Altman employed muted blues, browns, and oranges in *McCabe and Mrs. Miller* (1970) to create a sense of drabness, isolation, and despair in a small mining town, while Hill occasionally used sepia tones in *Butch Cassidy and the Sundance Kid* (1968) to suggest images from an old photo album. Other films that depend strongly on color to enhance the atmosphere of their various time periods include *A Clockwork Orange* (1971), in which Stanley Kubrick rendered a futuristic London in harsh shades of orange and blue, and *A Man and a Woman* (1966), through which Claude Lelouch suggested the changing moods of a human relationship by bathing individual scenes in particular hues—a golden yellow for lovemaking, for example. Luchino Visconti offered bold, heavy, and discordant hues in *The Damned* (1969) to suggest the unhealthy emotional and spiritual state of its major characters: Nazis and the members of a German industrialist family whom they try to coerce. Visconti turned to more subdued coloring in *Death in Venice* (1971), which deals with similar psychosexual conflicts (homosexuality in particular), but attempts to establish a more compassionate tone. In *The Garden of the Finzi-Continis* (1971), Vittorio de Sica used color to create several moods en route to contrasting a romantic past with the harsh realities of the present: the life of affluent Italian Jews before and after the rise of fascism.

Some filmmakers have moved beyond mood, atmospheric effects, and emotional tone to employ color as a symbolic reference. They have continued the tradition established by Griffith, Eisenstein, and other pioneer directors by exploring the psychological links between color and emotional response, and by establishing color motifs. The red in the decor of Ingmar Bergman's *Cries and Whispers* (1972), the green of the London park in Michelangelo Antonioni's *Blow-Up* (1966), and the blue and red of Teinosuke Kinugasa's *Gate of Hell* (1953) are so pervasive and so tied up in the messages of the films that it is impossible to analyze these works without reflecting on the colors themselves. Antonioni has said of his *Red Desert* (1964) that it was "born in color"—a suggestion echoed by Bergman in reference to his own *Cries and Whispers*.

Red Desert is actually an example of a film that goes even a step further than using color for symbol and motif. Here, as in Federico Fellini's *Juliet of the Spirits* (1965) and the children's classic *The Wizard of Oz* (1939), color is used to suggest the subjective experience and to provide us with a protagonist's–eye view of the world. Antonioni revealed the industrial Ravenna landscape as seen by Giuliana through the use of color—gray marshes, poisonous yellow smoke, and the vibrant but cold and sterile reds and blues of home and factory.

A few filmmakers have extended color as a motif by using it as a narrative or thematic element. In Hitchcock's *Marnie* (1964), the title character (Tippi Hedren) manifests a psychological aversion to the color red, which we learn is rooted in a traumatic childhood experience. Color also plays a prominent thematic role in Joseph Losey's *The Boy with Green Hair* (1948), about a war orphan rejected by society when his hair changes color. The boy's difference from others serves as a thematic base for examining prejudice and the need for international understanding.

One of the most dramatic yet underutilized possibilities of color is the juxtaposition of it with black-and-white cinematography. The most notable film to combine the two modes is *The Wizard of Oz*, in which the vibrant, surreal color of the Oz scenes not only characterizes the land of Dorothy's dream but also serves as a contrast to the everyday reality of her Kansas home, photographed in black and white. Otto Preminger achieved a notable surrealistic effect in his *Tell Me That You Love Me, Junie Moon* (1970) by placing a protagonist wearing a vibrant yellow and red striped shirt in a dream sequence in which all of the surroundings and even the other characters are colored in various shades of gray. The recent revival of Abel Gance's *Napoleon* illustrates an inspired if fleeting experiment in which the red, white, and blue fields of the French tricolor are superimposed over the black-and-white film's final scenes. French filmmaker Alain Resnais combined color and black-and-white cinematography in his 1955 documentary on Nazi concentration camps, *Night and Fog*, to establish a contrast between the horrors of the past, photographed in black and white, and the deceptively benign look of the abandoned camps in 1955, filmed in color. The color of the contemporary scenes emphasizes nature's healing (or perhaps, hiding) of the Holocaust scars. Except for Lindsay Anderson's color film *If . . .* (1969), which contains several black-and-white sequences reportedly as a result of economic stringencies, and a handful of color features containing brief black-and-white newsreel-type sequences (such as *How I Won the War* and *Newsfront*), few other filmmakers have tried combining color with black-and-white film in either narrative or documentary works.

Film is essentially a color medium today in the United States and it is quickly becoming the same in other film-producing nations. Technology and economics are partly responsible but the overriding influence has been television. When the film industry began competing with television in the late 1940s, the latter medium was limited to black-and-white broadcasting; to lure audiences away from their television sets and back into movie theaters, the film industry began using color in earnest (along with other technologies then unique to film, such as 3-D and the wide-screen processes) while abandoning the world of black-and-white cinematography. For many years a cinematography *non grata*, the black-and-white mode of filmmaking made a modest comeback in the late 1970s and 1980s with such films as Peter Bogdanovich's *The Last Picture Show* (1971) and *Paper Moon* (1973), Mel Brooks' *Young Frankenstein* (1974), and Woody Allen's *Manhattan* (1979). These films have used black-and-white cinematography to capture the mood or style of a particular time and place. For example, Bogdanovich's use of black-and-white photography perfectly accentuated the bleakness of a 1950s small Texas town in *The Last Picture Show* and the spirit of rural America during the Depression in *Paper Moon*. Mel Brooks took it one step further to help recreate the quality of a particular movie genre: Universal's horror movies of the 1930s (such as *Frankenstein* and *Bride of Frankenstein*), which he spoofed in his own *Young Frankenstein*. Director Martin Scorsese has long been concerned about the stability of color processes (that is, the extent to which colors in films retain their original hues and tones over the years), and Scorsese claims he will continue to make films in black and white, as he did for his *Raging Bull* (1980), until stabler color processes are available.

Focus and Recovery of Depth

Closely tied to lighting and color design are other photographic techniques that may modify the textural quality and surface detail of the image. Filmmakers may occasionally use soft focus to give images a desired surface quality or texture, for example, which they can accomplish through a variety of ways: using a telephoto lens, placing a filter or gauze in front of the lens, or employing a fast (that is, highly light-sensitive) film stock, which tends to be grainier and not nearly as smooth as a less sensitive stock. Lighting is only one of several elements that have contributed to the range in composition from the dusky naturalism of Robert Flaherty's *Moana* (1926) to the high-contrast hallmark of the American *film noir* style— the slick and sinister combination of crime and psychological intrigue that became a Hollywood favorite during the forties and fifties.

We should also say a word about the challenges that cinematographers have faced when working within, or compensating for, the two-dimensional nature of the film image. First of all, a number of filmmakers have found creative ways of exploiting the image's lack of depth. They have used it to manipulate natural proportions—size, shape, spatial relationships—of objects in the scene. The achieved effect is often some abstract design that would not be apparent if the image were truly three-dimensional. Filmmaker Busby Berkeley delighted countless audiences with the geometric designs he created by filming various groupings of dancers from directly overhead (see Fig. 2–22).

By reducing a sense of depth in their films, directors often make objects close to the camera seem superimposed as a design against the background of a scene, so that the foreground and background are seen as one. Lack of depth also allows special-effects cinematographers to create the illusion of a real scene or action through the use of models, miniatures, and rear-screen projection shots (the latter are actually composite shots in which, for example, an actor in the foreground is filmed against a translucent screen bearing the image of some setting). In other words, the medium's two-dimensionality allows filmmakers to trick the eye by combining images and objects of varying scale and dimension within the same shot. For instance, Peter Glenville fooled his viewers into believing they were looking at the ceiling of Canterbury Cathedral (or at least an elaborate studio replica of the same) while watching his 1964 film *Becket*. What they actually saw was a miniature ceiling painted on a panel suspended a few feet in front of the camera but strategically placed to fit the void of the ceilingless set.

Filmmakers can also suggest a sense of depth by carefully placing scenic details in front of, or behind, the subject and by strategically positioning the camera. Angle, perspective, balance, and scenic detail are basic to composition in all the graphic arts, and they are an important means of suggesting a third dimension in film.

Figure 2-22　A shot taken from directly overhead provides an unusual perspective for most action and may reveal interesting geometric patterns, as it does here in one of the many musicals that Busby Berkeley choreographed for Warner Brothers in the 1930s.

Although composition within the frame represents only one aspect of the filmmaker's creative control of the medium and must finally be considered in conjunction with other cinematic elements, it does suggest a considerable range of possibilities for creating designs, directing attention, and developing dramatic setting. D. W. Griffith, Sergei Eisenstein, and Abel Gance were among those who explored its potential during the days of the silent screen; it continues to be central to the creative use of the medium today.

MOVEMENT

> *"Films strikingly demonstrate that objective movement—any movement for that matter—is one of their choice subjects."*
>
> —Siegfried Kracauer, *Theory of Film*

Whether running a race, riding a horse, watching a ballet, spinning a top, or viewing a movie, we are absorbed in one of the basic and pervasive properties of stimuli: motion. The fascination with motion led to the invention of the optical toys that gave the illusion of moving images, which in turn resulted in the creation

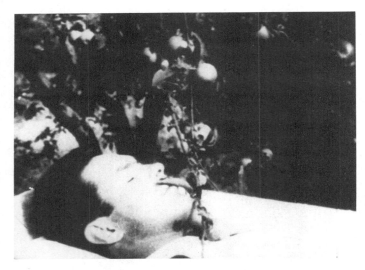

Figure 2-23 *Earth* (1930—Russian). Alexander Dovzhenko carefully emphasized details of setting in *Earth* to provide a clear symbolic function. He continually reinforced the sense of revolutionary rebirth in his film by presenting signs of new life. Here, the branches of a fruit-laden tree brush the face of the deceased young farmer.

of early cinematographic devices and the birth of the *movies, moving* pictures, or *motion* pictures, as the medium is variously called. In the pioneer days of Thomas Edison and the Lumière brothers, films depicting waves hitting the shore or horses in full gallop provided considerable fascination. Since then, filmmakers have relentlessly explored the implications of movement in film, refined the techniques for capturing motion, and greatly expanded the functions of motion. The importance of motion to all genres of film is so fundamental and obvious that we often take it for granted. Yet the movement of objects within the frame, the motion created by the camera, and the sense of movement brought about through the editing process together represent a substantial part of film's instructional, inspirational, and entertainment functions. By controlling motion, filmmakers are not only able to command viewer attention but can also compose within a "liberated" frame, establish or reinforce rhythm and sense of flow, and support the camera's role as expositor or voyeur by leading the eye to discoveries in physical reality or dramatic invention.

Movement Within the Frame (Primary Movement)

The direction, speed, kinetic quality, and symbolism of film actors and objects in motion provide important dramatic variables, though perhaps film theorists have made too much of their apparent psychological qualities. Downward movement is usually associated with depression, deflation, weakness, or death, while upward movement suggests exhilaration, authority, and life-giving force. Likewise, movement toward the camera is usually associated with aggression and the start of exploration, while movement away is associated with recession and completion of exploration. These psychological properties may be helpful guidelines to dance choreographers and film directors if they do not approach them as prescriptive and unalterable rules.

Whenever objects or actors move toward or away from the camera, they help provide a sense of depth to the two-dimensional image. When they move toward the camera, they also offer a gradual development of detail, thereby allow-

Figure 2-24 *Ben-Hur* (1925—American). Animal locomotion, and particularly the horse race or mounted chase, has been recognized as a quintessentially effective form of movement in film from the earliest flickering images. The chariot race from the 1925 version of *Ben-Hur* (seen here with its filming crew) remains a high point of screen excitement.

ing the filmmakers to control exposition. Psychologists tell us that left-to-right eye movements are more natural and restful than right-to-left, because of our years of conditioning by reading. Many filmmakers have played upon this observation by having objects and actors move from left to right during positive, harmonious scenes and from right to left to set up tension and disharmony. The effects of such movement, however, must finally be considered in light of other variables in composition, editing, sound, and decor, and should not be taken as isolated examples of psychological conditioning.

It is more difficult to define and categorize variables related to speed, kinetic quality, and symbolic associations of motion, yet the filmmaker, like the choreographer, has important choices to make in designing motion within the frame. Charlie Chaplin clearly understood this as shown in the balletic mastery of his "Little Tramp" character; Walt Disney learned it while bringing to life a host of animal and human characters with personalities developed largely through the ways they move and gesture; and Alfred Hitchcock demonstrated the ways that audiences could be manipulated by the carefully calculated movements of actors and objects.

In addition to the movement of actors or objects central to the narrative design, filmmakers can also give life to inanimate objects and reinforce the atmosphere of the setting through background movement. In Antonioni's *Blow-Up*, for example, the movement of rustling leaves in a London park (combined with the sound) creates a disquieting effect and imparts a menacing quality to the otherwise bucolic setting. Moreover, countless directors who have shot their films in big cities have used background movements of vehicles and pedestrians to create varying degrees of hustle-bustle, confusion, or both.

The movement of actors and objects discussed so far is certainly not unique to motion pictures; indeed, it relates also to theater, dance, and such sporting events as basketball, swimming, and tennis. Its uniqueness arises from the relationship of the camera to the moving object—including such factors as apparent distance, angle, and recording speed—and the ways that the relationship affects the nature of the movement.

The apparent distance between camera and objects contributes a great deal to the quality of the objects' movement. For instance, Lindsay Anderson accentuated the grueling and brutal nature of a rugby match in his *This Sporting Life* (1963) by bringing the camera into the middle of the action; in so doing, he continually crowded the frame with the frenetic thrashing of limbs and torsos. As noted previously, the choice of lens focal length, which affects the apparent distance between camera and object, will also affect the quality of motion. At critical points in *The Graduate* and *An Occurrence at Owl Creek Bridge*, the respective directors (Mike Nichols and Robert Enrico) filmed their protagonists with depth-flattening telephoto lenses to give the impression that the characters were almost running in place in a dreamlike fashion.

Camera angles also play important roles in affecting the quality of move-

Figure 2-25 *Superman II* (1981—American). Movement of objects and actors is not unique to film, but when combined with special effects, as it is in *Superman II* and most other science fiction, fantasy, and adventure spectacles, it provides a new dimension in thrills. In this scene, Superman (Christopher Reeve) is about to launch archvillain General Zod (Terence Stamp) into orbit while an approving audience watches.

ment by actors and objects. For example, filmmakers occasionally employ extremely low-angle shots during mounted attacks in myriad Westerns and adventure films, which they accomplish by placing the camera in a trench and having the mounted horses gallop over the trench. The resulting shots resound with energy and strength, as the horses appear to leap across the frame from bottom to top. An example from the opposite end of the spectrum is the extremely high-angle long shot of Yossarian (Alan Arkin) paddling a rubber raft, which concludes Mike Nichols' *Catch-22* (1970). By filming Yossarian from such a high angle, Nichols underscored the futility of the character's attempt to escape from World War II.

The running speed of the camera provides an additional means of control over motion within the frame. Some of the earliest screen directors were very much aware of the expressionistic and comic possibilities of slowing down, speeding up, or reversing the motion on the screen. Slow motion, which filmmakers occasionally use to give ordinary motion a quality of grace and rhythm, has become the hallmark of surrealism. Avant-garde filmmakers of the 1920s revealed how effectively slow motion could be used to suggest dream experiences, and many subsequent filmmakers have continued using it for this purpose. A dream sequence in William Friedkin's *The Exorcist* (1973), in which Father Karras (Jason Miller) imagines his mother ascending a subway staircase in slow motion, is only one of many examples of this tendency. Slow motion has also been of service to directors such as Jean Vigo, who employed it to heighten a memorable pillow fight at a boys' boarding school in *Zero for Conduct* (1933), and Leni Riefenstahl, who used it in *Olympia* (1938), her documentary of the 1936 Berlin Olympic Games, to help create a visual hymn to the human body in flight during the famous men's diving sequence (see Fig. 10–5).

The late 1960s saw the introduction of a macabre "dance of death" in films, in which directors placed the most brutal and bloody actions before the slow-motion camera. Particularly memorable if disquieting examples are the orgies of violence that conclude *Bonnie and Clyde* (1967), *The Wild Bunch* (1969), and *Straw Dogs* (1971), all of which were aesthetized into slow-motion ballets of vile destruction. Scenes of slow-motion violence are by turns fascinating and repellent, but their overuse by filmmakers has quickly lowered them today to the status of clichés.

As for fast and reverse motion, filmmakers have traditionally employed them for comic purposes, as the works of Georges Méliès, Mack Sennett, and countless other producers of screen comedy continually remind us. These filmmakers gave added momentum and absurdist flair to the comic chase in particular by speeding up its action; Sennett's Keystone Kops comedies still provide some of the best examples, with their fast-motion photography increasing the apparent danger as wildly careening cars narrowly miss such obstacles as telephone poles, other automobiles, and locomotives (see Fig. 1–3). A relatively recent manifestation of comic fast motion may be found in Kubrick's *A Clockwork Orange*, which features an artificially speeded-up lovemaking scene involving Alex (Malcolm McDowell) and two young women. Set to the trenchant strains of the "William Tell Overture," the orgy scene is over in less than a minute.

Several filmmakers have experimented with fast motion for dramatic purposes, but without much success. F. W. Murnau tried using it dramatically in his early film version of the Dracula saga, *Nosferatu* (1922), by speeding up the motion of the carriage that brings the protagonist to the vampire's castle. Though Murnau's presumed intent was to underscore the supernatural qualities of the environment the protagonist had just entered, the effect seems rather silly today. Filmmakers have had their best luck with fast-motion photography by using it for either comic purposes or revealing normally unseen motions or developments. They can achieve the latter effect by "undercranking" the camera or actually stopping it between frames, thereby revealing motion not normally visible because of the slow speed at which it occurs. Joris Ivens recorded the boiling and billowing of cloud formations in *Rain* (1929), his impressionistic study of a rain shower in Amsterdam, while countless science films and classroom "true-life adventures" have used time-lapse photography to record the opening of blossoms, sprouting of seeds, and hatching of eggs.

The freezing of motion also has both expository and narrative possibilities. Directors have used stop-motion photography in particular as a means of arresting movement to permit the scrutiny of an object that would otherwise be gone too quickly. For example, one of the camera operators who photographed the documentary *Gimme Shelter* (1970) accidentally captured an actual murder on film. The resulting image was so brief and indistinct, however, that the filmmakers used both slow motion and frozen motion in the completed film to make the event more observable to audiences. Filmmakers have also frozen motion whenever they have wished to offer a sense of permanence, completion, or nostalgia. After the young hero of François Truffaut's *The 400 Blows* (1959) finds himself trapped by the sea and realizes the futility of his escape attempt, Truffaut concludes the film by freezing the boy's image. Frozen motion also concludes *Butch Cassidy and the Sundance Kid*, after the title characters run from cover to their final encounter with their pursuers. To preserve the audience's warm feelings for these outlaws as they rush headlong into a fatal confrontation, director George Roy Hill froze the twosome into what becomes a sepia-tone photograph from a bygone day. A variety of filmmakers have shown that control of the speed of movement can serve multiple and diverse functions in both fiction and nonfiction films. It is an essential ingredient for what Siegfried Kracauer has called the "revealing function" of film.

Movement by the Camera (Secondary Movement)

Besides the movement that occurs within the frame, motion in film can also be realized through movement of the camera itself. After anchoring the camera to a fixed tripod, a filmmaker may pivot the camera from left to right or vice versa to produce what is called the *pan* shot, or vertically to create the *tilt* shot. When the filmmaker frees the camera from its fixed position on the tripod, several other types of moving-camera shots are made possible: the *dolly* shot, which involves movement of the entire camera toward or away from a stationary subject (see also our discussion of zoom lenses earlier in this chapter); the *trucking* (or *tracking*) shot, which concerns the horizontal movement of the camera parallel to a moving subject; and the *crane* shot, in which a platform-mounted camera moves above and around the subject in virtually any direction.

Identifying the "first" use of each moving-camera technique is difficult and probably not particularly enlightening, but the employment of the devices can be traced back to some of the earliest silent films. What is significant is that these initial uses of the moving camera were usually limited to such practical functions as keeping the action within the frame and following a moving subject. Examples of both these functions may be observed in Edwin Porter's *The Great Train Robbery*, in which the camera is mounted at one point on the tender of a stolen train. The movement of the camera past the wooded outdoor scene shortly gives way to a brief downward tilt as it follows the escaping bandits down the railroad embankment after the train has been stopped. Often cited and clearly more dramatic uses of camera movement may be found in D. W. Griffith's *The Birth of a Nation* (1915), including the slight pan of the camera that reveals Sherman's army on the march to Atlanta and the sea, and the spectacular trucking shots of the Ku Klux Klan riding to the rescue at the conclusion of the film.

Significant innovations in the use of the moving camera came about in Europe toward the close of the silent era. With the most advanced equipment and facilities, and under the most controlled of conditions, German filmmakers transformed the camera from passive observer to active participant, even to the point of revealing action as observed by one of the characters. In *Variety* (1925), for example, E. A. Dupont suspended his camera from a trapeze to present a circus aerialist's point of view, while F. W. Murnau strapped his camera to his cinematographer's chest to present a drunken subjective view in *The Last Laugh* (1924). In addition, the latter film opens with a spectacular sweep of the camera down an open elevator and across the lobby of a svelte Berlin hotel, thus permitting the viewer to become one of the guests, in a sense. France's Abel Gance provided some of the most audacious uses of the moving camera in his *Napoleon*, which featured shots from cameras strapped to horses and mounted on a trapeze-like mechanism similar to the one used by Murnau.

Technology and creative energy have together extended the functions of the moving camera over the years, and today we find filmmakers employing pans, dollies, and trucking shots for a variety of compositional, thematic, and psychological uses. The earliest and most obvious examples of the moving camera fall under the compositional category. When Edwin Porter briefly tilted his camera during the filming of *The Great Train Robbery*, for example, he clearly did so merely to keep the subject—the escaping bandits—within view. Since Porter's day, other directors have found different compositional purposes for the moving camera. A primary example is a filmmaker's camera tilt or pan across a relatively static subject to compensate for the fixed proportions of the frame. Although filmmakers must compose their shots within a fixed ratio, they can accentuate either the horizontal or vertical dimension by slowly panning the horizon or tilting the camera up a tall subject, such as the face of a skyscraper. The pan and the tilt have become cinematic clichés today because of the very liberation they afford from the fixed frame; indeed, our best directors have used them most judiciously. Filmmakers also use pans or tilts to emphasize either the spatial relationship between elements of the scene or to establish an associative value. In other words, they can create clear associations or show connections between two relatively static subjects by panning or tilting from one to the other.

Closely related to establishing spatial or other associative relationships is the use of camera movement to establish the center of interest and to focus attention on significant details of a scene. Filmmakers can bestow a "star status" on inanimate, nondescript objects—items that might otherwise escape the audience's attention—by filming them with tracking, dollying, or hovering cameras. In the early moments of *Earthquake* (1974), for example, a hairline crack in a California dam does not attract our attention until the camera moves in to exclude other components of the scene competing for our attention. Similarly, audiences would hardly give any notice to a tower clock that has stopped in an early scene in Lean's *Great Expectations* had the director not moved his camera during this and subsequent shots to establish that all of Miss Haversham's clocks have stopped at exactly the same time—on her wedding day. Of course, a filmmaker can tie a general scene to a specific detail by cutting from the larger scene to a close-up of the accented object, but the movement of the camera usually provides a smoother and more effective means of establishing physical links, particularly spatial relationships.

The filmmaker can use the moving camera for at least two other largely compositional functions: to create an illusion of depth and to give a sense of motion to static objects. We have already noted that a filmmaker can suggest depth by having subjects within the frame move toward or away from the camera, but an alternative—moving the camera into or out of the scene—will produce a similar result. In Akira Kurosawa's *Rashomon* (1951), for instance, forest branches part to allow the camera (and us) to pass, giving us a sense of the depth of the forest into which a Samurai bridegroom and his wife have wandered.

Narrative filmmakers have frequently employed the moving camera to suggest motion in static objects, but documentarists of the art world have perfected this technique. They have attempted to bring paintings and sculptures to life in countless films by allowing the camera to hover above or around details of the works before moving it on to explore other details. A particularly effective example may be found in the art documentary *The Titan*, in which Michelangelo's sculptures of the Pietà and David are made to appear more lifelike by the camera's constantly shifting perspective. In the scenes devoted to the statue of David, the filmmakers further accented the vibrance and power of the work by focusing on such motion-related details as arm and leg muscles and the slingshot in David's hand.

Directors may occasionally suggest a cause-and-effect relationship between two objects by panning or tilting from one to the other. A prime example is the "reaction pan," in which the camera shifts perspective from a stimulus to its receiver. Filmmakers have used this technique in situations ranging from verbal assaults to pie fights. In Jean-Luc Godard's *Weekend* (1967), the director linked the stimulus of a cello solo performed in a French barnyard to a group of farm hands and other onlookers through a complete 360-degree pan of the barnyard. The pan allows the audience to examine the various facial expressions, which range from boredom to rapture, before the camera returns to the object of the group's attention, the cellist. Dennis Hopper and Peter Fonda incorporated a similar 360-degree sweep of the camera in their *Easy Rider* (1969) to capture the reactions of commune members to another musical performance. If a filmmaker wanted to say in cinematic language, "The train came into view and the workers paused to watch it pass," that person might well pan from the train to the watching workers and perhaps, to make the causal relationship crystal clear, back once again to the train as the workers watched it pass. As an alternative, the filmmaker could establish a similar relationship by cutting from the train to the workers and then back to the train. Though the space between the train and the workers would be broken up through the editing process, this latter method is perhaps less self-conscious than the former, due to its high familiarity with audiences.

Filmmakers may also use the moving camera to establish or reinforce some thematic concept. They might employ it, for example, to introduce visual details gradually to suggest the growth of an idea. At the conclusion of *Citizen Kane*, the camera slowly glides over the contents of the Xanadu basement storeroom in a single shot and thereby accomplishes several things. It not only reaffirms Charles Foster Kane's lifelong obsession with collecting *objets* both *d'art* and *d'trash*, but it also embodies a symbolic search for the key to the enigma of that life and the mystery of the dying man's words. In another scene from the same film—the debut of Susan Alexander Kane at the Chicago Opera House built for her by her husband—the camera initially records the frantic scurrying on stage as the overture swells. It then drifts upward with the rising curtain to reveal two stagehands standing on a catwalk, one of whom holds his nose in a wordless comment on Susan Kane's singing.

A number of filmmakers have made the traveling shot a favorite means of handling opening-scene exposition, and it often provides a spectacular trip into the core of the film. In such a shot, the director often begins the camera movement with a sweeping panoramic view to help establish the setting of the film before eventually settling on some detail within the setting. The traveling shot thus creates the effect of whisking the viewer directly into the heart of the film, which directors Robert Wise and Alfred Hitchcock accomplished effectively in their respective films *West Side Story* (1961) and *Frenzy*. With the aid of a helicopter, each director began his film with a traveling shot consisting initially of a broad view of a large city (New York in the former film, London in the latter) that eventually became a close view of a considerably smaller event within the city. Laurence Olivier used the device to give his audience an aerial view of Elizabethan London before lowering his camera through the top of the Globe Theater in his *Henry V* (1945). Directors pursuing a popular variation on the technique reverse the movement and allow close-ups to give way to increasingly broader views. John Schlesinger used a novel and ironic approach in *Midnight Cowboy* (1969) when he began the film with a completely blank screen and pulled back to reveal the screen's location: a movie drive-in theater, complete with a children's playground in front of the screen. We quickly learn that the theater is set in a lackluster western town where the protagonist Joe Buck (Jon Voight) works as a short-order cook. The director of *The China Syndrome* (1979), James Bridges, achieved a similar effect by starting and ending the film with close-ups of a television test pattern consisting of vertical color bars. In both instances, the filmmakers reminded the audiences (at least fleetingly) that the stories they are viewing are indeed *mediated* stories.

Filmmakers may also use camera movement to establish symbolic detail or action by moving in on, or away from, the details of a scene. In Fred Zinnemann's *From Here to Eternity* (1953), to cite one example, the camera avoids a sexual encounter between an Army sergeant and his company commander's wife by pulling back through an open window. The withdrawal of the camera from sexual intimacies to focus on an open window has won cliché status (especially if it is raining) because it has proven a triple threat for so long: it establishes aesthetic credentials by introducing symbolic details; it satisfies the censors by not presenting explicit lovemaking in front of the camera; and it leaves so much to the viewer's imagination. Before the technique became a cliché, E. A. Dupont used it subtly and masterfully in *Variety* (1925) when he established the first illicit meeting between a handsome trapeze artist and the wife of another performer. At that point in the film, Dupont moved the camera to the open window where the fluttering curtains become still as the door to the hotel room is closed. Such an indirect suggestion of the beginning of an intimate relationship is far more effective than a shot of the closing door or perhaps even of an actual embrace.

An indispensable use of the moving camera in narrative design is to facilitate a transition between scenes. By using the camera to search out and link a detail of one scene to the same or similar detail in the next scene, filmmakers follow a standard if often cliché-ridden means of moving the viewers smoothly from one time or place to the next. Many modern feature-film directors have bypassed the device in favor of cutting more directly and spontaneously from scene to scene.

In addition to demonstrating the compositional and thematic functions of camera movement within the shot, filmmakers have shown that it also has significant psychological implications. To help increase the tension of a scene, for example, a director will frequently use a slowly panning or trucking camera to heighten our expectations. Alfred Hitchcock provided a fine example in *Frenzy*. A man whom the audience knows is a killer has invited a young woman into his second-floor apartment located on the edge of London's busy Covent Garden produce market area. The camera leads us away from the anticipated murder, and thereby increases our suspense, by slowly descending the apartment staircase in a long trucking shot. The camera continues out into the street, where it quickly becomes apparent that the noise from the bustling marketplace would completely obliterate the woman's cries for help. Filmmakers also use camera movement to create a tempo enhancing a certain mood or atmosphere for a scene. It ranges from the lyrically paced camera movement contributing to the serenity and romantic ambience of such period films as *Elvira Madigan* (1967) and *Barry Lyndon* (1975) to the choppy, frenetic movement underscoring the violence of *Straw Dogs*, *The French Connection* (1971), and *Taxi Driver* (1976).

Besides using camera movement to put the audience in an appropriate mood, filmmakers often employ it to invite the spectators to role-play. The moving camera can simulate the eye movement of a character and permit the viewers to see and experience the action from that character's perspective *within* the scene. The subjective experience has long played an important part in screen drama, and an example may be found in *Variety* when cinematographer Karl Freund put his camera—and thus his film audience—on the Winter Garden trapeze. In this film, the spectators see not only the protagonist's actual view of the Winter Garden audience, but also his fantasies. Similarly, the audience viewing *An Occurrence at Owl Creek Bridge* experiences the twilight world of that film's protagonist by seeing virtually all of the action through his eyes.[9]

Filmmakers are quite able to extend our role-playing beyond the characters on the screen. Via camera movement, directors can transport us to propitious vantage points that afford omniscient views. With improved camera mobility and zoom lenses, filmmakers today are able to permit their audiences to shift perspectives continually while frequently allowing them the most realistic, involving, revealing, or otherwise advantageous views of the action.

Whether we are looking through the eyes of a single film character or seeing the action from a godlike, all-knowing perspective, modern filmmakers frequently give us the sense that we are watching a spontaneous occurrence they captured on celluloid. Greatly assisted by the development of highly portable camera equipment, directors such as John Cassavetes and Robert Altman have demonstrated that the spontaneous and unrehearsed quality so often found in documentaries need not be limited to such films but can add a new dimension in realism to the fiction film as well. In *Dr. Strangelove*, for example, Stanley Kubrick photographed much of a military assault on an Air Force base with a hand-held camera to give it a realistic, documentary-like veneer. Gillo Pontecorvo employed the same technique throughout *The Battle of Algiers* (1966), a narrative film depicting various stages of the Algierian revolt against the French from 1954 to 1962. With the help of jittery hand-held cameras and grainy film stock—elements we frequently associate with documentaries—Pontecorvo created a powerful sense of immediacy and realism in this film.

Apparent Movement Through Editing (Tertiary Movement)

Directors wishing to imbue their films with life and a sense of flow are by no means limited to recording action in front of the lens or to moving the camera. A critical source of movement in motion pictures is created through the editing process. Indeed, the entire field of *animation* is founded on the principle of apparent motion through editing. Whether animators work with three-dimensional clay models, two-dimensional drawings, or simple inanimate objects, the procedure they follow is basically the same: a slight adjustment of the subjects (sometimes only a fraction of an inch) while the camera is off, followed by the exposure of a few frames of film. Repeated ad infinitum, this painstaking *in-camera* editing process endows the static subjects with a remarkable—indeed, magical—illusion of movement when the finished film is projected.

Filmmakers also create a significant part of the motion in movies by cutting from one shot within a scene to another, thereby shifting the audience's per-

Figure 2-26 *Dr. Strangelove* (1964—American). Stanley Kubrick used hand-held camerawork while filming the attack on Burpelson Air Force Base to give that sequence from *Dr. Strangelove* a texture found in many documentaries.

spective and attention with the scene. Other significant aspects that lend the sensation of motion to the medium—and help distinguish it from the other arts and media—are the movement in time and space from scene to scene and even the intellectual leap the audience must make between two disparate images juxtaposed to create a metaphoric message (the image of a politician followed immediately by the image of a fox).

All of these devices and techniques are closely tied to the editing process. Because of this, we will explore them in the broader context of montage theory and practice (that is, the nature and rationale for the selection, arrangement, and length of individual shots) in the chapter that follows.

NOTES

[1]Hugo Mauerhofer, "Psychology of Film Experience," in *Film: A Montage of Theories*, ed. Richard Dyer MacCann (New York: Dutton, 1966), pp. 229-35. Mauerhofer centers on the lack of competing stimuli, absorption in the screen image, distention of time and space as steps leading to the more acute powers of imagination.

[2]Soviet filmmakers and theorists adopted the term "montage" to describe not only the physical process of editing but also the creative rationale or theory of film construction through the editing process.

[3]Béla Balázs, *Theory of the Film: Character and Growth of a New Art*, trans. Edith Bone (New York: Dover, 1970), pp. 52-60.

[4]James Stewart, "Actor James Stewart Talks About Movies and America," *U. S. News and World Report*, Nov. 15, 1976, p. 86.

[5]Balázs, *Theory of the Film*, pp. 52-60.

[6]André Sennwald, "The Future of Color," in *Introduction to the Art of the Movies*, ed. Lewis Jacobs (New York: Noonday Press, 1960), pp. 232-35.

[7]Ibid., p. 235.

[8]Sergei Eisenstein, *The Film Sense* (New York: Harcourt Brace & Co., 1942), p. 121.

[9]Subjective camera work is also essential in introducing the viewer to Guido's fantasies in Federico Fellini's $8\frac{1}{2}$ (1963) and Isak Borg's nightmares in Bergman's *Wild Strawberries*. In Robert Montgomery's cinematic treatment of Raymond Chandler's *Lady in the Lake* (1946), the view becomes completely subjective; we see only what the protagonist Philip Marlowe sees throughout the entire film.

3

FILM PROPERTIES AND FUNDAMENTALS OF TECHNIQUE: editing and sound

EDITING

Developing Functions

Film differs from photography and painting in that it is a temporal as well as a spatial medium. Since film involves progression and change over time, film-makers must make decisions regarding the starting and stopping of action, its integration with other units of action, and the most effective ways of transporting the viewer from one location or time period to the next. Editing is without doubt a critical function of the cinematic process. Indeed, film's status as an incredibly flexible means of expression is due in large measure to the great range of possibilities in the selection and arrangement of individual shots.

The physical act of editing is easy to describe and nearly as simple to accomplish; it basically involves the joining of the end of one piece of film with the beginning of the next (accomplished with film cement or splicing tape) so that the second shot will follow the first when projected. *Editing* is used interchangeably with the term *cutting* to describe that part of the filmmaking process which involves the splicing together of shots that will eventually make up the finished film.

The *rationale* for editing choices, however, makes the procedure considerably more complex. The choices begin with the selection and arrangement of shots to create basic units of action in time and space called *scenes*. In addition, filmmakers must decide on the arrangement of the individual scenes to create *sequences*. (Both narrative units are imprecise, but the former usually refers to a collection of shots unified by time and place, while the latter refers to a collection of related scenes leading to a major climax in the film.) Finally, filmmakers must decide on the length and arrangement of sequences within the film itself. The conclusion of one sequence and the commencement of the next is usually characterized by a major shift in time, location, or both.

The arrangement of shots may involve an even more complex set of associations between them. The filmmaker's choices may include creating relationships between ideas, forms, physical movement, and duration as well as those of basic narrative construction. Besides basic continuity and smoothness in either exposition or narrative progression, filmmakers are concerned with creating pace and rhythm, timing cuts for dramatic emphasis, and drawing on various associations of images. Thus, filmmakers move well beyond the mere mechanics of shot-linking, often to explore various expressive means of editing.

Though editing initially took the form of simple and straightforward linking of related shots, it quickly became a key element of the earliest attempts at screen storytelling. The pioneers of filmic storytelling—Georges Méliès in France, Edwin S. Porter in America, and Cecil Hepworth in Great Britain—were also the first to explore the role of editing in narrative construction. Méliès went beyond the single-shot film, for example, by linking several of his so-termed "artificially arranged scenes," thereby introducing progression that involved changes in location and lapses in time. In 1899, he produced the screen world's first *Cinderella*, a "motion tableaux" film consisting of 20 scenes. His film *A Trip to the Moon* is recognized today as a milestone in film history in part because through it Méliès demonstrated the technique of selecting and combining several units of an action to complete a multiple-scene story extending over several minutes. The scenes include a meeting of the "Royal Astronomical Society," the foundry where the rocket is produced, the launching pad, the lunar surface, a cave of the Selenites, the lunar launching site, the ocean "recovery area," the docking, and the homecoming celebration. By linking these scenes through the editing process, Méliès had developed a relatively complex story line that stretched across many different locales.

Edwin Porter took an important step further than Méliès by first establishing several units of action in his *The Great Train Robbery*, including a telegraph office, a dance hall, the baggage compartment of a train, and a wooded glade. He then proceeded to move his narrative back and forth among the locations until the action reached a satisfactory climax and conclusion. In two subsequent films, *The Ex-Convict* and *The Kleptomaniac*, Porter extended the use of cutting back and forth between separate scenes—called *crosscutting*—to compare and contrast the two central situations of each film. In the former film, he contrasted the lifestyle of a rich industrialist with that of a man released from prison, while in the latter, he made a similar point regarding social inequities by crosscutting between a judge's disposition of two cases of theft—an affluent shoplifter and a woman stealing bread for her family.

Building on the work of Méliès, Porter, and others, David Wark Griffith opened up a broad range of functions for film editing in the 450 films he made for the Biograph Company between 1908 and 1913. He refined the use of cross-cutting by controlling the length of the shots to create tempo and heighten the tension inherent in his melodramatic subjects. He introduced the flashback to screen narrative, and he dared to cut into and away from an action already in progress. He also developed a kind of visual punctuation between scenes by using such devices as the *fade*, through which the image gradually darkens until the screen becomes completely black, and the *iris*, a circular masking device that gradually closes off the view of one scene before opening up on the next.

Griffith's most significant contributions to narrative construction through editing, however, were his shifting of perspective within the scene and his understanding that each individual scene could be composed of several bits of incomplete action. The order and selection of these actions could be governed by the requirements of the drama, and their meaning could arise from their juxtaposition or relationship with one another. Griffith's emphasis on the individual shot as the basic building block of narrative construction served as the point of departure for many of his successors and imitators, particularly the young Soviet filmmakers who were themselves to make the most significant contributions to the art of editing during the 1920s.

The key characteristic of the body of cinema and theory that emerged from the Soviet Union during this time was the belief that editing (or *montage*, a term the Russians borrowed from the French, which roughly means *assemblage*) was the central and paramount creative act in filmmaking. Sergei Eisenstein and V.I. Pudovkin, leaders of both the theoretical and practical dimensions of the movement,[1] extended the uses of editing in daring and dramatic ways. Whereas Griffith would photograph a scene in medium or long shot and use the close-up for exposition or dramatic impact, Pudovkin would obtain impressive and meaningful drama by constructing a scene entirely from the accumulation of relevant details. He developed a theory of relational editing that built on the Griffith and Porter methods of contrast and parallel construction but that also dealt with the creation of symbolism through shot juxtaposition. He employed this latter technique in his own film, *Mother* (1925), in which scenes of marching workers united in their resolve are intercut with scenes of ice floes breaking up on Russian rivers during the spring thaw. By such juxtapositions, Pudovkin was perhaps attempting to make the point that the revolutionary spirit was just as inevitable as the spring thaw, and that its potential for shattering the old order was just as strong as that demonstrated by the river current's shattering of the ice. Pudovkin shaped these and other torrents of visual details into powerful montage constructions that were as revolutionary in style as they were in theme.

Like Pudovkin, Eisenstein believed that a film was not shot but built piece by piece (that is, shot by shot) through editing, with the meaning of the scene arising from the accumulation and arrangement of detail. But whereas Pudovkin stressed the importance of encouraging the viewer to accept the filmmaker's point of view through a generally *invisible* linkage of shots (a smoothly flowing series of shots in which the editing does not call undue attention to itself), Eisenstein insisted on grabbing the audience's attention through a highly noticeable editing style in which the shots collided with one another. He built his theories of editing on the *dialectical construct* posed by Georg Hegel and Karl Marx, which suggests that meaning arises out of the juxtaposition and reconciliation of opposites. Their general formula read somewhat like this: Thesis "A" followed by its opposite, Antithesis "B," equals Synthesis "C." As adapted by Eisenstein to film, it became: Shot "A" followed by Shot "B" equals not AB but something new—Concept C. If a shot of a person greedily devouring food is followed by the shot of a pig gorging itself at a trough, for example, a new concept not inherent in the individual shots—such as "that person eats like a pig" or "that person *is* a pig"—arises as a result of their juxtaposition.

Eisenstein's films actually reveal a more eclectic approach to editing than his treatises on montage might suggest. In addition to the "collision of images," his films display an understanding and effective use of parallelism (cutting back and forth between two events occurring simultaneously), connotation through the use of close-ups of symbolic detail (such as the dangling *pince-nez* of the ship's doctor in *The Battleship Potemkin*, described in Chapter 2), the expansion as well as the contraction of time through editing, and the creation of rhythm and tempo by control of shot length.

Further invention, refinements, and experiments followed the efforts of these editing innovators, resulting in the basic approaches and methods of film editing that still serve us today, including:

1. Basic construction—the design of the film, whether narrative or not, to provide an orderly and meaningful exposition or statement of theme.
2. Dramatic emphasis—through the use of shot breakdown, relational editing, rhythm and tempo, to increase the effectiveness of the filmed action on the observer.
3. Creative montage—recognizing the natural association that one assumes exists among juxtaposed images, to create, through the accumulation of details, an object, place, or abstract idea not present in the individual shots.

Implicit in all of these methods is the creation of associative values through the linkage of images. In dealing with both the basic design of the film and its dramatic emphasis, directors often create their own filmic space and filmic time, items that may have no perfect correlates in the real world. In other words, the editing process enables filmmakers to create locations and senses of time that may not necessarily exist in real life. An example of the former, which pioneers such as Pudovkin called "creative geography," may be found in the domestic scenes of Michael Cimino's 1979 film, *The Deer Hunter*. Ostensibly set in a small western Pennsylvania town, these portions of the film actually consist of footage recorded not only in that part of the state but also in Ohio and Oregon. Edited together, however, the scenes appear to represent one general location (but only if one is willing to overlook the fact that mountains are not snowcapped year-round in western Pennsylvania).

Regarding the creation of filmic time, we should note that filmmakers actually work with two time frames different from the real time in which the recorded action unfolds:

1. The filmic or dramatic time (that is, the time covered by the story), which may extend to centuries and even millennia, as Mel Brooks' *History of the World, Part I* (1981) and Stanley Kubrick's *2001: A Space Odyssey* (1968) have demonstrated; and
2. The mental or psychological time that appears to elapse while an action is being

observed. The action of the famous "Odessa Steps" sequence of *The Battleship Potemkin* would probably have taken only a few seconds in real life, for example, but Eisenstein chose to stretch it out over several minutes of screen time, presumably for several reasons: to heighten the tension and suspense of the moment, and to simulate our perception and cognition of the event were we there watching it happen in real life.

Through shot selection and control of the length of the shots, therefore, filmmakers are able to create their own locations for action and can also extend or compress the length of time in which it will occur. They will also frequently use the natural association that viewers will make between joined images to create certain inferences. In addition to spatial and temporal inferences arising from shot relationships, filmmakers may allow for conceptual inferences that involve visual symbols and enable the filmmakers to deal with abstract ideas (such as that arising from the politician/fox shot-juxtaposition suggested earlier).

Filmmakers can perform these editing functions by accomplishing four basic tasks: (1) Selecting the shots they will use in the finished film; (2) trimming excess footage from the beginning and end of each shot, if deemed necessary; (3) choosing the section of the film to insert the shots; (4) arranging the shots within that section. Yet it should be apparent that the simplicity of these variables belies the complex and extensive range of editing possibilities.

Basic Forms

NARRATIVE CONSTRUCTION.   If we look at the ways in which present-day film editors select, arrange, and time their shots, we find that the same categories that early filmmakers and theorists used to describe the works of their day still serve quite adequately. Choosing the overall design or structure of the film is still a fundamental activity that filmmakers must undertake. In his book *The Film Sense*, Eisenstein spoke of the "need for connected and sequential exposition of the theme," and today's directors find that the organization of time and space for purposes of general continuity and progression are immediate and central concerns. On the most fundamental and practical level, a filmmaker builds a scene from an accumulation of details of an action. Unless the purpose is to leave the audience in a state of uncertainty, a filmmaker will probably edit the details together smoothly and naturally, making sure that the scene is free of disruptive breaks in tempo, ambiguous relationships, and disorienting shifts in focus. The filmmaker is usually interested in giving the illusion of continuous action and eliminating extraneous shots in order to focus on that detail which best conveys the meaning of a scene.

Through the natural association of images, the filmmaker is able to establish spatial, temporal, and thematic links that will help convey a message not evident in the individual shots. D. W. Griffith provided many excellent examples of the ways these several means to basic design and continuity could be employed. In the sequence depicting the assassination of Abraham Lincoln in *The Birth of a Nation*, Griffith skillfully brought together four units of action to recreate a historic event in a clear, smooth, and convincing manner. Using a replica of Ford's Theater as the setting, Griffith cut from the action on the stage to Phil and Elsie Stoneman in the audience. From there he cut to the Presidential party in the theater box and then to the action involving Lincoln's bodyguard and John Wilkes Booth just outside the box. Within several seconds, Griffith smoothly and quickly introduced the essential units of action. The fateful climax of the scene then unfolds with a quickening tempo while the film audience observes all the action from a constantly shifting, omniscient vantage point.

John Ford provided an equally masterful if less momentous example of smooth and direct exposition in the opening of *The Informer* (1935), his study of the effects of poverty on friendship during the Irish rebellion. With well-chosen visual detail, Ford offered the basic exposition and character motivation in a minimum of screen time. The story takes place in the fog-enshrouded environs of 1922 Dublin, where the taunting and flirtatious Katie (Heather Angel) has dreams of sailing to America. Hard-drinking Gypo Nolan (Victor McLaglen), desperate in his lack of funds with which to buy drinks and keep Katie happy, sees a window display advertising ship passage to America for twenty pounds. He also discovers a poster offering a twenty-pound reward for information leading to the capture of his friend, Frankie McPhillip. Perhaps too pat by today's standards, this scene does a most effective job of presenting basic exposition through editing (see also Fig. 7-5).

In both the Griffith and Ford films, editing is critical to exposition and plot progression. Both illustrate the ways that directors can build the action and message of a scene by gathering select details logically related by cause and effect. There is, however, an important difference between the two scenes just described; the details in Griffith's Lincoln assassination sequence are all part of the same limited physical setting, while those in the Ford film are not. Griffith used editing to unite four separate actions within the context of one general setting and, to a limited extent, to provide dramatic emphasis. Ford's method included the kind of creative montage that draws its meaning from a collection of thematically related images that are not part of a single, limited setting.

Moviemakers usually observe some basic rules of "grammar" when building a scene effectively through editing. When constructed successfully, the scene will provide a logical flow of images in which the action of one shot smoothly matches the action of the next. Filmmakers can accomplish an economy of expression by eliminating extraneous detail while observing the rules of continuity that prevent a scene from becoming a jumble of shots. The rules they usually follow constitute what has become known as *psychological editing*. In other words, traditional filmmakers believe that the most natural and unobtrusive means of editing a scene is to present it in such a way as to resemble the spectators' psychological processes. If a seated person in a close shot begins to stand, for example, the filmmaker will usually cut to a wider-angle shot, or at least a shot from a different perspective, to keep the person in the frame. If the filmmaker cuts on the movement, the editing would mimic the way the spectators would normally shift their attention if they were watching a person rise from a chair in real life. If, on the other hand, the filmmaker cuts *before* the movement, the mimicking quality would be lost and the editing (and through it the filmmaker's presence) would subsequently become more apparent to the audience. In both cases, the filmmaker determines to a large extent what the spectators will see, but the former editing approach is considerably subtler and more "invisible" than the latter.

Filmmakers have explored other ways of linking shots for purposes of narrative progression, such as the many visual and aural montage devices that Orson

Welles used in *Citizen Kane* to allow the narrative to cover sizable periods of time. To show Charles Foster Kane's mounting interest in Susan Alexander, for example, Welles presented a scene of Susan performing at an upright piano in her modestly furnished apartment after the two have just met. He then follows this with the scene featuring more elegant surroundings (including a grand piano) depicted in Fig. 3–1. Susan performs the same song through the transition.

DRAMATIC EMPHASIS.   Welles and many other creative filmmakers have frequently gone beyond the basics of construction to more imaginative uses of montage. British director Karel Reisz underscored this point when he wrote, "Although mechanical rules of cutting must be kept in mind, the decisive consider-

Figure 3–1   *Citizen Kane* (1941—American). Orson Welles gave cohesion and flow to *Kane's* intricate narrative through a variety of visual and aural montage devices. He succinctly underscored the growing infatuation of Charles Foster Kane for Susan Alexander by combining a scene of Susan performing on an upright piano in her modestly furnished apartment on their first meeting with this scene of more elegant surroundings. Susan is heard continuing the same song through the transition.

ation at the junction of any two shots must be that the transition be motivated by dramatic necessity."[2] "Dramatic necessity" for many of today's filmmakers means an intentionally frenetic, seemingly disjointed, often cryptic association of images to reflect the mood and temper of the times. The rationale for scene construction in such films may be less apparent, even though the filmmaker is following a carefully planned and often complex design.

One way the filmmaker can step beyond the bare mechanics of scene building is to use editing to increase the scene's dramatic intensity. The filmmaker can control the timing of the individual cuts and the spacing of events within the whole narrative to reveal a series of actions at the psychologically appropriate moment. Scientists have proven empirically what directors such as Alfred Hitchcock have known intuitively for years: that a film viewer's anxiety level increases dramatically during the *anticipation* of an event, object, etc., rather than during its actual appearance on the screen.[3] Hitchcock's reputation as the "master of suspense" came largely from his ability to predict audience responses and tolerance levels and to know exactly when to conceal and when to reveal details of an action. The control of timing is not in the province of directors who create suspense thrillers alone, however. Filmmakers can heighten the emotional impact of any narrative form—dramatic, tragic, or comic—through the editing process.

Moviemakers can use timing to influence the spectator in another way by establishing pace and rhythm within the scene. D. W. Griffith intuitively understood the dramatic potential of controlling shot length and used it to give an added sense of urgency to the climactic moments in many of his works. In his famous early short film *Lonely Villa* (1909), Griffith presented two events occurring simultaneously: bandits menacing a woman and several of her children in their unguarded home, and the woman's husband riding home to the rescue. In addition to cutting back and forth between these events, Griffith made sure to make each succeeding shot just a little bit shorter than the previous one until the events eventually converged (that is, until the husband finally arrived home to rescue his family). Through this editing technique, which has been popularly labeled the "last minute rescue," Griffith helped instill a breathless quality into this and countless other melodramatic situations. His most famous last minute rescue is tied to a highly controversial subject: the Ku Klux Klan, when dozens of its members ride to the rescue of some white people menaced by blacks at the conclusion of *The Birth of a Nation*. Strongly influenced by Griffith's editing procedures, Sergei Eisenstein conceptualized several "methods of montage," two of which concerned pace and rhythm in film. The first of these is termed *metric*, in which the filmmaker virtually ignores any motion within the frame while editing and instead measures out each shot according to some preplanned formula (such as Griffith's last minute rescues, wherein each shot, regardless of content, is somewhat shorter than the previous one). The second is called *rhythmic*, whereby the moviemaker indeed takes into account motion within the frame when establishing the tempo of the film. For example, a filmmaker may decide to keep a motion-filled shot on the screen longer than a static one since the audience may not apprehend all the information in the former situation as quickly as in the latter. Interestingly, Eisenstein described the construction of film in these and other writings in very much the way a composer might characterize the creation of a musical score.[4]

Directors today will vary pace and establish tempo through editing in order to accent the dramatic intensity of key moments of conflict and to bring to life scenes that might otherwise remain uninvolving. Despite Eisenstein's prescriptive elaborations on metric and rhythmic montage, there are usually few rules regarding rhythm and tempo in film construction. Yet the nature of the shot content will frequently influence the speed of cutting, and when motion is present within the shot, cutting to the rhythm of the action will help reinforce the action itself. An example may be drawn from *The River* (1937), a documentary focusing on the Mississippi River and related topics such as soil conservation and flood control. During the flood sequence, the filmmaker, Pare Lorentz, employed a rapid succession of images to reinforce the drama and urgency of that event. A deliberate and relatively long look at a single drop of water falling from an icicle gives way to a trickle of water, a small stream, a tributary, and finally the mighty flow of the raging Mississippi. As this series of shots progresses, the shots become shorter. Similarly, the lumbering sequence from the same film begins with a long take of an ax cutting into a single tree and progresses to a massive river logjam with the tempo quickening as the cuts become more frequent.

In another documentary classic, *Night Mail* (1936) by Harry Watt and Basil Wright, the inherent rhythm of locomotive wheels—in this case the mail express between London and Glasgow—provides the tempo for a number of elements: the cutting, the accompanying poetic verse written by W. H. Auden, and the music by Benjamin Britten.

The filmmaker may also provide dramatic emphasis by cutting the scene to suggest the subjective experience: that is, to reproduce the visual experience of a specific character in the film or to represent the mental process itself. Film theorist Ernest Lindgren attaches primary importance to this function of editing: "The fundamental psychological justification of editing as a method of representing the physical world around us lies in the fact that it reproduces this mental process in which one visual image follows another as our attention is drawn to this point and to that in our surroundings."[5] Lindgren's point is that the filmmaker cannot only provide a glimpse of the real world but can also reveal it in the "*manner* in which we normally see it" through editing. Unlike the camera used in a classic Hollywood pan shot, the human eye does not travel smoothly from point to point. Instead, it moves in quick, involuntary jumps called *saccades*. The filmmaker in effect mimics the eye's saccadic movement by cutting from object to object, which makes for a more natural way of redirecting audience attention than by panning.

The filmmaker may take the subjective experience to its limit by rendering it in the form of an altered state of consciousness. For example, directors have depicted dream states and madness in films at least as early as Edwin Porter's *Dreams of a Rarebit Fiend* and Robert Wiene's *The Cabinet of Dr. Caligari*, respectively (see Figs. 1–4 and 2–20), and have found favor with countless other moviemakers since. In his 1967 screen version of James Joyce's *Ulysses*, Joseph Strick attempted an elaborate subjective experience akin to Joyce's celebrated "stream of consciousness" passages by editing together bits of action that represented Leopold and Molly Bloom's daydreams and fantasies as well as their real-life activities. As in other situations, the filmmaker does not usually create the subjective experience exclusively through editing but draws on a variety of controls: composition, camera perspective, sound, and lighting, to mention the more prominent.

The rhythm of a film may reflect not only a specific action or subjective experience but also the larger cultural context of the society in which the work was produced. The rapid, choppy editing characteristic of many Russian films produced during the decade following the Revolution reflects to some degree the upheavals of that society, just as the more lyrically paced films of some Far Eastern directors—most notably the Japanese director Yasujiro Ozu—suggest the importance of harmony in their societies.[6] Western audiences, particularly in America, have come to expect rapidly paced films loaded with action and thus may feel uncomfortable with the more deliberately paced films common to other countries. A kind of culture shock occurs when an audience used to viewing such thrill-a-minute films as *Raiders of the Lost Ark* and *Superman* is exposed to the leisurely paced films of Ozu and Indian director Satyajit Ray, or vice versa. Such a "shock" may result from the fact that the works of these latter directors are far more tranquil, at least on the surface, than many of their American counterparts.

(It would be unfair to suggest, however, that *all* American films are rapidly paced. Bob Rafelson began his 1972 film *The King of Marvin Gardens* with a tight close-up of Jack Nicholson as his character tells a story—fabricated, as we eventually learn—of how he and his brother allowed their grandfather to choke to death. This "talking-head" shot lasts an incredibly long time by Hollywood standards—more than five and one-half minutes—and seems longer due to Nicholson's soft monotone, the lack of an interesting background, and the paucity of any kind of movement. It establishes the slow, downbeat quality that permeates the entire film.)

CREATIVE EDITING.   One of the greatest challenges facing any director is the task of dealing with abstractions. Filmmakers tend to draw on various cinematic techniques in the course of grappling with the problems of presenting these intangibles, and editing usually plays a central role. For example, a filmmaker can create an abstract idea through the synthesis that occurs when joining seemingly unrelated shots. The combination becomes more than the simple sum of the joined shots; instead, the filmmaker fashions a new concept not apparent in either of the separate shots. The works of the Soviet directors Eisenstein and Pudovkin abound with this method. In Pudovkin's *Storm Over Asia* (1928), a colonialist power manipulates a descendant of Genghis Khan as a political pawn. To demonstrate the smothering restrictions under which the young Mongol must operate, Pudovkin included a scene in which his character collapses from weakness and, in reaching for support, pulls a tablecloth and fish tank to the floor with him. By combining the images of the collapsed man with those of fish out of water, the director suggests the effect of the suffocating restraint on the young captive.

In his interpretation of the Russian revolution entitled *Ten Days That Shook the World* (1927), Eisenstein wanted to show Alexander Kerensky, head of the short-lived provisional government sandwiched between the czarist and Bolshevik regimes, in a very unfavorable light. To accomplish this task, the director employed editing techniques that compared Kerensky with such things as an ornamental peacock, to make an obvious comment on Kerensky's personality, and a bust of Napoleon, to show his lust for power and empire building. Near the conclusion of his famous "Odessa Steps" sequence from *The Battleship Potemkin*, in which automaton-like czarist soldiers fire their rifles into a crowd showing its support for the mutinous *Potemkin* sailors, Eisenstein combined shots of three stone lions: one sleeping, a second awakened, and a third fully roused. In so doing, he suggested the awakening revolutionary fervor of the proletariat in response to this latest atrocity committed on behalf of the old government.

Like Eisenstein, Stanley Kubrick has used creative editing for political and ironic purposes. His most notable achievements in this area are found in *Paths of Glory* (1957), a film set during World War I but with antiwar ramifications extending far beyond that conflict. In this work, Kubrick frequently cut from an elegant, ornate French villa, where several generals plan a disastrous campaign, to the twilight world of the perpetually bombarded trenches where battle-weary enlisted men and lower officers must carry out their orders.

The construction of dramatic irony through creative editing is also central to Charlie Chaplin's *Monsieur Verdoux* (1947). Here, Chaplin plays a debonair and charming Frenchman who turns out to be a murderer of women whom he marries for their wealth. Much of the film's irony arises from Chaplin's careful linking of shots that contrast the delicate and tasteful airs of the title character with his grisly deeds.

Creative editing through the direct association of images and by way of contrasting or "contrapuntal" images has become an indispensable tool for filmmakers who wish to go beyond the obvious and the directly observable. It has become an invaluable aid in delivering to the audience abstract ideas and conceptual reasoning that defy easy visual representation. It is a function of editing at the heart of what Eisenstein called "intellectual montage."

Special Montage Devices

Among the many ways that filmmakers can use editing for basic design, psychological impact, and intellectual statement are several that have become standard tools of the filmmaking trade; they deserve special mention. One form that has found particular favor is the construction of the montage sequence sometimes called the "Hollywood montage." Especially popular during the thirties and forties, the technique grew out of the Russian system of creating some object, place, or idea out of the accumulation of details. Moviemakers in America, particularly Yugoslavian émigré Slavko Vorkapich, adopted and modified it to provide a quick impressionistic overview of some subject through the collection of separate but related shots. The device proved particularly popular with filmmakers wishing to offer quickly some necessary link in exposition (such as some scene-setting or transitional requirements of the screenplay), especially when a detailed elaboration on the scene would lack dramatic force.

Orson Welles' opening sequence of *The Magnificent Ambersons* (1942) is an example of the method used to set quickly the necessary background of both the film's story and the spirit of the era invoked by the Booth Tarkington novel on which the film is based. In just a few minutes of screen time, Welles captured a whole way of life in turn-of-the-century America by bringing together a wealth of detail. At the same time, he managed to establish the prominence of a particular family—the well-to-do Ambersons—in a particular Midwest town. In *Butch Cassidy and the Sundance Kid*, George Roy Hill employed a montage sequence as a transitional device to move the principal characters from a western setting to one in Bolivia. At the same time, Hill gave the viewer just a glimpse of some of the fun and high jinks that the travelers enjoyed along the way.

Directors have discovered limitations in the use of such montage sequences, however. As a means of "visual shorthand," the Hollywood montage tends to be artificial, facile, and lacking in the conviction of straight narrative, particularly in otherwise realistic dramas. It also has become cliché-ridden, as films marking a journey or the passage of time with spinning newspaper headlines, animated maps, hyperkinetic clocks, churning locomotive wheels, fluttering calendar pages, changing seasons, and ashtrays magically filling with cigarette butts have become legion. Primarily for these reasons, the Hollywood montage, once a popular form of cinematic grammar, has fallen into disuse.

Moviemakers can accomplish another method of time compression by combining elements of the montage sequence with the concept of accumulating thematically related details within the same setting, though the details may have occurred many years apart. Within a few minutes of screen time in *Citizen Kane,* Orson Welles presented the gradual disintegration of Charles Foster Kane's first marriage by showing Charles and Emily in the same situation and setting—having breakfast in their dining room—over a period of several years. At first, the duo sit close together, but by the end of the sequence the older and grayer couple are at opposite ends of the table. The camera appears to pan rapidly back and forth from Charles to Emily to reveal the growing estrangement; the method is actually one of montage, however. Similarly, directors Anthony Asquith and Leslie Howard visualized the change of Liza Doolittle from Cockney flower seller to countess in *Pygmalion* (1938) primarily through montage consisting of various shots representing stages of her transformation.

Filmmakers can pursue yet another means of compressing time by cutting between two similar actions (also known as *match cutting*), even though the actions may be far removed from one other in terms of setting and situation. Alfred Hitchcock provided an excellent example of this technique at the conclusion of his 1959 film, *North by Northwest.* In the final shot of the famous Mount Rushmore sequence, he presented Roger Thornhill (Cary Grant) reaching down to pull up Eve Kendall (Eva Marie Saint) while both cling precariously to the facade of the monument. Hitchcock then cut to a shot of Thornhill completing the action by pulling Kendall up to his berth in a railroad passenger car. Though the contexts for the actions are completely different, the film moves smoothly from one setting to the other via Hitchcock's match-action editing (see Fig. 3–2).

Many times moviemakers wish to expand or draw out an action to delay some climactic moment and thereby create suspense. The method they often follow also involves selecting relevant details of the scene. In *High Noon* (1952), for example, repeated shots of clocks not only help expand the time in which the limited action takes place but also raise expectations and tension over the inevitable arrival of the gunmen aboard the noon train. The time covered by the story and the time it takes to tell it are about the same, a fact that on first appearance suggests no time elongation at all. Yet director Fred Zinnemann and scriptwriter

Figure 3–2 (A & B) *North by Northwest* (1959—American). A cut can be motivated by a shift in time and/or location. It can be executed so that the form or line of movement in the first scene gives way to a similar configuration or thrust in the succeeding one. In Alfred Hitchcock's *North by Northwest,* the climactic rescue involving Roger Thornhill and Eve Kendall (Cary Grant and Eva Marie Saint) on the faces of Mount Rushmore gives way to a romantic conclusion in the upper berth of a railway sleeping car. Through careful match editing, Thornhill's acts of hoisting Kendall up the monument and pulling her up into the train berth appear as a single continuous movement.

(A)

(B)

Carl Foreman did indeed expand time in this film, almost excruciatingly so, by dwelling extensively on details. (This situation becomes more apparent after one considers that Hollywood directors hardly ever make complete narrative films consisting of only one and a half hours or so out of their characters' lives.) The frequency of the clock shots, along with shots of the townspeople and the protagonist anxiously awaiting the train's arrival, physically extend the action of the screenplay and psychologically draws attention to the impending danger of confrontation at the appointed hour.

The expansion of time is an effective means of accentuating the importance of an event as well as increasing tension. As we have already noted, Eisenstein expanded time (and thereby our suspense) during the Odessa Steps sequence of *The Battleship Potemkin* to great dramatic effect. Another example may be found near the conclusion of Michelangelo Antonioni's *Zabriskie Point* (1970), when an explosion turns a fancy mountain home into a shower of fiery debris. Antonioni amplified the dramatic impact of this otherwise very brief event by repeating it several times.

In the interest of going beyond traditional narrative progression, a number of modern directors have experimented with several forms of nonlinear construction. The most generally recognized "violation" of the traditional chronological pattern of screen storytelling occurs whenever moviemakers edit glimpses of past or future occurrences into the present story. Shots of past events so inserted are *flashbacks,* while shots of future events are the comparatively rare *flashforwards.* Modern directors have usually used these devices to reveal quick views of past and future action through the thoughts, dreams, or memories of one or more characters of the story.

Filmmakers may handle flashbacks in several ways; they may use them sparingly or may carefully develop lengthy and elaborate ones as key portions of the film. Vittorio de Sica used them briefly and judiciously in his 1971 masterpiece *The Garden of the Finzi-Continis,* which focused on a wealthy Jewish family living in fascist Italy. He employed one near the end of the film when the fascists are rounding up the Jews and detaining them in a large, unidentified building. Amid the many apprehensive detainees squeezed into one of the rooms are Nicole Finzi-Contini (Dominique Sanda) and her grandmother, whom she comforts. As the young woman looks about the crowded room, a flashback lasting only a few seconds shows that Nicole used to attend classes in that very room as a child. Despite the brevity of the flashback, de Sica made his point clearly and poignantly.

Other filmmakers have relied extensively on lengthier and far more detailed flashbacks. Such segments frequently carry a major burden of exposition, as in the dream sequences in Ingmar Bergman's *Wild Strawberries* and the memory sequences in Sidney Lumet's *The Pawnbroker* (1965). These segments provide important contexts for the present anxieties of the central characters of these films. In the Bergman work, aged professor Isak Borg (Victor Sjöström) is about to receive an award for his lifelong service to science. En route to the award ceremony, he experiences several dreams that reveal his romantic disappointments as a youth and doubts about his professional abilities, among other concerns. In *The Pawnbroker,* Rod Steiger plays Sol Nazerman, a Jewish pawnbroker striving to find some meaning to his life in a decaying and crime-ridden section of New York City. Lumet set his character's present anguish against the past atrocities that Nazerman experienced in a Nazi concentration camp.

Moviemakers may become carried away with the device at times, resulting in the creation of hard-to-follow films. In *Sorry, Wrong Number* (1948), Anatole Litvak actually presented a flashback within a flashback, in which a character remembers a situation featuring another character remembering still another situation. Whether the result of carelessness or painstaking design, such a multilevel narrative construction presents a real challenge to the audience's ability to follow the story.

Some filmmakers will present their stories primarily in the flashback mode by inserting them within "framing devices" consisting of present-tense openings and closings. Examples of this sort abound, including Dupont's *Variety*, Luis Buñuel's *That Obscure Object of Desire* (1977), and David Lean's *Lawrence of Arabia* (1962). The latter film, for instance, begins with the untimely death of legendary British officer T. E. Lawrence (Peter O'Toole) following a motorcycle accident. After the funeral, Lean devotes much of the remainder of his nearly four-hour movie to exploring Lawrence's Middle Eastern adventures during World War I. A variation is the extended dream sequence integral to such children's classics as *The Wizard of Oz* and the many screen versions of *Alice in Wonderland*.

The nonlinear structures of *Citizen Kane, Rashomon, Catch–22,* and many of Alain Resnais's films, including *Night and Fog, Last Year at Marienbad* (1962), and *Providence* (1977), are further extensions of the method. Such films move freely between the past and the present and, in the case of *Slaughterhouse Five* (1972), the future as well. The latter film tells the story of Billy Pilgrim (Michael Sacks), a mild-mannered, middle-aged optometrist who becomes "unstuck" in time and finds himself moving between such events in his life as his World War II experiences in Dresden, the courtship of his future wife, a jet crash later in his life, and his abduction to another planet by unseen aliens who then request him to mate with Montana Wildhack (Valerie Perrine), a stripper also kidnapped from Earth. The film, which first-time viewers often find disorienting because of its constant shifts in time, uses carefully matched action and overlapping sound (sounds occurring at the end of one sequence extend into the beginning of the next) to help link its nonlinear sequences.

Slaughterhouse Five is one of the few films containing flashforwards. Others include *Easy Rider* and *They Shoot Horses, Don't They?* (1969). Each of these films presents one or more glimpses of what the future holds for the principal characters. *Easy Rider* provides a fine if brief example after Billy and Wyatt (Dennis Hopper and Peter Fonda), high on wine, embark on a mystical visit to a New Orleans brothel. Billy's eagerness to find a prostitute contrasts sharply with Wyatt's ruminations on God and death. After the camera pans past the pensive Wyatt to a death-related inscription on a nearby wall ("Death only closes a man's reputation and determines it as good or bad"), we see a very brief shot of a fiery motorcycle crash. Presumably Wyatt's vision, this flashforward presages an event that concludes the movie.

At times, filmmakers attempt to bring together two actions occurring simultaneously instead of in the present and past or future. "Simultaneity," as Pudovkin called it in his discussions of relational editing, continues to provide a challenge for directors working in all kinds of films. Directors have traditionally handled simultaneity by cutting between the actions, yet some have explored a different editing technique: the split screen. This device, which can show two or more events occurring at the same time, has been around at least since 1913, when

Phillips Smalley used a version of it called a *triptych* in a film entitled *Suspense*. A triptych divides the screen into three triangles, with the dominant action occurring in the largest triangle in the center of the screen and two lesser events happening concurrently in the smaller triangles on either side. This particular device is rarely seen today, though the idea of presenting two images side by side has always intrigued filmmakers. In recent years, director Brian de Palma has been the primary advocate of the split screen, using the device in such Hitchcock-inspired odes to violence and eroticism as *Sisters* (1973) and *Dressed to Kill* (1980). Despite the split screen's long history and its promise of bringing scattered but related elements into a single field of view, the technique remains a clumsy way of presenting two or more actions occurring simultaneously. For one thing, it demands that the audience divide its attention between two or more discrete parts of the frame, resulting in considerable confusion; for another, movies featuring the technique look terrible on television—the inevitable mode of exhibition for most films—since much of the imagery must be cropped to fit the film into television's 3 x 4 aspect ratio. This is a problem for all wide-screen films but is particularly acute for those employing the split-screen device.

In summation, the importance of the choices related to editing can hardly be minimized. When working with the more conventional sequential story patterns, the filmmaker finds the control of movement in time and space and the linkage of shot, scene, and sequence a demanding process. In the more inventive forms of narrative construction—demonstrated in films ranging from *Citizen Kane* to *Catch-22* to *Slaughterhouse Five*—the challenge to filmmaker and viewer alike can be even greater.

SOUND

Evolving Functions

Sound provides the filmmaker with a separate channel with which to record the real world and create a fictional world of voices, melodies, and noises. We use the word "separate" to suggest distinct or discrete rather than divorced from or isolated, because sound is almost always complementary to, or an adjunct of, some visual image. The natural association of sound and image was without doubt a contributing factor in the creation of the film medium; indeed, Thomas Edison's initial interest in motion pictures was to develop a system whereby pictures could be produced to accompany the music and dialogue reproduced by his recently invented phonograph. Other inventors and innovators also looked for ways of yoking sight and sound into a single, controlled medium, and Edison himself developed a synchronized system as early as 1911, which he used to record several Mother Goose nursery rhymes and even a speech by the mayor of New York City.[7] These early successes were undermined by lingering synchronization problems and the difficulty of sufficiently amplifying the sound for group exhibition. Hence, these problems, along with economic factors, delayed the arrival of a viable sound-film process until 1927, some thirty years after movies had found their first audiences.

The sounds that did reach the ears of movie patrons during this thirty-year period were provided by orchestras or organists, in the case of larger urban theaters, or piano accompanists in the smaller theaters. Originally taking their cues directly from the projected silent image itself, these performers provided music to reinforce the mood of the picture, to create or support its rhythm or tempo, or simply to eliminate the unnatural silence of the screen performance and mask the noises produced by the spectators and the projectors. Producers of the more ambitious and elaborate films often had musical scores specially composed, thereby standardizing the sound component and relieving the theater pianist or organist of having to improvise at the keyboard. In addition, film exhibitors would occasionally lend a note of aural realism to their otherwise silent films by creating sound effects on the spot to accompany the goings-on in the film. The most interesting quality in the evolution of sound in the "silent" cinema is that two basic functions were operating from the very beginning: expressing mood and reinforcing rhythm.

The filmmakers' new capability to capture sound and image on the same piece of film led to a novel range of possibilities. In addition to providing music appropriate to the mood and tempo of the film, moviemakers could now record and synchronize voices with the lip movements of the actors, as they could with sound effects and their sources. These directors soon discovered that they could introduce sounds independent of, even in contrast to, the images on the screen. The new sound era saw experimentation with what were to become the major aural components of the film medium: synchronous sound, asynchronous sound, and background sound. The third of these, background sound, comes closest to what the live music of the silent cinema had already provided: an appropriate musical score. Synchronized sound made the dialogue film or "talking picture" a reality and transformed film acting from mime to fully realized performance akin to that provided in the legitimate theater. Finally, asynchronous sound in the hands of the more creative director meant an infinite variety of possibilities for commenting on the visuals rather than simply duplicating their messages.

The basic advantages of sound film became immediately apparent; this new channel of communication permitted moviemakers to present more complex and detailed stories while simultaneously allowing those stories to unfold in more natural ways. Directors could now use the soundtrack—particularly dialogue—to handle most of the exposition and character-revelation burdens, and performers learned that the spoken word facilitated a more realistic and intimate acting style. Sound effects could make available an array of naturalistic detail to give the scene an added realistic sense. At the same time, filmmakers could extend the dimensions of the scene beyond the limits of the frame by creating sound effects out of the range of the camera. On the whole, synchronous sound made more direct, natural, and detailed filmic messages possible.

With the advantages and creative potential of "sync" sound came some problems and shortcomings. Some of these were related to the technology and were quicky overcome. These included the limitations on the mobility of both the camera and the actors because of the fixed position of early microphones and the necessity of anchoring the camera in an immobile soundproof enclosure to prevent the microphones from picking up camera noises. (These enclosures were popularly dubbed "iceboxes," presumably because the cameras were "frozen" inside them.) Other shortcomings stemmed from the natural tendency to exploit the more obvious potential of the new form, particularly the new capability to record and reproduce the speaking film actor (an interest reflected in the term "the talkies," the popular name for early sound films) and to provide a deluge of sound and musical effects. As audiences' initial fascination with talk, slamming doors, and rattling teacups wore thin, these problems in exploitation also faded (see Fig. 3-3).

A third problem concerned the filmmakers' own conception of the range of creative possibilities for using sound. Film directors, editors, and sound technicians could easily take all of their sound cues from the visual imagery, and often did. Some never used sound beyond the level of allowing audiences to see and hear a barking dog, or saturating the sound track with mood music, or filling every minute of screen time with dialogue, resulting in what Hitchcock and others have referred to as "talking-head shots." The medium's major sound-era creative talents, including Hitchcock, Fritz Lang, René Clair, and Richard Lester, partially solved the problem by making sound something more than a complement and extension of visual imagery. But the problem continues to offer challenges to everyone who uses the medium as a means of creative expression, whether documentarist, experimentalist, or narrative filmmaker.

Characteristics of Form

Before moviemakers can meet the challenge of using sound creatively, they must recognize the several forms of sound available and their characteristics. The general categories of voice, sound effects, and music are well known, but within each of these forms are specific styles that have had their own particular uses in storytelling, documentation, and other functions that the medium serves.

VOICE.   The addition of the human voice to film gained the greatest attention with the arrival of synchronous sound in the late 1920s. Since that time, filmmakers have explored and adopted several approaches to the use of human speech. With the synchronization of sound and visuals, directors found that they could easily record on camera actors speaking their lines, and they quickly made sound an important element of their films. *Dialogue* in film could bring acting a step closer to the theatrical performance and allow the fuller range of expression and character development that theater has traditionally afforded. At the same time, however, filmmakers began taking advantage of the microphone's ability to pick up natural speech without the amplification necessary in the theater; in so doing, they began clearing the way for a more naturalistic performance style that eventually set apart screen acting from its more flamboyant counterpart in the theater.

Indispensable parts of screen characterization continue to be the quality of the voice and the nuances of delivery. Greta Garbo, James Cagney, Mae West, Edward G. Robinson, W.C. Fields, and Henry Fonda were known in their early sound roles as much by voice as their image on screen. Speech and its effect on character delineation were important considerations in the careers of many performers, particularly in screen comedy where speech brought about a revolution in the genre. Favorite silent-screen comics such as Buster Keaton, Harold Lloyd, and even Chaplin's cherished "Little Tramp" were eventually replaced by comics with voices and repartees, including W.C. Fields and the Marx Brothers (see Fig. 3-4).

Monologues and narration, which have been integral elements of documentary films ever since the 1930s (see Chapter 10), became important alternatives

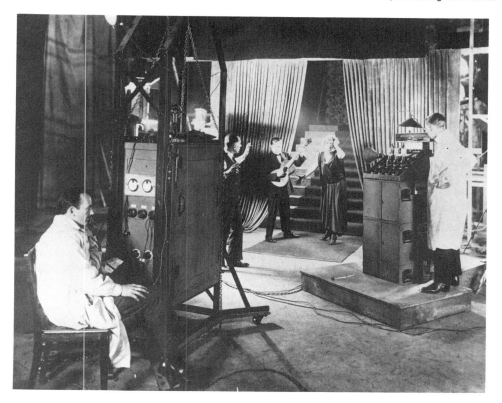

Figure 3-3 The arrival of sound brought new dimensions and constraints to screen drama. The sound technicians as well as the director are calling the shots in this German talking-picture screen test which features a vocalist accompanied by guitar.

to dialogue in film comedy and drama. In dramatic films, narration allowed a character, both on screen or off, to assume the role of storyteller by directing the audience's attention and commenting directly on the action. Filmmakers use the internal monologue extensively in films today to serve much the same function as the theater soliloquy; in other words, the device enables a character to provide exposition and a personal perspective on the developing action. By using a "voice-over" technique, in which the audience hears but does not see the speaker, the director does not have to stop the action to let the character deliver an aside to the audience as the soliloquy requires. Yet the internal monologue, like the soliloquy, offers the audience direct access to the thoughts of the character and is a useful expository and transitional device from the first-person perspective.

A number of films have employed voice-over narration without falling into the trap of unduly relying on it and becoming bogged down in excessive verbiage. In Billy Wilder's *Double Indemnity* (1944), Fred MacMurray plays a wayward insurance investigator who begins the film by speaking his confession of murder into an office dictaphone. This activity quickly and efficiently sets the background for the film's story, told largely in flashback. In another Wilder film, *Sunset Boulevard*

Figure 3-4 *Modern Times* (1936—American). Charlie Chaplin's ability to keep his tramp character speechless for a full decade into the sound era is testament to his genius as a pantomimic actor. Though Chaplin did not speak in *Modern Times*, he did provide sound effects and composed a score for the film. He had begun this practice with *City Lights* in 1931 and continued it in all his sound films.

(1950), the murder victim himself provides the exposition of events leading to his demise. The film opens with a shot of the victim's body floating in the swimming pool of a former Hollywood star; the victim then explains, by way of voice-over narration, how he got there.

In the process of adapting plays into films, moviemakers have learned that voice-over monologues can be effective substitutes for theatrical soliloquies, but only if they are tailored to meet the needs of the medium. The spoken word in cinema has never reached the primacy that the spoken word enjoys in the theater, and it probably never will; indeed, most film directors, scriptwriters, and theorists are agreed that lengthy stretches of narration, though common in theater, are anathema in cinema and need to be shortened. As for the on-screen monologue or aside to the audience, screen comics from the Marx Brothers to Mel Brooks to Woody Allen have turned them into effective comedic devices. At one point in the Marx Brothers' *The Big Store* (1941), for instance, Groucho turns to the camera to inform the audience that the scene he is in would have looked better in color but unfortunately "Technicolor is sooooo expensive." We often find moments like this funny because we do not expect them; actors seldom address the camera directly in Hollywood films. The humor of the example from *The Big Store* is also reinforced by a strong reflexive quality, since Groucho's comment refers to the very film the audience is watching.

A form of voice recording generally associated with documentaries produced since the late 1950s is the extemporaneous recording of unscripted, naturally existing speech. This type of speech has long fascinated feature-film directors and has provided a challenge for the more adventurous. As far back as Orson Welles' 1942 production of *The Magnificent Ambersons,* directors have experimented with running their actors' conversations together and even overlapping them to suggest a more natural exchange of dialogue and to give additional credibility to the screen action. Robert Altman has turned this means of presenting dialogue into something of a trademark, using overlapping and frequently indistinct dialogue in films ranging from *M*A*S*H* (1970) to *McCabe and Mrs. Miller* (1971) to *Nashville* (1975). In these and other works, Altman has created rich tapestries of sound to accompany his carefully chosen and decorated locales. The textures of sound and image complement one another so well that they create a

Figure 3-5 *Horse Feathers* (1932—American). A perfect balance of mime and repartee put the Marx Brothers in the forefront of early sound comedy and allowed their routines to remain popular through today. In this scene from *Horse Feathers*, Harpo, Groucho, and Chico inflict their lunacy on a hapless bartender.

special ambience rarely found in other narrative films. This pervasive ambience contributes to the audience's eventual sense of presence with the actors in the world Altman has created. He may well be trying to replicate the way we normally hear sounds in the real world: sometimes clearly, often unclearly. One gets the impression from his films that words themselves are not all that significant; the most important consideration is not what is said but how it is said.

Our discussion of voice in film would not be complete without covering a far more pervasive and heated controversy: the translation of foreign films. The battlelines on both sides of the argument have been clearly drawn. Proponents of the dubbed film argue that the most direct and least disruptive way of conveying the verbal messages of a foreign film is to have actors rerecord the dialogue in the domestic language and then replace the original sound track with it. They point out that audiences are frequently distracted from the important content of images when it is required to read subtitles (printed transcripts on the bottom of the screen), particularly when they are often so poorly produced and usually cover one-half or less of the original dialogue. (Subtitled films would have nonstop captions zipping across the bottoms of their screens if they were translated word for word.) Proponents of the subtitled film, on the other hand, argue that the dubbers are often inferior actors having no involvement in the film situation. This factor along with the distraction of poorly matched lip movements and the loss of the original background noises make dubbing an inferior alternative. They also suggest that the texture of the original language becomes lost through dubbing; part of the Bergman experience, for example, is the sound of the Swedish language itself. One way of circumventing this problem would be to use headphones through which audiences could hear a simultaneous translation of the dialogue, United Nations style. This method as well as improvements in film subtitling will likely play a role in future foreign-film exhibition systems. Such technical innovations, however, are not likely to end the controversy.

SOUND EFFECTS.   Since music and sound effects require no translation, they are not a part of the dubbing/subtitling controversy. Yet many of the advantages, limitations, and challenges associated with speech are also related to the use of sound effects in narrative motion pictures. Filmmakers' initial fascination with their new ability to synchronize sounds and visuals extended beyond human speech to include all sorts of noises, and it led to many faithful recordings and reproductions of sounds naturally emanating from the filmed subjects. This preoccupation gradually faded, but the interest in using sound effects to provide more than a faithful, "realistic" rendering of the aural dimension of a scene continues unabated through this day. We put "realistic" in quotation marks because many theorists, critics, and filmmakers from the advent of sound up to the present time have argued that the reproduction of every sound that might occur in a particular scene is neither realistic nor aesthetically valid. They suggest that selectivity is the key to cinematic realism as well as a more aesthetically satisfying use of sound. Theorist Ernest Lindgren argued the point when he observed: "All the sounds within audible range are striking our ears all the time and are able to be heard; which of them in fact we hear depends on a purely mental process of selection that allows some sounds through and stops others, that may even on occasion stop all sounds, according to the preoccupations that hold our attention at that moment."[8]

The early sound directors who were striving to show that film art did not die with the coming of sound generally followed the selectivity principle and also experimented with nonsynchronous sound. They believed that combining the image of one object with the sound of another gave them considerable latitude in expression and restored any loss that came about when they gave up mime and other elements of silent-screen expression. Much of the creative potential of sound effects today continues to be tied to selectivity and nonsynchronous sound.

In addition, filmmakers may choose sound effects from varying perspectives, just as they do for visual composition. Natural sounds such as street noises, locomotive whistles, and distant thunder may help provide a fuller and more detailed semblance of the setting and at the same time open up that setting by suggesting objects and actions out of camera view. Mike Nichols created a fine example in *Carnal Knowledge* (1971) when he rendered a tennis game between Jonathan (Jack Nicholson) and Sandy (Art Garfunkel) in a shot lasting exactly two minutes. Though we can clearly hear the sound of their feet on the court, the bouncing ball, and their voices as they playfully taunt one another, we never actually see them play; instead, the camera holds for most of the lengthy shot on two women who wordlessly watch them from the sidelines: Cindy (Cynthia O'Neal) and Bobbie (Ann-Margret). Director Sidney Lumet employed a similar technique in *The Verdict* (1982) after Mickey (Jack Warden) learns that Laura (Charlotte Rampling) has been paid to spy on him and his fellow lawyer, Frank (Paul Newman). When Mickey stops Frank in the street to tell him of his discovery, Lumet elected to obliterate their conversation with street noise. Through this technique, Lumet avoided redundant verbal information while inviting the audience to "fill in the blanks" of the lawyers' conversation about Laura.

Directors might also use symbolic or atmospheric sounds that go beyond naturalistic detail and suggest some abstraction or motif. The screech of a cockatoo is only one of several forms of symbolic and nonrepresentational uses of sound in *Citizen Kane.* Still another choice might be the sounds that suggest the subjective experience, such as electronically distorted noises and sounds recorded in echo chambers. Through such means, filmmakers allow the audience to perceive the world through both the eyes and ears of a character. In *Repulsion* (1965), Roman Polanski suggested that the rape of a mentally deteriorating young woman (Catherine Deneuve) occurred only in her mind through the use of a loudly ticking clock as the primary element of the sound track during that sequence (perhaps suggesting she is a human time bomb) followed by an unnaturally loud sound of a bell awakening her from her fantasy. Finally, filmmakers who create creatures or objects not a part of our world, such as the myriad denizens of *Star Wars*, must often resort to highly imaginative uses of both sound effects and voices to characterize them. Audio technicians created the voice of the title creature of Steven Spielberg's *E.T.* by electronically distorting the voice of an 82-year-old woman.

MUSIC. Music is perhaps the most challenging form of sound for filmmakers because of its abstract nature and the range of functions it can serve. As we have noted, music has been a part of the film experience from the very beginning. Before and during the salad days of cinema, stage directors frequently used music in melodramatic plays to set mood and reinforce action. Following this tradition, silent-film directors used the same pit piano to draw on the natural association of movement and sound to reinforce rhythm and create mood.

In sound films, directors have used music in three basic ways that can fulfill the same general functions as those described under sound effects. The first of these, *source music*, refers to the music that occurs naturally within the context of the film story. Filmmakers often use source music the same way they employ sound effects: to offer naturalistic detail and to open up and give an added dimension to the scene. At other times, directors use it as an integral element of the plot. A whistled tune from Edvard Grieg's *Peer Gynt* becomes a sinister motif in Fritz Lang's *M* (1931), a harrowing tale of a child murderer (Peter Lorre) pursued by both the police and the underworld. Lang did not explicitly show the killer in the opening of the film; instead, he established the murderer's presence through shadow, off-screen voice, and the melody he nervously whistles. The audience quickly learns that the murderer is nearby and about to kill again every time it hears the eerie tune.

The second, *incidental or background music,* is by far the most pervasive form of film music and at the same time the least understood and most abused. This type of music is often performed by a full orchestra and added to the film after the latter has been shot and edited. Unlike some of the musicians who perform souce music, incidental-music performers are not actually present on-screen. The general rule that Hollywood and other filmmaking communities have followed regarding this type of music is that it should be just as "invisible" as its performers; in other words, the music should not call undue attention to itself. Moviemakers have used it in various ways: to comment on the action, to reinforce mood and atmosphere, and, all too often, to mask the dullness of a film. Filmmakers' original preoccupation with "wall to wall" music has waned, but much of the challenge of discovering inventive ways of employing incidental music remains.

One relatively recent innovation has been the prominent display of popular songs as backgrounds for both comic and dramatic scenes. Without necessarily establishing a special link between song and plot, filmmakers have used such musical backdrops to help create a particular mood or atmosphere. In this way, films such as *Breakfast at Tiffany's* (1961), *The Graduate*, and *Butch Cassidy and the Sundance Kid* become showcases for tunes such as "Moon River," "Scarborough Fair," and "Raindrops Keep Fallin' on My Head." The songs not only contribute significantly to the unique moods of their respective films but they also share star status with the performers.

The final form, called the *production number*, puts music at the center of attention. Production numbers range from the elaborate routines of Busby Berkeley (see Fig. 2–22) and the magical grace of Fred Astaire and Gene Kelly to the more modest interludes of harp and piano music provided by Harpo and Chico Marx in many of their comedies. The musical performances of such rock documentaries as *Monterey Pop* (1969) and *Woodstock* (1970) also fall within this category.

The production number is its own *raison d'etre* and often makes little pretense of playing an integral part of the drama; source music and incidental music, on the other hand, often serve dramatic requirements. Incidental music in particular can serve as a means of commenting on character, place, or object, and it often establishes motifs that can be reintroduced later in the film to direct attention to some character or particular detail. Steven Spielberg employed a menacing, low-register motif performed on a bass fiddle to establish the presence of a killer shark in *Jaws* (1975) and then used it as a periodic reminder of the shark's continued threat to a New England coastal community. Filmmakers have also used music extensively to set mood and suggest mental or emotional states. A particularly memorable example is Carol Reed's use of zither music in *The Third Man* to help evoke the spirit—mainly the intrigue and the uncertainties—of postwar Vienna (see Figs. 2–11 and 3–6).

Armed with an understanding of these forms and characteristics of sound, moviemakers are better prepared to use voice, effects, and music to support either visual storytelling or documentation. Since the advent of sound, filmmakers have learned a great deal about selectivity, free association of sound and image, and the primacy of visual stimuli. Although there are exceptions to this last factor, most directors recognize that sound usually plays a supportive role in film communication. Japanese director Akira Kurosawa spoke for many filmmakers when he discussed the way he perceived the relationship of sound to pictures:

> In motion pictures both image and sound must be treated with special care. In my view, a motion picture stands or falls on the effective combination of these two factors. Truly cinematic sound is neither merely accompanying sound (easy

Figure 3-6 The zither score of *The Third Man*, arranged and performed by Anton Karas, became as celebrated as the story and stars of Carol Reed's 1949 film. The score captured both the melancholy and the intrigue of the postwar Vienna drama by Graham Greene. Karas is seen playing during a *Third Man* recording session.

and explanatory) nor the natural sounds captured at the time of simultaneous re-cording. In other words, cinematic sound is that which does not simply add to, but multiplies, two or three times, the effect of the image.[9]

Special Uses

Whether filmmakers use sound merely for dialogue purposes or to express a particular mood, they *always* use it in conjunction with images and *often* employ it in association with some other form of sound. Recognizing these links between sound and image, and between sound and sound, moviemakers have developed and refined a number of special montage devices. These are discussed next.

TRANSITIONS.   Filmmakers pursue a prominent form of linkage when-ever they combine sound and images to create transitions and provide continuity in narrative progression. A classic example occurs in Hitchcock's *The 39 Steps* when he shifted scenes from that of a landlady discovering a murder victim to the speed-ing train on which the alleged murderer is fleeing. Hitchcock made the switch by juxtaposing the sound of the train whistle with the final shot of the screaming woman before cutting a second later to a shot of the train entering a tunnel. In *Citizen Kane*, Orson Welles used what appears to be continuous dialogue or sound effects at several points to bring together otherwise highly disparate scenes. At one point, he used the two phrases of a single line of dialogue—"Merry Christmas, Charles, and a Happy New Year"—to combine two scenes about fifteen years apart. Throughout the film, Welles incorporated written and spoken recollections to provide the links between a reporter's investigation of "Rosebud," the last word to pass from the lips of Charles Foster Kane, and the extended flashbacks that make up the bulk of the film. In *The Graduate*, Mike Nichols allowed a few words of the dialogue of a new scene to intrude on the previous action, producing strange and frequently amusing results. For example, we see the youthful Benjamin (Dus-tin Hoffman) at the bottom of his parents' swimming pool at the same time we hear his voice on the telephone as he arranges his first illicit meeting with Mrs. Robinson.

IRONY.   In both theory and practice, Sergei Eisenstein, V.I. Pudovkin, René Clair, and Rouben Mamoulian all affirmed the potential for nonsynchronous sound. These and other directors have linked seemingly unrelated or incongruous sound and image for humorous and frequently ironic intent. Hitchcock created a humorous if macabre example in *Frenzy* when he combined the sound of cracking bread sticks with the account of how a murderer broke his victim's fingers to re-trieve an incriminating stickpin.

Moviemakers have often used music to make ironic statements. By ex-ploiting the associations called up by certain musical styles, tempos, and specific scores, directors can make music particularly effective in this function. Stanley Kramer used the tune "Waltzing Matilda" throughout his film *On the Beach* (1959) as an aural motif to help evoke the "down under" spirit of the Australians awaiting the effects of an atomic blast that has devastated the rest of the world. The popular Australian song eventually takes on ironic overtones after the island-nation has finally succumbed to the fallout and met the fate of the rest of the planet. The final rendition of the tune contrasts sharply with the empty streets and particularly with a large banner hanging over a deserted area and which reads: *There is still time, brother.* By combining the music with this relic from an earlier demonstration against nuclear weapons, Kramer created a cogent if unsubtle message.

Stanley Kubrick used source music to great ironic effect in A *Clockwork Orange* by having Alex (Malcolm McDowell) perform the life-affirming "Singin' in the Rain" while he and his droogs viciously assault a man and a woman (see Fig. 3–7). In the same film, Kubrick juxtaposed recordings of Beethoven's Ninth Symphony with other violent scenes, while in the opening of *Dr. Strangelove* he used the song "Try a Little Tenderness" to underscore the airborne mating of a bomber and a refueling plane.

PLOTTING AND MOTIF.   Sound probably plays its most dramatic role in films that use it directly as a plotting device, either to provide exposition or to affect the twists and turns of the narrative progression itself. Pudovkin recognized the *leitmotif* as a form of structural editing that involved the reiteration of some theme. Filmmakers used themes in the form of sound effects and music as a way to focus viewer attention on some person, place, idea, or object by establishing an initial association between image and sound, and then allowing the sound to serve as a substitute for the image. Renowned film composer Bernard Herrmann estab-

Figure 3-7   *A Clockwork Orange* (1971—American). Stanley Kubrick reached a peak in "ultra-violence" in *A Clockwork Orange* during a surprise visit by Alex (Malcolm McDowell) and his droogs to the suburban home of a radical writer and his wife. According to the director, Alex's stomping of the writer while singing "Singin' in the Rain" was an improvisation added during the shooting of the scene. The same ironic counterpoint of action and music also occurs each time Beethoven's Ninth Symphony inspires Alex to new acts of violence.

lished musical motifs in *Citizen Kane* not only for the major characters but also for Xanadu and Rosebud. Even today, the "Tara" theme from *Gone With the Wind* (1939) provides for the instant recall of a picturesque antebellum mansion and even a whole way of life as depicted in that film.

In addition to its more general function of suggesting atmosphere, sound—particularly music—may function as a foreshadowing device. We are often alerted to some impending danger by the sound of tremulous strings or some other sinister and foreboding musical signature or effect. We also may be reassured by the soft and melodic strains of woodwinds that the danger has passed and the threat is held in abeyance, at least for the moment.

Hitchcock coined the term *MacGuffin* to label a plot device in his films that helps keep the intrigue spinning. It is usually something that the audience does not care about but is consistently on the minds of the characters, such as a secret formula or a piece of incriminating evidence (for example, the stickpin in *Frenzy*). In the works of Hitchcock and several other directors, the MacGuffin is occasionally a sound or musical motif. A tune whistled by an Alpine serenader turns out to be a secret treaty in Hitchcock's *The Lady Vanishes* (1938), while the music he used to introduce a music hall memory artist in *The 39 Steps* becomes the key to a secret spy organization.

Fritz Lang proved his expertise at turning sounds into plot elements early on; indeed, his pioneering sound work *M* is a veritable catalogue of sound plotting devices. As we have noted, Lang frequently established the presence of *M*'s murderous central character by having him whistle a few bars from *Peer Gynt*. The tune later proves to be his undoing, after it is recognized by a blind balloon seller (see Fig. 3–8). In addition, Lang simultaneously suggested the death of an early victim—a little girl—and underscored the mounting anguish of her mother by repeating the mother's off-screen cry of "Elsie!" as it echoes loudly through the hallways and stairwells of her apartment building. He also dramatized the killer's frenzy through the noises he makes while trying to escape from a locked storeroom in the film's final chase. The reporting of police procedures, the alarm that alerts the police, and the accused's agonized confession and appeal before a kangaroo court are among the other ways that Lang used sound in *M* as considerably more than auditory embellishment.

Such works as *Pygmalion*, Arthur Penn's *The Miracle Worker* (1962), François Truffaut's *The Wild Child* (1970), and Gus Trikonis' *Touched by Love* (1980) have reaffirmed the central role of sound in screen storytelling. In all four films, the challenge of learning human speech provides the basis for conflict and eventual victory. Consider their dramatic highlights: Liza Doolittle abandoning her Cockney accent to pronounce "The rain in Spain stays mainly on the plain," Helen Keller overcoming her multiple disabilities to learn to say "water," the wild boy Victor learning to utter "milk," and Karen, a preadolescent stricken with cerebral palsy, conquering her disorder to speak the name of her therapist. It is difficult to imagine any of these working as silent films (see Fig. 3–9).

SUBJECTIVE AND SYMBOLIC SOUND.   The use of sound to suggest the subjective experience or to provide some symbolic reference is part of its expositional function, but it is worthy of special mention here. Just as the camera can reveal an action from the point of view of a character in the film, so can the sound

Figure 3-8 *M* (1931—German). Audiences of Fritz Lang's *M* have quickly learned to associate a nervously whistled tune from Grieg's *Peer Gynt* with the presence of the film's child murderer (Peter Lorre). The tune eventually leads to the murderer's downfall, however, after a blind balloon seller recognizes the tune and identifies him.

track suggest what a character hears or does not hear. A Hitchcock movie once again provides the classic example. In *Blackmail* (1929), Hitchcock's first sound film, Alice White (Anna Ondry) fatally stabs an assailant. Later, when the young woman overhears bits of a nearby conversation, Hitchcock suggested her anguish over the outcome of her self-defensive act in a unique way; he amplified a key word—"knife"—uttered repeatedly in the otherwise innocent and rather indistinct conversation while showing Alice's face in close-up as she reacts to the word. We may find another prominent example in Robert Enrico's adaptation of the Ambrose Bierce short story, *An Occurrence at Owl Creek Bridge*. In this relatively brief film, Enrico distorted voices and natural sounds (as well as sights) to allow the viewer to share Peyton Farquhar's experiences as he faces a military detail responsible for his execution.

Moving beyond the strictly subjective experience and taking on symbolic significance are the hollow and echoing sounds of the Thatcher Memorial Library and Xanadu in *Citizen Kane*. In both situations, Welles used the effect to suggest the emptiness and sterility of the lives that these "monuments" represent. In *Wild Strawberries*, Bergman represented Isak Borg's recognition of the emptiness of his

Figure 3-9   *The Wild Child* (1970—French). In this "docu-drama" about the "wild boy of Averyron"
by François Truffaut, the uttering of human speech becomes a dramatic highlight. The film also
features the first-person offscreen narration of Dr. Itard (Truffaut himself) who chronicles the stages
of the boy's socialization.

own life and his fear of death by employing the recurring sound of the elderly
professor's heartbeat during his nightmares and fantasies. While Bergman used
sound to symbolize the life-death conflict, Michelangelo Antonioni used it to represent a young photographer's struggle to distinguish fantasy from reality in *Blow-
Up*. At the conclusion of that film, the photographer, Thomas (David Hemmings),
observes a group of mimes act out an imaginary game of tennis and ends up hear-
ing the illusory ball as they "hit" it back and forth across the invisible net. Antonioni then allowed the audience to hear the sound as well—just before he whisked
Thomas from view through cinema trickery.

SILENCE.   A director can employ an important dramatic device by removing sound from a film at key moments. Ironically, the use of silence was un-
available to silent-era filmmakers. Antonioni used silence for dramatic effect in
Blow-Up when Thomas wordlessly examines his enlarged photographs of two people in a London park and gradually becomes convinced that a murder took place.
In *Dressed to Kill*, Brian de Palma employed a long, wordless sequence in an art

museum where a sexually frustrated wife (Angie Dickinson) finds herself attracted to a mysterious, handsome man. Photographed largely from her point of view, the sequence presents them discreetly pursuing one another through the museum galleries and hallways, the atmosphere thick with risk and eroticism. Cloaked in a false casualness, their silent mating behavior becomes a surprisingly intriguing game of cat-and-mouse as they alternate between the roles of pursuer and pursued.

When not using silence for more serious or dramatic purposes, filmmakers sometimes employ it to poke fun at audience expectations regarding sound. René Clair provided much pleasure for his viewers in such early sound films as *Le Million* (1931) and *À Nous la Liberté* (1932) by withholding expected sound and mismatching sound with image. His efforts and those of other imaginative directors such as Hitchcock, Jacques Tati, and Luis Buñuel have lent support to film theorist Béla Balázs' suggestion that silence is one of the most effective dramatic devices of the sound film.

NOTES

[1] The major theoretical works of these two Russian filmmakers are Eisenstein's *Film Form* (New York: Harcourt Brace & Co., 1949) and *The Film Sense* (New York: Harcourt Brace Jovanovich 1942), and Pudovkin's *Film Technique and Film Acting* (London: Vision Press, 1954). *The Battleship Potemkin* and Eisenstein's own analysis of its construction in *The Film Sense* provide an excellent model of his montage method.

[2] Karel Reisz, *The Technique of Film Editing* (New York: Focal Press, 1958).

[3] For further information on this topic, see Martin F. Norden, "Toward a Theory of Audience Response to Suspenseful Films," *Journal of the University Film Association*, 32, nos. 1 and 2 (Winter-Spring 1980), 71–77.

[4] See Eisenstein, *Film Form*, pp. 72–83.

[5] Ernest Lindgren, *The Art of the Film* (London: Allen & Unwin, 1963), p. 67.

[6] For a summary of the literature focusing on this latter observation, see Kim Wolfson and Martin F. Norden, "A Rules Approach for Measuring Responses to Filmed Interpersonal Conflict," in *Intercultural Communication Research*, ed. William Gudykunst and Young Kim (Beverly Hills, Calif.: Sage Publications, Inc., in press).

[7] Martin F. Norden, "New York Mayor William J. Gaynor and His City's Film Industry," *Film Reader*, in press.

[8] Lindgren, *Art of the Film*, p. 131.

[9] Akira Kurosawa, "On Sound and Image," *Cinema* (August-September, 1963), p. 27.

4

FILM PROPERTIES
AND FUNDAMENTALS
OF TECHNIQUE:
setting and actor

SETTING

Form and Function

The basic elements of visual design such as composition and perspective are significantly affected by the filmmaker's selection of settings and their details. Of all the elements directors must consider when conceptualizing and realizing their audiovisual messages, the one most difficult to avoid is the setting or environment. Filmmakers have created many works without color, sound, or special lighting, but few if any have tried to photograph an action without a setting. To put it another way, directors must fill the frame with some background. Song-writers, novelists, playwrights, and sculptors *may* create settings for their works but are not bound to do so; filmmakers are, unless they are working in some abstract style. Whether working in a studio, on a back lot, or on location, movie-makers use settings to establish a context for the action and help complete its meaning (see Fig. 4–1).

Film researchers and critics frequently overlook the roles, functions, contributions, and limitations of film settings. Film criticism, developing primarily out of the literary and theatrical traditions, has customarily emphasized the qualities of plot, character, acting, theme, and form. Setting, when dealt with at all, usually comes in last. Yet few would deny, on reflection, that settings play significant roles

Figure 4-1 *Old Ironsides* (1926—American). Filming exteriors and shooting on location provides ready-made settings and lends authenticity to the scene. It also raises problems in logistics and control of natural elements. Here, a filming crew is set up on a barge for filming scenes featuring the frigate, "Old Ironsides."

in cinema. This is true in terms of both the financial considerations involved in the making of a film and the resulting "look" of the final product. As suggested by John Fell, a typical film producer usually "devotes his early attentions to set design . . . where investment is most visibly apparent to the audience."[1] At their simplest, film settings supply the environment for the film narrative; at their most sophisticated and dynamic, they help generate the mood that permeates the entire film or function as leitmotifs. In some instances, settings are comparable to, and may even surpass, plot, character, and theme in importance.

A filmmaker's treatment of settings range from the direct recording of action in the exact location in which it naturally occurs to the highly stylized and even abstract studio creations of the expressionist variety. Setting selection depends on the extent to which the filmmakers are following a formalistic or realistic approach; that is, how closely they are suggesting an imagined or real world by their imagery. Like the history of film itself, the history of film settings developed along the lines of the famous if timeworn Lumière-Méliès dichotomy. Since the earliest days, filmmakers have had to choose either real locations or artificial sets as the backdrops for their films, or perhaps a combination of the two. Any decision would be fraught with limitations. In the case of the Lumière *frères* and other early "realists," their choice of settings was limited to those locations drenched with light. Due to the relative slowness of their film stocks, these filmmakers had to avoid places with low-level lighting. Thus, most of their subjects centered on activities occurring naturally in the outdoors. Likewise, film-stock slowness was the bane of the earliest "studioists," whose use of artificial settings gave rise to a different array of problems. For example, Thomas Edison had made about 60 films by 1894, but their content was determined mainly by what he and his assistants could most easily film with a largely immobile camera in his cramped "Black Maria" studio, which could be rotated to follow the sun.

Leon Barsacq, a set designer for such notable film directors as René Clair, Jean Renoir, and Marcel Carné, has suggested that a pendulum has frequently swung between the poles of real locations and artificial sets.[2] Let us briefly examine some of the more promient "swings," en route to an analysis of the virtues and limitations of film settings.

Many of the one- and two-reeler slapsticks and melodramas produced during the first twenty years of the twentieth century used real locations as the settings. The fundamental plots and characterizations within each genre were remarkably similar; indeed, one of the chief variables among these films was the choice of setting out of which filmmakers could develop various bits of business. For instance, Charlie Chaplin has written of his early work with slapstick king Mack Sennett: "'What do you think of this for an idea?' Sennett would say, or 'There's a flood downtown on Main Street.' Such remarks launched a Keystone Comedy. It was this charming alfresco spirit that was such a delight—a challenge to one's creativeness. It was so free and easy—no literature, no writers—we had just had a notion around which we built gags, then made up the story as we went along."[3]

It is not unreasonable to assume that these filmmakers frequently spun the stories, or at least significant parts of the stories, out of the locations themselves. Initially, many of these locations were in the East: New York, Massachusetts, New Jersey. Later, Southern California became more attractive to filmmakers for a number of reasons, not the least of which was the exceedingly wide range of locales from which they could choose: mountains, fields, ocean fronts, deserts, forests. This factor along with the area's abundant year-round sunlight, then as now an all-important consideration, proved irresistible to filmmakers.

The "charming alfresco spirit" of the early American films faded in stark contrast to the heavily studio-centered offerings of several Western European nations during the World War I era. The Italian cinema presented lavish spectacles such as *Quo Vadis?* (1913), *Cabiria* (1914), *Theodora* (1919), and *Messalina* (1923), which often featured mammoth outdoor settings recreating the splendor of ancient Rome. Such artificial sets were quite different from the ones built in Germany during roughly the same period. The Germans had the technological capabilities for constructing and equipping the world's best studios. These studios, especially the giant government-subsidized Ufa, enabled directors such as Robert Wiene, Fritz Lang, Ernst Lubitsch, and Paul Wegener to work under highly controllable filming situations. They made their films almost entirely indoors using elaborate theatrical sets and lighting. These combined elements gave rise to an "enclosed" feeling that frequently permeated these films and often contributed to a brooding, festering tone. Though the settings ranged from the starkly stylized expressionist backdrops of *Caligari* and Lang's *Metropolis* (1927) to the "studio realism" of *The Last Laugh* and *The Joyless Street* (1925), the Germans' dedication to "studioism" set a trend that strongly affected the American film of the following two decades.

Finally, in France, commercial filmmakers by the 1920s had discarded the tradition of the painted-canvas setting (which had been a part of the Georges Méliès legacy) largely as the result of the influence exerted by an influx of Russian filmmakers. Perhaps more noteworthy was the rise of the French avant-garde cinema, through which Germaine Dulac, Jean Epstein, Jean Cocteau, and Marcel L'Herbier frequently featured fanciful, sometimes surreal tales set against artificial sets that were alternately realistic or unworldly (see Fig. 4–2).

At the same time that the Germans and the French were meeting the challenge of creating elaborate and intricate exteriors within the confines of the studio, Swedish filmmakers were showing equal dedication to using natural landscapes as backdrops for action and as integral parts of their narratives. Mauritz Stiller and Victor Sjöstrom gained prominence in the Swedish silent film through their adaptations of novels steeped in the traditions of Sweden's culture and in its landscape. Modern Swedish director Ingmar Bergman had continued to make the natural elements and settings of his native land—such as the stark, windblown, thinly populated countryside and the choppy seas that surround it—into central and pervasive elements of his original screenplays. The childhood summer home in *Wild Strawberries* and the isolated island settings of such films as *Shame* (1968) and *The Passion of Anna* (1969) are notable examples.

As for Russian filmmakers of the 1920s, they exhibited far less concern for introspection than their Swedish counterparts, but they nevertheless eschewed artificial settings as well. Soviet directors such as Eisenstein and Pudovkin, dedicated to the filmic celebration of their nation's recent past, frequently shot their films on location in the streets of Moscow and Leningrad and on collective farms. For example, Eisenstein used a real factory building as the main setting for his 1924 film *Strike*. He and others often photographed their works on the actual sites of key events in the revolutionary movement or locations chosen for their lyrical qualities and allegorical connotations (see Fig. 4–3).

The large and well-equipped American film companies of the thirties and forties followed the German example and began turning out decidedly studio-bound films. With the aid of imported German production personnel, the major studios developed elaborate and efficient production systems. Given the sensitive and cumbersome nature of early sound equipment, filmmakers then shot virtually all of the initial sound films indoors in huge barn-like sound studios, which were dressed as if they were products of a factory assembly line (see Fig. 4–4). The standardization was such that moviegoers could even identify styles in settings by studio. The heavy reliance on artificial surroundings frequently led to a strong aura

(A)

(B)

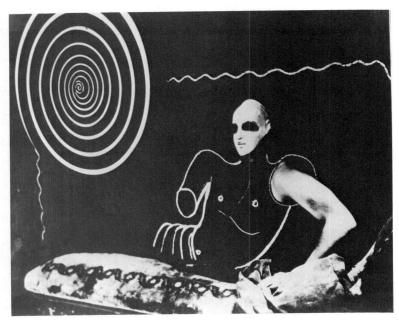

Figure 4-2 (A & B) *Quo Vadis?* (1913—Italian) *I Blood of a Poet* (1930—French). The early Italian film industry's extravagant outdoor settings contrasted sharply with the bizarre indoor surroundings employed by a number of French avant-garde filmmakers in the years that followed; both, however, represent ways that early filmmakers incorporated artificial surroundings into their works. Fig. A shows a scene laden with phallic imagery from Enrico Guazzoni's epic *Quo Vadis?*, while Fig. B. shows a highly stylized backdrop from Jean Cocteau's journey into an inner self called *Blood of a Poet.*

Figure 4-3 *October* (1927—Russian). Eisenstein's use of real locations often gave a documentary-like quality to his fictional films, as seen in this view from his ode to the Russian revolution, *October*.

of staginess in these films, just as it did in the German films of the late silent period. Directors later alleviated this problem somewhat by shooting all of the close-ups and critical dialogue scenes indoors on sound stages while filming the nondialogue passages on real locations. Though still heavily dependent on the perfect acoustics of the sound stages, these directors could now return to the trail blazed by American silent-era filmmakers and take advantage of the veracity of natural scenery, as John Ford did with the grandeur of Monument Valley in many of his Westerns.

Following World War II, many filmmakers turned from the studio and toward shooting scenes on specific and recognizable locations (favorites were Rome, Paris, New York, and London) or some general locations that suggested the region and geographic detail required by the screenplay, such as deserts, oceans, and jungles. Moviemakers based their move to location shooting partly on aesthetic developments and partly on industrial conditions. For example, the style of Italian neorealism, one of several postwar film movements to return to real locations, was based mainly on that country's physical and economic devastation during and following the war. Eager to deal with the social problems of their postwar nation but lacking adequate capital and studio facilities, directors such as Roberto Rossellini, Vittorio de Sica, and Luchino Visconti used the war-ravaged, rebuilding cities and towns of Italy and Sicily as the actual backdrops for their films. Michelangelo Antonioni, who helped extend the practice of shooting on location beyond the orig-

Figure 4-4   *Top Hat* (1935—American). Studio settings provide control over all elements of
production and give free reign to the imagination of the scenic designer. The design, dressing, and
lighting of the set can occasionally provide the ultimate in chic, as it does in this setting from *Top
Hat.*

inal neorealist movement, indicated the importance of real settings in his works:
"I am very susceptible to landscape. When I am shooting a film, I always try to
establish a rapport between characters and landscape."

Other postwar European film movements were just as absorbed in bringing a sense of the immediacy and spontaneity of life to the screen. In France
during the 1950s, youthful writers working for the influential film journal *Cahiers
du Cinema* negatively criticized the heavily studioized offerings of the traditional
French film industry. These same critics showed a marked preference for the pre-
war works of such French directors as Jean Renoir and Jean Vigo, in part because
they frequently used natural surroundings as settings. In 1959, a number of these
critics, including François Truffaut and Jean-Luc Godard, became feature filmmakers themselves and helped carry the legacy of Renoir, Vigo, and other "heroes"
onto the screen by avoiding artificial sets. This movement, popularly called the
French *nouvelle vague* or "New Wave," roughly coincided with a similar movement in Great Britain. Developing from the short-lived but highly influential British Free Cinema documentary movement of the mid-1950s, "Kitchen-Sink
Realism" unsentimentally explored the plight of the British working class against
the backdrop of harshly realistic locations (see Fig. 4–5).

Recent technological and industrial developments within the film and television industries have tended to support filmmaking out of the studio and on lo-

Figure 4-5 *Breathless* (1959—French). A number of young French and British filmmakers eschewed artificial sets in favor of real locations during the 1950s and 1960s. Jean-Luc Godard was one such director, who filmed *Breathless* in the streets of Paris. The actual urban background enhanced the life-on-the-run tale of a small-time French hoodlum and his American "moll" (Jean-Paul Belmondo and Jean Seberg).

cation. The rise of television created the need in the film industry to compete on a grander, more expansive scale; one result was the wide screen with its panoramic vistas that only outdoor settings could provide well. At the same time, more maneuverable cameras, recording equipment, and lighting techniques eliminated or reduced many obstacles that outdoor shooting had previously presented. The rise in independent film production and the corresponding drop in big-studio production supported the move outdoors.

Whether artificial or real, all film settings carry with them aesthetic, functional, and economic limitations under which filmmakers must work. However, as we shall see, the limitations are not always negative or detrimental to the quality of the film. In fact, moviemakers frequently exploit the limitations of their selected settings for a desired effect, particularly in the areas of fantasies and musicals.

Limitations of Artificial Sets

LACK OF REAL AUTHENTICITY.   Whenever a film is shot on an artificial set, the art director often has difficulty replicating the exact "feel" of the real location. Indeed, this priority appears to have been very low on the list for the earliest set designers, whose main concern was simply to allow for adequate lighting. As previously noted, the first film stocks were relatively slow. This, combined with inadequate or nonexistent electrical lighting, caused considerable difficulties when filmmakers attempted to work with artificial settings. One solution was to use "solar power" for interior scenes as well as exterior ones. The settings had to be highly portable for filmmakers to make the most efficient use of the sun's rays. Set designers adapted simple yet highly maneuverable two-dimensional painted backdrops from theater for this purpose. The earliest permanent studios that followed also made use of sunlight by virtue of the huge skylights built into their ceilings. As far as lighting was concerned during the earliest years of film, moviemakers were usually interested merely in having enough light to obtain a recognizable image. Not until the mid-teens did filmmakers such as Cecil B. DeMille, Thomas Ince, and D. W. Griffith go beyond that level by experimenting with lighting as a dramatic and evocative tool.

Since those times, set designers have generally strived for a more faithful representation of reality. In their quests for greater authenticity, however, set designers are often impeded by a number of variables with which they must deal: the illusion of depth, on which they must frequently improve; the necessity of using set materials that are easy to set up and take down; the selection of color schemes that correspond to the proper photographic effect; and, to facilitate the work of the electricians and sound personnel, the usual lack of set ceilings. The artificiality of constructed sets is often heightened by other factors. The actors on the set may be too evenly lit to be passed off as having been filmed on a real location, for example, or the camera work may be too smooth. This artificiality is particularly noticeable whenever filmmakers attempt to replicate the quality of a real location with artificial materials. Director Alan Parker acknowledged and overcame this problem during the making of the 1978 film *Midnight Express* (see Fig. 4–6). The movie's primary setting was an abandoned fort in Malta that the film crew transformed into a replica of Istanbul's Sagmalcilar Prison. The crew added a third wall built of real stone to the original fort. According to Parker, the reason for that undertaking was that "there is a texture to real stone that you can never match, no matter how brilliant the art director."[4]

Set designers may convert this general limitation into a virtue, however, if the aim is not to present "real authenticity" but something beyond that, as in fantasy films, musicals, even period films. As film producer and historian Kenneth Macgowan has noted, "The public all over the world has learned to expect from Hollywood—and save the mark, enjoy—something more than fidelity to life, something beyond reality, something glamorous and extravagant."[5] As further argued by Ralph Stephenson and J. R. Debrix, "For a fantasy like Lang's *Metropolis* or a ballet or a musical film, film scenery can successfully be as artificial and formalized as any stage setting or any painting. It is when the artificial is posing as real that the camera is liable to give it away."[6]

COST OF CONSTRUCTION.   This is another limitation of studio filmmaking that looms large, but for a different reason: money. As suggested by Ivor Montagu, "The degree of reality of the set will depend on the cash of the producer,"[7] among other factors. Wages, raw materials, research, furniture and properties, and

Figure 4-6 *Midnight Express* (1978—American). The set designers of *Midnight Express* supplemented the film's main setting—an abandoned Malta fort—with a new wall built of real stone. The wall may be seen in the background.

miscellaneous decoration expenses all contribute to a significant percentage of a film's total cost. The more elaborate and expensive the set, the greater the risk; for if the resulting film does poorly at the box office, the financial loss obviously would be greater. Films such as *Intolerance, Cleopatra* (1963), and *Heaven's Gate* (1980) have left indelible impressions on Hollywood and its ways of making films. In the long run, a production company might save money by using a given set over and over, but this practice leads to a severe limitation:

INADVERTENT RESEMBLANCE AMONG FILMS USING THE SAME SETS. During Hollywood's Golden Age, production companies found several ways to save money on production costs. One was the scene dock, where filmmakers would store parts of old sets before taking them out and rearranging them in some new pattern for another movie. The *standing set* used to be a major cost-cutting measure. It was based on the belief that some settings, such as western streets and European villages, could serve a variety of purposes and need not be rebuilt every time they were needed. Still applicable today to a limited degree, such strategies may nevertheless prove detrimental if the resulting films look too much alike. This is particularly true of low-budget films whose directors and producers may have to settle for whatever previously used sets are available. Art directors can diminish the problem by altering a number of the details of the set, such as the storefront signs on a western town set, but the basic structure of the original setting usually remains. One way around this problem is to use the original set under entirely different circumstances in another film. For instance, the giant Skull Island gate set used in the original *King Kong* came to a fiery end as a disguised part of the Atlanta skyline in *Gone With the Wind* (see Fig. 4–7).

THE "CLOSED-IN" FEELING.   This is a limitation endemic to indoor studio situations. Set designers often have difficulty creating a light, airy mood when working within the confines of the studio. Even a film such as *The Wizard of Oz* has difficulty transcending the closed-in feeling. If left unchecked, a constructed set may give rise to strong feelings of claustrophobia and entrapment, which is fine for films like *The Diary of Anne Frank* (1959) and *M* but may be at variance with the themes of a host of other studio-bound films. Some of the best examples of films that have overcome this problem are those that have been shot on extremely large and well-lit sets, such as the "globe-tossing" sequence from Chaplin's

Figure 4–7   *Gone With the Wind* (1939—American). Any survey of spectacular settings in cinema would have to include the extreme long shot of the mass of wounded at an impromptu hospital in *Gone With the Wind.* Equally memorable is the scene of Rhett Butler and Scarlett O'Hara leaving Atlanta for her Tara plantation after General Sherman has put the torch to the city.

The Great Dictator (1940) and the Busby Berkeley extravaganzas. There is no question, however, that the set designers for films like these are fighting a tough, uphill battle to overcome the closed-in feeling. They are not assisted at all by the fact the often cramped studio space limits the mobility of both the camera and the actors, which is also reflected in the final film.

LACK OF FORTUITOUS CONTRIBUTIONS TO THE FILM. This limitation of studio settings deals to a large degree with the sources of ideas for the film story. Instead of the story arising naturally out of the setting, as in the case of Italian neorealism films, filmmakers impose the story on the setting. When this happens, the director may find that it limits new ideas worthy of inclusion in the film. A director may avoid using the studio set and instead turn to natural locations simply to take advantage of any fortuitous situations and events, as in the case of the Keystone comedies mentioned earlier. Any director will attest to the difficulty of planning each and every aspect of a film before the cameras roll. Instead of attempting to do so, a filmmaker may choose to shoot at least part of the film on location in the hope of discovering and using some element of the location that might have been completely unanticipated. Steve Rash, director of *The Buddy Holly Story* (1978), observed, "I'd really like working on location because a location can be a good source of ideas. You can even get ideas for the film during the scouting phase. But when you work on stage, you're limited to exactly what you can bring in. There is very little serendipity; you just follow the planned input. And sometimes it's the serendipitous events that really make things work."[8] (see Fig. 4–8).

Limitations of Real Locations

UNCONTROLLABLE SITUATIONS. If filmmakers are working on a studio set they can control to a strong degree such considerations as camera movements, lighting, design of buildings, traffic patterns, and even the weather. This is frequently not the case for those filmmakers working on location. They often face problems with bad weather, inadequate lighting, awkward camera work, and groups of people and vehicles that may be difficult to manage. For example, the story of *I Wanna Hold Your Hand* (1978) was set in New York City during the Beatles' invasion of the United States during the early sixties, yet the film was actually shot in California. Director Robert Zemeckis faced the considerable problem of trying to sell Los Angeles locations and back-lot constructions, particularly the replica of the Plaza Hotel, as New York City. Yet he found it preferable to shoot on the back lots rather than on location in Manhattan, for as he explained:

> I couldn't shoot across the street at the New General Motors Building; I couldn't dress our own traffic on Fifth Avenue; we wouldn't be able to stop traffic on 59th Street; and where are you going to put a thousand extras to change their clothes? It would have been a major event to shoot a scene like that on Fifth Avenue. I think we would have gone a week over schedule. At least we had a controlled situation on the back lot.[9]

Yet directors will occasionally turn this liability of real locations into an asset. Concerning indoor shooting, for example, Michael Ritchie, director of such

Figure 4-8   *The Buddy Holly Story* (1978—American). Filmmakers who produce period films must usually plan everything—including settings—well in advance of the shooting, and may thus deprive themselves of ideas to be found in natural settings. Steve Rash, director of *The Buddy Holly Story*, managed to shoot part of his film on location, but relied heavily on studio sets recreating the look of 1950s environments.

films as *Downhill Racer* (1969), *The Candidate* (1972), and *Smile* (1975), has stated his preference for working with location interiors: "I think that's an advantage. It forces you into camera positions which are realistic. I'd much rather work in a real room precisely because the shooting is limited and will probably be more real."[10]

SOUND RECORDING.   Of all the uncontrollable situations, sound recording is perhaps the most troublesome and warrants separate mention. Filmmakers often have difficulty obtaining a quality sound track while filming on location, such as Paul Mazursky, who shot *An Unmarried Woman* (1978) entirely on location in New York City. According to Mazursky, most of the location problems had to do with sound: "It's no problem in [studios], but when you go into a loft in SoHo that's maybe a hundred years old and has one-inch gaps in the walls and floor, you pick up sounds that happen blocks away. We had to do some reshooting for that reason."[11] The Italian neorealists of the forties and fifties circumvented this problem by postdubbing their films in sound studios, but often the "too-perfect" aural conditions of the sound studios and lack of ambient sound conflicted with the gritty realism of the visual imagery. Today, filmmakers often use miniaturized wireless microphones hidden underneath the actors' clothing, but, as indicated in the Mazursky anecdote, the limitations of recording sound on location have yet to be fully worked out (see Fig. 4–9).

NIGHT PHOTOGRAPHY.   Since the days of the Lumières Brothers, location photography has usually been characterized by a light, open mood. Only recently have filmmakers been able to shoot under dark or murky conditions while on location, which is largely the result of the development of highly light-sensitive film stocks and camera lenses. Yet night photography continues to be a problem for directors working on location. If a night scene needed to be filmed in a studio setting, the traditional answer was to shoot "day for night"—in other words, to shoot under regular lighting but after inserting a darkening filter behind or on the camera lens to give the impression that the scene had been shot at night.

Audiences, already accepting the artificiality of the sets, would probably find minimal objection to this method. But shooting "day for night" on location, especially in urban areas where there would normally be light from office windows, neon fixtures, etc., poses a different set of problems. Shooting day for night might severely detract from the otherwise highly realistic qualities imparted by actual locations. Walter Hill's *The Warriors* (1979) serves well as a case in point. This film

Figure 4-9   *An Unmarried Woman* (1978—American). Sound recording can be an occasional pitfall for location filmmakers. According to director Paul Mazursky, the acoustics of the actual Soho loft he used in *An Unmarried Woman* were so problematic that some reshooting and rerecording were necessary.

was shot almost entirely on location in New York City, but the script called for all of the action to occur at night. To help retain the grimy realism of nighttime New York, Hill and his cinematographer, Andrew Laszlo, decided to shoot actually at night instead of day for night. This posed a particular problem for Laszlo; his average f-stop setting for his camera lens was two, which provides a very shallow depth of field, or area in focus. The low-level lighting of this location work brought with it some advantages, however, as perceived by Laszlo: "The interesting thing was that with the advances in film sensitivity, and the capabilities of the lab, and the super-speed lenses, I had to reduce the amount of lighting equipment rather than take more on: I had to reduce the light level rather than build it up. And this gave us an interesting result: instead of the feel of a back lot, where the action takes place and then the rest falls off in the distance, in this case the light level in the distance was virtually the same as the foreground where the action was taking place."[12] Thus, the near-equal lighting in the foreground and background can compensate somewhat for the shallow depth of field, but night photography on location is, like sound recording, an area that needs considerable improvement.

ECONOMICS AND LOGISTICS.   As suggested earlier, the cost of set construction may induce filmmakers to use real locations as settings. But location-work costs, mainly in terms of transporting personnel and equipment, housing, food, and securing shooting permission from the owners of the location, are very real as well. Filmmakers who choose to shoot their films against artificial backgrounds in a studio are spared many of these financial and logistical headaches. For example, both economics and logistics played a part in Richard Donner's decision to shoot the Smallville, Kansas, scenes of his movie *Superman* (1978) in Calgary, Alberta, despite that Canadian province's decidedly un-Kansas-looking rolling countryside. His reasons: "First because it was cheaper to take an English crew to Canada than to use an American crew in America. Second, Calgary is not only located in the heart of Canada's wheat belt, it's also equidistant from the lakes and mountains of Lake Louise and Banff, and if need be only a short drive from desert terrain. So you have several different locales nearly in every direction."[13]

UNSUITABILITY TO FANTASIES AND PERIOD FILMS.   Except when settings have a timeless quality, most real locations are poorly suited to fantasies and period films. Sidney Lumet's *The Wiz* (1978) serves well as an example of the former. In this updating of the popular fantasy *The Wizard of Oz*, the filmmakers decided to shoot many of the sequences on location in New York City, with added decorations. The Manhattan depicted in the film was supposed to be a mixture of realism and fantasy, but according to production designer Tony Walton, this led to the biggest production problem of the film: getting the feeling of fantasy while using the textures of reality. This problem was diminished somewhat by using unusual locales in New York, such as the old World's Fair grounds and the plaza of the World Trade Center, but difficulties remained. As Walton explained: "Even God-given growing things like trees and grass were taboo as far as we were concerned. I don't know why, but they are immediate destroyers of fantasy."[14] The locations actually used in New York required a liberal amount of "doctoring," such as an extensive use of yellow linoleum-vinyl on the streets of Manhattan and Albert Whitlock's carefully crafted glass paintings (see Fig. 4–10).

Figure 4-10   *The Wiz* (1978—American). The fantasy of Oz and the reality of Manhattan collide in Sidney Lumet's revision of *The Wizard of Oz* entitled *The Wiz*. Production designer Tony Walton employed a grimy back alley for the latter film's version of the "poppy field" sequence, which features bidirectional, windowless taxis and several dozen of Poppy Street's exotic denizens.

Real locations are often no better suited to period films, particularly when the filmmakers are striving for a high degree of authenticity. Working on a fifties period film amid locations in the seventies was no picnic for Steve Rash when he made *The Buddy Holly Story*:

> I don't like doing period location. It turned out to be even more of a pain than I had imagined. There are just so many things that seem to have been around forever; but when you try to be authentic you realize how ancient the 50s really were. You scout a location, try to see everything and make sure everything is covered, but the minute you set up and look through the lens there's a neon fixture you *know* wasn't around in the 50s.[15]

Polly Platt, production designer for many of Peter Bogdanovich's films, including *Targets* (1968), *The Last Picture Show* (1971), *What's Up, Doc?* (1972), and *Paper Moon* (1973) adds:

A period picture is more difficult because you don't have the freedom of choice in terms of where you can shoot it if you're on actual location. You have to find a town that doesn't have too much modernization so you're spending a lot of money on sets to cover up buildings that don't look right. There are tremendous limitations in doing a period picture that result in it being a challenge economically and creatively—and I love that. You have all these incredible problems which become fun. However, I always breathe a sigh of relief when a picture is not period because I realize that I have complete freedom.[16]

Special Uses

Filmmakers will always face limitations regardless of their choice of settings, yet some of the most brilliant set designs and uses of real locations have occurred as a direct result of the tension generated between the requirements of the film script and the limitations of the setting. Such settings often depend on refinements in *special-effects cinematography* for their effectiveness. Filmmakers from Méliès to Welles to Spielberg have looked on moviemaking as a "conjurer's art" by which to create illusions as well as record settings and actions. As early as the first decade of film history, directors such as Méliès and Ferdinand Zecca suggested both underwater travel and space flight through special techniques of the camera, editing, scenic design, and laboratory processing. Through these areas, moviemakers have continued to create not only the more fanciful and exotic settings for horror, science fiction, and disaster-type films, but also countless special scenic effects in more conventional genres. By combining rear-screen projection with live action, by painting background scenery directly on glass (called *matte painting*), or by employing models, miniatures, mock-ups, and limitless other inventions of special effects departments, filmmakers can transport film audiences into interplanetary space travel and into the jaws of a hungry shark. These same devices have simulated countless plane, train, and car journeys staged in the studio and have been responsible for many naval battles that took place in studio watertanks.

Special-effects cinematography is usually a joint effort on the part of the scenic designer, cinematographer, editor, and various other technicians to bring to the screen an environment or suggested action that will satisfy story needs that cannot be met by regular camera recording and editing. In suggesting either an exotic or very ordinary world, filmmakers must combine their talents to create a cohesive and convincing environment. With modern audiences growing more sophisticated and demanding, the task of creating believable settings has become an even greater challenge.

Whether working with special effects in the studio or striving for authenticity on location, filmmakers will be trying to achieve a credible environment for the action. V. I. Pudovkin, writing on "The Environment of the Film," suggested: "All the action of any scenario is immersed in some environment that provides, as it were, the general color of the film," and he underscored the importance of the filmmakers' "ability to saturate the film with numerous and correctly observed details."[17] The care in providing details of a scene as well as the general "color" or atmosphere is generally the mark of major directors. For example, Steven Spielberg's carefully detailed "bedroom community" settings for *Close En-*

counters of the Third Kind (1977), *Poltergeist* (1982), and *E.T.* evoke the Middle America of his own youth while serving as the backgrounds for visits from other worldly beings (see Fig. 4–11).

Besides helping create an appropriate environment for character and action, filmmakers also use settings for expository purposes in narrative films. We are often kept informed on the progress of screen actions and their relationship with one another by recognizing the settings in which they occur. Viewers of *Citizen Kane* can make sense of the film's elliptical and seemingly disjointed structure by using the settings (the Colorado homestead, the *Inquirer* offices, the "El Rancho" night spot, the Chicago Opera House, Xanadu, etc.) to help identify the various characters and time periods of the movie. In chase films, the constant change of scenery helps reinforce the sense of pursuit. In his famous picaresque thriller *North by Northwest* (1959), Alfred Hitchcock used a variety of conveyances—plane, train, jet, private automobile, taxi—to move his characters across equally varied locations, including the United Nations building in Manhattan, a Chicago railroad station, an Illinois cornfield, and Mount Rushmore in South Dakota. Ironically, Hitchcock shot very little of the film on location. He created the settings in the studio with the assistance of rear-screen photography and Albert Whitlock's intricate glass paintings while filming the cornfield sequence near Bakersfield, California. Hitchcock's suggestions of famous settings have become something of a trademark, however, and they range from the English countryside sites of his pre-1940 films to the Covent Garden and Los Angeles settings of his last two works: *Frenzy* and *Family Plot*, respectively.

Settings will occasionally go beyond a supportive function in building a story and will become central to the conflict itself. Many of the silent-screen adaptations of the novels of Swedish author Selma Lagerlof used the natural settings and the vagaries of the elements—fire, blizzard, flood—as prime plot devices. *The*

Figure 4-11 *Close Encounters of the Third Kind* (1977—American). The suburban environment has played a prominent role in a number of films associated with Steven Spielberg. In this scene from *Close Encounters of the Third Kind,* the "everyman" character played by Richard Dreyfuss is involved in a close encounter of a motorized kind in his otherwise placid suburban neighborhood.

Grapes of Wrath (1940), John Ford's brilliant study of dust-bowl Oklahomans migrating to California during the Great Depression, along with the more recent spate of disaster movies such as *Earthquake* and *The Towering Inferno*, allow the setting, however briefly, to become the center of attention (see Fig. 4–12).

In addition to narrative or atmospheric function, setting often serves as a means of linking the place where an action occurs with some figurative or symbolic meaning or to help articulate the film's theme. In *Citizen Kane*, for example, the Chicago Opera House actually has more than a narrative function; it also symbolizes the way Kane manipulates, controls, and generally uses other people to support his very large ego. In William Wellman's *The Ox-Bow Incident* (1943), the stark silhouette of a gnarled tree stands as a constant reminder of the ugliness of lynch-mob psychology.

The challenge directors face in choosing and designing a setting for a film is to avoid clichés and to make the setting an integrated and meaningful part of the total *mise-en-scène*. To our more creative filmmakers, this means going beyond selecting an appropriate geographical location and design for the film's action. It includes making the location and its rendering on the screen a cohesive part of

Figure 4–12   *Earthquake* (1974—American). The environment is the real star of this famous Irwin Allen disaster epic. Actually, many of the special effects in this scene were achieved through the magic of Albert Whitlock's incredibly detailed matte paintings (see text).

the film's total form and content. It requires seeing the setting as an environment in which the action evolves rather than as a backdrop against which it is played. The danger of familiar or photogenic settings and those that help "open up" the film is that they will turn it into a travelogue with story, weighted down by self-consciously applied atmospheric and symbolic effects accumulated through the obligatory wanderings of its characters. Screenplays buried in their own scenery are legion.

SCREEN ACTING

Among the many cinematic elements that help convey meaning and give dramatic dimension to narrative films, the screen actor is one of the most central and yet least understood. Actors who represent people drawn into struggles with other people, with forces of nature, or with forces within themselves are essential to screen storytelling, yet their exact roles and contributions to an aesthetics of film are still subject to much debate.

Screen actors have always served a broad range of functions. In the earliest silent films, they provided the two types of motion that became basic to all story-telling films: physical movement and movement in the form of narrative progression. As they emoted for the silent hand-cranked cameras, the first film players seldom gave subtle performances; instead, they frequently employed the broad, exaggerated gestures of stage actors. Such performances reflected the then-widespread view that film was primarily a recording medium for theater and that individual films should consist mainly of long and medium-long shots to show as much of the actors' physical presence as possible.

To remain financially solvent, however, filmmakers eventually stopped regarding film as "canned theater" and started incorporating subjects and techniques inaccessible or difficult to accomplish in theater (see Chapter 8). One of these was the close-up, which brought with it the need for a different style of acting, one far subtler than that usually associated with theater. At the same time, the film industry quickly learned that the actor could also function as the star, creating a role tied to the personality of the performer and forming certain archetypes and stereotypes that could be reworked or simply repeated in subsequent films. Directors usually had only a few minutes to establish character and were often loath to rely on title cards to convey dialogue and character-revealing descriptions; these and other factors facilitated the rise of stock characters ("Mother," "Ingénue," "Hero," etc.) and attendant stereotypes, through which qualities of character could be instantly communicated to the audience.

Silent-screen actors occasionally transcended stock characterizations, however, with some of the most notable achievements occurring in American comedy. This genre provides some of the best examples of actors who went beyond stereotypes to serve as key creative forces. Charlie Chaplin and Buster Keaton are obvious choices of truly creative screen performers of the silent age. They elevated the art of mime to new heights, with their humor often arising from their interactions with objects both small (clocks, canes, and shoes in Chaplin's case) and large (ladders, locomotives, and steamboats in Keaton's). These and other early film artists demonstrated that, when screenplay and direction allow, acting can also become cinematic invention in which actors use the medium to best effect instead of allowing it to expose, manipulate, or otherwise control them.

As the silent era of film matured, actors gained increased responsibility by conveying inner conflicts. A prime example is Emil Jannings, who infused the character he played in *The Last Laugh* with psychic torment (see Fig. 4–13). At the same time, directors such as Griffith and Eisenstein demonstrated that actors could also serve as part of the set dressing and decor, lending them detail, "color," and authenticity. Eisenstein often selected his performers primarily by the way they appeared, regardless of their acting ability. While his films are unquestionable triumphs of editing and composition, the acting found in them is usually limited to such unsubtleties as fist-shaking, gun-shooting, and running.

With the arrival of sound and the addition of dialogue as a means of character delineation, the basic nature of screen acting changed. Not only did actors have to look the part but they also had to sound it. In addition, directors found it easier to work with relatively long runs of the camera when editing the aural and visual components of their films. The craft of cinema acting thus became increasingly demanding; though no longer called upon to improvise their scenes (the burdensome nature of sound equipment temporarily ended that common practice of the silent era), actors now had to give sustained performances through both speech and body movement. Though rather stilted and declamatory at first, sound-era film acting quickly developed into a more natural means of dramatic expression.

Films of the post-World War II period in particular became renowned as showcases for naturalistic acting styles. Many of the Italian neorealist directors of the forties and early fifties used nonprofessional actors in their films. The freshness and believability of their performances—to say nothing of the authenticity of their appearances—continue to exert an enormous impact on filmmakers and actors around the world.

Figure 4-13 *The Last Laugh* (1925—German). Without speaking a line of dialogue, German actor Emil Jannings became an international favorite of film audiences in the mid-1920s for his commanding performances in such films as *The Last Laugh* and *Variety.*

Another post-World War II development in film was the emergence of an acting style known simply as *the Method*. Initially developed by Constantin Stanislavsky in Russia, the style was nurtured by New York City theatrical acting teachers during the 1930s and adapted to the film medium by Elia Kazan during the 1950s, where it has prospered ever since. It stresses the bond between the actor's own personality and life experiences and those of the character that is portrayed. Under the tutelage of Kazan, Lee Strasberg, and other Method proponents, actors such as Marlon Brando, James Dean, Rod Steiger, and Dustin Hoffman have drawn on feelings similar to those experienced by their characters to help shape their performances. Other hallmarks of the Method include a sense of true interaction between performers, the actors becoming or living their roles after thoroughly researching them, and improvisation during the rehearsal stage. This latter characteristic has often led to a rather cavalier attitude toward the scripted dialogue, as exemplified by the famous "mumbling" performances of Dean and Brando. Nevertheless, Method actors have given many startlingly realistic performances and continue to demonstrate that actors can assume a major responsibility in building cinematic drama (see Fig. 4–14).

Improvisation in front of the camera (as opposed to Method actors' improvisation during rehearsal) made a comeback during the 1960s in many of the French New Wave films. Jean-Luc Godard and François Truffaut in particular

Figure 4-14   Following the principles of "method" acting, James Dean gave stunning performances in the three films that made him famous: *East of Eden* (1955), *Rebel Without a Cause* (1955), and *Giant* (1956).

were quite successful in eliciting very realistic performances from their actors by occasionally allowing them to make up their own dialogue while the cameras rolled. More recently, a number of American directors have relied heavily on improvised dialogue and acting—most notably, John Cassavetes and Robert Altman. They will often "feed" the scripted lines of dialogue to their actors and then ask them to adapt the dialogue in ways that feel comfortable to them. Sometimes these directors will give the players only a general idea of what they want conveyed before the actors put the dialogue in their own words. In so doing, filmmakers such as Cassavetes and Altman have offered their performers a strong degree of creative freedom and a significant share of the drama-building process. In return, the players have frequently given performances so powerful and realistic that audiences are hard-pressed to remember that they are watching fiction films, not documentaries.

Approaches to screen performance and the contributions of actors are varied, but the most important considerations are probably the relationship between actor and director, and the extent to which such cinematic elements as composition, editing, and sound are used not just in support of the role but in its creation (see Fig. 4–15).

Figure 4-15 *Autumn Sonata* (1978—Swedish). Cinematic devices pale before the powerful performances of Liv Ullmann and Ingrid Bergman in Ingmar Bergman's *Autumn Sonata*. Although his mastery of cinematic devices is not to be minimized, Bergman, who has directed in theatre as well as film, is widely regarded as an actor's director.

The relationship between screen and stage acting is discussed further in a later chapter dealing with film and theater, but it is readily apparent even without a detailed comparison of the two acting forms that stage actors are responsible for conveying a larger share of a drama's messages than their film counterparts. In short, the performances are built differently. Screen characterizations as otherwise diverse as Paul Muni's Emile Zola, Laurence Olivier's *Henry V*, C3PO from *Star Wars*, and Chaplin's *Little Tramp* are alike in that they are composites of bits and pieces of performances previously recorded before a cold and unresponsive camera lens. Differences arise with regard to acting styles, range, and the extent to which the players control and dominate the action, or contribute, along with camera positioning, lighting, shot sequence, and sound, to building a characterization and an action. Many of the affinities of film and controls involving composition, editing, sound, and setting support characterization; for example, a filmmaker could make a short actor such as Alan Ladd appear taller and more heroic by filming him from a low angle or by having his leading lady stand in a trench while photographing the couple from the waist up. Yet these same techniques also render the actor as just another object on the set. In a sense, an actor becomes one object among others when filmed by the camera, but this statement is not meant to suggest that the actor's performance will automatically become flawed or be lacking in aesthetic merit. It simply means that the director rather than the actor is in charge and is "calling the shots." A few screen artists like Olivier in *Hamlet* (1948) and *Henry V* (1945), Welles in *Citizen Kane* and *The Lady from Shanghai* (1948), along with Charlie Chaplin and Woody Allen in most of their films, have enjoyed having it both ways by directing themselves in their own works.

NOTES

[1]John L. Fell, *Film: An Introduction* (New York: Praeger, 1975), p. 174.

[2]Leon Barsacq, *Caligari's Cabinet and Other Grand Illusions: A History of Film Design* (Boston: New York Graphic Society, 1976), p. 121.

[3]Charles Chaplin, *My Autobiography* (New York: Simon & Schuster, 1964), p. 153.

[4]Cited in Neal Nordlinger, "The Making of 'Midnight Express,'" *Filmmakers Monthly*, 12, no. 1 (November 1978), p. 19.

[5]Kenneth Macgowan, *Behind the Screen: The History and Techniques of the Motion Picture* (New York: Delacorte, 1965), p. 305.

[6]Ralph Stephenson and J. R. Debrix, *The Cinema as Art*, rev. ed. (Baltimore: Penguin, 1969), p. 152.

[7]Ivor Montagu, *Film World: A Guide to Cinema* (Baltimore: Penguin, 1964), p. 47.

[8]Cited in Steve Mitchell, "Making 'The Buddy Holly Story,'" *Filmmakers Newsletter*, 11, no. 10 (August 1978), p. 31.

[9]Cited in Steve Mitchell, "Making 'I Wanna Hold Your Hand'," *Filmmakers Newsletter*, 11, no. 8 (June 1978), pp. 20-21.

[10]Cited in Larry Sturhahn, "The Making of 'Smile': An Interview with Michael Ritchie," *Filmmakers Newsletter*, 8, no. 12 (October 1975), p. 20.

[11]Cited in Cecile Starr, "Paul Mazursky's 'An Unmarried Woman,'" *Filmmakers Newsletter*, 11, no. 6 (April 1978), p. 30.

[12]Cited in Chuck Austin, "Andy Laszlo: Night Cinematography for 'The Warriors,'" *Filmmakers Monthly*, 12, no. 3 (January 1979), p. 19.

[13]Cited in Steve Mitchell, "Richard Donner: The Making of 'Superman,'" *Filmmakers Monthly*, 12, no. 4 (February 1979), p. 20.

[14]Cited in Judith McNally, "Tony Walton: Designing 'The Wiz,'" *Filmmakers Monthly*, 12, no. 2 (December 1978), p. 22.

[15]Cited in Mitchell, "Buddy Holly, " pp. 30–31.

[16]Cited in Donald Chase, *Filmmaking: The Collaborative Art*, The American Film Institute Series (Boston: Little, Brown, 1975), pp. 159–60.

[17]V. I. Pudovkin, *Film Technique and Film Acting* (New York: Grove Press, 1960), p. 124.

5

FILM AS STORYTELLING

FILMIC CONVENTIONS AND THE NARRATIVE TRADITION

Film historians have speculated that if such early entrepreneurs as Thomas Edison and the Lumière brothers had followed their own inclinations in charting the course of film form and function, they would have quickly if inadvertently relegated the medium to the graveyard of scientific curiosities. It would have remained one of the countless novelties that have caught the public's fancy through the ages, run their course in the marketplace, and then faded from attention almost as quickly as they appeared. Though Edison contributed significantly to the development of motion-picture apparatuses and their early marketing, his vision of the long-range future of the medium was considerably myopic. He initially showed little interest in developing an auditorium-type projection system for his kinetoscope; instead, he thought of motion pictures as a popular and lucrative addition to the amusement parlor trade.

The Lumières were even less visionary. They had very little interest in exploring the ways that cinema could be used to tell stories; rather, they were primarily concerned with the technological development of the new medium. Auguste Lumière told the great filmic storyteller Georges Méliès that cinema "can be exploited for a certain time as a scientific curiosity but, apart from that, it has no commercial future whatsoever."[1] The Lumière brothers made very few films after the turn of the century, since, as Louis Lumière noted, "films turned more and more toward the theatre and toward the use of staged scenes, compelling us to abandon production since we were not equipped to do this kind of thing."[2] In a 1948 interview conducted shortly before his death, Louis Lumière summed up his approach to film: "My work has been in the direction of scientific research. I have never engaged in what is termed 'production.' I do not think I would fit into a modern studio."[3]

Creative pioneers such as Méliès, Edwin Porter, and D. W. Griffith, who saw in movie making the potential for more than recording bits of reality or staged business, were not so much trying to bestow aesthetic credentials on the new popular form as to save it from oblivion. These and other filmmakers introduced and developed the single-reel narrative film, which allowed them to weave stories within a span of approximately ten minutes each. Though their stories were elemental, these moviemakers helped save the medium from the junk heap after the novelty of "living pictures" had worn off.

However, the possibility of the medium's stagnation arose once again during its early years when many conservative companies that dominated the American film industry balked at the prospect of permitting their directors to make films longer than one reel. In response, the more daring of the filmmakers, inspired by several enterprising European counterparts who began producing longer films (most notably, *Quo Vadis?* and *Les Miserables,* two 1913 multireel films produced respectively in Italy and France), joined more progressive production companies or formed their own. Working in the more favorable climate provided by these new companies, these directors expanded the format for screen storytelling and pushed the movies themselves beyond the single reel to lengths of two, three, four, and ten—even, in the case of Griffith's *Intolerance,* a 13-reel length.

Most film historians agree that these early screen storytellers simply embellished and expanded on those traditions in visual storytelling such as theater, comic strips, wild west shows, and slide presentations. By placing film in direct succession and lineage to the storytelling media, filmmakers not only assured its place in a showcase of its own (the storefront theater, the nickelodeon, the moving-picture palace, the neighborhood theater, the multiscreen "mall" theater, television) with its own large, devoted, and continuous following, but it also led to the development of a versatile and unique means of narrative communication, entertainment, an eventual art form in its own right.

The push beyond the one- and two-reel length in film storytelling was critical because it allowed filmmakers considerable freedom to do a number of things: to explore the fuller range of narrative techniques, to adapt traditional designs in dramatic construction to the medium, and to satisfy more fully those expectations and demands of audiences that relate to narrative design. Depending on certain cultural variables, audiences usually anticipate and respond to specific narrative patterns or formulas. American musicals prior to 1970 almost always conclude on positive and reassuring notes while gangster films of any vintage frequently end in orgies of death and destruction, for example; were such films to end differently, they would clash with audience anticipations. Many of the more basic expectations go back to the earliest forms of narrative. Although we should not regard them as formal rules of narrative construction, they do represent patterns that have gained wide and long-lasting acceptance and constitute the foundations of a "good story."

These expectations include first of all some kind of narrative movement or progression of the story. In any form of storytelling, we have come to expect that the presented events will follow one another in some ordered sequence, that such ordering will be governed primarily by the cause-and-effect relationship of events, and that such events will lead somewhere. Progression in film and other narrative media may vary from simple, physical forms such as chases and rescues to those that mark some emotional or intellectual change, such as a character's developing awareness of some aspect of the world around him or her. Alfred Hitchcock built many of his films on the premise of physical progression, ranging from an exciting chase between a bus and a train in *Number Seventeen* (1932) to the frequent change of locale in *North by Northwest* (see Fig. 5–1). The latter film, with its movement from New York to Illinois to South Dakota, is a particularly vivid illustration of a narrative strongly tied to the physical journey, though its story-telling form is by no means new; writers such as Homer, Boccaccio, and John

Figure 5-1 *Number Seventeen* (1932—British). A little known early film by Hitchcock, *Number Seventeen* becomes a spoof of the suspense thriller and therefore a self-parody as well. The first half features mysterious comings and goings in an old dark house, with much of the action taking place on one of Hitchcock's favorite sets—a staircase. The second half involves a spectacular race between a bus and a train that ends with the train crashing into a coastal ferry.

Bunyan used it centuries before in such literary milestones as *The Odyssey, The Decameron,* and *Pilgrim's Progress,* respectively.

In other literary and filmic works, the progress involves not so much physical movement as increased emotional involvement, estrangement, or detachment that reflects the change in the way the characters relate to one another, their environment, or whatever else to which people have emotional attachments at some time in their lives. Films that stress character over plot, such as those of Yasujiro Ozu, the Italian neorealists, and the early French New Wave, involve progression of this kind.

Another type of progression concerns intellectual or philosophical growth, in which a character may experience an increased awareness of some concept or phenomenon. The travels of Don Quixote are clearly more than a physical journey, a situation that also holds true for a woodcutter's trip from forest to courtroom to Kyoto Gate in Akira Kurosawa's *Rashomon.* These three forms of narrative progression are not mutually exclusive; indeed, many stories are often composites of physical, emotional, and intellectual journeys, with the physical progression serving as a framework for the more complex and subtler forms. In fact, many of the best narratives in literature and film have involved all three forms of progression. For instance, the combination of the physical journey, mental or emotion conflict, and progress toward some philosophical insight makes both John Ford's *Stagecoach* (1939) and Ingmar Bergman's *Wild Strawberries* such rewarding experiences (see Fig. 5–2). In the case of the Bergman film, the physical journey of the aged doctor to the University of Lund, where he is to receive an honorary degree, is in itself flat and not particularly memorable. What gives the work stature are the emotional conflicts that exist between the doctor and those closest to him and the ways they are resolved. On yet another level, the film transports the audience, through the protagonist, to a new perspective on certain philosophical issues, including an examination of the meaning and values of one's life, and accepting its shortcomings and eventual end. Not all films will have a narrative structure this rich and complex, but clearly no meaningful storytelling can take place in any film without some form of progression.

A second ingredient of storytelling that shapes a part of our expectations involves the formal design of the narrative. In addition to our interest in a narrative work's sense of progression and completion, we as audience members gain considerable satisfaction from certain established patterns that filmmakers and other narrative artists have repeated or extended. As with novels, plays, and short stories—not to mention such nonnarrative forms as painting, sculpture, and musical composition—films are more apt to hold attention and gain aesthetic approval if they are organized and follow some predetermined pattern. Indeed, film viewing is a pleasurable experience partly because it satisfies our sense of orderliness and provide us with a feeling of participation. Narrative filmmakers create (or, perhaps more appropriately, recreate) patterns and designs and allow us to recognize them and anticipate their extension and completion; the filmmakers then complete the patterns to meet our expectations. Among the many design methods are parallel opening and closing sequences, plot devices such as Hitchcock's "MacGuffin" (that is, an item on which the central characters focus much of their attention, such as a stolen rocket-fuel formula or an incriminating piece of evidence, but which concerns the audience only minimally), and such standard plot structures as a young,

Figure 5-2   *Wild Strawberries* (1957—Swedish). Narrative progression in Ingmar Bergman's *Wild Strawberries* combines a physical journey with an emotional one. Here the protagonist, Isak Borg (Victor Sjöstrom) is seen in a nightmare trial scene where the aged doctor finds himself judged incompetent by his peers.

innocent character on a quest of some sort or a "good" outsider intervening in the affairs of others. Ernest Lindgren has suggested that we are entitled to expect that film as a work of art will have unity and be a thing complete in itself that can be appreciated for its own sake, "every part falling into place to create a satisfying pattern unmarred by redundancies, irrelevancies or omissions."[4] Yet the nature of unity will vary from one type of film to another; with the exception of many modern Hollywood films, which hew to preordained formulas to maximize profits, narrative patterns are today considerably less predictable than in earlier times. Jean-Luc Godard has taken a familiar Aristotelian notion—that a good story must have a beginning, a middle, and an end—and set it on its ear by suggesting that these fundamental elements need not be presented necessarily in that order. We have in fact learned to expect the unexpected in narrative design; indeed, today's average viewer can easily take in stride unorthodox structures that may have bamboozled audiences of a previous era, such as the fugue-like, four-part, parallel construction of *Intolerance* or the story-within-a-story framework of *The Cabinet of Dr. Caligari.*

Progression and design are ingredients that are most closely associated with the form and structure of the film; the other two ingredients that stimulate and satisfy expectations in narrative are more closely linked to content. The first of these involves the viewers' identification with particular story detail and the links that they establish between the imitation of action on the screen and their own real-life experience. Regardless of which of the two traditional approaches—realist or formalist—one cares to follow, the concept of viewer identification is so fundamental to the theory of film communication (as it is to all forms of communication arts and media), that the only meaningful approach to it in the limits of this work is in terms of the unique ways in which viewer identification is affected by the characteristics peculiar to the film medium. This will be discussed more fully in the section on screen realism.

The other factor related to content that forms part of our expectations in film is *voyeurism*. The term is used here in its broader sense, to describe the anticipation and gratification one experiences from surreptitious viewing of not only nudity and sex, but any detail or act that is considered too intimate, or is denied to the onlooker because of social stigma or taboo status. The French film theorist André Bazin suggests it's like looking through half-open blinds. Voyeur appeal is certainly not unique to film, but it is a motivational factor that is probably stronger here than generally recognized, and one that has special application. The camera, as an extension of our vision, has a special facility for probing, uncovering, moving in for a closer look. Using it in a way that will satisfy viewer expectations and emotional needs and at the same time meet aesthetic requirements has escaped many filmmakers. Renoir, Fellini, Buñuel, and Hitchcock are among the major *auteurs* who have had particular success in allowing us to experience vicariously assorted acts of violence, sexual aberrations and grisly or indelicate detail, but usually within the realm of acceptable standards of taste. Their success has been not simply in knowing the threshold of tolerance, but in their mastery of the medium—knowing not just what to show but how to show it.

The evolution in screen storytelling through the several decades of its silent and sound forms has been inspired by the traditional approaches to dramatic construction found in the other arts. The development of screen narrative has also been guided by an increased understanding of how the properties unique to film can offer special approaches to narrative design. As mentioned earlier, the Victorian novel and late nineteenth-century stage melodrama and popular fiction had a significant influence in molding the early screenplay. The traditional approaches to theatrical and literary fiction had been tried and proven; they were understood and expected and therefore served as a natural blueprint for meeting audience needs and expectations in the film medium as well. Like its theatrical cousin, the film melodrama focused on crime and the plight of the city worker or the dangers and challenges of the frontier, thus establishing early two basic and durable genres—the crime thriller and the western. Moreover, like its stage counterpart, the film melodrama had a simple plot line, clear and direct moral issues, clearly and externally defined characterization, and costuming, setting, and gesture given simple symbolic reference. Suspense, which was a key ingredient, was supported by quick scene changes and a general attention to tempo.

The dime novel, like stage melodrama, provided simplistic moral tales with a somewhat broader and more fanciful range that encompassed disaster, horror, supernatural, and science-fiction subjects. Such topics provided popular and durable fare in early one- and two-reel screen dramas; strong, direct plotting, intense but straightforward conflict, suspense, pace, and rapid scene changes were characteristics quickly assimilated by the new medium. The novel, with its visual detail, shifting perspective within a scene, and occasionally elaborate transitional requirements, provided both inspiration and structural guidelines for the more complex screenplays that evolved in the multireel film.

With multireel screenplays came further exploration of a fuller range of film forms, techniques, and stylistic detail that tested approaches to narrative that filmmakers drew from the medium's own unique qualities. The Germans centered on visual style and matters of camera perspective, lighting, setting, and acting. The Russians gave their attention to montage and allowed the selection, juxtaposition, and length of individual shots to carry the major responsibility for conveying meaning. The documentarist and neorealist filmmakers of the thirties and forties gave emphasis to naturalistic detail and spontaneity in design that the New Wave and the modernist directors further explored and modified. Though varying widely in style and final design, each approach has demonstrated special and at times unique characteristics of screen storytelling. The influences of television along with film and video experimentalists today have helped extend the range in approaches to screen narrative and genre types. The simple stories of Porter's *The Great Train Robbery* and Griffith's first film, *The Adventures of Dollie*, have given way to the structural intricacies of the *Last Year at Marienbad* and *Slaughterhouse Five*, and the emotional and intellectual density of *Wild Strawberries* and *The Wild Child*. The modern screenplay is a multidimensional, diverse, and multisensory construct that continues to meet the needs and expectations of audiences by drawing from the medium's own potential for dramatic involvement while still drawing from the traditions in dramatic construction offered by the older, established arts.

A closer look at those characteristics of design common to all dramatic modes will be our next step. It should help make an examination of screen storytelling—particularly the application of general narrative techniques to film—more meaningful.

FUNDAMENTALS OF DRAMATIC STRUCTURE

Drama, Aristotle tells us in his *Poetics*, is the imitation of an action that is created according to certain means, objects, and manners. Means, he suggests, include such devices as color, voice, and rhythm, while objects are "the actions of men" and manners of presentation are either by narration or imitation. Imitation, he says, is the representation of the author's characters as "real, and employed in the very action itself."[5] The definition sets down the fundamentals for both structure and content of not only drama in the theatrical sense, but dramatic action that is manifest in all story forms from ancient fable to contemporary screenplay. What renders a drama unique according to its medium is found to the greatest degree in the *means*. In literature the means are literary tropes, descriptive idioms, and other linguistic forms of signification, or the connotative and denotative uses of *language*. In the film the means are camera composition, lighting, editing, sound, and setting. We may find unique properties in the manner of presentation, but

Figure 5-3 *Close Encounters of the Third Kind* (1977—American). Among the screen narratives that have tradtionally challenged the imagination are those that deal with otherworldly inhabitants.

perhaps to a lesser degree. Aristotle suggests that the dramatization can be offered through use of either narration or imitation, and although either manner would be common to several narrative forms, the nature of their employment would differ. The soliloquy is common to both stage drama and film, but its use differs; the film version is usually a "voice-over" technique in which the actor is seen thinking rather than speaking the lines. Least suggestive of the unique properties of the film medium is the object of the imitation, which Aristotle defines as "the actions of men" and which he goes on to amplify as "the imitation of an action that is important, entire, and of a proper mangitude"[6] in its tragic form. Film theorists have come remarkably close to the Aristotelian prescription in defining the nature of film's structure and its key ingredients. "The imitation of actions" of which Aristotle speaks is echoed in Kracauer's description of the film story's "strong concern for human characters and human interaction."[7] Lindgren similarly speaks of the function of the fiction film, "to present an imaginary story of the thoughts and actions of individual human beings."[8] While allowing considerable latitude for the source of a film's unity, most contemporary film theory also follows closely to Aristotle's model:

> An imitation of an action that is one and entire, the parts of it being so connected that if any one of them be either transposed or taken away, the whole will be

destroyed or changed; for whatever may be either retained or omitted, without making any sensible difference, is not properly a part.[9]

Ernest Lindgren has previously been quoted in this book as calling for "satisfying patterns. . . unmarred by redundancies, irrelevancies or omissions." John Howard Lawson, Hollywood screenwriter, has also suggested that, "as long as films are performed by people, they must give some order and sequence to human action" and that "the total rejection of a story. . .can only lead to a breakdown of cinematic form."[10]

The Aristotelian requirements of storytelling and tragedy in particular serve quite effectively as a model not only for the general nature of form and content, but also for the specific components of contemporary screen narrative. The six elements of tragedy listed by Aristotle include "fable. . .character. . .language. . .thought. . .setting. . .and melody." The cinematic counterparts of these elements are clearly defined by theorists and practitioners in film. "Fable" or plot, which Aristotle says consists of "complication and development," provides the framework or vehicle upon which the action or series of actions will be placed, while "character" provides the human expression, through the screen actor, by which the imitation of action will take place. The other elements, with perhaps the exception of "melody," also have their counterpart as central and critical parts in film narrative. On the subject of "thought" or theme, Lindgren has reminded us that "not all films have an explicit moral purpose, but they all have an implicit one."[11] And Lawson has stated that "a film is organized in order to meet the requirements of its theme."[12]

The purpose of linking the nature of screen narrative to Aristotle's work is neither to legitimize the form and establish its lineage, nor to establish some prescription for what storytelling via the medium must include. Rather, we wish to make clear that certain narrative traits common to a variety of early dramatic forms have become standard fixtures in screen storytelling. They have evolved from the special requirements of the film medium but have also satisfied the expectations that our exposure to other media/arts has produced. We are not simply paying homage to Aristotle by defining a story film as an imitation of an action that, through language, character, and setting, will develop some thought through orderly progression from beginning to middle to end; such a definition helps describe how the form has developed in both unique and universal ways.

The Film Story

Although other dramatic forms share film's basic storytelling design, the filmmakers' employment of narrative technique becomes authentically cinematic through their ability to compose and construct in the medium's own terms. Filmmakers can translate, or transmute, narrative from play and prose fiction, but they can also create their own stories and tell them in a largely cinematic way. The medium's degree of success in telling a story will depend on the extent to which it exhibits three qualities: clarity, unity, and credibility. The first two, clarity and unity, can be roughly equated with the plot and theme; the third, credibility, embraces the larger issue of screen realism and involves the total film message.

Filmic Approaches to Plotting

Imitating an action or series of actions that have progression and causal relationship is known in film, as in other narrative forms, as *plot*. Plotting involves not only the ordering of events into a satisfying pattern but also moving the audience from beginning to middle to end (or from exposition to involvement to crisis to climax to resolution—to use the terms that identify the traditional plotting elements). The challenge is to accomplish the journey while keeping the viewers reasonably well informed as to where they are and what is going on.

Major concerns for filmmakers in handling plot design and details are smoothness and clarity of purpose, and the medium has innumerable ways of assuring that these requirements are met. Moviemakers occasionally define their plots according to the limits of time or space (or both) as required for their films' action to be completed. We identify film as a "plastic" means of expression in part because of its facility for getting from one location to another, or one time period to another, without interruption or delay. A range of narrative films would serve to illustrate the point, but Griffith's *Intolerance* provides a quintessential example. Here, Griffith established four separate and distinct story lines, with the action flowing back and forth among them. Labor strife and personal tragedy in a contemporary American city give way to activities in the French court of Charles IX and the scheming Catherine de Medici. This story becomes interwoven, in turn, with incidents surrounding the attack on and fall of ancient Babylon. A fourth "story" taken from incidents in the life of Christ provides some basic counterpoint but is otherwise undeveloped. Narrative progression involves not only cutting among the four settings and their major action, but also intercutting between incidents within the three more fully developed story lines. The film stands today as one of the most complex narrative designs ever attempted in film. Though initially confusing to audiences, it illustrates on careful examination just how fully aware Griffith was of movement in film: movement of camera, of the action placed

Figure 5-4 *Great Expectations* (1947—British). The opening scene of David Lean's *Great Expectations* serves the dual function of providing basic exposition for the Dickens tale and also riveting the attention of the viewer. Lean has said of the scene, "If I can get the interest of the audience in those first three minutes, I am halfway there to holding them. Pip's first meeting with Magwitch, the convict in the cemetery, seems to be remembered by everyone." Cited in Gerald Pratley, *The Cinema of David Lean.*

before the camera, and particularly movement in narrative progression and the flow and rhythm that could be created by interweaving distinct stories from different ages.

Camera movement and editing were both essential to Griffith in providing the necessary emphasis on detail, and making the required links between details in this most intricate screenplay. Today, the close-up, flashback, and crosscutting from detail to detail enable filmmakers to keep viewers reasonably well informed while moving through the web of subplots or related actions in the more intricately designed films. Clarity of plot detail is not the province of camera placement and editing alone; sound, setting, lighting, color, costuming, makeup, acting, and dialogue all support exposition and help make the screenplay of greater density and complexity fathomable. Composition and montage, however, are the critical elements.

Our "maneuverability" in the story film also includes the shifting of perspective within a particular scene. Not only can the angle from which a filmmaker records an action suggest a subtle change in perspective, but it can also provide choices between the first- and third-person point of view, allowing the viewer to observe the action from the most revealing position. The action of the drama is more meaningful to us because we can be moved directly into the action—even, at times, into the shoes of the protagonist. In our earlier discussion of basic film properties, we cited *Occurrence at Owl Creek Bridge* as a film in which perspective is critical to plot. Other films in which the positioning of the camera serves more than a supportive function and provides extensive first-person perspective include Bergman's *Wild Strawberries* and *Hour of the Wolf*, short narrative films like Chris Marker's *La Jette,* and the single film effort by Samuel Beckett, *Film,* which is seen almost completely through the eyes of its protagonist.

Filmmakers have also shown considerable talent for creating and extending *tension* and *suspense.* The technique of suspense, the more easily identifiable plotting device, raises audience expectations concerning plot progression by drawing attention to certain details while temporarily withholding other information the audience needs to understand fully the implications of an action or where it will lead. Editing and manipulation of the camera are once again the principal means by which suspense can be realized. For example, we along with James Stewart become increasingly aware that something sinister is going on in an apartment across the courtyard in Hitchcock's *Rear Window* but are deprived of the vantage point from which we can understand the full implications of the action. Other elements less exclusively cinematic, particularly music, provide strong reinforcement for suspenseful situations. Associations established between music and a particular character or situation will serve as effectively in raising expectations and keeping an audience on tenterhooks as any tricks of camera or montage. The shark and the bass-fiddle musical motif in *Jaws* are prime examples.

Tension, somewhat more elusive as an element in dramatic construction, is concerned less with specific details of plot and more with the general *mise-en-scène* or atmosphere in which the plot action takes place. Even before we are supplied with any plotting detail to raise questions about past or future events, we often experience a sense of foreboding, uneasiness, or even fear by the "climate" of the scene. The opening scene of *Great Expectations,* described earlier, immediately sets up certain tensions in the viewer, even though there is no way of anticipating in these early moments what the action is all about. Tension involves

(A)

(B)

an emotional involvement with a dramatic situation that is less dependent on conscious recognition of specific plotting details than suspense. Film technique, particularly compositional and editing devices, can effectively accommodate plot complexities and at the same time promote clarity, giving the viewer a sense of participation and understanding. At times such technique will, by a kind of deliberate villainy, produce a sense of anxiety by leaving the viewer at least temporarily in the dark.

Cinematic approaches to plot construction are applicable to a variety of types of plot situations or story forms, but certain forms lend themselves particularly well to cinematic representation. The earliest screen storytellers established the chase, in both its comic and dramatic form, as a "cinematic subject par excellence,"[13] to use Kracauer's phrase. The directness of progression makes this a continued favorite as a basic plot design. The ability to reveal and withhold detail and provide for intricate interweaving of plot and subplots make the mystery or suspense thriller another most durable and serviceable form. "Sleuthing," as Kracauer has called it, works particularly well on film because it draws upon the medium's ability to focus on visual detail (collect evidence) and control atmosphere and viewer perspective. It also often incorporates the chase, making it a double threat as plotting material. Another form that succeeds in using the medium to particular advantage as storyteller and extends beyond any particular genre is the fairy tale or fable. Moralistic tales of adventure, physical adversity, and triumph have an established and accepted design and still accommodate a wide range of specific generic forms from tales of the Arabian Nights to those of the untamed West, with countless legendary kingdoms and forbidden islands or planets in between.

Storytelling and the Plotless Film

Michelangelo Antonioni, in speaking of his approach to filmmaking, observed, "It is the story which fascinates me most. The images are the medium through which a story can be understood."[14] Anyone who has seen an Antonioni film must wonder why he, of all directors, would place such an importance on story when his films are so lacking in conventional elements of plot construction and for many viewers (and some critics) seem to go nowhere. The reason for the seeming contradiction is that when Antonioni speaks of story, he is not concerned with the manipulation of formulas but with the exploration of a condition or circumstance. He is beginning his story not with "Once upon a time" but with "What might happen if?"

Story is not synonymous with plot in either film or other dramatic forms. A basic difference is that a story relates a sequence of events but, unlike the plot, these events are not necessarily related by cause and effect. An often repeated example of the distinction is that of the two simple narratives: "The Queen died and then the King died"—the story; and "The Queen died and then the King died of grief"—the plot. Although both suggest narrative sequence, the difference is that in the second form causality is established between the two events. In fact,

Figure 5–5 (A & B)   *Intolerance* (1916—American). One of the most ambitious attempts at narrative construction was Griffith's fugue-like interlacing of the four stories of *Intolerance*. The attack on the city of Babylon frequently gives way to scenes of court intrigue involving the planning and final execution of the St. Bartholomew's Day Massacre in Paris.

the only events relevant to the relating of a plot are those involving a cause-and-effect relationship. The story draws its meaning from a broader range of details, particularly from the delineation of character and the establishment of *mise-en-scène*. Narrative devices in films like Antonioni's may give the appearance of plot but they usually reject the conventional plotting elements—opening exposition, climax, and denouement are the usual victims—and concentrate instead on giving meaning to the human experience. Some film theorists have suggested that the structure of a film is not strengthened, and may be weakened, by plot devices characteristic of other narrative forms.[15] Whether or not this can be accepted as a principle of film construction, Antonioni, Bergman, Satyajit Ray, Eric Rohmer and Robert Altman are among the filmmakers who have clearly demonstrated that the plot is not a necessary requirement for filmic unity.

Theme has become more prominent as a means of organizing film content and providing it with cohesion and unity. Theme is the idea behind the portrayed action and assumes some perspective or point of view (the director's, unless otherwise specified) and a mood or emotional or intellectual climate for the action. Theme is not necessarily a film "message" in the moralistic sense of the word, but it does draw from the dramatized human action some social, psychological, or philosophical significance. The plot of *Bicycle Thieves* is a thin narrative about a young father who searches vainly for the stolen bicycle that is a necessary requirement for his employment as a bill poster. The theme of the film is human anxiety, disillusionment, compassion, and understanding, revealed mostly through the relationship of father and son. *Rashomon*, on a plot level, is about the death of a man and the encounter of the man's wife with a bandit, and how these events are related in a police court by the various parties involved. The theme of the film concerns the nature of truth, suggesting that truth is what each individual chooses to believe or to have others believe. *Citizen Kane* as plot also involves separate and sometimes overlapping accounts of the events in a man's life. Thematically, it dramatizes, like *Rashomon*, that one's perspective on events will be influenced by the nature and degree of one's involvement. More significantly, however, it becomes an ironic comment on the loss in meaningful human relationships experienced by a man of great physical wealth and power. Bergman's *Wild Strawberries* is virtually plotless, involving an uneventful car journey (except for a minor auto accident) of a retired scientist and his daughter-in-law to a ceremony where he is to receive an honorary degree. Thematically, Bergman has provided a rich study in the emotional scars left by past events and the fears of the future—death, and a life unfulfilled.

Conflict, Character, and Motivation

All drama involves a story of human conflict. Any film that goes beyond the simple relating of events to ask (and sometimes answer) questions about cause and effect in human experience—how or why people influence, or are affected by, a conflict with their environment, with other human beings, or with themselves—is exploring a theme. Whereas plot is a narrative and descriptive process, theme is analytical and goes beyond the relating of the conflict to search for its meaning in terms of human motivation. *The Great Train Robbery* has a plot centering on the conflict between a group of bandits who have stolen a train and the posse that has been alerted to apprehend them. With a little stretch of the imagination we might even say that the film has a message: "crime does not pay!" It is without a theme, however, in that there is no exploration of human motivation undertaken. Griffith's *Intolerance* has four major plots with several subplots interwoven with two of these, but it has a single theme, summed up in the one word of its title. Erich Von Stroheim's *Greed* (1924) is another opus that explores the theme suggested by its title, but, in spite of its original ten-hour length, concentrates on a limited number of characters—Trina, McTeague and Marcus—and their lust for gold. Such seemingly plotless films as Bergman's *Persona* (1966) Antonioni's *Red Desert* (1964), and Fellini's 8 ½ (1963) are psychological case studies in which the conflict is so internal that the physical and visual events portrayed give only a hint to the real struggle going on. This is not to say that the visual detail is unimportant. The unity of films such as these is realized from details of character, event, setting and total sense of *mise-en-scène*. The conflict is finally reflected in, and draws its meaning from, all of these.

Using the screen image to explore emotional conflict may seem to raise insurmountable obstacles and work against the very nature of film. But filmmakers aware of the medium's fuller capabilities have used dialogue and limited movement to deal effectively with psychological stress and emotional turmoil. By control of camera perspective, movement in time as well as space, and by careful selection of details placed before the camera, they have demonstrated that a conflict of mind and will can have as much dramatic impact, and cinematic impact at that, as a physical one.

SCREEN REALISM

Regardless of the dichotomy between the realist and formalist traditions in film theory, all theorists recognize a potential for making the imitation of real-life situations a legitimate and satisfying use of the medium. It calls for an approach universally described as "screen realism" but defined in a variety of ways. The extent to which the story film offers such an approach will depend on the nature and degree of faithful and true representation from a rather broad range of possiblities. This range, generally speaking, has at one extreme the concrete, mechanical photographic authenticity of the visual document, and at the other a much more abstract notion of philosophical truth.

The various approaches to realism in narrative film often overlap, but it may prove helpful if we identify those characteristics that help provide for the more genuine and credible dramatization of an action and isolate those qualities by which the term "realism" has been identified. If we proceed generally from the concrete to the abstract, the first of these draws from the medium's affinity for concreteness and photographic authenticity, and obviously has its greatest relevancy to the documentary tradition. But it is also the foundation for the entire realist approach to film theory. Michael Roemer, writing on "The Surface of Reality," speaks of "true film images, derived from life and rendered in concrete, physical terms."[16] Kracauer, emphasizing the unique ability of the camera to represent nature builds his theory of film on "the redemption of physical reality."[17] In screen narrative (or "fiction" film as we sometimes call it) this level of realism manifests itself in a photographic rendering of detail which "particularizes" for greater authenticity, density, and thematic accent. In films as diverse in style as Martin Scorsese's *Taxi Driver* (1976) and Louis Malle's *Pretty Baby* (1978) there is a common concern for capturing detail that best preserves the physical characteristics of each film's environment: a contemporary New York City subculture and a turn-of-the-century bordello in the New Orleans Tenderloin district, respectively. Virtually all of the affinities and controls of the medium can aid in the redemption of physical reality, but the selection of setting and set detail and the use of an exploring camera are of greatest importance.

A second level of realism is in the extent to which the camera explores the intimacies that we are often denied even in real life because they are hidden away by the dictates of moral convention, or simply by physical distance. Besides persuading us of the authenticity of detail, the close-up may also probe beneath the surface reality to reveal subtleties and intimacies normally hidden from view. Béla Balázs speaks of rediscovery of the subtleties of human expression through the use of the close-up camera in his essay on "The Faces of Men,"[18] while Michael Roemer suggests that film thrives on intimate detail.[19] Such subtleties and intimacies are clearly a basic component of major film statements on so-called "adult themes." They are also at the heart of some nonstory films that provide an exposé on hidden or forgotten subjects. They include the bizarre film journals (*Mondo Cane* and *Women of the World*) as well as the semidocumentary studies of the drug culture (*Cool World*) and other social afflictions. In searching out and revealing things that normally go unseen, such films give added dimension to screen realism in a broad range of film styles.

A third quality in film drama that goes under the name of screen realism involves the capturing of some of the spontaneity and immediacy of real life's random and unplanned experiences. The direct, unobtrusive approach to recording real-life events has become an established tradition in the documentary form, but such approaches have influenced narrative styles as well. The "new realism" that had its beginnings in the Italian cinema of the late forties (see Fig. 5–6) and spread to other European, American and third-world genres was often characterized by an unrefined, often ragged look that ranged from the casual to the chaotic and provided the fiction film with some of the sense of authenticity that the modern documentary had enjoyed. *Bicycle Thieves*, Cassavetes' *Faces* (1968), and even one of Richard Lester's Beatles film—*A Hard Day's Night* (1964)—were reflections of the unordered, ironic, sometimes contradictory and even chaotic nature of life off the screen. Today, directors will still turn to using the hand-held camera, high-grain film stock, spontaneous screenplay with improvised dialogue, and a direct and functional editing style to give the look of unstaged reality to narrative films that depict either real or imagined events. A step beyond the sense of witnessing unstaged reality is the sense of direct involvement in that reality. Psychologists and film theorists have recognized this illusion of the personal experience as an important factor in the fascination that many narrative films have on us. Although we identify with situations and details in the other arts, film is unique in its ability to draw us directly into the action and to shift our perspective from that of detached observer to active participant. Motion, the close-up, and other controls of camera and editing are key factors in producing the sense of realism that makes the film event a part of our own real-life experience. Psychologists point out, however, that the very nature of the film viewing experience, with its darkened au-

Figure 5-6 *Rome: Open City* (1945—Italian). Roberto Rossellini's *Rome: Open City* helped usher in the movement that became a hallmark in realist expression in post World War II cinema. Rossellini shot the film on location, using many nonprofessional actors. The resulting film revealed through its sparse narrative line what its screenwriter, Cesare Zavattini, called, "a direct look at living social facts."

ditorium, luminous rectangle, and lack of other competing stimuli, facilitates the identification and participation with what's going on on the screen. When the image offers film viewers the opportunity to "discover" and sort out details for themselves, the sense of involvement may be even stronger. André Bazin has suggested the deep-focus photography in *Citizen Kane* forces the spectator to participate in the film by searching for significant detail within the scene and thereby making it a more involving and real experience.[20] The moviemaker can transport the viewer not simply into the scene but into the "shoes" of the protagonist by using subjective camerawork, expressionistic settings, and editing that suggest shifts of attention and private associations that the character might be experiencing. Expressionistic sound and use of internal monologue will also help to suggest the subjective, first-person experience. Together, image and sound in the darkened theater provide transport to the "real" world of storied characters.

For many filmmakers, realism goes beyond the direct observation of concrete, immediate, and intimate detail of either objective or subjective varieties to a sense of discovery in composition, motion, sound, and the associative possibilities among images. This sense of discovery is voiced by Luis Buñuel when he speaks of "an integral vision of reality" that will "increase my knowledge of things and beings, and will open to me the marvelous world of the unknown, which I can neither read about in the daily press nor find in the street."[21] Fellini also professed his interest in "showing the things behind the things, not just to make statements of what can be seen," while Carl Dreyer wanted to "wrench the film out of the embrace of naturalism."[22]

All three filmmakers have demonstrated, not just by these statements, but through their films as well, that realism in film may be extended to include an understanding of the world—including human activity and motivation—not necessarily found in the record or simulation of the immediate experience. Such a realism may be abstracted from concrete or imagined detail and provides insight into human experience that may not be so easily captured directly by the camera. When Dreyer introduced us to the supernatural world of *Vampyr* (1921) and Buñuel to his surrealistic world of *The Exterminating Angel* (1962), they did so by way of what Kracauer calls "special modes of reality." Although the term *surrealism* is often used to describe this extension of the real beyond physical appearances, the term has perhaps been tied too closely to dream imagery and the subjective experience to provide adequate latitude. It is a world of the imagination made real by visual dynamic organization or, as Slavko Vorkapich has put it, by "making the visual parts go well together."[23] It can be a world as complex as that of Kubrick's *Clockwork Orange,* or as simple as the revolutionary one suggested by three stone lions in *Battleship Potemkin.* Such dynamic organization of material requires not only imagination but a command of the medium as well. It is the challenge of abstracting from reality to provide an impression of the world that would otherwise go unrealized.

Related to the sense of dynamic organization is a kind of realism that extends one's identification and involvement in film a step further and might be called *intellectual honesty.* It is that quality in filmic representation that makes things acceptable to our sense of reason about the nature of things social, psychological, and philosophical. It represents things that satisfy our perceptions about human motivation and certain philosophical truths. In *The Cinema as Art*, Ralph Stephenson and J. R. Debrix speak of "recognition in film of a mental truth . . . as important or more important than the physical reality."[24] This mental truth provides films with the kind of credibility or ethos that satisfies not simply one's sense of what is real, but what is right: that which is faithfully portrayed in a philosophical sense.

In his *Poetics*, Aristotle observes that "it is not the poet's province to relate such things as have actually happened, but such as might have happened."[25] Seizing on the same theme, S. H. Butcher, in his notes on Aristotle's *Theory of Poetry and Fine Art*, relates the reaction of the detractors of poetry who say, "These creations are not true to life," and Aristotle's response: "not real, but a higher quality."[26] Aristotle holds that the truth of poetry is essentially different from the truth of fact. According to Butcher's notes, "Things that are outside and beyond the range of our experience, that never have happened and never will happen, may be more true, poetically speaking, more profoundly true than those daily occurrences which we can with confidence predict."[27] Aristotle's suggestion that poetry need not concern itself with fact but with probability serves as a point of departure for this natural extension and final level of realism in film, in that this type of realism does not concern itself with a literal translation of specific experiences and observations of life, but is a representation of those that have universal meaning. The concern here is not with the reality of setting, dress, or even language, but rather with the ways in which people respond to their environment and to one another. It is the "moral probability" that depends on human nature and character motivation of which Aristotle speaks. On this level, the successful imitation of human action and thought and not the literal translation of details attracts us to a film narrative.

One work that has had successful renderings in several dramatic forms because of the inherent simplicity and universality of its theme is *Rashomon* (see Fig. 5–7). It began as a short story, an eight-page narrative by Ryunosuke Akutagawa, which Akira Kurosawa combined with two other works to make the 1952 film that received considerable critical acclaim around the world. It was adapted to the stage in 1959 by Peter Glenville, and in 1964 was readapted to film with an American western setting starring Paul Newman and called *The Outrage. Rashomon* is, in itself, a questioning after the meaning of truth. It is set in tenth-century Japan, before the crumbling gate of the city of Kyoto. Here we find a woodcutter and a priest in the rain discussing a murder trial to which the former has been called to testify. The appearance of a wigmaker provides an opportunity for relating, through flashback, the details of the case. The preliminaries are not in doubt: a samurai, traveling with his young bride through a forest, is waylaid by a bandit, who ties him up and rapes his wife. The husband is impaled on his own sword. Later, at the trial, four different versions of the incident are related. The bandit boasts that he killed the samurai in fair combat; the wife claims she killed her husband rather than face his contempt; the husband, speaking through a medium, insists that he killed himself when he saw his wife attracted to the bandit; and the woodcutter tells a completely different version in which the bandit is a braggart, the samurai a coward, and the wife a harlot. The wigmaker states the theme of the story: "Everyone tells what he wants the world to believe." Even the woodcutter's version contains a lie to cover the fact that he stole the sword implanted in the samurai's chest.

Here is a work that provides the kind of "impossible probability" of which Aristotle speaks. In the hands of a masterful director like Kurosawa it becomes a film to which we find ourselves drawn, not through its representation of daily occurrences and familiar detail, but through its ability to delineate elements of

Figure 5–7 *Rashomon* (1951—Japanese). Realism in film may go beyond authenticity of setting and action to become the expression of some universal truth. In *Rashomon*, director Akira Kurosawa examined the nature of truth by having each of the film's principals relate a personal account of the death of a samurai and the possible rape of his wife.

human nature easily recognizable to us all. Here we can sum up the universal meaning in a single phrase: the truth is what we want others to believe.

Although film clearly has a special affinity for physical reality, its range in expressing a recognizable, credible, and acceptable world extends more abstract notions of dynamic organization and truth. The range is perhaps best summed up by Ivor Montagu: "Realism is not a single style or a technique; it is a content shaped by a style appropriate each time to its chosen aspect and with a mastery of requisite technique."[28]

SUMMARY OF NARRATIVE FUNCTIONS

The evolution of several functions in narrative cinema provides a useful approach for establishing more specific generic patterns. Although an application of the traditional dichotomy of film functions—formalist and realist—may at times become tenuous, it is helpful when looking at the basic needs met by screen storytelling, before going on to sort out and identify particular genres.

In the spirit of the realist tradition, filmmakers have, since the beginnings of film narrative, involved themselves in screen dramas that exploit the ability of film to record or imitate physical existence. Where some actual past circumstances provided more than simply a backdrop for some other function, directors were learning to use the story film to provide a reconstruction of historical events. *Birth of a Nation* thus became the story of the Civil War and the Reconstruction period as Griffith's *America* (1924) later became the story of the American Revolution. Eisenstein's *Battleship Potemkin* and *Ten Days that Shook the World* provided stories of the abortive revolution of 1905 and the Bolshevik uprising of 1917. Although such films can hardly be thought of today as providing the best examples of the realist approach to film construction, they do illustrate the dedication of their creators to a more or less faithful representation of actual happenings. Griffith in fact prided himself on the accuracy of detail in the presentation of such events as the Lincoln assassination and the signing of the surrender of Lee at Appomattox, while the sequence in *Ten Days that Shook the World* depicting the storming of the Winter Palace has a strong documentary-like flavor. More recently, features such as *In Cold Blood* (1967) and *All the President's Men* (1976) have made storytelling generally akin to, if not synonymous with, the recounting of causally related real-life events.

Stories of events frequently do not make for the most unified, cohesive, and absorbing of screen dramas. The fact that they are frequently expansive composites or collages of individual human conflicts often makes them seem episodic and even arbitrary in their design. Screen dramas that are more successful in suggesting real-life experiences, at the same time telling a more direct and cohesive story, are generally those that limit their focus to the depiction of a specific social conflict (such as *Grapes of Wrath* or *Shoeshine*), or those psychoanalytical case studies where the focus narrows even further to the individual within the social setting (*The Informer, Autumn Sonata*). Such social and psychological studies, particularly those that avoid plot intrigues in favor of the direct case-study approach, seem to work against the tradition of storytelling. Those that succeed as both narrative and dramatization of real-life events are those in which the story seems to grow naturally out of genuine social and psychological conditions. *Bicycle Thieves* and Kurosawa's *Dersu Uzala, The Hunter* (1975) satisfy as both stories and social documents because events evolve naturally (if not intricately) from a given set of circumstances.

Film narrative that follows more in the formalist traditon includes those forms in which the story serves as a vehicle to a less than realistic world of romance, adventure, or voyeuristic indulgence. Much dramatic fiction on the screen provides for identification that satisfies basic human needs to enjoy human relationships, while at the same time it allows us to observe and experience vicariously what is taboo and potentially dangerous. From *The Great Train Robbery* to *Close Encounters of a Third Kind*, audiences have had the pleasure of experiences with the dangerous and unknown, and at times the erotic and spiritually uplifting. We go to the movies to be amused, frightened, emotionally stirred, sexually aroused, and, finally, assuming the scriptwriter has not betrayed our expectations of the traditional formula, made to feel secure.

Ultimately, we become willing listeners and observers to screen narrative because of our love of a good story. The satisfaction we experience is of the well-spun yarn; with the identification of significant patterns; with the anticipation of effects and final resolution; with the recognition of quasi-enigmatic situations and an acceptable denouement. We have learned, particularly in recent years, that if the experience can be both funny and frightening, so much the better. Over the past several decades it has become increasingly difficult to distinguish the screen comedy from serious drama. *The Graduate, Bonnie and Clyde,* and *Outrageous* attest to the mixed nature of today's cinematic storytelling. Whether or not Aristotle would approve of the mingling of comic and dramatic forms is another question.

NOTES

[1] Cited in Maurice Bardèche and Robert Brasillach, *The History of Motion Pictures,* trans. and ed. Iris Barry (New York: W. W. Norton & Co., Inc. and the Museum of Modern Art, 1938), p. 10.

[2] Ibid. pp. 8–9.

[3] Cited in Harry M. Geduld, *Film Makers on Film Making* (Bloomington: Indiana University Press, 1967), p. 25.

[4] Ernest Lindgren, *The Art of the Film* (London: Allen & Unwin, 1963), p. 43.

[5] S. H. Butcher, *Aristotle's Theory of Poetry and Fine Art* (London: Macmillan, 1923), p. 11.

[6] Butcher, p. 31.

[7] Siegfried Kracauer, *Theory of Film: The Redemption of Physical Reality* (New York: Oxford University Press, 1960), p. 218.

[8] Lindgren, *Art of the Film,* p. 46.

[9] Aristotle, p. 31.

[10] See John Howard Lawson, *Film: The Creative Process* (New York: Hill & Wang, 1964), pp. 285–89.

[11] Lindgren, *Art of the Film,* p. 54.

[12] Lawson, *Film,* p. 290.

[13] Kracauer, *Theory of Film,* p. 42.

[14] Michelangelo Antonioni, "There Must Be a Reason for Every Film," *Films and Filming* 5:7 (April 1959), p. 11.

[15] See, for example, Lawson, *Film,* p. 289.

[16]Michael Roemer, "The Surfaces of Reality," in *Film: A Montage of Theories*, ed. Richard Dyer MacCann (New York: Dutton, 1966), p. 259.

[17]This phrase is the subtitle of Kracauer's *Theory of Film*. According to Kracauer, cinema "redeems" reality by enabling us to view the world around us in new and different ways.

[18]Béla Balázs, *Theory of the Film: Character and Growth of a New Art*, trans. Edith Bone (New York: Dover, 1970), pp. 60–88.

[19]Roemer, "The Surfaces of Reality," p. 257.

[20]André Bazin, *What Is Cinema?*, *Volume II*, trans. and ed. Hugh Gray (Berkeley: University of California Press, 1971), p. 8.

[21]Luis Buñuel, "Cinema: An Instrument of Poetry," Vol. 46, *Theatre Arts* (July 1962), p. 18.

[22]Carl Dreyer, "Thoughts on My Craft," *Sight and Sound* 25:3 (Winter 1955–56), p. 128.

[23]Slavko Vorkapich, "Toward True Cinema," in *Film: A Montage of Theories*, p. 175.

[24]Ralph Stephenson and J. R. Debrix, *The Cinema as Art*, rev. ed. (Baltimore: Penguin, 1969), p. 211.

[25]Butcher, p. 101.

[26]Butcher, p. 168.

[27]Ibid.

[28]Ivor Montagu, *Film World: A Guide to Cinema* (Baltimore: Penguin, 1964), p. 295.

6

NARRATIVE PATTERNS
AND GENRE TRAITS

GENRE CLASSIFICATION

Describing and Prescribing Genres in Film

As film storytelling expanded in style and subject matter, it became more detailed and varied in dealing with time and place of action, types of characters, nature of action, and visual quality of its rendering. Writers, producers, and audiences soon began to look at individual works in relation to the ever increasing number of works that had gone before, and to draw comparisons among those that had recognizable traits in common. When motion pictures were becoming a major industry in the United States, studies began to show increasing interest in product control and marketability, which led to repetition of tested formulas, standardization of story patterns and, in general, a recycling of old properties and methods. These two tendencies—classification and formulization—established what is known today as film genres and the genre film.

The term *genre* serves as both noun and adjective to both name and describe on the one hand the type, class, or category into which a film may be placed, and on the other, the formula or blueprint that serves as a basis for its design and, in some instances, a prescription for its detail. Thus, *High Noon* falls within the category (genre) of the western and as a genre film follows certain characteristics

137

associated with that class. The genre film is recognized as one that fits within an established and accepted pattern, but when the term *genre* is used as a means of sorting out films according to class and subclass, every film becomes a "genre film" in that it will inevitably be grouped with others of similar characteristics.

Serving in its descriptive function, genre is a system of classification and categorization that identifies characteristics common to a particular group of films while distinguishing them from other groups; in its prescriptive function, genre is a formula that evolves from a history of usage and becomes a model for future films. Because it repeats certain easily recognizable patterns, the genre film also becomes an invitation to audience expectations. In defining genre, Stanley Solomon calls it, "the recognizable ordering of narrative patterns to produce related experiences from film to film."[1] We might add to this "related *and expected*," in defining genre from the audience's point of view.

Value of Genre Identification

The values of having a system of classification for screen narrative are several. First, it allows those involved in the process—both creators and viewers—to sort out groupings of film according to more meaningful patterns than some chronological, alphabetical, or other equally arbitrary method that reflects little about the nature of the work. But such classification serves more than a clerical function. By such identification, we are able to establish links between a specific work and the general category into which it falls. As previously mentioned, familiarity with the basic design on which a film is patterned provides for easy orientation and identification and establishes in the viewers a set of expectations that they can be assured will be met. We needn't have seen more than a couple of the Warner Brothers musicals of the 1930s to be reasonably assured that the one we are about to see for the first time will involve a conflict no more sinister than trying to get a cast assembled and ready for the opening of a show while trying to find or hold onto the required financial backing. We can also expect that once the show is put together, we will be treated to elaborate, kaleidoscopic production numbers that will severely strain our suspension of disbelief (that is, that all this could be mounted on a Broadway stage and actually seen by the theater audience—see Fig. 2-22).

In addition to the appeal that the repetition of familiar patterns has for audiences, established and easily recognizable generic patterns also lead to an economy in narrative exposition, or a kind of cinematic shorthand. One test of the good director, one that distinguishes the hack from the *auteur*, is whether he or she has sufficient understanding and control of the medium to know when to draw from traditional generic patterns and when to set these aside or modify them.

The director who knows how to use old formulas in new ways, and who has the conviction to do so, can move an audience quickly into narrative exploration without the otherwise necessary but undramatic and time-consuming exposition. Hitchcock can, within seconds of a scene's opening, establish both circumstance and mood by the introduction of devices that have appeared in his films from the very beginning (a staircase, a close-up of a ringing telephone) and yet never appear as clichés.

As a critical approach to film, genre identification provides a study of variations on familiar patterns and evolution in style (see Chapter 12). An initial look at the basic ways in which narrative films can be grouped and labeled, however, may be useful in discovering the extent to which materials and structures—narrative patterns, themes, characters, milieu or setting—lend themselves to filmic representation. To coin a phrase, certain subjects and designs may be found to be more "cinematogenic" than others.

Siegfried Kracauer has identified certain "cinematic subjects par excellence," namely "the chase" and "dance," as particularly well suited to the medium.[2] Georges Méliès learned as early as 1900 that imaginary voyages to the moon, the North Pole, and other exotic and fantastic locales could be facilitated through the miracles of cinematography. The ability of the camera to record detail that we tend to ignore—what Kracauer calls "refuse"—has likewise opened up a range of styles that draw their dramatic impact from what comes under the general heading of *photographic realism*. And when Béla Balázs wrote about the rediscovery of the human face through cinema,[3] he was illustrating how, through use of the close-up, the art of mime became a significant part of the communication process in film.

The links between film genres and particular affinities of the medium are at times tenuous, often complex, and inevitably overlapping. Still, recurring techniques, themes, and designs in the more successful examples of a particular genre do help to explain how the perceptive film storyteller can draw from past models in fashioning new creations. And, if an element is found to be a part of nearly all the important films of a particular genre, we may assume that the element is an integral and critical rather than incidental ingredient of the genre. So the very essence of the western genre is dependent on its geographical setting, just as the musical film requires song and dance.

Of course some filmmakers who understand generic traits will draw from these familiar patterns to gain fresh perspective on a subject, while others will simply revive the familiar formula and stock ingredients. Genre critics have founded their approach to film precisely on the basis of this distinction. We find it helpful here to view genre definition and classification as a purposeful reintroduction of patterns that have, because of an affinity of the medium and a successful track record in past works, become a signature or a hallmark of the class.

Because of its tendency to group films and to focus on associative values, genre identification also encourages the person with more than a casual interest in films to step back and gain some perspective and a better understanding of individual works and the aesthetic, psychological, and sociological implications of the genre of which they are a part. Our awareness of the development of genre patterns can increase our understanding and appreciation of how the medium has dealt with certain themes. This in turn can make our viewing of a particular film within the genre a more rewarding experience because we see it in relation to other works and in the evolution of the genre. Viewing a film with this kind of perception is an on-going experience from one film of the genre to the next.

As an analytical tool, genre identification goes beyond the medium and provides a means of studying the ways in which film mirrors social and psychological conditions and thought. The prototype of the western hero tells us something more than the way in which the medium and the genre have treated one of its favorite protagonists; it also tells us a good deal about basic human motivations, anxieties, and the nature of hero worship. Robert Warshow's essays on "The Westerner" and "The Gangster as Tragic Hero" are two excellent and celebrated studies.[4] The extent to which films of a particular genre explore or choose to ignore a particular social condition or phenomenon likewise tells us something about our society as well as about our cinema. Kracauer's book *From Caligari to Hitler* is an exploration of how the German film of the twenties reflects the collective psychological paralysis of the country in the postimperialist, pre-Nazi period.[5] The American industry failed to include in one of its most cherished genres more than a single major feature (*The Green Berets*) on the Vietnam War until several years after its end, even though the conflict preoccupied this nation for more than a decade (See Fig. 1–5).

Problems

There are pitfalls in the use of genre both as a means of suggesting or prescribing formula or format and as a system of classification. As in almost any system of sorting and filing, the placing of films into categories raises the problems of finding distinct boundaries between groups of films and determining at what point similarities and differences will dictate the grouping of works under a single heading or their separation into different ones.

In the case of films that deal in some way with crime and its detection, critics have used numerous and overlapping generic terms to identify variations of the story form and its style of presentation; these include crime drama, private-eye film, gangster film, suspense thriller, detective film, and even *film noir*. The problem is often compounded by the use of the term *genre* to describe both larger and smaller groupings (unlike the scientist who classifies according to genus, species, family class, subclass). The tendency is to make generic distinctions among drama, comedy, and melodrama at one moment, and among spy, gangster, and "whodunit" the next.

A further complication is introduced by the shifting and varied basis for genre identification that might place a film about crime not only in one of the several categories just enumerated, but also in groupings that identify director, studio, national origin, location, period, origin of screenplay, and, with the labeling today of "women's films," even sex. Godard's *Breathless*, Penn's *Bonnie and Clyde*, and Hill's *The Sting* are all films that make the assigning of genre labels difficult.

The problem that arises in using genre to set the pattern and the requirements of future films is that it can limit the horizons of both filmmaker and viewer and become no more than a recycling of previous works with superficial modifications that allows an old and often worn work to be given a new title and new cast of characters. Generic "requirements" will also lead viewers (and critics) to think that by virtue of the genre label they have the right to expect particular detail in design that has come to be associated with films of the class but that would not necessarily improve their quality and effectiveness as screen drama.

Such expectations have been reinforced throughout the history of film storytelling by the practice of formula filmmaking that provides a production-marketing system for studios and uses past popularity as a criterion for future formats. Early filmmakers quickly discovered that by refurbishing old screenplays that had proved popular, they were assured of speed and economy, both in terms of the creation of "new" screenplays for their rigorous production schedules, and in terms of familiarity and acceptance by audiences who looked for comfortable old themes, characterizations, and details. The result of such standardization and recycling was often the establishment of stereotypes in both characters and situations. For example, most American films that have portrayed Chinese people have character-ized them in the most basic of stereotypes: gentle and pure souls (a "type" made famous by Richard Barthelmess in D.W. Griffith's 1919 film *Broken Blossoms*), obedient houseboys, efficient laundrymen, self-effacing detectives, exotic prin-cesses, decadent opium smokers, Communist automatons, and, in the case of the redoubtable Dr. Fu Manchu and his ilk, villains of the most unspeakable evil (see Fig. 6–1).

Formula filmmaking enabled the Hollywood industry to meet production and marketing demands of a rapidly growing industry. When methods fell into a catalogue of superficial traits and repetitive designs, they became clichés. Creative filmmakers resisted the easy accommodation of film cycles and formula, however; by using familiar and accepted patterns to elaborate, reinterpret, and offer fresh perspectives, they not only developed designs more durable than the short-lived cycles, but they also created genres of film like the westerns and gangster movies that became mythic.

Figure 6-1 *The Mask of Fu Manchu* (1932—American). A film cycle which promoted one of the screen's most legendary villains dealt with the schemes of the nefarious Dr. Fu Manchu. Fu's first screen appearance came in 1923 with the British serial, *The Mystery of Dr. Fu Manchu.* Paramount established Fu as an American screen favorite in 1931 with Swedish actor Warner Oland in the role. MGM had Boris Karloff take over the characterization the following year in *The Mask of Fu Manchu* (pictured). The cycle continued with a serial by Republic Pictures in 1940 and a series of British features in the mid-1960s. Peter Sellers revived the role in the early 1980s with *The Fiendish Plot of Fu Manchu,* his last film.

Classification and the Evolution
of Genre Types

Generic roots go back to the popular arts and media of the nineteenth century. The history of storytelling in fact is the history of genre development and evolution. Narrative patterns are established, repeated, and modified. The groupings that film began to separate into in most instances preceded the medium itself. In narrative development a fundamental division (too fundamental, finally, to be useful as generic distinction) was between the comic and dramatic modes. This in fact provided the only real distinction between films that were produced in the days of one- and two-reel production. As screen storytelling expanded and followed literary methods and adapted literary works, the separation among epic, lyric, and dramatic modes became evident.

But generic identification was not to be limited to the patterns set by earlier arts and media alone, and the grouping and patterning of films developed along broad and diverse lines. Subject content has and continues to be a major determinant. With conflict, the necessary ingredient of any story, we may classify content according to the nature of that conflict. The crime, gangster, or detective film suggests by such labeling that the conflict here will be between lawbreaker and representatives of the social and legal order. Although the nature of conflict is less obvious, we know the screen romance will involve an emotional struggle of some sort that may or may not lead to actual physical encounter. The adventure film may lead us to a confrontation between individuals, but may also represent the struggle between an individual and the natural elements. The term *psychological drama* tells us that the conflict will likely be more mental than physical and may indeed be an internal struggle within the protagonist.

We may thus make a basic division according to the nature of the struggle in terms of the traditional categories of conflict—person versus person, person versus nature, and person versus oneself. Such distinctions produce genre groupings such as survival films, social dramas, psychodramas, and psychological thrillers. The survival film, in which the major conflict is with natural (or supernatural) elements, is the least complex and perhaps the least interesting in terms of human motivation. Robinson Crusoe, Icarus, and their progeny who battle for food, clothing, shelter, and protection from fire, water, and falling from high places do draw from film's ability to suggest menacing situations, but these are usually predictable, episodic, and finally uninvolving. Films ultimately depend on some human interaction or self-examination to make them work successfully. Filmed biographies of personal triumph over adversity, from *The Life of Emile Zola* (1937) to *Patton* (1970), usually turn out to be struggles of conscience and will or conflict with other persons or institutions. The adventure and disaster films likewise depend on the struggle of will to give them continuity and momentum.

Other specific genre labels such as war films, horror films, and even bedroom farce go beyond basic delineation of conflict to say something about the setting, style, or attitude toward the struggle. These other factors will at times identify a unique grouping or subgenre of works, but they will more likely represent a cross-reference with characteristics common to other, and sometimes quite dissimilar, genres. The western, for example, uses location as a means of classification for a film group that has maintained certain clear and discrete characteristics. To identify a work as a jungle film or an eastern, on the other hand, tells much less about either attitude or style, or about the nature of the conflict. Still,

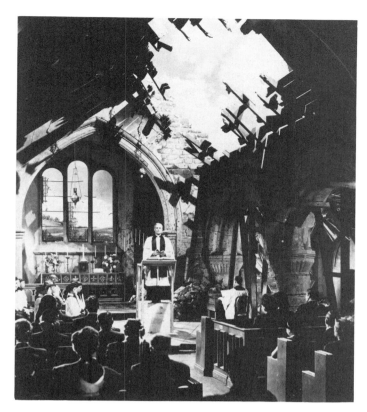

Figure 6-2 (A & B) *Mrs. Miniver* (1942—American) / *Apocalypse Now* (1979—American). The war film genre embraces a great range of styles and sentiments. The many romantic and inspirational studies of courage and faith stand in marked contrast to the grim and nihilistic accounts of war. Here we see war's victims keeping the faith in *Mrs. Miniver* and *Apocalypse Now.*

(A)   (B)

location, time, and nationality of films can be used to signal something about the manner of storytelling and the setting in which an encounter is to take place, even though it may not reveal much about the nature of the conflict itself. A Japanese period film, we can expect, will not only have a special style in detail of setting and costume but in tempo, musical background or other complementary sound, movement and gesture of actors, and perhaps even in the way scenes are lit or otherwise composed. In the case of futuristic films, we have learned from works as diverse in style as Lang's *Metropolis*, Godard's *Alphaville*, and Kubrick's *2001: A Space Odyssey* that a formalistic approach will likely be evident. A generic label that identifies an occupation such as a "doctor film," "newspaper film," or film about deep-sea fishermen is likewise going to suggest something about both the setting for the action and the kind of people who will be involved.

In addition to grouping films by period, location and nature of conflict, critics have a tendency to make generic distinctions among films that generally follow the realist tradition and are identified by some ideological, sociopolitical, or cultural statement. Such a thematic or conceptual grouping of films has increased as filmmakers have turned from plot-oriented works to those exploring ideas. The periodic emergence of social issues also helps to create new genre identification. "Sex in cinema," "the Indian film," "women's films," and "Cinema and the Black Experience" are popular labels today, and they reflect an interest in searching out the links among films on social themes and films that dramatize ideological rather than physical conflict. Such classification and grouping of films draw their common bond not from physical design, detail, and other specific traits, but rather from their theme, idea, or message; as a result, they are more difficult to pin down and identify in a concrete way.

Some genre groupings have very little to say about the nature of film, but those that seem the most durable and meaningful identify and draw from qualities of the medium itself. Vachel Lindsay, in his vintage work on the nature of the "photoplay," makes generic distinctions that, while seeming a bit quaint today, identify associations tied to affinities of the medium. The "action photoplay," he suggests, is based on the out-of-doors chase; the "intimate photoplay," he states, is "the medium for studying the half relaxed or gently restrained moods of human creatures"; in "the motion picture of fairy splendor," Lindsay points to the medium's ability to "take in the most varied of out-of-door landscapes"; and in "motion pictures of crowd splendor" he finds the motion picture "is powerful in conveying the passions of masses of men."[6]

More recently, such venerable genres as the western and gangster films have effectively illustrated common characteristics tied to the nature of the medium itself. We have a tendency to assume, however, that such genres are quintessentially cinematic because of their durability and general responsiveness to cinematic rendering. Stanley Solomon suggests that "gangster films illustrate the principle that a genre may be inherently cinematic."[7] This is to invite the details that have become a traditional part of the genre to set the standards of what is cinematic and essential to its durability and critical acceptance. In a system of formula filmmaking, directors and screenwriters repeated narrative elements and detail because collectively they seemed to work. In a sense these elements did begin to work in that they met expectations that had gradually been built up in audiences, but their special cinematic credentials may well have been overstated. It would perhaps be better to say that gangster films illustrate the principle that

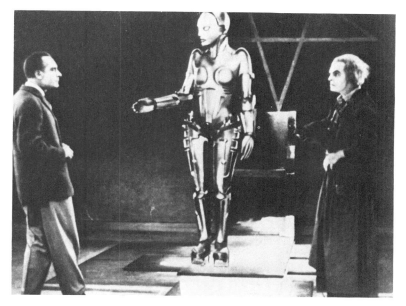

(A)

Figure 6-3 (A & B) *Metropolis* (1927—German) / *Star Wars* (1977—American). Revolution in film content and refinements in design and technique will not obscure certain enduring genre traits. Fritz Lang made an impressive early attempt to instill life into a robot in *Metropolis,* while fifty years later a kindred spirit named George Lucas made stars out of robots C–3PO (seen below) and R2D2 in *Star Wars.*

(B)

a genre may *contain elements* inherently cinematic. In other words, genres like the western and gangster film are particularly accommodating to plotting elements, technique, and visual detail that work particularly well on film. For example, the earliest experimenters in cinematography recognized the attractiveness of galloping horses, whose perfect suitability to the medium undoubtedly gave rise to the western genre in film. The shoot-out, another highly "cinematic" situation, has become an indispensable part of virtually every western and gangster film ever made. Other details may well have become part of the tradition of the genre by the practice of formula filmmaking but not by any proven effectiveness.

The cult status of the western hero may be explained in sociological terms, but in cinematic terms any number of other character types are equally able to affect some sort of conflict and a chase, the latter of which is a supremely cinematic element. In examining the nature of screen narrative within genre groupings, we need to look at traits that extend beyond the single genre and to discover a commonality in genre clusters as well as to define what is unique about the more limited format. When Solomon says of the private-eye film, "In this genre, representatives of the dark world of hypocrisy and greed impinge upon the moral order until the hero is alerted and single-handedly sets about restoring the proper moral balance,"[8] he could be talking about any number of genres that fall generally into the class of crime or detection. The description, in fact, would fit an even broader range of dramatic films in several generally recognized genres, including the western.

In facing the hazards of genre identification, we should note that both bona fide generic characteristics and incidental (and perhaps uncinematic ones) have a way of becoming a part of the label, and ultimately a part of our expectations. When these characteristics become prominently displayed, repeated, and generally accepted as a part of the breed, they then invite not only further interpretation and imitation but also spoofing. Films like *Young Frankenstein*, a parody of both the horror genre generally and Universal's "Frankenstein" movies of the 1930s (in particular, *Frankenstein* [1931] and *Bride of Frankenstein* [1935], both directed by James Whale); *Cat Ballou* (1965), which spoofs the western; and *Take the Money and Run* (1969) and the *Pink Panther* series, which take the crime drama to task, all depend on recognition of what have become standard generic patterns for their humor. It is not possible to satirize something without the audience having some degree of familiarity with, and general acceptance of, its characteristics.

ENDURING AND ENDEARING GENRE TRAITS

Without further extending the mythic proportions of such classic types as the horror, Western, gangster, or musical films, it should be possible to detail the design and some of the characteristics of generic trends or groupings based on types of appeal particularly well suited to filmic representation. This approach should make room for the unique qualities of both narrower categories and those that extend to broader classes that include two or more traditionally recognized genres. Such a "wide-angle" view of genre related to motivation should provide us with a better look at elements of narrative film construction that help draw together individual genres as well as those that tend to keep them distinct. The groupings that we use

Figure 6-4 *Young Frankenstein* (1974—American). Familiarity and acceptance of some generic patterns and formulas lead inevitably to parodies of the film. In *Young Frankenstein,* Mel Brooks not only spoofed the horror genre but also used the original 1931 *Frankenstein* as a model for his tongue-in-cheek sequel.

for this purpose are *spectacle,* which draws from visual design and sometimes from larger-than-life phenomena for its dramatic impact; *sleuthing,* which centers on plot intricacies and uses tension and suspense in the process of problem solving and the chase for its effect; *social exploration,* which depends on the "redemption of physical reality" and the articulation of social issues; and finally, *psychological introspection,* which involves itself with character delineation, motivation, and a tour of the mental landscape.

Spectacle and Fantasy

Vachel Lindsay, in describing film's potential for "splendor," provides a fair assessment of the medium's range: "It can give every ripple of the lily-pond. It can show us cathedrals within and without. It can take in the panorama of cyclopaean cloud, bending forest, storm-hung mountain. In like manner it can put on the screen great impersonal mobs of men. It can give us tremendous armies, moving as oceans move."[9] Filmmakers recognized the potential of the screen for such splendor and spectacle from the very beginning and quickly exploited them; these qualities in turn became central to a number of genre types. They included the historical spectacle and adventure films traceable to such historical recreations as Edison's reenactment of *The Execution of Mary Queen of Scots.* They also include tales of the supernatural and extraterrestrial, which have evolved into the fantasy, horror, and science-fiction films of today. They extend also to the musical, dance, and theater spectacle films that came into their own as a distinct and popular genre with the arrival of sound. These genres, which generally followed the formalist tradition, depended on qualities of sensual appeal and the visual representation of imagined worlds, or at least the real world freely interpreted. Kracauer, in spite of his emphasis of the medium's function in the "redemption of physical reality," has recognized the concept that "film is better equipped than other representational media to render visible things that have been imagined."[10]

The historical spectacle follows the tradition of epic narrative, is well suited to film's ability to deal with panoramic storytelling, and provides a range of diverse settings and actions. It is a form of screen narrative pioneered by Griffith in works like *Birth of a Nation, Intolerance, Orphans of the Storm* (1921) and *America*. Eisenstein's Soviet revolutionary epics extended it, along with Cecil B. DeMille's Hollywood biblical epics, and the sprawling westerns, particularly those of John Ford, produced on both Hollywood sound stages and such real-life vistas as Monument Valley. As epic narrative has traditionally drawn heavily from national legend and folklore, western expansion and the taming of the frontier provided a natural basis for a considerable proportion of the sweeping spectacles of the screen in this country, particularly during the medium's formative years.

In these early forms, film's ability to create settings and phenomena larger, more exotic, or otherwise beyond the normal range of real-life experience was central. This holds true for spectacles of more recent vintage: *Gone With the Wind,* the remakes of *Ben-Hur* (1959) and *The Ten Commandments* (1956), *Lawrence of Arabia* and *Dr. Zhivago* by David Lean, and even the nonepic spectacle of disaster such as *Earthquake* and *The Towering Inferno*. Set design and dressing and the magic of special-effects cinematography are of course critical factors, but the complete range of cinematic effects—aural as well as visual—helps meet the requirements of expansive content and epic flow. Within specific genres, particular cinematic means to splendor gain prominence. The drama of the swashbuckler sea adventure depends on the sound of waves, gulls, and creaking rigging, the sight of flapping sail and dipping horizon, and a general sense of motion to capture some of the mysteries of the deep and the capricious nature of the elements. The war film depends largely on pyrotechnics for its effects; when the battle is in the air, however, the sense of movement is so completely absorbing that it becomes a quintessential adventure in motion, surpassing even the ride aboard a speeding train or galloping steed. The "crowd splendor" of which Vachel Lindsay spoke involves the deployment of large numbers of actors, effectively illustrated in Griffith's Babylon, Eisenstein's Odessa, and DeMille's Roman amphitheater. In all cases, the exhilaration of the extraordinary in sensory experience makes these factors cinematic.

Beyond the range of the extraordinary or larger than life is the supernatural and extraterrestrial, which are also within filmmakers' creative capabilities. As we have seen, the interest in film as the art of the conjurer began with Méliès and the chase and trick films of other Frenchmen, as well as some early experiments by American pioneers. It reached feature-film proportions and aesthetic recognition with Wiene's *Caligari*, Murnau's *Nosferatu* (the original screen *Dracula*) and Carl Dreyer's *Vampyr*. It developed as popular entertainment in the sound era when Hollywood filmmakers, some of whom were German immigrants who had worked in the Expressionistic movement, made the horror film a distinct genre in the thirties and gave the science-fiction film genre status by the forties.

The enduring quality of screen fantasy is tied to escape and the invitation to the free reign of imagination and the exploration of other-worldly phenomena. Within the horror film, it reveals the medium's ability to deal effectively in phantasmagoria and create stories of supernatural and hallucinatory creatures, places, and events. Horror came to film from a time-honored place in drama and literature. It finds accommodation in movies in two significant ways. First of all, the nature of most film viewing—the darkened theater, size of images, and subtle effects of our judgment of time and space—makes conjuring up demons or simply creating anxiety-producing settings a relatively easy task. Along with such preconditions, the horror film also gains its effect by giving physical presence to the fantasy and nightmare world.

Set designer, cinematographer, makeup artist, lighting designer, scriptwriter, director, and actor all help create appropriately sinister settings as well as the demons that inhabit them. Monster films have provided a substantial part of screen horror thanks to the photogenic quality of the title characters from *Nosferatu* and *King Kong* to *The Creature from the Black Lagoon* (1954), *The Thing* (1951 and 1982), and *The Abominable Snowman* (1957), abetted by tricks of camera and editing. During the late 1970s and early 1980s, makeup artists took filmic horror one step further by combining their traditional art with developments in technology to create "special-effects makeup" through which actors appear to metamorphose into other beings directly on camera. The most prominent examples are *Altered States* (1980), in which a psychologist (William Hurt) gradually changes into a lower humanoid creature, and *An American Werewolf in London* (1981) and *The Howling* (1981), two updates of the durable werewolf saga. In all three films, we actually see what appear to be the actors' muscles undergoing preternatural spasms as their faces and bodies become physically distorted during the transformation process—all accomplished by their "makeup in motion" as the cameras rolled.

Even inanimate objects and structures may take on monstrous proportions through set design, shot composition, and the added effects of wind, rain, and the organ fugue or other appropriate musical background. Vachel Lindsay observed that "great structures may become villains"; indeed, the screen's collection of "killer architectures" ranges from such historic settings as the Paris Opera House in *Phantom of the Opera* and Notre Dame cathedral in the several screen versions of *The Hunchback of Notre Dame* to the Gothic structures of *Dracula* (1931) and *Psycho* (1960) to the plush, billowy Victorian settings of Great Britain's Hammer Studio horror films of the 1960s and early 1970s. In the case of *The Shining* (1980) and *The Amityville Horror* (1979), buildings have distinct personalities and are as much the "stars" of their respective films as the actors.

The motion picture may also produce a sense of foreboding if not actual terror long before our conscious recognition of lurking dangers. Indeed, the horror of unseen monsters is the effect that draws most fully from the resources of film. The truly horrific film is tied to our anticipation of unseen terrors, such as the venerable creaking door and coffin lid of early forms, and the tip of a shark fin breaking the surface of the water in both the original version of *Jaws* and its sequels. These techniques may create anxiety-laden involvement equalling or surpassing that experienced during the actual appearance of monsters or other horrifying detail—a point supported by considerable empirical evidence.[11] Dreyer's *Vampyr*, William Friedkin's *The Exorcist*, and the variety of occult films currently popular speak to the terror of unseen demons and the capabilities of film to bring these to viewer consciousness.

Although lacking the broader appeal of the horror film, the science-fiction film has the added appeal of gadgetry and the visual manifestations of advanced technology. In writing on the genre, Susan Sontag noted, "One job that fantasy can do is to lift us out of the unbearably humdrum and distract us from terrors, real or anticipated—by an escape into exotic, dangerous situations which have last-minute happy endings."[12] The "sensuous elaboration" of which Sontag also speaks is the strength of filmed science fiction. And, like the western, it also has the appeal of the frontier. Here the frontiers are the microcosm of the human body through which miniaturized people travel in *Fantastic Voyage* as well as the macrocosm of outer space in *Star Wars*.

The musical spectacle or fantasy film also depends on "sensuous elaboration" for its appeal, but here sound—music in particular—becomes a central element. The film musical joined the western as a staple of the American film with the arrival of sound. It has evolved through a variety of forms with varying degrees of cinematic quality and with generally little pretense of reflecting serious storytelling. Musicals tend to divide into screen originals and adaptations from the variety and musical stage, with the former generally regarded as the more successful and cinematically valid. Films like *Top Hat* (1935) and *Singin' in the Rain*

Figure 6-5 *Flower Drum Song* (1961—American). The Broadway stage has traditionally been a primary source of material for musical comedy in film. Juanita Hall and Jack Soo are seen here in a dance routine from *Flower Drum Song*, the last of the many Rodgers and Hammerstein collaborations to make it to the screen.

(1952) have become classics as well as popular favorites because of their effective integration of song, dance, scenic design, and the talents of key performers.

The screen musical works in several ways. It may serve as a showcase in which song or song-and-dance routines are developed into production numbers of modest or sweeping scale. In many originals and adaptations from theater, the individual numbers are the real substance of the film. Such elaborate musical-production numbers as "I Only Have Eyes for You," from *Dames* (1934), "New York, New York," from *On the Town* (1949), and the incredibly acrobatic dance routines of the "barn-raising" scene from *Seven Brides for Seven Brothers* (1954) are undoubtedly the most memorable moments of these films (see Fig. 6–6).

As part of a system built on the promotion of stars, the musical film may also function as a vehicle for a star singer or dancer. Fred Astaire, Gene Kelly, James Cagney, Judy Garland, the Beatles, and Barbra Streisand have found screenplays of varying quality as settings for their talents. On occasion they have used their own talents to dramatize those of other performers in musical biographies. James Cagney won an Oscar for his performance as show-biz wiz George M. Cohan in *Yankee Doodle Dandy* (1942), as did Barbra Streisand in 1968 for her portrait of singer-comedienne Fanny Brice in *Funny Girl*.

The musical may also demonstrate an interplay of musical form and cinematic devices in which the filmmakers orchestrate composition, editing, scenic design, props, and lighting to reinforce the mood, tempo, and "meaning" of the musical score. Busby Berkeley was a pioneer in this area; his many breathtaking musical numbers often featured dozens of scantily clad chorines arranging themselves into intricate geometric patterns against a nonrealistic background while his camera filmed them from unusual and frequently erotic angles. In *42nd Street* (1933), for example, Berkeley had the women stand in a circle front-to-back while he passed the camera through their parted legs. In addition, Berkeley often sup-

Figure 6-6 *Seven Brides for Seven Brothers* (1954— American). The original screenplay for *Seven Brides for Seven Brothers* combined song and dance of the musical extravaganza with the spectacle and grandeur of the frontier adventure. The resulting film remains a challenge to the confines of the stage and the small TV screen, despite the recent TV series based on the same vehicle.

plied his female performers with bizarre props ranging from interlocking grand pianos and violins lined with neon lighting to huge plastic bananas. The cumulative effect of carefully choreographed performances, cinematic devices, props, settings, and music was often one of surrealism. In addition to Berkeley's films, many others that have served as settings for star and musical routine owe their success to carefully employed cinematic techniques to enhance the quality of music and dance on the screen.

Walt Disney's feature-length animated work *Fantasia* (1940) is another example of a film employing a complex mixture of visual and musical elements while exhibiting a minimal concern for plot. Though often brilliant in its attempts to visualize various musical forms, *Fantasia* appalled many aficionados of fine music, particularly when it linked the music with the antics of Mickey Mouse and other typically Disneyesque creatures. Fans of Ponchielli's graceful "Dance of the Hours" were considerably less than pleased to see cartoon images of demure hippopotamuses dressed in ridiculously short tutus dancing to it.

The term *realistic musicals* may seem a contradiction, but recently we have witnessed the development of musical films in which the singing and dancing are natural parts of the stories, and the stories themselves are as important as any found in other genres. *Saturday Night Fever* (1977) features the dynamic dancing of disco king Tony Manero (John Travolta), whose proficiency on the dance floor contrasts sharply with his humdrum job as a paint salesman in Brooklyn. In *Cabaret* (1972), director and choreographer Bob Fosse told the story of Sally Bowles (Liza Minnelli), an American performing in a Berlin nightclub during the early 1930s. Fosse frequently used the cabaret performances of Bowles and others as counterpoints to the grim realities outside the club as Hitler's Nazi party rose in power. At one point in the film, Fosse cut back and forth between the nightclub's emcee (Joel Grey) playfully spanking female performers in a musical number and several Nazi bullyboys outside the cabaret beating up the nightclub's owner who had thrown them out. With its carefully matched action and contrapuntal sound (we continue to hear the music as the Nazis brutalize the owner), this masterful sequence helps illustrate how filmmakers can use a musical film, which might normally be considered a harmless bit of fluff, to present a strong social statement.

The musical genre, like the horror and fantasy types, has characteristics well suited to filmic representation, primarily those reflecting a strong sensory appeal. Except for more recent (and realistic) musicals, however, the narrative role of the genre is usually very basic and often minimal. What unity the genre exhibits comes from the performances and from its visual and aural design, not the story. Kracauer has said of the genre that "it pretends to unity and threatens to fall into pieces,"[13] but allows it legitimacy as cinematic entertainment. With its potential for combining visual spectacle, color, motion and melody, the musical has found broad appeal and moderate critical acceptance even when storytelling is the least of its concerns.

One final form that draws much of its appeal from direct sensory stimulation is animation. Of all the formalistic approaches in filmmaking it provides the greatest freedom in creating imagined settings, characters, and actions because it is the least beholden to the physical reality before the camera lens; it is a completely synthetic form. Its major stylistic elements are those of drawing and painting (or in the case of 3-D animation, shaping flexible forms) in in-camera editing.

Figure 6-7 *Fritz the Cat* (1972—American). One of the relatively few animators to produce cartoons intended for adult audiences is Ralph Bakshi. In this scene from Bakshi's X-rated *Fritz the Cat,* the celebrated title character finds himself beset by silhouetted police and street people.

It is actually closer to the older graphic and plastic arts than live-action cinematography.

What distinguishes animation most from other formalistic types is in the creating of character. Through the wizardry of scenic design and special effects, photographed forms can create an imagined setting complete in every detail. There are limits, though, to what even the most talented of actors can accomplish. Animators, on the other hand, bring characters of their imagination to the screen. These are often animals with human attributes, the most endearing and long-lived of which have been those with distinct personalities. In a sense, the star system prevails even here, as many Disney favorites as well as those of the UPA and Hanna-Barbera studios have demonstrated. The omnipotence and indestructibility that we share with cartoon characters is another satisfying part of the experience. Innumerable cartoon characters have been flattened by infernal machines, walked on air (until they look down), and been propelled by countless explosions and then returned in pristine shape to fight new battles. Wile E. Coyote is a creature of many lives who returns again and again to become a victim of the diabolical plots he himself hatches in order to eliminate his foe, the Roadrunner.

Although the animated film (except for *Fantasia*) has been mostly limited to the comic cartoon in America, it has found broader application in more serious, often esoteric, functions in other production centers. The National Film Board of Canada and the Zagreb Studios in Yugoslavia are important sources today of more diversified and experimental forms of animation. The limitless potential for design makes animation a favorite medium for experimentalists to work in, but the considerable costs of production limit its use in longer films. This naturally means limitations in the use of animation in screen storytelling. But where budget and time permit, screen animation provides an approach to filmic representation—particularly where more fanciful and imaginative renderings are desired—that knows no bounds.

Puzzle Solving and the Chase

Beyond its basic sensory appeal, a special part of film's staying power is its ability to attract and hold attention by providing a pattern of progression for viewers to anticipate, follow, and to fill out on their own. This appeal of direct involvement in narrative progression includes the *chase* and *problem solving*. Not only does everyone like a good story, most everyone also likes to be involved in formulating the links of narrative progression. The affinity of film for the physical chase, for the progression dependent on the relationship of pursuer to pursued, should require little elaboration. The chase was on in single-reel comedies and melodramas before directors had established the narrative film as a viable and central form of film communication and entertainment. They have since extended the chase to embrace many forms of pursuit. Part of the appeal of a good story in any medium is the exercise it provides in solving a problem or puzzle, in the discovery of causal links in narrative, or to use Kracauer's coinage, in "sleuthing."[14]

Filmmakers' ability to limit or extend our range of vision and to shift perspective and uncover "things normally unseen" makes the medium an effective means of providing those enticing exercises in puzzle solving, exploits in the science of deduction, and other forms of "sleuthing" that extend the filmic chase beyond the limits of physical pursuit. The chase is on when Robert Donat steps aboard the *Flying Scotsman* in *The 39 Steps* in pursuit of a secret spy organization and the person responsible for the murder for which he is suspected; but the chase is also on when Richard Harris boards the *Britannic* in *Juggernaut* (1974) to mastermind the disarming of explosives timed to blow up the liner within hours of its sailing. The exercise extends to the enigmas that face screen protagonists in less adventuresome pursuits than those just cited. The reporter who goes in search of the mystery of "Rosebud" in *Citizen Kane*, young Pip's conjecture and discovery concerning his benefactor in *Great Expectations*, even the pursuit of a bicycle in *Bicycle Thieves*, are forms of chase that involve the viewer in the linking of action to motivation and provide the satisfaction of working out cause/effect relationships if not final solutions to problems and the ultimate resolutions to stories.

Although problem solving and mental chase extend over several genres of film, the suspense film or crime and mystery thriller best illustrates the characteristics of the medium that accommodate the form. When the physical chase is combined with the intellectual exercise in sorting out evidence, it becomes an especially durable hybrid of what Kracauer means by "sleuthing" and shows screen storytelling at its most intricate and absorbing.

Moviemakers can effectively provide the framework and ingredients necessary to the drama of detection. The general strategy involves revealing just the right amount of information at the strategic time to involve the viewer more directly in the process of detection or problem solving. At the same time, an appropriate atmosphere renders the whole procedure more immediate, more intense, or, to use the much overworked term, more suspenseful. The specific plotting elements include the creation of some enigma or sense of the unknown, creating a sense of confinement or isolation for the protagonist, providing clues to problem solving, and laying down false leads and ironic conclusions.

Artists working in any medium have often demonstrated that a work can be more absorbing if they initially withhold key information. Providing basic information for initial involvement and then leaving a viewer, reader, or listener with some enigma to work out is an especially important element of all narrative forms. Film is particularly good at revealing and withholding detail, and in the mystery or suspense film the process can be most creatively applied. By the control of camera placement and movement, filmmakers can direct audience attention and reveal detail when it suits their purpose, but through the same controls can also withhold information and leave the audience to work out causal links, obscured details, and other unknowns on its own. Through care in selection and arrangement of shots, moviemakers can also employ the editing process to the same ends. In Fritz Lang's *M*, the director revealed the abduction of a little girl through a series of close-ups of a deserted loft, an empty courtyard and stairwell, a man's shadow falling across a "wanted" poster, and a balloon caught in telephone wires. In the early moments of the scene, Lang balanced the explication of the action through details by suggesting the terror of the unknown. Later in the film, when we know the identity of the murderer, our involvement in detection and puzzle solving continues, replete with uncertainties concerning the killer's actions as he becomes the target of a chase, and also with the methods of detection carried out by both police and the underworld.

In much detective fiction, both in literature and on the screen, the enigma centers on the identity of the criminal, and the orderly cataloguing of clues leads to his or her discovery by both protagonist and reader/viewer. Agatha Christie is a particular favorite among writers of the form. Hitchcock, on the other hand, has largely ignored the whodunit approach. While perhaps sacrificing some of the intrigue of the unknown culprit, he has made up for it by creating in us the terror of *knowing* that the life of the unsuspecting protagonist is in jeopardy each time the villain appears on the scene.

In the case of both approaches, our direct participation in the intrigue comes about through a sense of the unknown—either the identity of the criminal or the fate of the protagonist. Filmmakers create this sense of the unknown not only through the revelation and withholding of material clues, however; the appropriate *mise-en-scène* is also an important factor. Literature and the screen abound in old dark houses, desolate moors, and shadowy, rain-slicked streets that provide the appropriately sinister setting for the terrors that can't be seen but are surely lurking. Here again, in his perverse and inimitable way, Hitchcock turns the table on the traditional use of the device and allows the most diabolical of crimes to occur in sunny, open settings, such as a cornfield in *North by Northwest* and the Covent Garden market in *Frenzy*. Terror by the babbling brook has in fact become a critical part of the Hitchcock signature and has proven itself an effective means of manipulating audiences' expectations.

Our involvement in dramatic situations is finally dependent on identification with people rather than on setting. The fate of the protagonist with whom we identify or at least empathize makes participation in "sleuthing" more absorbing and immediate. Moviemakers intensify our identification and involvement through a sense of confinement, isolation, or both at some point in most thrillers. Edgar Allan Poe obviously recognized the potential for terrorizing readers by placing them with the protagonist in some confining and lonely spot. "The Pit and the Pendulum," "The Cask of Amontillado," and particularly "Premature Burial" combine isolation and confinement to make problem solving a fearful and deadly business. The isolation of darkness, fog, myopic vision, and the confinement of prison cells, railway carriages, and blocked mine shafts have enhanced our terror in countless stories.

These restrictions are not limited to physical design of the setting; they are often the result of plotting, particularly where the protagonist is a suspect of the crime he or she is trying to solve. The so-called *wrong-man* theme is a favorite of mystery writers and finds a ready place in screen narrative because of the medium's strong affinity for physical movement and the chase. O.B. Hardison, writing on the Hitchcock thriller, notes: "Two defining characteristics of the thriller, then, are its setting, which is alien, and its hero, who is typically a victim rather than an agent."[15] Actually, the protagonist is both in nearly half of Hitchcock's films—the proportion of his works that feature the wrong-man theme. In fact, many Hitchcock protagonists are hampered in their efforts to solve a crime because they themselves are suspected of it. *The 39 Steps, The Wrong Man, North by Northwest, Spellbound, To Catch a Thief* and *Frenzy* are notable examples.

A final attraction of the wrong-man theme is that it provides appropriate tests of the invincibility of the protagonists. To keep themselves (and the viewer) free to continue learning new information before ultimately apprehending the villains, the heroes must overcome prodigious obstacles placed in their paths. Such obstacles initially extend and reinforce our anxiety but have the added value of reinforcing the ethos or reputation of the protagonists as well.

After establishing an appropriately menacing and enigmatic situation, directors working on films devoted to "sleuthing" must next provide clues to problem solving that will relieve the confinement of the protagonists, reveal the identity of the villains, and offer conclusive evidence of their guilt. We discover the clues in the visual and aural detail of setting, dialogue, events, even in musical notifs (Lang's *M* and Hitchcock's *The Lady Vanishes* as well as *The 39 Steps*), and the hidden recesses of the mind (*Marnie, Spellbound, Suddenly Last Summer*). The search for clues is at the heart of "sleuthing" and filmmakers may bring any number of cinematic devices into play to facilitate detection. The control of camera and particularly the use of the close-up direct our attention and bring necessary detail into focus. John Fell suggests that "in a detective story the close-ups become the 'clues.' "[16]

Although not central to detection and problem solving, another attraction that often becomes a bonus of clue hunting is the appeal to voyeuristic needs. In addition to our identification with the qualities of omnipotence and indestructibility in the protagonists, we will also find satisfaction in sharing their view of things; of being able to observe details otherwise denied us by physical barriers, social taboos, or both. Sexual excesses and deviation and a range of indulgences related to violence and morbid subjects are easily revealed by the "innocent eye" of the camera, and all in the name of good police work (see Fig. 2–1).

Our final satisfying experience with a good thriller is being party to, and even temporarily victim of, some twist of plot, false lead, or ironic situation. We delight in being led down the garden path by a false lead or red herring so long as we are allowed to recover and are given genuine leads relatively quickly. We find even greater satisfaction in the discovery of the irony of a situation to which our pursuit of evidence has led us. *The 39 Steps* is a catalogue of ironic situations and verbal exchanges. "Can I come home with you?" asks Miss Smith of Richard

Hannay outside a London music hall. "Well, it's your funeral," he responds. After the murder of Miss Smith in Hannay's apartment, Hannay tries to enlist the aid of a milkman to help him elude the murderers who are still outside. Hannay tells him what has happened, but the disbelieving milkman comes to Hannay's aid only after the hero invents a story of a clandestine meeting with a married woman. In the same film, the safety of a police station becomes a trap and the innocent fun of a memory artist becomes a deadly game of espionage. Dramatic irony, of course, is not the exclusive province of the film of crime and detection, but where "sleuthing" is in progress, some ironic situation is almost sure to develop.

"Sleuthing" itself extends into many forms of narrative film; indeed, the ingredients just outlined play a significant part in the plotting of several film genres. It doesn't matter whether it's a gangster film, suspense thriller, private eye, or detective thriller (the more obvious genres in which "sleuthing" is involved); or the western, adventure or science-fiction forms. As long as progression centers on problem solving, these elements that enhance the chase may be applied. George Fenin and William Everson, in describing the western film, observed, "The Western theme, based on the triplex system of the hero, the adventure, and the law, has at all times been fascinating to movie audiences."[17] As adventure, the western provides much of the same intrigue and involvement with the isolation and confinement of the hero as other forms provide, with the added attraction of the chase, usually on horseback; it becomes as cinematic a form as can be found anywhere. With its conflicts centering on bank robbery, cattle rustling, Indian threats, and challenges to the fastest gun in the West, the genre usually follows patterns similar to other forms employing the chase or hunt. An important difference, perhaps, is that its clean lines in narrative progression and character motivation tend to render conflict more direct, and the enigmas of the crime thriller may be less in evidence. Although the western heroes may be complex and driven by conflicting motivations, the society in which they function and the values they represent are relatively direct and simple. The world of their city cousins—the private detectives—is generally a more complex one and the pursuit of lawlessness is often complicated by hidden crosscurrents in motivation. In style, the chase is not substantially different whether East or West. In substance, motivational factors and the kind of moral ambivalence for which Hitchcock's characters are known often set the two forms apart.

Film as Social Document

Social awareness and the celebration of causes are not a requirement for film to be a viable and popular means of storytelling. A work need not even be fraught with social, psychological, or political significance to be granted legitimacy as an aesthetic form. The creation of popular films with very little "on their minds" except to delight audiences with aural-visual patterns and narrative designs has been, and should be, considered a legitimate function of the medium. When done with care and discrimination, it can also be an artistic one.

Yet filmmakers can give their works added dimension by exploring real-life experiences and shedding light on conflicts that are a part of our everyday world. They can bring their stories out of the shadows of history and fantasy and give them a substance and sometimes a durability that separates the major and timeless works of a genre from the numerous exercises in storytelling or the show-cases in design that make up the larger proportion of feature films.

In describing the nature of the Italian neorealist cinema, Cesare Zavattini made the distinction between the films that take a direct look at things as they are and those that are simply "superimposing dead formula over living social facts."[18] The movement of which Zavattini spoke illustrates a form of social documentation close to one end of the spectrum. It in fact comes as close as possible to the documentation of actual events while remaining within the fictional form. Still, the distinction Zavattini made between looking at real events and reworking a formula is a useful one when considering the qualities and directions of film storytelling beyond the narrative for its own sake.

Before examining the ways filmmakers use their medium to explore social realities directly and consciously, we need to consider narrative film itself as a social phenomenon. The ways in which the medium indirectly reflects the society that produced it, not to mention the effects of film treatment and subject on audiences, raise extremely complex issues beyond the scope of this study. Identifying the major factors that determine the extent to which film storytelling will also tell something about the temperaments and times in which it was made should help to make film's mission as social observer (and advocate) more meaningful. These factors include the economic and aesthetic influences exerted on filmmakers as well as the social and political climate in which films are produced. To say it simply, the demands of an industry, the requirements of the medium, and the needs of the viewer are all going to affect filmmakers' perspective on social issues. A producer, considering a screenplay in which the subject of abortion or homosexuality is featured, will be very much concerned with public acceptance of a film on such a controversial issue and with ultimate effects at the box office. Directors concerned with finding the most effective way to dramatize a conflict on the subject will be guided by their understanding of the capabilities of the medium and ways of bringing new insight to the topic. Producer, director, and spectator will all be influenced by the sociopolitical climate of the times. Such influences might include the rating a film might receive from the industry's own rating administration (or censorship board in the case of many foreign film industries). The filmmaker's judgment on how to treat potentially offensive subjects and the moviegoer's ability to relate to and accept that perspective and treatment are additional considerations. In language, action, and thought, films such as *Pretty Baby* or *Saturday Night Fever*, which seem acceptable today, would have been problematic from the viewpoint of both producer and viewer just a few years ago. Changes in perspective, styles, and purposes of screen narrative, and also the climate in which filmmakers create their works, will affect the ways films function as social documents.[19]

Historically, narrative film has been socially involved in a number of ways. As screen storytelling proceeded from single to multireel forms, filmmakers needed to flesh out their stories with greater detail and to put the action in some larger context. The social milieus they created as backdrops for their films gave greater depth and realism to the action and also often helped explain character motivation expeditiously. For instance, D.W. Griffith set the actions of a ruthless businessman in *A Corner in Wheat* (1909) against the backdrop of the free-enterprise system and the fever of the commodity exchange. Filmmakers may establish the social context of a film by placing an original screenplay within a particular time and place, or, as in the case *The Grapes of Wrath*, by building on the social context of a work adapted from another medium (see Fig. 6–8). Even when they are not directly exploring a social condition, moviemakers must often acknowledge it as an obvious and expected part of the drama. A screen narrative will frequently touch base with some social condition and eventually allow some aspect of it to become a plot device by triggering one or more actions outside the immediate personal story. For example, Haskell Wexler used film footage of the 1968 Chicago riots outside the Democratic national convention in his *Medium Cool* (1969) to give added dimension to the film's personal drama. When the screenplay goes beyond the individual and personal drama to deal with conflicts involving groups of people and institutions, the social function of the narrative film becomes greatest.

Filmmakers have been inserting social commentary into their works ever since the earliest days of screen storytelling, and they continue to examine the conditions of the world around them today. We have broken down their attention to social issues into three basic categories—*incidental, gratuitous,* and *exploratory*—that are discussed below.

Incidental social commentary has been a part of those dramas that only require a social backdrop against which the action can be placed. Here a casual reference to people, places, and issues provides us with an orientation in time and space as well as a kind of social dressing and "realistic" dimension for the action. Countless screen dramas have given some passing reference to issues large and small—from corrupt politicians to world wars—without allowing them to become more than reference points or parts of the decor.

We use the term *gratuitous* to describe the type of social commentary that goes beyond set dressing and becomes a means of working out the narrative de-

Figure 6-8 *The Grapes of Wrath* (1940—American). The plight of Oklahoma sharecroppers who face the pain of relocation and exploitation as migrant workers is central to the John Ford film, *The Grapes of Wrath,* and the John Steinbeck novel on which it is based. Ford's intimate and affectionate study of the Joad family has made it a classic among screen social dramas.

velopment and of explaining character motivation without the need for close examination. Here a social condition may play a significant role in determining the direction of the story and the fate of principal characters, but the issue itself and its causes will not come under close examination. Filmmakers have staged countless Indian raids in Western films without the least interest in exploring the true relationship between the races and the motivation behind the raids. In the same genre, lynchings have provided the required dramatic involvement without becoming studies in lynch-mob psychology and how otherwise honest and decent people can be driven into a frenzy of hate and blood-lust by a rabble-rouser or two.

In *The Ox-Bow Incident,* William Wellman went a step beyond using a lynching as set decoration and plot machination to examine the phenomenon of mass persuasion and the psychology of a group of townspeople bent on their own brand of justice for three presumed criminals. Although the film's concern is more with the *drama* of the event and its effects on those involved, rather than with uncovering deep-seated motivations, it does explore, at least nominally, the dynamics of vigilante justice in an untamed land. *Exploratory* social commentary is not really typified by this film, but it begins here and extends to the more intensive and uncompromising studies in social phenomena that have graced the screen from Porter's look at the plight of a former prisoner in *The Ex-Convict* to several of the screen dramatizations in third–world nations of political oppression and revolution today.

Westerns, gangster films, revolutionary epics, and satiric comedies and farce have all been among the genres known to take more than a casual look at social themes. *Social drama* and *social comedy* are not really generic labels but rather describe a degree of awareness that a film within a particular genre has of the world around it.

Aside from its historical ties, the western, which Fenin and Everson call "the purest and most original genre of the American cinema,"[20] frequently pro-

Figure 6-9 *Black Legion* (1936—American). The Hollywood studios rarely gave serious attention to race relations in their films until after World War II. A notable exception was Warner Brothers' *Black Legion,* in which a factory worker (Humphrey Bogart) and others encounter a secret Klan-like organization. The film's screenplay was based on an actual incident in Detroit.

vides a clear and simple study of the forces at work within an evolving society. It provides a microcosm of social stresses and how they are met. Issues and the human drives that create them are usually clean-lined and not complicated by the intricacies of urban, industrial civilization. The western is concerned with taming the wilderness associated with both physical adversity and the social order.

The western form varies in style and purpose from the austere, naturalistic, and hard-hitting dramatizations of Thomas Ince to the romantic, fanciful, and musical reveries of Roy Rogers. In his study of the form, Robert Warshow points out that the romanticism of such westerns has been replaced by a realism that exposes the drabness of setting and the pressures of obligation and also shows horses that "grow tired and stumble more often than they did."[21] Such realistic detail has long been associated with film's role in social exploration; Griffith's *Musketeers of Pig Alley* (1912), Mervyn LeRoy's *I am a Fugitive from a Chain Gang* and Martin Scorsese's *Mean Streets* (1973) all exude a kind of authenticity resulting from their attention to realistic detail and journalistic style.

Yet realism goes beyond the surface reality of visual detail and a documentary style reportage. In fact, complexities of narrative and seriousness of tone may have little to do with the significance of theme in a film. Important social documents have come in the form of comic divertissements, including many of Chaplin's later works, such as *Modern Times, The Great Dictator, Monsieur Verdoux,* and *A King in New York* (1957). Social awareness embraces both the mordant wit of these films and such anti-war satires as Kubrick's *Dr. Strangelove* and Richard Lester's *How I Won the War* (1967), and the nihilistic farce of the Marx Brothers' *Duck Soup.*

In such films the entertainment function can hardly be separated from its social role, and the humor is so dependent on a social awareness that the works extend beyond the gratuitous form and become important social documents. Although they are not exploratory in the true sense of the word, they have the weight of social documents because they provide a concentration of individual or group perspective and attitudes on some of the issues of our times. Even when their heart is in storytelling and the amusement of audiences, the creators of such films have their minds on real world issues, values, and idiosyncrasies. By design or accident their films may say a good deal about not only their own views but also their perceptions of their viewers' attitudes.

We should note that the dramatization of social events and conditions is very different from the recording of their real-world counterparts, documentary-style. Even after the most careful planning, documentarists often encounter unexpected situations as they explore some aspect of the world around them. While this is one of the documentary film's most exciting qualities, it does not afford the control that staging provides. Staging an event allows filmmakers to anticipate the way the action will unfold and offers virtually complete control over camera placement, lighting, lenses, sound, and the action itself (see also Chapter 10).

While the aspect of staging often sets apart social-minded narrative and documentary filmmakers, an important consideration for both groups is the plasticity and control afforded through editing. With the freedom to begin and end an action where they choose and the ability to arrange the order of actions, filmmakers can select and integrate those details that best represent the action and their attitudes toward it. When Porter dramatized the plight of the title character in *The Ex-Convict,* he made his point about society's failure to deal with this person's readjustment to life on the outside by linking shots of the former prisoner and his struggling family with those of the rich industrialist who refuses to give him a job. In this way, montage can provide the ordering of visual and aural detail that enhances the dramatic quality and narrative continuity while simultaneously drawing attention to the ideas behind the action.

Several film theorists, most notably Béla Balázs and Jean Mitry, have argued that film is not well suited to representing abstract ideas and social thought; film is encumbered by the requirement to show some visual manifestation of the subject with which it is dealing, preferably something in motion.[22] Yet when ideas need pinning down, particularly when some concrete visual reference or documentation is desired, film's flexibility in rendering visual detail and making it a part of some larger drama make the narrative film with a social conscience a viable and useful form.

Psychodrama and the Mental Landscape

Since all drama concerns itself with conflict, we may assume that conflict in its broadest sense pertains to social issues generally and their application to groups of people, institutions, and the ways the latter serve (or fail to serve) the former. On a more intimate level, human conflict involves the struggle among individuals as well as the personal drama and internal conflict within the lone person.

Widest in scope are those social dramas of epic proportion, or at least general enough in treatment that no one person stands at the center of the conflict. Using only war films for illustration, we find this level represented by such early efforts as Griffith's *Birth of a Nation* and *America* and Eisenstein's *Battleship Potemkin* and *Ten Days That Shook the World*. Somewhat narrower in scope are Kubrick's *Paths of Glory* and even his *Dr. Strangelove*, which look at the institutions that plan and carry out the business of waging war. Other institutions that have come under scrutiny in social dramas are religion, big business, big government, the legal, journalistic, and medical professions—even the oldest profession, prostitution. The ability of the medium to provide a dramatic rendering of the larger sweep of events as well as more precise and intimate detail makes it a useful means of conveying ideas about human conflict in both the broader societal and more limited institutional range.

A more intimate level of social drama centers on conflicts among and within individuals—topics over which filmmakers face some of their greatest challenges. Intimate dramas centering on mental struggles would seem ill-suited to the medium since film thrives on visual detail and motion. Yet the history of film has demonstrated that some directors have had considerable success in revealing hidden conflicts that would not normally appear to lend themselves to filmic representation. A famous example is also one of the last great films of the silent era: Carl Dreyer's *The Passion of Joan of Arc*. In this work, Dreyer dramatized the conflict of wills and the personal anguish of one of Christendom's most famous martyrs by having his cinematographer, Rudolph Maté, frequently photograph Joan (Marie Falconetti) in tight close-up as she underwent her famous inquisition. Her face and all the emotions and conflicts it revealed had a powerful effect on audiences of the time, as they still do on audiences today (see Fig. 2–3).

Other silent-era European films that charted the mental landscape include

Robert Wiene's *The Cabinet of Dr. Caligari,* F. W. Murnau's *The Last Laugh,* and Erno Metzner's *Überfall* (1929). This latter film tells the story of a man down on his luck who finds a coin, takes it to a gambling hall, and parlays it into a considerable amount of money. His good fortune is short-lived, however, after thieves quickly beset him. The film contains a significant number of subjective shots, including several visually distorted ones representing his hallucinations after the assault (see Fig. 2–7).

In America, films as diverse as *A Bill of Divorcement* (1932), *Harvey* (1950), and *Three Faces of Eve* (1957), while not all that important as social dramas, demonstrated the capabilities of the medium in extending the personal drama to provide close scrutiny of the individual psyche. As for the stylistically diverse film genres of post-World War II Europe, they showed a decided tendency to get away from plot-for-plot's-sake. Many even attempted to escape the broader categories in social drama to provide close studies of conflicts between individuals and in themselves. Directors specializing in what critic Penelope Houston referred to as "emotional strip-tease"[23] have included Ingmar Bergman, François Truffaut, Alain Resnais, and Michelangelo Antonioni. These directors have all described their interest in exploring the mental landscape and bringing it to the screen. Resnais has said on the subject:

> For me film is an attempt, still very crude and primitive, to approach the complexity of thought and its mechanism. But I stress the fact that this is only a tiny step forward by comparison with what we should be able to do someday. . . . I find that as soon as we delve into the unconscious, an emotion may be born.[24]

Other directors from American, European, Asian, and third-world film industries have joined these explorers of the mental condition and found that making internal conflict a subject for film is not only possible but also dramatically valid. Again, the flexibility of the medium in terms of its perspective and the plasticity in construction puts such exploration within reach of filmmakers and their audiences.

Many moviemakers are able to create a tension by using camera perspective, editing, and other cinematic devices to provide a close, sometimes omniscient look at personal and even internal struggle. When they wish to suggest the subjective experience, filmmakers possess the wherewithal for revealing how characters in conscious, unconscious, or hallucinatory states experience objects or actions. Early on, Edwin Porter and Robert Wiene provided wildly distorted worlds as seen by a glutton and a madman in their respective films, *Dreams of a Rarebit Fiend* (1906) and *Caligari* (see Figs. 1–4 and 2–20); since those times, mental aberrations have been central to films as diverse as Resnais' *Providence,* Hitchcock's *Spellbound,* and Kubrick's *The Shining.* Dennis Hopper and Peter Fonda gave us a glimpse of what the world looks like to people under the influence of hallucinogenic drugs in *Easy Rider* by rapidly intercutting grainy shots of religious figures, naked women, cemeteries, and themselves, while their offscreen voices recite prayers. These and other narrative filmmakers concerned with presenting altered states of consciousness on celluloid are indebted to experimental filmmakers, many of whom have shown particular interest in creating visual representations of the subconscious world. Luis Buñuel and Salvador Dali plumbed their subconsciousnesses for imagery that eventually went into their famous surrealistic short subject *Un*

Chien Andalou (1929), which overflows with such dreamlike subjects as a hand crawling with ants and two people blending into a seashore. Modern experimentalist Jordan Belson, who has stressed his ability to put his meditative visions on film with a strong degree of accuracy, has produced a number of films with nonrepresentational images that evoke the meditative condition. Indeed, experimental film critic P. Adams Sitney has suggested that most experimental filmmakers have devoted their artistic careers to reproducing the workings of the human mind.[25] (See also Chapter 11.)

Not all "mental landscape" filmmakers are concerned with creating unusual mental states or aberrations primarily through cinematic technique; many have explored mental stress and seemingly uncinematic psychological conflicts that depend more on the performers' acting abilities. These films are usually notable for their lack of plot development and physical action, and are characterized by a close scrutiny of a handful of individuals in a confined and ambiguous setting. Orson Welles' 1963 film adaptation of Franz Kafka's *The Trial*, which concerns an individual in a nameless country accused of an unspecified crime, comes immediately to mind, as do many films by Bergman, Resnais, and Antonioni. These works depend as much on the actors as on the directors and screenwriters to bring the normally hidden and elusive drama of psychological conflict and stress to the screen in a relatively naturalistic way. Directors and scriptwriters for such dramas are more concerned with the emotional stress that can be suggested by a glance, a handshake, or a passing remark than with the density of the plot complications or the ways they can keep everything in motion.

As for the actors, a close study of the individual psyche has historically provided some of the screen's most memorable roles and continues to offer the potential for tour-de-force performance. Swedish actress Harriet Andersson gave such a performance as a former mental patient in Bergman's Oscar-winning *Through a Glass Darkly* (1962). The woman spends a summer on a remote island with her father, husband, and younger brother, who eventually learn that she is tragically reverting to her former condition. Andersson's touching portrayal of a person "slipping back into darkness" added immeasurably to this film (see Fig. 6–10).

Films in which conflict and chase are carried out on a mental landscape, like the broader range of social dramas, are not limited to particular genres. It does seem, however, that the more durable films of any genre are those that involve protagonists and audiences in psychological as well as (if not in place of) physical struggles. Early gangster classics like *Little Caesar* (1930) and *The Public Enemy* (1931), memorable westerns such as *High Noon* and *The Gunfighter* (1950), and such great favorites that elude generic labeling as Jean Renoir's *Rules of the Game* (1939) and *Le Grande Illusion* (1937), Welles' *Citizen Kane*, and Bergman's *Autumn Sonata* are primarily struggles of conscience and will.

The "villains" in these films are frequently the demons within all human beings. We may attribute the durability of the classic western as much to its opportunity for study of cowboy heroes and their complex, often enigmatic natures as to the drama of their gun battles. Our identification with the antihero of the gangster film likewise satisfies vicariously our appetite for thrills and chills and our need to break the bonds of conventional rules of behavior; it also offers us a perverse kind of pleasure in being able to share with the protagonist the anxieties

Figure 6-10 *Through a Glass Darkly* (1961—Swedish). Exploring the mental landscape is central to much of Ingmar Bergman's work. In *Through a Glass Darkly,* he examined the growing insanity of a young woman and its impact on those closest to her. She is seen here in the hull of a rotting boat after making incestuous advances toward her brother, who himself suffers serious emotional scars from the incident.

over success, loyalty, and social ostracism that we all sometimes face. But perhaps the most severe challenge to narrative filmmakers is to bring film viewers into struggles in which very little appears to be happening on the screen.

NOTES

[1]See Stanley Solomon, *Beyond Formula* (New York: Harcourt Brace Jovanovich, 1976), pp. 2–7.

[2]Siegfried Kracauer, *Theory of Film: The Redemption of Physical Reality* (New York: Oxford University Press, 1960), pp. 42–43.

[3]See Béla Balázs, *Theory of the Film: Character and Growth of a New Art,* trans. Edith Bone (New York: Dover, 1970), pp. 60–80.

[4]Robert Warshow, *The Immediate Experience* (Garden City, N.Y.: Doubleday, 1962).

[5]Siegfried Kracauer, *From Caligari to Hitler: A Psychological History of the German Film* (Princeton, N.J.: Princeton University Press, 1947).

[6]See Vachel Lindsay, *The Art of the Moving Picture* (New York: Liveright, 1970), pp. 37–68.

[7]Stanley Solomon, *The Film Idea* (New York: Harcourt Brace Jovanovich, 1972), p. 209.

[8]Ibid., p. 210.

[9]Lindsay, *Art of the Moving Picture,* p. 58.

[10]Kracauer, *Theory of Film,* p. 83.

[11]Martin F. Norden, "Toward a Theory of Audience Response to Suspenseful Films," *Journal of the University Film Association,* 32, nos. 1 and 2 (Winter-Spring 1980), 71–77.

[12]Susan Sontag, "The Imagination of Disaster," in *Film and the Liberal Arts,* ed. T. J. Ross (New York: Holt, Rinehart & Winston, 1970), pp. 275–91.

[13]Kracauer, *Theory of Film,* p. 146.

[14]Ibid., pp. 274–80.

[15]O. B. Hardison, "The Rhetoric of Hitchcock's Thrillers," in *Man and the Movies,* ed. W. R. Robinson (Baltimore: Penguin, 1969), p. 143.

[16]John L. Fell, *Film and the Narrative Tradition* (Norman, Okla.: University of Oklahoma Press, 1974), p. 62.

[17]George N. Fenin and William K. Everson, "Contents and Moral Influence of the Western," in *Film and the Liberal Arts,* p. 260.

[18]Cesare Zavattini, "Some Ideas on the Cinema," in *Film: A Montage of Theories,* ed. Richard Dyer MacCann (New York: Dutton, 1966), p. 217.

[19]For a detailed discussion of film as a social document, see Thomas W. Bohn and Richard L. Stromgren, *Light and Shadows: A History of Motion Pictures,* 2nd ed. (Sherman Oaks, Calif.: Alfred Publishing Co., 1978), pp. 146–72 and 267–309.

[20]Fenin and Everson, "Contents and Moral Influence," p. 266.

[21]Warshow, *The Immediate Experience,* p. 97.

[22]For summaries of these theorists' positions on this issue, see J. Dudley Andrew, *The Major Film Theories: An Introduction* (New York: Oxford University Press, 1976), pp. 91 and 197–202.

[23]See Penelope Houston, *The Contemporary Cinema* (Baltimore: Penguin, 1964), pp. 182–95.

[24]Alain Resnais, in an interview with R. M. Franchi, *New York Film Bulletin* (March 1962).

[25]P. Adams Sitney, *Visionary Film: The American Avant-Garde,* 2nd ed. (New York: Oxford University Press, 1979).

7

FILM AND LITERATURE

CONNECTIONS

The influences of other arts and media on narrative film are considerable and varied. Although a basic distinction is usually made between the "original screenplay" and the "adaptation," it finally tells little about the kinds and extent of influences that have been at work in shaping the screenplay that becomes the model or blueprint for the film itself. The adaptation may find its model in a poem, short story, song, novel, ballet, biography, play, essay, and even, as in the cases of *Requiem for a Heavyweight* (1962) and *Marty* (1955), television drama. The extent to which screenwriters use a work in some other form as a model will range from casual references to attempts at direct translation. Even the most original screenplay, as the product of a literate human being, will be shaped indirectly and subconsciously by exposure to other arts and media.

Of all the arts and media, literature reveals the closest and most extensive relationship to film. In addition to providing the inspiration and structural model for narrative films, literature has also been the source of many of the techniques that transform the relating of events or simple exposition into the creation of drama. The relationship of language to the dialogue film is an obvious link; the manipulation of time and space, the control of perspective, and the providing of connotative meaning are others. Literature has clearly given the scenarist and film director the means of enriching the dramatic quality of the film, if not the actual method of execution. With the expansion and refinement of narrative technique in cinema in recent decades, there is evidence of film having brought about changes in contemporary literary forms. Even more recently, authors have created literary works with one eye on the eventual screen adaptations and have even created novels from works already planned or created for the screen. This idea was new in 1968 when Arthur C. Clarke based his novel *2001: A Space Odyssey* on the screenplay of the same name that he and Stanley Kubrick had previously written (which had in turn been based on a short story by Clarke); it has since become a standard procedure for the Hollywood industry to commission authors to write novels based on popular films, which we may interpret as a result of the "conglomeratization" of Hollywood that commenced in the 1960s. For instance, Paramount Pictures distributed *Star Trek: The Motion Picture* in 1979, the same year that Pocket Books published a paperback novel based directly on the film's screenplay. Both Paramount and Pocket Books' parent company, Simon & Schuster, are owned by Gulf & Western, a huge conglomerate with fingers in many pies.

Any attempt to establish a direct correlation between the quality of literary works and the quality of films based on them is both dangerous and finally misleading. Even a cursory examination of some notable works within the two forms will show that a negative correlation often exists. Great books like *Don Quixote, Madame Bovary, Moby Dick, War and Peace,* and *Ulysses* have not made great films, while such pulpy potboilers as *Psycho, The Clansman,* and *Badge of Evil* have formed the basis for some cinematic masterpieces (*Birth of a Nation* and *Touch of Evil,* in the case of the latter two works). Ingmar Bergman has suggested that film has nothing to do with literature and has underscored his point by creating some of greatest screen dramas from original ideas. A number of other screen classics, such as *Citizen Kane, Rules of the Game,* and *The 400 Blows,* have likewise had "nothing to do with literature."

Yet a substantial portion of narrative screenplays are adapted from or inspired by literary works (estimates range from 10 to 40 percent), including such substantial and durable screen dramas as *The Magnificent Ambersons, The Grapes of Wrath,* and *Rashomon.* For better or worse, the relationship between the screen image and the printed word has been a close one, from the formative years of the one- and two-reel silents to the contemporary feature films based on modern popular novels, short stories, nonfiction works, and the literary classics.

The following listings provide some sense of the range of literary sources that have been the inspiration, guide, or blueprint for narrative films in both the silent and sound eras. They also suggest that many prominent directors have had their turn at fashioning films from literary works.

Literary Sources for Selected Silent Films

TITLE OF FILM	TITLE OF LITERARY SOURCE IF DIFFERENT	AUTHOR	DIRECTOR OR PRODUCING CO.
After Many Years (1908)	*Enoch Arden*	Alfred Tennyson	D. W. Griffith
Birth of a Nation (1915)	*The Clansman*	Thomas Dixon	D. W. Griffith

TITLE OF FILM	TITLE OF LITERARY SOURCE IF DIFFERENT	AUTHOR	DIRECTOR OR PRODUCING CO.
A Corner in Wheat (1909)	The Pit	Frank Norris	D. W. Griffith
The Corsican Brothers (1898)		Alexandre Dumas	Anonymous
The Count of Monte Cristo (1912)		Alexandre Dumas	Famous Players
Damnation of Faust (1903)	Faust	Goethe	Georges Méliès
Faust et Marguerite (ca. 1900)	Faust	Goethe	Georges Méliès
Faust and Marguerite (ca. 1900)	Faust	Goethe	Edwin Porter
Greed (1924)	McTeague	Frank Norris	Erich von Stroheim
Leatherstocking (1909)		James Fenimore Cooper	D. W. Griffith
Les Miserables (1913)		Victor Hugo	Pathé Frères
Male and Female (1919)	Admirable Crichton	James M. Barrie	C. B. DeMille
The Necklace (1909)		Guy de Maupassant	D. W. Griffith
Nicholas Nickleby (1903)		Charles Dickens	Biograph
Pippa Passes (1909)		Elizabeth Browning	D. W. Griffith
The Prisoner of Zenda (1913)		Anthony Hope	Famous Players
The Resurrection (1909)		Leo Tolstoy	D. W. Griffith
Rumpelstiltskin (1915)		Grimm Brothers	Thomas Ince
The Sacrifice (1909)	"The Gift of the Magi"	O. Henry	D. W. Griffith
The Scarlet Letter (1926)		Nathaniel Hawthorne	Victor Sjöstrom
Variety (1926)	The Oath of Stephen Huller	Alex Hollander	E. A. Dupont

Literary Sources for Selected Sound Films

TITLE OF FILM	TITLE OF LITERARY SOURCE IF DIFFERENT	AUTHOR	DIRECTOR (*SCREENWRITER)
The African Queen (1951)		C. S. Forester	John Huston *James Agee
All About Eve (1950)	"The Wisdom of Eve"	Mary Orr	Joseph Mankiewicz
All Quiet on the Western Front (1930)		Erich Maria Remarque	Lewis Milestone *Maxwell Anderson and George Abbott

(continued)

TITLE OF FILM	TITLE OF LITERARY SOURCE IF DIFFERENT	AUTHOR	DIRECTOR (*SCREENWRITER)
Anna Karenina (1935)		Leo Tolstoy	Clarence Brown
Barry Lyndon (1975)		William Makepeace Thackeray	Stanley Kubrick
Becky Sharp (1935)	*Vanity Fair*	William Makepeace Thackeray	Rouben Mamoulian
The Big Sleep (1946)		Raymond Chandler	Howard Hawks *William Faulkner, *et al.*
The Bridge on the River Kwai (1957)	"B over RK"	Pierre Boulle	David Lean
The Caine Mutiny (1954)		Herman Wouk	Edward Dmytryk
Dr. Jekyll and Mr. Hyde (1932)		Robert Louis Stevenson	Rouben Mamoulian
Dr. Zhivago (1965)		Boris Pasternak	David Lean *Robert Bolt
Don't Look Now (1973)		Daphne du Maurier	Nicolas Roeg
Double Indemnity (1944)		James Cain	Billy Wilder *Billy Wilder and Raymond Chandler
Frankenstein (1931)		Mary Shelley	James Whale
From Here to Eternity (1953)		James Jones	Fred Zinnemann *Daniel Tardash
Gone With the Wind (1939)		Margaret Mitchell	Victor Fleming, *et al.*
Grapes of Wrath (1940)		John Steinbeck	John Ford *Nunnally Johnson
Great Expectations (1946)		Charles Dickens	David Lean
How Green Was My Valley (1941)		Richard Llewellyn	John Ford
The Hunchback of Notre Dame (1939)		Victor Hugo	William Dieterle
The Informer (1935)		Liam O'Flaherty	John Ford *Dudley Nichols
Kind Hearts and Coronets (1949)	"Israel Rank"	Roy Horniman	Robert Hamer
Little Caesar (1930)		R. W. Burnett	Mervyn LeRoy
Lolita (1962)		Vladimir Nabokov	Stanley Kubrick
Lost Weekend (1945)		Charles Jackson	Billy Wilder *Billy Wilder and Charles Brackett
Little Women (1933)		Louisa May Alcott	George Cukor
The Magnificent Ambersons (1942)		Booth Tarkington	Orson Welles
The Manchurian Candidate (1962)		Richard Condon	John Frankenheimer

TITLE OF FILM	TITLE OF LITERARY SOURCE IF DIFFERENT	AUTHOR	DIRECTOR (*SCREENWRITER)
Moby Dick (1956)		Herman Melville	John Huston
The Night of the Hunter (1955)		Davis Grubb	Charles Laughton *James Agee
Odd Man Out (1947)		F. L. Green	Carol Reed
Oliver Twist (1948)		Charles Dickens	David Lean
The Ox-Bow Incident (1943)		Walter van Tilburg Clark	William Wellman
A Place in the Sun (1951)	*An American Tragedy*	Theordore Dreiser	George Stevens
The Postman Always Rings Twice (1946; 1980)		James Cain	Tay Garnett; Bob Rafelson
Psycho (1960)		Robert Bloch	Alfred Hitchcock
Rebecca (1940)		Daphne du Maurier	Alfred Hitchcock
The Red Badge of Courage (1951)		Stephen Crane	John Huston
Slaughterhouse Five (1972)		Kurt Vonnegut	George Roy Hill
Spellbound (1945)	*The House of Dr. Edwards*	Francis Beeding	Alfred Hitchcock
Stagecoach (1939)	*Stage to Lordsburg*	Ernest Haycox	John Ford
They Shoot Horses Don't They? (1969)		Horace McCoy	Sydney Pollack
To Kill a Mockingbird (1962)		Harper Lee	Robert Mulligan
Tom Jones (1963)		Henry Fielding	Tony Richardson *John Osborne
A Tree Grows in Brooklyn (1945)		Betty Smith	Elia Kazan
2001: A Space Odyssey (1968)	"The Sentinel"	Arthur C. Clarke	Stanley Kubrick
War and Peace (1956; 1968)		Leo Tolstoy	King Vidor; Sergei Bondarchuk
The Wizard of Oz (1939)		L. Frank Baum	Victor Fleming
Wuthering Heights (1939)		Emily Brontë	William Wyler *Ben Hecht and Charles MacArthur

Certain works are so durable and timeless that they have enjoyed frequent cinematic interpretation, as in the cases of Goethe's *Faust*, Hugo's *Hunchback of Notre Dame* (see Fig. 7–1), and Stevenson's *Dr. Jekyll and Mr. Hyde*. Others have inspired a cycle of films or sequels to the original, such as *Frankenstein, Robin Hood,* and Raymond Chandler's Philip Marlowe character, whose adventures as a private detective have been given several filmic renderings.

Figure 7-1   *The Hunchback of Notre Dame* (1923— American). The various film and television versions of Victor Hugo's classic tale of misunderstood passions attest to its durability as screen drama. The original and most successful Hollywood version was produced in 1923 with a famous human chameleon named Lon Chaney in the title role.

Other works as diverse as *Rashomon* and *Gentlemen Prefer Blondes* have moved freely, if with varying degrees of success, through several media. The Kurosawa film was itself based on two short stories, "Rashomon" and "In a Grove," by Ryunosuke Akutagawa. The film inspired the Broadway production by Fay and Michael Kanin, and in 1964 Metro-Golden-Mayer produced the much inferior film, *The Outrage,* directed by Martin Ritt, which drew from the original stories as well as the earlier film and play. Screenwriter Anita Loos, responsible for the creation of scripts for several early studios and silent stars, went on to create one of the most adaptable works in the arts. Her novel *Gentlemen Prefer Blondes* became a Broadway play in 1926, a movie in 1928, a stage musical in 1949, a movie musical in 1953, and a new stage musical in 1974.[1] Loos had written or collaborated on each version.

In addition to providing the works that have found their way to the screen, many prominent as well as lesser known men and women of letters have earned screen credit as scenarist as well as for original authorship. They include William Faulkner, F. Scott Fitzgerald, James Agee, Nathanael West, Dylan Thomas, and Jean-Paul Sartre. Literary figures have become authors of cinema in another sense as well. John Osborne, Alain Robbe-Grillet, and Marguerite Duras are among the writers for New Wave films who have followed the literary approaches to cinema suggested by Alexandre Astruc's 1948 essay, "Le Camera Stylo":

1

Figure 7-2 *Great Expectations* (1947—British). Production designer John Bryan effectively created the world of cobwebs and decay that has shut Miss Haversham away from the world in David Lean's filmic rendering of *Great Expectations*. Soviet filmmaker Sergei Eisenstein credited Charles Dickens with a cinematic style of writing, making his novels particularly well-suited for adaptation to the screen. The author's careful attention to visual detail has frequently provided filmmakers with a complete picture of the major settings of his novels.

The cinema . . . becomes bit by bit a language. By a language I mean the form in which and through which an artist can express his thoughts, however abstract they may be, or translate his obsessions, just as in an essay or a novel . . . . The film will . . . become a means of writing as supple and subtle as the written word.[2]

Although Charles Dickens never wrote a screenplay, he is among the several nineteenth-century novelists who have been cited by film theorists as writing cinematically. In his celebrated essay "Dickens, Griffith, and the Film Today," Eisenstein has illustrated the close links between the verbal imagery that helps the reader visualize the world of Dickens' novels and the visual imagery that leads to meaningful narrative in cinema.[3]

But we should caution that similarities in filmic and literary means of narrative construction and the communication of detail soon give way to significant differences. In *Novels Into Film*, George Bluestone observed: "Between the visual image and the concept of the mental image lies the root difference between the two media."[4] The relationship between film and literature effectively shows how two things can be quite similar and at the same time completely different. As Bluestone notes: "Like two intersecting lines, novel and film meet at a point, then diverge. At the intersection, the book and shooting script are almost indistinguishable. But where the lines diverge, they not only resist conversion; they also lose all resemblance to each other."[5]

Film and literature are joined by accident and design in various ways; the links are easily illustrated and hardly at issue. The extent to which we may carry the analogy between film and written language and the ways the cinematic and literary forms compare as means of storytelling are considerably more problematic, however, and warrant further examination. To aid in such a study, we have grouped the essentials of storytelling under four headings that illustrate the similarities and differences of the two forms in their approach to narrative and in their relationship to the audience for whom the narrative is intended. The first two, *flexibility* and *perspective*, emphasize the similarities between the two forms; the latter two, *presentation* and *public vs. private experience*, emphasize the differences.

FLEXIBILITY

An immediate and certainly critical link between the literary and cinematic forms is their *flexibility of expression*. When we consider the ways that other arts are anchored to temporal and spatial parameters, film's easy movement in time and space is similar to the novel's storytelling fluidity, but not absolutely identical. (Filmmakers' imaginations are limited to where they may bring their cameras, among other factors, while those of the writers have absolutely free reign.) Yet in both theory and practice, Eisenstein and Pudovkin demonstrated that filmmakers can realize some of the fluidity normally associated with literary forms through the key cinematic means of montage, the creative selection and arrangement of individual shots.

The opening passage of Booth Tarkington's *The Magnificent Ambersons* provides a leisurely, nostalgic account of values and lifestyles in a small Midwestern city of the 1870s. Orson Welles, who saw the Tarkington novel as "a lament for the sense of moral values which have been destroyed," used a montage sequence to suggest a sense of the times, paying particular attention to the changing styles of men's and women's fashions and grooming that the author had developed: "Every house still kept its bootjack, but high-topped boots gave way to shoes and 'congress gaiters'; and these were played through fashions that shaped them now with toes like box-ends and now with toes like prows of racing shells."[6]

Through the use of close-ups and editing untied to a single time and setting, Welles, like Tarkington, set the stage for the action while also establishing a major theme of the work: the inevitability of change. Welles successfully used the device throughout the film, beginning with changes in dress, grooming, architecture, and modes of transportation, extending through the metamorphosis in lifestyles, and culminating in the "comeuppance" and change of George Amberson Minafer himself.

Through the composition and arrangement of individual shots, the filmmaker can also replicate some of the fluidity of literature by moving freely in space and extending the range of the setting to suggest the broader expanse of the epic novel. From the finely drawn detail of the emotional strain experienced by Ma Joad and her family in *The Grapes of Wrath* to the expanse of their pilgrimage from their Oklahoma farm to their new life in California, John Ford demonstrated the capabilities of the camera to reflect both panoramic and intimate scenes. Whether working with original screen material or that adapted from some other form, Ford and other creative filmmakers have shown that, in Bluestone's words,

Figure 7-3   *The Magnificent Ambersons* (1942—American). Booth Tarkington's novel about the changing way of life in America at the turn of the century provided Orson Welles with a follow-up project to *Citizen Kane*. Due to studio tampering, the final few minutes of *Ambersons* conflict with the spirit of the rest of the film; however, much of Welles' screen adaptation powerfully evokes Tarkington's characters and settings.

"the camera can see over a hundred miles of prairie, or count the eyelashes on an actor's lid."[7]

Theorists have often compared film's shot, scene, and sequence constructions to the way that authors use words, sentences, and paragraphs to shape the dramatic event. For example, André Levinson has noted:

> The film has in common with the novel, a mixed literary form: the abolition of all the unities—place, action, time; and, quite like the novel, it rescues from this complexity and apparent incoherence its inner reality, that of design, and a harmony of parts which should concur in forming a whole endowed with an organic life. The composition of a novel is equivalent to the continuity of a picture, each chapter, paragraph, or other division forming a "shot."[8]

Theorists like Pudovkin and Eisenstein have even suggested that individual shots are comparable to individual words, in the sense that words and shots *by themselves* are vague and may carry a wide range of possible meanings. When a word is inserted into the context of a sentence, however, its juxtaposition with other words narrows its meaning considerably, just as a shot's juxtaposition with other shots sharpens its meaning.

Although we may find such comparisons initially helpful in understanding how film functions as a *visual language,* such links are obviously limited. Modern theorists such as Christian Metz have argued that a shot of a lion, for example, is not really equivalent to the word "lion." A shot is actually closer to a statement, such as "Here is a lion!" in this case. Nevertheless, the comparison of film and literature's basic building blocks is useful when examining the ways that film, like poetry, is able to abandon logical sequence, to deal with abstractions and figurative meanings, and to develop a unity through rhythm and sense of flow. But here, too, we must study the links in light of corresponding limitations and not overextend them.

PERSPECTIVE

Before turning to the more serious limitations of film as a narrative form and its contrasts with literature, we need to focus our attention on a second primary link: *perspective*. As outlined earlier, filmmakers not only have the ability to record and reveal action but can also control the perspective from which they observe the action. They accomplish this through a range of techniques including camera placement and movement, shot selection and arrangement, lighting, set design, and sound. In literature, such means as tense (past, present, future), person (first, third limited, third omniscient), number (singular, plural), and voice (active, passive) make us aware of perspective as well as the presence of the author. John Howard Lawson had pointed out that in film, "the spectator knows that someone invented and guided the action, but this consciousness is submerged in the emotional effect of what is seen and heard," but in literature, "someone must be telling the story and the narration is a mode of remembering."[9]

In the opening pages of *How Green Was My Valley*, Richard Llewellyn remembered what life was like in the small Welsh mining village where he grew up. Through his recollections, he continually shifted from the past to the present tense. "I am going to pack my two shirts. . .and I am going from the Valley," begins the narrative. It continues in the following paragraphs with such shifts in perspective as "It has always seemed to me. . . ," "But all I have felt this past hour. . . ," and "My father met her when she was sixteen and he was twenty."[10] This shift of tense and person continues with simple past tense giving way to such subtle variations as "*I have often stood* outside the door. . ." and "All the women *used to dress up* specially. . ." (our emphasis).

Filmmakers can suggest similar distinctions in tense, person, number, and even voice, but such shifts are seldom easily accomplished. The flashback is a useful means of moving into the past tense, but once we have been delivered into the action of a time gone by, it quickly becomes the present; moviemakers have no equivalent of a verb form to keep us in the past. They can use camera angle, quality of movement, montage, and sound to represent their points of view but, unlike authors, they cannot reproduce the thought process directly. In other words, filmmakers can suggest the subjective experience and mental reality but cannot translate them directly into cinematic terms.

Let's examine two examples. In the written version of *The Magnificent Ambersons*, George Minafer's last walk up National Avenue is filled with rememberances (for Booth Tarkington if not for George himself): "In this alley he had fought with two boys at the same time, and whipped them; in that front yard he had been successfully teased into temporary insanity by a Sunday-school class of pinky little girls." In adapting this scene for the film, Orson Welles resorted to providing the memory through his own voice as narrator. In Ambrose Bierce's short story "An Occurrence at Owl Creek Bridge," the author suggested speculation rather than remembrance when he led the reader directly to the central character's thoughts: "If I could free my hands," he thought, "I might throw off the noose and spring into the stream." In the screen adaptation of this work, director Robert Enrico simply deleted Peyton Farquar's speculation about his immediate future. Both instances illustrate filmmakers' lack of a perfect cinematic equivalent to the thought process. George Bluestone has summed up the problem faced by filmmakers in representing mental reality this way: "Dreams and memories, which exist nowhere but in the individual consciousness, cannot be adequately represented in spatial terms."[11]

As we noted earlier in this book, surrealist filmmakers working in the original avant-garde film movement as well as the experimentalists of more recent times have shown some interesting approaches to representing the thought process in visual terms. In narrative films, however, such attempts tend to result in cumbersome and self-conscious exercises.

Film's advantage in immediately rendering concrete detail from a given perspective is offset by the burden of that detail when subtle shifts in perspective are desired. In the literary form of *The Caine Mutiny*, Herman Wouk suggested Willie Keith's preoccupation with the growing irrationality of Captain Queeg with the following lines:

> The sea was the one thing in Willie's life that remained larger than Queeg. The Captain had swelled in his consciousness to all-pervading presence, a giant of malice and evil; but when Willie filled his mind with the sight of the sea and the sky, he could, at least for a while, reduce Queeg to a sickly well-meaning man struggling with a job beyond his powers. The hot little fevers of the *Caine*, the deadlines, the investigations, the queer ordinances, the dreaded tantrums, all these could dwindle and cool to comic pictures, contrasted, with the sea—momentarily.[12]

The film version of *The Caine Mutiny*, unlike that of *The Magnificent Ambersons*, has no narrator to translate into words the thoughts and emotional stresses of its characters, but instead relies on dialogue, action, and the close-up scrutiny of subtleties of expression. The fuller meaning of the passage just quoted must necessarily be lost in cinema; indeed, director Edward Dmytryk and scriptwriter Stanley Roberts made no attempt to bring it to the screen (see Fig. 7–4).

It is somewhat ironic that although the novel has the ability to shift perspective easily, it will usually keep to a single point of view, generally that of the first- or third-person observer "remembering" events of the past. Film, on the other hand, avoids extended use of the first-person subjective view and shifts perspective, frequently through shot variation within the scene, such as in the reverse angle shot of two characters engaged in conversation. Such changes in camera angle do not come close to the subtle shifts in perspective that literature is capable of providing. Sound, and more particularly the use of an off-screen narrator, does help to close the gap, and as uncinematic as the device may be, it allows the unseen storyteller to serve his or her function via the sound track.

PRESENTATION VS. REPRESENTATION

The filmmaker, like the novelist, is frequently interested in extending the meaning of an action or an object from its objective, denotative meaning to a figurative or connotative meaning or significance in order to create some abstract idea, mood, or emotion. The filmmaker, like the writer, will turn to motifs, metaphors, and tropes that serve essentially the same function they do in literature. But the literalness of the motion-picture camera becomes most apparent here, and the fun-

Figure 7-4 *The Caine Mutiny* (1954—American). In this scene from *The Caine Mutiny*, Willie Keith (Robert Francis) silently reflects on the paranoid behavior of his commanding officer, Captain Queeg. In the novel on which the movie was based, Herman Wouk offered a precise description of Willie's thoughts; the film version, however, provides only a suggestion of the young officer's anxiety.

damental differences between film as a means of direct visual and aural presentation of the world and literature as word symbols that offer a representation of that world can be most dramatically illustrated. Ingmar Bergman has made this distinction: "The written word is read and assimilated by a conscious act of the will in alliance with the intellect; *little by little* it affects the imagination and the emotion. The process is different with motion pictures. When we experience a film, we consciously prime ourselves for illusion. . . . The sequence of pictures plays *directly* on our feelings," (emphasis ours).[13]

The directness and literalness of film are useful as exposition and documentation of people, places, and events, but these become problematic when some freedom from concrete and immediate (denotative) significance is required. When Ambrose Bierce reflects on the nature of death before a body of executioners, he says, "Death is a dignitary who when he comes announced is to be received with formal manifestations of respect, even by those most familiar with him." Such metaphoric language has no direct counterpart in film.

Thus film frequently becomes tied to the literalness of what the filmmakers put before the lens and also to the detail of the object or action. When, near the conclusion of "An Occurrence at Owl Creek Bridge," Bierce wrote of Peyton

Farquar, "He stands at the gate of his own home," he detailed the scene no further; he offered no description of either gate or home, preferring instead to allow the reader to fill in the information. When filmmakers place a character before a gate and house, they become slaves to the detail that such a setting will inevitably offer. The gate and house must be of a specific size and design, and seen from a particular perspective. If they try to modify the amount of detail that the scene provides, this will itself be seen as just that: a modification of what the camera would otherwise record in all its literalness.

In *The Caine Mutiny*, Wouk easily isolated the detail to which he wanted to draw attention by giving the reader no other. For example, "The bellboy turned on the lights, opened the closets, and left Willie alone with the sunset and his bags." Providing such selectivity is a greater challenge for the moviemaker and risks becoming an artificial masking of unwanted detail.

As we have suggested, such limitations in abstraction, generalization, and literary metaphor do not preclude the filmmaker's discovery of some cinematic alternative. Visual metaphors in film range from the direct allegory of Bergman's *The Seventh Seal* (including a character who plays Death) to the cryptic allusions to bisecting paths or the double-cross in Hitchcock's *Strangers on a Train* or to hunger and food in his *Frenzy*. Filmmakers can create visual abstractions and metaphors through various cinematic means. Griffith and Eisenstein were particularly good at demonstrating the uses of montage to provide the meter of poetry and even to make objects "rhyme" by matching composition and movement of two actions. As we noted in Chapter 3, Pudovkin created a brilliant metaphor by alluding to spring floods to provide a visual key to the spirit of revolution in Soviet Russia in his film *Mother*. Alexander Dovzhenko surpassed Pudovkin with his own ode to rebirth in *Earth* through the use of cleansing rain and fruit-laden orchards.

Bergman's warning notwithstanding, film *does* have something to do with literature, but major differences begin to appear in the visual *presentation* of film and verbal *representation* of literature. Subjective and metaphoric expression magnifies the contrast. The section of Joyce's *Ulysses* that finds Molly Bloom absorbed in a "stream of consciousness" is denied a direct visual rendering in film. Aside from the injury it would do to the general rhythm and flow, such literal and concrete detail would destroy the subtle suggestiveness and spontaneity of the represented daydream. Furthermore, our moral and aesthetic sensibilities would likely be offended by the sight of Molly performing fellatio on the statue of a saint. While film has difficulty with certain literary forms, literature has difficulty with subtleties in visual expression. Words can never fully capture the camera's discovery of the human face and other forms of human expression through movement, gesture, and mime. The problem of adapting *Ulysses* to the screen matches the improbability of a literary adaptation of Chaplin's *The Gold Rush*.

PRIVATE VS. PUBLIC EXPERIENCE

We may find the most substantive contrasts between film and literature in the ways we experience the two media. Reading a literary work is a very private experience and one controlled by the reader. It takes place at a time and location of the reader's own choosing, progresses at a speed set by the reader, and may continue through single or multiple reading sessions with skips, rereading of passages, and even the reading of passages out of sequence. The reading is also done alone, and except for the possibility of some previous or subsequent communication with other readers of the work, provides no sense of group response or interaction during the reading. The group reading, popular in both informal gatherings and as a part of literary guild presentations in the days before mass media, is infrequent today.

The film spectator is bound by much closer limitations of time and place. The viewing usually occurs in a public theater or screening room and continues for a fixed period of time at a single sitting and at a pace and in a sequence determined by the filmmaker and not usually subject to modification. Significantly, the viewer often becomes aware of the responses of others, despite the darkness and general feeling of anonymity. Horror films and comedies are usually more enjoyable when shared with others who are responding, sometimes visually as well as audibly, to the happenings on the screen. (This phenomenon reaches its zenith during presentations of the 1976 cult hit, *The Rocky Horror Picture Show*, when costumed audience members scream out memorized lines of dialogue and hurl food and other items at the screen—and, unavoidably, at each other—during the movie's key moments.) Our response to the film experience, then, is not only a more controlled response; it is also shared and affords considerably less individual initiative and imagination than sitting down with a good book.

Our expectations and psychological set also influence our film viewing in a way quite different from reading. Besides being a private experience, reading is also a more casual one which does not require the planning, physical exertion, and financial investment of going to the movies. Because of the wider public attention given to popular films—publicity, promotion of stars, reviews, awards—preconditioning to a film is also usually more extensive than to literature. Films, even mass-entertainment ones, come and go and eventually reappear on television; literature is less demanding of public attention but more accessible to casual and extemporaneous perusal.

In addition to the expectations and requirements set by film audiences, the film industry has established others that further distinguish the film experience from its literary counterpart. The profit motive and a sensitivity to material that might prove objectionable to the larger, more heterogeneous audience have significantly influenced content and treatment on the screen. High cost and accessibility to the public forum require that most narrative films find and satisfy a larger audience; literature can still afford to be more selective.

ISSUES IN ADAPTATION

Given the considerable distance between filmic presentation and literary representation, the challenges in adapting literature to the screen become quickly evident. Such challenges are extended and become problematic through the demands that have traditionally been placed on a work adapted from another medium. George Bluestone has called them the "assumptions which blur the mutation process." They are the assumptions that "incidents and characters in fiction are interchangeable with incidents and characters in the film; that the novel is a norm and the film deviates at its peril."[14]

The assumption that success in adaptation is tied to a faithful translation from one medium to another is not easily overcome. Even when we are aware that film comes equipped with its own means of dramatic expression, we may still have a tendency to judge accomplishments of the film in terms of faithfulness to the original action, setting, character development, language, and other physical detail. Such a tendency almost invariably casts the adapted film in an unfavorable light, since filmmakers rarely if ever can capture all the dimensions of the original novel. If a filmmaker were to adapt every scene out of a typical novel for inclusion in one film, the resulting film would probably run ten hours or more. Scriptwriters and directors have to make concessions to keep their films to manageable lengths (and budgets); these concessions usually take the form of axed subplots and a tightening of the main story. For example, the literary version of *Jaws* contained numerous land-based subplots, the most notable of which was an affair between the sheriff's wife and a visiting ichthyologist. Those responsible for adapting the film cut out most of these vignettes, leaving behind a film as streamlined and powerful as its central creature. The challenge in adaptation, as well as in the critical re-

Figure 7-5 *The Informer* (1935— American). Gypo Nolan (Victor McLaglen) asks forgiveness from the mother of the friend he has betrayed (Una O'Connor) in the concluding moments of *The Informer*. Director John Ford and screenwriter Dudley Nichols successfully translated Liam O'Flaherty's Irish rebellion novel to the screen in 1935.

sponse to it, is to find analogous techniques that will draw from the medium's own potential and render something of the mood, temper, and theme of the original that inspired filmmakers to turn to it in the first place.

We have already suggested that the works of some authors seem to anticipate visual rendering, and finding analogous means of expression in cinema is fairly direct in these cases. Uncinematic material, on the other hand, is usually found in works dependent on language-bound observations that resist physical representation. The final judgment of what will survive the journey, however, will depend on the filmmakers' understanding of how their own medium can provide something of the experience of the original, rendered in its own terms. It will also depend on the viewer's understanding and acceptance of the mutation process. John Howard Lawson put it succinctly when he said, "When the difference between the two modes of expression is recognized, it becomes possible to analyze the tremendous contributions which one art can make to the other."[15]

NOTES

[1]The ill-fated Broadway musical was called *Lorelei*.

[2]Cited in Penelope Houston, *The Contemporary Cinema* (Baltimore: Penguin, 1964, p. 97.

[3]Sergei Eisenstein, *Film Form* (New York: Harcourt Brace Jovanovich, 1949), pp. 195–255.

[4]George Bluestone, *Novels into Film* (Berkeley: University of California, 1961), p. IX

[5]Bluestone, *Novels into Film*, p. 63.

[6]Booth Tarkington, *The Magnificent Ambersons* (Garden City, N.Y.: Doubleday, 1918), p. 5.

[7]Bluestone, *Novels into Film*, p. 15.

[8]André Levinson, "The Nature of Cinema," *Theatre Arts Monthly* XIII, 9 (September 1929), p. 693.

[9]John Howard Lawson, *Film: The Creative Process* (New York: Hill & Wang, 1964), p. 211.

[10]Richard Llewellyn, *How Green Was My Valley* (New York: Macmillian, 1966), pp. 1–3.

[11]Bluestone, *Novels into Film*, p. 47.

[12]Herman Wouk, *The Caine Mutiny* (Garden City, N.Y.: Doubleday, 1954), pp. 336–37.

[13]Ingmar Bergman, "Film Has Nothing to Do with Literature," in *Film: A Montage of Theories*, ed. Richard Dyer MacCann (New York: Dutton, 1966), p. 144.

[14]Bluestone, *Novels into Film*, p. 5.

[15]Lawson, *Film*, p. 218.

8

FILM AND THEATER

THE TRADITION

In 1896, May Irwin and John Rice embraced to recreate for film's first audiences the mildly erotic kiss from the stage production of *The Widow Jones*, in which they were currently appearing. In that same year, which marked the first public showing of motion pictures in the United States, Joseph Jefferson was providing the screen with another characterization that he had created for the stage, Washington Irving's hero, Rip Van Winkle. Within a few years, famous stage roles were being performed before the camera with little concern for the inability of the medium to provide more than a few moments of the play's action; Desdemona, Macbeth, Parsifal, and Cyrano all became screen personalities within the confines of the narrative clips that ran anywhere from a few seconds to the ten- to twelve-minute limit of the single reel.

By 1907 a French company calling itself *Film d'Art* undertook a noble experiment in filmed theater. Turning the camera on the company of the *Comédie Francaise* and many of the major artists of the French National Theater, it attempted to bring to a largely skeptical audience great players in great plays. Although a failure in artistic as well as popular terms, the movement was instrumental in lending the film medium an air of respectability and, perhaps more significantly, in extending the narrative film to the unprecedented length of four reels, almost three-quarters of an hour in length.

The appearance of the American Film Theater in 1973 showed that after nearly eighty years of evolution, the motion-picture medium could still accommodate "canned theater" and provide the larger film audience with an opportunity to see major stage works without going to the legitimate theater. Although such American Film Theater productions as O'Neill's *The Iceman Cometh*, Ionesco's *Rhinoceros*, and Genet's *The Maids* never won wide popular support, they did help reaffirm film's function in providing a means of recording and distributing, and more significantly in preserving works from the other dramatic arts (see Fig. 8–4).

But the association of film and theater goes far beyond these two movements and the many other attempts to bring stage performances, including ballet, opera, musical theater, and television drama, to the screen. The screen adaptation of works written originally for the stage has formed a significant part of our legacy in film and has frequently illustrated the ways that the two forms approximate one another in dramatic presentation and the points at which they diverge. The close relationship of film and theater is illustrated by the following listing of some of the films produced since the coming of sound that are based on significant stage works, or in some cases, works that have gained some prestige or critical acclaim as films but come from plays of little note.

Theatrical Sources for Selected Sound Films

PLAY	PLAYWRIGHT	DATE OF FILM RELEASE	FILM DIRECTOR
Abe Lincoln in Illinois	Robert Sherwood	1940	John Cromwell
Androcles and the Lion	George Bernard Shaw	1952	Chester Erskine
Anna Christie	Eugene O'Neill	1930	Clarence Brown
Becket	Jean Anouilh	1964	Peter Glenville
Blackmail	C. Bennett	1929	Alfred Hitchcock
Born Yesterday	Garson Kanin	1950	George Cukor
The Boys in the Band	Mart Crowley	1970	William Friedkin
Brief Encounter (Still Life)	Noel Coward	1946	David Lean
Butley	Harold Pinter	1974	Harold Pinter
Butterflies Are Free	Leonard Gershe	1972	Milton Katselas
Caesar and Cleopatra	George Bernard Shaw	1946	Gabriel Pascal
The Children's Hour	Lillian Hellman	1962	William Wyler
Cry Havoc	A. R. Kenward	1943	Richard Thorpe
Death of a Salesman	Arthur Miller	1951	Laslo Benedek
Deathtrap	Ira Levin	1982	Sidney Lumet
Desire Under the Elms	Eugene O'Neill	1958	Delbert Mann
Detective Story	Sidney Kingsley	1951	William Wyler
Dial M for Murder	Frederick Knott	1954	Alfred Hitchcock
Dracula	J. Balderstone and C. Deane	1931	Tod Browning

Theatrical Sources for Selected Sound Films

PLAY	PLAYWRIGHT	DATE OF FILM RELEASE	FILM DIRECTOR
Edward, My Son	R. Morley and N. Langley	1949	George Cukor
The Emperor Jones	Eugene O'Neill	1933	Dudley Murphy
The Glass Menagerie	Tennessee Williams	1950	Irving Rapper
Golden Boy	Clifford Odets	1939	Rouben Mamoulian
The Great White Hope	Howard Sackler	1970	Martin Ritt
Hamlet	William Shakespeare	1948	Laurence Olivier
		1969	Tony Richardson
Harvey	Mary Chase	1951	Henry Koster
A Hatful of Rain	M. V. Gazzo	1957	Fred Zinnemann
Heaven Can Wait	R. Ackland	1943	Ernst Lubitsch
Henry V	William Shakespeare	1945	Laurence Olivier
Johnny Belinda	Elmer Harris	1948	Jean Negulesco
Julius Caesar	William Shakespeare	1953	Joseph L. Mankiewicz
		1971	Stuart Burge
Key Largo	Maxwell Anderson	1948	John Huston
Macbeth	William Shakespeare	1950	Orson Welles
		1971	Roman Polanski
A Man for All Seasons	Robert Bolt	1966	Fred Zinnemann
The Man in the Glass Booth	Robert Shaw	1975	Arthur Hiller
The Man Who Came to Dinner	George S. Kaufman and Moss Hart	1941	William Keighley
Marat/Sade	Peter Weiss	1967	Peter Brook
A Midsummer Night's Dream	William Shakespeare	1935	Max Reinhardt
		1966	Dan Eriksen
The Miracle Worker	William Gibson	1962	Arthur Penn
The Odd Couple	Neil Simon	1968	Gene Saks
The Petrified Forest	Robert Sherwood	1936	Archie Mayo
Play It Again, Sam	Woody Allen	1972	Herbert Ross
Pygmalion	George Bernard Shaw	1938	Anthony Asquith and Leslie Howard
Romeo and Juliet	William Shakespeare	1936	George Cukor
		1954	Renato Castellani
		1966	Franco Zeffirelli
		1966	Paul Czinner
Seventh Heaven	A. Strong	1937	Henry King
Stalag 17	D. Bevan and E. Trzcinski	1953	Billy Wilder
Strange Interlude	Eugene O'Neill	1932	Robert Z. Leonard
A Streetcar Named Desire	Tennessee Williams	1951	Elia Kazan
Suddenly Last Summer	Tennessee Williams	1959	Joseph L. Mankiewicz
Sweet Bird of Youth	Tennessee Williams	1962	Richard Brooks
A Taste of Honey	Shelagh Delaney	1962	Tony Richardson
Tea and Sympathy	Robert Anderson	1956	Vincente Minnelli
Wait Until Dark	Frederick Knott	1967	Terence Young

(*continued*)

Theatrical Sources for Selected Sound Films

PLAY	PLAYWRIGHT	DATE OF FILM RELEASE	FILM DIRECTOR
Watch on the Rhine	Lillian Hellman	1943	Herman Shumlin
What Price Glory?	Laurence Stallings and Maxwell Anderson	1952	John Ford
Who's Afraid of Virginia Woolf?	Edward Albee	1966	Mike Nichols
Whose Life Is It Anyway?	Brian Clark	1982	John Badham
You Can't Take It with You	George S. Kaufman and Moss Hart	1938	Frank Capra

The extent to which these films owe their design structure and detail, as well as their origins, to theater varies widely. All in some way help illustrate the bonds between stage and screen as means of dramatic expression, or emphasize the ways that each is unique and the challenges in moving from the one form to the other.

PHYSICAL PROPERTIES AND CONTROLS

The similarities between film and play are easily stated. In their traditional form, both provide some sort of human activity arranged in narrative form and acted out before an audience seated in a darkened theater. Although contemporary experimental forms of both suggest significant exceptions to the rule, both stage and screen play are of roughly the same length and follow the Aristotelian principles of dramatic unity, and have a beginning, a middle, and an end. In comparison with the novel, which often attains epic proportions, both are usually more limited to scope in terms of time, place, and action, making Brecht's *Mother Courage*, Griffith's *Intolerance*, and Altman's *Nashville* special cases rather than representatives of the norm.

Although the works in each form are often marked by the style of a single creative artist—in film it is usually the director, in theater, the playwright—both are nonetheless collaborative arts drawing from the talents and technical expertise of writers, actors, producers, scenic designers, costumers, and a host of other production personnel. In other words, they both involve a production organization with all of the intricacies and hazards of group dynamics that such a corporate effort implies. In their most visible form—major film studios and professional theater organizations—they are also tied both to an economic base and strong business interests.

In addition to being collective arts and industries, film and theater are social activities in which audiences gather for performances, mingle, and interact. One becomes part of a social event, responding to the events on stage or screen and frequently being influenced by responses of others in the gathering. Furthermore, going both to the theater and to the movies requires planning, the investment of a fixed period of time, physical exertion in getting to and from the theater, and a considerable financial investment. The significance of such expenditure of time, money, and energy is amplified when comparing film and theater to the television experience (see Chapter 9).

In spite of these similarities and the long association of the two forms, the development of cinematic technique has been largely away from the conventions of the theater. The divergence of the two forms was described by one theater critic in a 1929 article on "The Nature of Cinema":

> The screen is clearly opposed to the stage. They differ completely in their methods, as in their object, even when both treat the same situations. It is neither the subject nor the theme which is the essential quality either of theatre or cinema; it is the mode of expression, and in this they part at the same point as do music and sculpture.[1]

Differences in the mode of expression are indeed at the center of what distinguishes the screen from the stage work. A major distinction is between the two-dimensional recording of screen action and the three-dimensional live action of the stage. A significant part of the distinction involves the nature of the performance and the viewer perspective, which we will treat separately. These considerations aside, the presentation of recorded images of an action that took place some time in the past and the live performance are significantly different in terms of the psychology of the viewing experience. In the theater the relationship between audience and stage action is based on the suspension of disbelief. We accept the actor as a person involved in the creation of a role, and the set and decor as a *representation* of a setting for the action. Our tolerance in theater for role-playing is broad enough for the versatile performer to portray a broad range of characters in various age groups. By the same token, the barest and most highly stylized setting will be accepted as sufficient in suggesting either the time or place of the action. The Elizabethan theater's simple platform with men performing in women's roles effectively illustrates the point.

As film viewers, we recognize that the movie about to unfold before us will be a recording of action that has taken place some time in the past. Once the film has begun, however, we are easily propelled into the immediacy of the event and fail to distinguish between the actor and the character portrayed. The ability of the camera to provide a faithful representation of the subject before the lens provides the ethos or believability for the camera recording, providing the setting and action are rendered in reasonably natural or realistic terms.[2] This sense of screen realism, in contrast to the theatrical illusion accounts for the major difference between the film and theater experience as far as the spectators are concerned.

The theatrical and film experiences also differ for the spectators in terms of the vantage point from which they observe the action. In the theater, the spectators remain in a single, fixed position and at a specific distance from the action. If a theatrical director wants to draw their attention to one area of the stage, he or she must stage and light the action there. If detail is small and intricate, the director can do little to bring it into range of the spectators for closer scrutiny, particularly those spectators in the last row of the theater.

In film, the close-up is the key to exposition, and, through the editing process generally, the filmmaker can provide the viewers a variety of vantage points from which to observe the action. By moving the spectators into and around the action, the filmmaker not only provides access to intricate detail but also makes the spectators first- or third-person participants or omniscient observers, unlike theater observers, who find themselves barred from crossing the curtain line and kept a fixed distance from the stage action.

Although the film medium would seem to hold the advantage with regard to vantage point, we should note that the psychological distancing in theater allows us to maintain the necessary perspective for the suspension of disbelief to take effect. We can more easily accept the artifice of the theatrical production because we are forced to keep our distance.

A spatial continuity within the stage setting may also be lost when the scene is broken down into a series of close-ups, as it is in film. Editing of the film scene may move the spectator into the action, but with constant shifts in perspective, establishing and maintaining the overall composition or larger perspective of the scene may prove difficult. Filmmakers often overcome the problem by using the "master shot" or reestablishing shot, but the device may appear arbitrary, since it may pull the spectators away from action that deserves close scrutiny. A move in filmmaking of the thirties and forties toward "deep-focus photography" allowed for close-up attention to elements of the setting in the foreground while rendering background detail in acceptably sharp focus. The practice helped overcome the dissociation of scenic detail that editing may produce and helped regain some of the spatial continuity that might otherwise have been lost. It is an approach to scenic composition used sparingly by filmmakers today.

The nature of performance and the progression of the drama provide another significant point at which we may examine the separate qualities of screen and stage. After a period of extended rehearsal, the actors present the play before an audience in a single, unalterable performance of from generally two to three hours. The basic performance unit for the stage actor is the scene, and for the leading performers these may extend to the full length of the act, with intermissions providing the only break in performance. With the assistance of backstage crews, the play is in the hands of the actors and completely out of the hands of its director once the curtain has been raised.

For the screen actor the performance comes in much smaller units—shots—which are created out of the mayhem and complexities of the studio or location setting. These shots, often taken out of sequence, are painstakingly set up and run through for technical modifications and then often repeated several times in front of the impersonal and unresponsive camera. The cycle is then repeated over a period of weeks and even months until shooting is finished. The actual presentation of the drama before an audience is delayed even longer, until the film is finally assembled and released for showing. In a sense, the film performance is a more "synthetic" form in which even a single action may consist of a collection of shots taken at different times and finally put together into what resembles a single playing of the scene. In this process the talents of the director, and presumably an editor, come into play long after the actor has completed the role. Once the film is completed, or "in the can," it remains the single, unalterable work that all viewers will see in exactly the same form. In theater, each production of the play and indeed each performance of the production renders something unique in the interpretation of the drama.

The interpretation of a written text and the function that the stage play and the screenplay serve provide another useful perspective from which we may examine differences in the two forms. At the heart of the stage drama is the text. The actors, and more specifically the dialogue and stage directions that guide their performances, provide the center of focus for both the director and audience. In film, the function of the screenplay is more variable, ranging from the barest outline of action to detailed script. But even in its most detailed and refined form, the film script has an essentially visual base, guiding the director in the selection and arrangement of units of action from varying perspectives. Here the actors are only one of many elements that the director considers in the creation of the scene. They in fact may not be present at all, and yet the "drama" will continue. There's a great deal going on in the opening sequence of Kubrick's *Dr. Strangelove* (the "mating" of two jets) or the doomsday closing of Kramer's *On the Beach* without the aid of actors.

In theater, the director places the play in the hands, or more accurately in the voice by way of the line readings, of the performer. Theater requires actors for the meaning and progression of the play. Film, on the other hand, may ignore the actor and make a "star" of either the setting or some inanimate objects. Through lighting, camera positioning, and sound, but mostly by use of the close-up camera, an object or set detail may "upstage" the actor and even steal the scene. The ticking clock in *High Noon*, the burning sled in *Citizen Kane*, and countless unanswered telephones in Hitchcock's films are among the many examples.

The way characters experience an action or think is frequently a part of

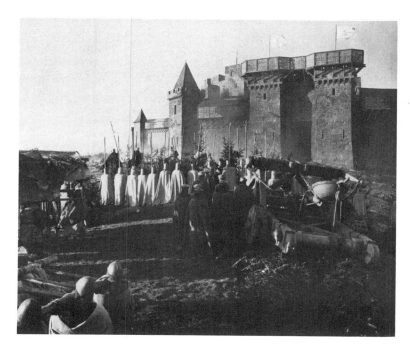

Figure 8-1   *Macbeth* (1971—British). One of the more original conceptions of Shakespeare's *Macbeth* to reach the screen was Roman Polanski's 1971 Columbia/Playboy production. The visual spectacle of Birnam Wood moving toward Macbeth's castle was easily executed on the screen.

both stage and screen drama. The traditional means of suggesting such subjective experience on the stage is necessarily through language and more specifically through the use of the aside or soliloquy. Filmmakers are capable of conveying mental reality or the characters' inner world quite effectively without the aid of the actors themselves—even if they are excluded from the scene entirely. In such instances, the camera doubles for the actors and may even become the star, as it does in the scenes from the Winter Garden trapeze in Dupont's *Variety* or during space travel in George Lucas' *Star Wars*.

Yet such alternatives in film do not preclude the possibility of great screen performances. When screenplay and director allow, the screen actor, abetted by the appropriate placement of the camera, can take advantage of various cinematic conventions and steal the show. The long runs of the camera employed by directors as otherwise diverse as Chaplin, Rossellini, Bergman, Cassavetes, Jancsó, and Altman call for sustained acting performances, often in close-up. Bergman has dwelled on the magnificently expressive face of Liv Ullmann in many films (see Fig. 4–15 and 8–2), and she has rarely failed to give a complex, moving performance based on such subtleties as a look in the eyes and a furrow in the brow, the impact of which would largely be lost on theatrical audiences. Indeed, Ullmann's range of expressions is so great that Bergman frequently turned to it in his *Scenes from a Marriage* (1973) to indicate passages of time; instead of relying on tried-and-true devices such as fade-outs and "X Years Later" title cards, Bergman would cut from a shot of Ullmann expressing one emotion to a shot of her expressing a completely different one. The audience quickly learns that each emotional clash, such as of Ullmann ecstatic in one shot and weeping in the next, signifies a major shift in time. Ullmann's work here and elsewhere is only one example of the ways that the screen has provided a showcase for the talents of great performers.

Perhaps the most obvious difference between film and theater has to do with the environments in which their actions take place. The physical restrictions of the stage contrast markedly with the range and flexibility of the film setting;

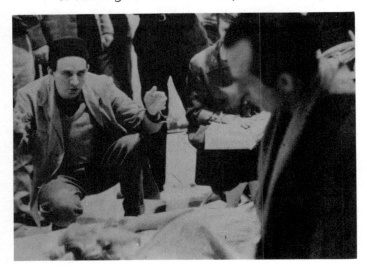

Figure 8-2   Sweden's Ingmar Bergman is one of the few directors who frequently employ long runs of the camera and require their actors to give relatively sustained performances.

yet if art thrives on its limitations, as many aestheticians argue, then film may not necessarily hold the advantage. Aside from the implications of the thrust stage and audience participation in some modern theaters, the form has traditionally used the stage as a performance area for the actors, the proscenium arch as a frame, and the curtain line as a divider between the real world of the spectator and the illusory one of the actors. In comparison with film, the stage is limited in its ability to make shifts in time and space. This distinction has at times been overstated, but it remains a fundamental difference in the ways directors in film and theater stage actions, handle transitions in time and space, use details to convey information, and create *mise-en-scène*. The issue of settings is at the heart of the ethos of the two forms: the sense of realism we as spectators experience as part of a theater or film audience.

SCREEN REALISM
AND THEATRICAL ILLUSION

The distinctions between stage and screen just outlined form the basis for what we might term *screen realism* and *theatrical illusion*. Susan Sontag has stated that "theatre deploys artifice while cinema is committed to reality."[3] In deploying artifice, however, the creator in theater is still involved in the imitation of real human thought, action, and interaction; in other words the artifice is an allusion to or interpretation of the real world. In actual practice, each form has realistic and artificial qualities. As already outlined, film has a particular affinity for physical reality and thrives on detail, yet its performers are only shadows on the screen and its directors have frequently relied on camera and editing trickery and special-effects wizardry.

On the other hand, theater employs flesh-and-blood actors and follows more closely the unities of time and space (and therefore might be regarded as more "realistic"), yet it requires its audience to accept a considerable number of conventions that simply would not work in film. Our point is that film *tends* toward realism while theater *tends* toward illusion, and that these general tendencies will affect the nature of each form's stories, the settings in which they occur, the characters who carry out the action, and the ways the spectators identify (or are denied identification) with them.

We have already dealt to some degree with the basic role of film and theater actors in Chapters 2 and 4, but beyond the performer-centered perspective is the association between performer and spectator. Aided by the close-up camera, screen performances tend to be individualized, marked by the peculiar features of performers and by nuances of gesture and expression. Stage actors depend mostly on conventionalized and stylized expression in both voice and movement. Acting on the screen frequently gives the "illusion of unstaged reality"; stage acting conveys the "reality" of role-playing. This aesthetic distance and recognition of role-playing permit the stage actor to portray a wider range of roles. Just as Elizabethan audiences accepted men playing women's parts, we would have little problem today accepting a 30-year-old actor portraying King Lear on the stage, as long as the actor, in suitable makeup, possessed the abilities and presence required for the role. That same actor would have much more difficulty convincing film audiences of his veracity as an aged monarch, however, because the close-up camera would reveal as false those items that theater audiences readily accept: the makeup, the wig, the young actor's approximation of an old man's demeanor. As Kracauer has suggested, film actors are more dependent on their natural physical appearances than their theater counterparts.[4]

Sontag's distinction between artifice and reality becomes the most apparent with regard to setting. On occasion the theater reaches for naturalistic detail to provide an appropriate atmosphere for its action but has little chance of competing with film in this regard. The theatrical setting is acknowledged, filled out, and interpreted in its larger context by the mind's eye and then allowed to take a back seat to the performance. The film setting, because of its verisimilitude and propensity for change, is constantly reasserting itself and may compete with the players as the star of the film. In films such as Malick's *Days of Heaven* and Kubrick's *Barry Lyndon*, which respectively feature Texas wheat fields rippling gently in the wind like ocean waves and the rolling rocky countryside of Ireland, it often succeeds.

The way the viewer relates to the action or the nature of identification finally separates the film from the theater experience. As the more literary of the forms, theater tends to be verbally oriented; film, more dependent on visual communication, is more action oriented. Theater asks us to suspend disbelief, imagine and share ideas; film asks us to relax, surrender to the detail it can provide, and experience the recreation of an action. For all its ideological intent, *The Battleship Potemkin* puts us directly into the action on board the cruiser and on the Odessa Steps. In *Oedipus Rex*, on the other hand, the playwright focuses our attention more on the broodings and self-examination of the protagonist than on the limited action of the play.

Finally, we discover a significant difference in the aging process of material created for the two forms. Movies, because they provide a relatively permanent record of a past action, age rather quickly. Even such classic films as *The Grapes of Wrath* and *Rules of the Game*, which express timeless sentiments, are tied to specific and concrete detail. As a result, they come to us as echoes out of the past despite their universal themes. The theater is continually providing fresh perspective and a contemporary context for old ideas. The theatrical performance of a play of some substance therefore offers a fresh interpretation of timeless issues and can be as current as today's headlines. Films grow old, while plays—good plays, at any rate—are in a constant state of rebirth.

THE ADAPTATION

The foregoing discussion of the historical links between film and theater and the disparity in styles and functions that frequently marks the two forms begs the question: "How can a work designed for theater successfully make the transition to film?" In writing on "Film and Theater," Susan Sontag has stated, "Because one can make a movie 'of' a play but not a play 'of' a movie, cinema had an early but, I should argue, fortuitous connection with the stage."[5] The observation that film has something to do with theater (as well as literature) is supported by more than the historical accident of their association, however. Throughout the history of the medium, films have found their inspiration, form, and even their detail in the stage work.

The screen adaptation of a work written for the stage continues to offer new challenges for the modern filmmaker and a new battleground for the film critics. The issues surrounding *canned theater*, as the adaptation is sometimes termed, are relatively simple. Critics opposing the screen adaptation, either generally or by individual example, argue that film's need to render everything in concrete and visual terms violates the essence of drama: the theatrical illusion. They frequently find the screen adaptation overblown, overdressed, and sacrificing the discipline and beauty of the *text* for the ease and bravura of cinematic device. Wilfrid Sheed wrote of the Franco Zeffirelli production of *The Taming of the Shrew* (1967) that, "There is no excuse for turning this domestic trifle into a costume extravaganza. . . . *The Shrew* is a difficult, cranky little play that has to be done to scale, if it is to be done at all."[6] Theater producer-director Tyrone Guthrie suggests that "while it is pleasant to see clearly, in the movies, especially since wide screen came in, we tend to get too much of an eyeful."[7] Guthrie is among many artists who see the requirements of economics and mass appeal as well as technology bringing about a debasement in film and in the adaptation in particular.

On the other side of the argument, both critics and creators have seen the adaptation as a natural, useful, and aesthetically valid extension of film's function. They sometimes base their argument for the adaptation on the same works as those used to challenge it. Hollis Alpert says of the Zeffirelli *Shrew*, "It has turned out to be not only a quite literally gorgeous piece of filmmaking, but a quintessential rendering of the play that could hardly have been dreamed of in the past."[8]

Filmmakers usually make the case for the adaptation on the grounds of film's potential for "opening up the play"; that is, using the plasticity offered through controls of camera and editing in particular to free the play from the tyranny of language, and to give a fuller rendering of the drama through a more flexible, complete or "realistic" interpretation. Critics will sometimes credit a film for its superior rendering of the text through line readings that are spoken under optimum conditions. Yet the major case for the adaptation does not rest on the basis of line reading. Recognizing the fundamental differences between the two forms, the proponents base the success of the screen adaptation on the filmmaker's ability to find cinematic equivalents for theatrical means of expression. In Susan Sontag's words, "The success of a movie version of plays is measured by the extent to which the script rearranges and displaces the action and deals less than respectfully with the spoken text."[9]

The 1957 screen version of *Macbeth*, which director Akira Kurosawa entitled *Throne of Blood*, was a particularly daring adaptation, not only because of its rearrangement and displacement but also because of the reverence in which the original is held (see Fig. 8–3). The reception that critics afforded the film was mixed. J. Blumenthal wrote in *Sight and Sound*: "Akira Kurosawa's *Throne of Blood* is the only work, to my knowledge, that has ever completely succeeded in transforming a play of Shakespeare into a film."[10] Stanley Kauffmann was respectful of the imaginative Kurosawa approach but wrote: "The film's inherent contradiction is that it continually reminds us of *Macbeth* and thus the wide difference from it; it becomes a moderately interesting curiosity rather than an artistic experience."[11]

Figure 8-3 *Throne of Blood* (1957—Japanese). A freer adaptation of *Macbeth* than Polanski's 1971 version was created by Akira Kurosawa under the title *Throne of Blood*. Kurosawa preserved the Shakespearean play's basic characters and action, but set them within the context of the feudal wars of twelfth century Japan.

Besides those making the case for the adaptation on the basis of cinematic interpretation there are those, such as André Bazin, who see filmed theater as an alternative means of "staging a play" rather than "adapting a subject." The point of the argument here is the ability of the film medium to bring living theater to a vastly wider audience. "Shakespeare now has a popular audience no one prior to 1930 could ever have dreamed of," wrote Alpert.[12] In writing on filmed theater, Pauline Kael chides its detractors when she says, "Filmed plays are often denigrated, somewhat dishonestly, by people who learn a little cant about what is said to be proper to the film medium and forget about the pleasure they've been getting from filmed plays all their lives."[13] Faith in film (and television) as a valid means of bringing theater to a virtually limitless audience is dramatically illustrated by the program undertaken by the British Broadcasting Company to film and broadcase the entire repertoire of Shakespeare plays over a six-year period. It has been calculated that more people will see a single telecast of one of the plays than the total of theater audiences who have seen the work performed since it was written.

But canned theater does not preclude the opportunity for creative cinema using stage works. Directors such as Laurence Olivier (*Hamlet, Henry V, Richard III*), William Wyler (*The Little Foxes*), and Jack Clayton (*Look Back in Anger*) have used film to do more than provide a medium for wider distribution of living theater. They have met the challenge, at least in part, of creative interpretation according to the affinities and characteristics of the medium. At the same time they have left themselves open to close scrutiny and possible censure concerning their responsibilities to the work from which the film was adapted or on which, however loosely, it was based. The degree to which the filmmaker deserves censure for rearranging, editing, opening up, or otherwise taking liberties with the original text will depend largely on intent and the recognized relationship between the original and the screen version. The film's opening credits will often announce this relationship: "based on," "adapted from," "a screen version of," "from an idea suggested by." Franco Zeffirelli certainly invited comparison and the slings and arrows of the critics when he chose to have a title credit introduce "William Shakespeare's *Romeo and Juliet.*"

Whether stated or not, a filmmaker's indebtedness to another work will come under scrutiny in direct proportion to the viewer's familarity with the original. The reception from there on will vary according to the viewer's or critic's disposition toward or against canned theater generally, and the extent to which theatrical convention or cinematic invention are held in esteem. Laurence Olivier protected both his flanks in bringing *Henry V* to the screen. He took his cue from Shakespeare's apology for the cramped and inadequate features of the "wooden O" (the Globe Theater), and the invitation to use one's imagination in recreating the "vasty fields of France." He let his camera function as both recording and creative instrument. By way of camera movement and editing, he literally lifted the action out of the confines of the Globe and transported it to a setting that better accommodated the action and also the film's ability to deal with that action. At the same time, he maintained a theatrical style in setting, decor, and even in action and speech that preserved the integrity of the work as a piece of theater. Such a mixed-media approach is clearly not a solution to all adaptations; it was even here only partially successful. It does, however, show that the qualities of film and theater are not mutually exclusive and may be found at work within a single filmed play, whatever its original incarnation may have been.

FILM'S INFLUENCE ON THEATER

The longstanding notion of a one-way relationship between film and theater is understandable; the instances of films acting as the inspiration or blueprint for stage plays seem relatively rare. Nevertheless, there is evidence of film exerting an influence on modern theater. The dedication of much contemporary theater to naturalism—in playwriting, acting, and decor—appears an obvious link, but the periodic swing in theater toward realism and naturalism predates the arrival of motion pictures and suggests a tendency that the cinematic approach may reinforce but which we could hardly cite as a causal factor.

The basic design and progression of many modern plays provide stronger evidence of film's influence on theater. The free flow of modern stage action often suggests the plasticity in time and space for which film is noted. Through lighting, scrims, and quickly modified settings, the theater becomes less anchored to the conventional scene shift carried out with the lowering of the scene curtain. Plays as diverse in style as *Death of a Salesman* and *Equus* have experimented with the flashback, long a staple of screen storytelling. "Blackouts," a popular format for stringing together comic vignettes in variety shows of the 1930s, has its modern counterpart in the free association of stage actions having thematic, though not necessarily temporal or spatial, relationships. Theatrical directors have accomplished such vignette collages by controlling lighting and changing settings rapidly, and the effects closely resemble the kind of plastic expression that filmmakers bring to their medium through editing.

One might look at the means of moving the stage action closer to the spectators, such as the thrust stage, as a link with film's most basic device: the close-up. Here again, the link is speculative, as periods in theater which predate

(A)

Figure 8-4 (A, B, & C) A major effort to bring stage works to the screen was undertaken in 1973 and 1974 under the name of the American Film Theatre. The productions which more closely resembled filmed plays rather than screen adaptations, were shown in movie theaters on a reserved seating, limited engagement basis. Fig. A: Eugene O'Neill's *The Iceman Cometh* (1973—American) presented Lee Marvin, Fredric March, and Robert Ryan playing under the direction of John Frankenheimer. Fig. B: Anton Chekhov's *Three Sisters* (1970—British); released in the United States, 1974) was directed by Laurence Olivier and featured Alan Bates along with Olivier and Joan Plowright. Fig. C: *Rhinoceros* (1974—American) starred Zero Mostel, Gene Wilder, and Karen Black in this adaptation of Eugene Ionesco's absurdist play, directed by Tom O'Horgan.

(B)

(C)

film have shown attempts to abandon the traditional placement of performers and audience on either side of the proscenium. Still, the coming together of many "cinematic"styles and techniques in today's theater, together with the movement of writers and directors back and forth between the two forms, suggests that the new look in theater has something more than a casual and coincidental relationship with filmic means of expression.

A notable example of a modern playwright whose works bear the influence of cinema is Tennessee Williams. He has freely admitted his lifelong fascination with movies, and, as many other major twentieth-century playwrights have done, he worked as a Hollywood scriptwriter—in his case, briefly during the early 1940s. During his stint in "Tinsel Town," he completed an original screenplay entitled *The Gentleman Caller,* which he offered to Metro-Goldwyn-Mayer with the prediction that the potential film would run two or three times as long as *Gone With the Wind.* After the M-G-M production chiefs rejected the script (claiming a lack of interest in making another Southern epic), Williams eventually reworked *The Gentleman Caller* into the play for which he is best remembered: *The Glass Menagerie.*

The theatrical version of *The Glass Menagerie* stands as a rather strange example of a play exhibiting filmic characteristics. Williams combined his particular fondness for silent movies with the lessons learned under Erwin Piscator at the New School for Social Research to create a script with techniques akin to the multimedia devices of Piscator and Bertolt Brecht. *Menagerie's* most expressionistic device is also the most filmic: a screen on which various words and images would be projected while the play progressed. Williams' apologia for the screen, which was never actually used during the play's Broadway incarnation, made the device sound justifiable:

> The legend or image upon the screen will strengthen the effect of what is merely allusion in the writing and allow the primary point to be made more simply and lightly than if the entire responsibility were on the spoken lines. Aside from this structural value, I think the screen will have a definite emotional appeal. . . . A free, imaginative use of light can be of enormous value in giving a mobile, plastic quality to plays of a more or less static nature.[14]

As notable as this idea sounds, however, the projection of images and verbal commentary throughout the play was unfortunately an ill-chosen cinematic effect. As Gerald Weales has argued:

> Unless [Williams'] purpose in *Mengerie* is to mock his characters (which hardly seems likely), his device would be a failure, for the screened comments seem designed to reduce all the scenes—even the tenderest—to ludicrous parodies. For instance, in the dinner scene, when Laura, panic-stricken at the idea of sitting down with the gentleman caller, drags herself unwillingly toward the table, Williams calls for this legend: "TERROR!" As she stumbles and Amanda and Tom cry out, the screen says, "AH!" This would put us back with the Gish sisters in the silent movies and not, as the device suggests, with Piscator and Brecht on the edge of the Epic Theater.[15]

A number of Williams' later plays have scenes that use cinematic devices to better effect. As an example, Williams occasionally employed the spotlight as a means of focusing attention on a character in much the same way a filmmaker would use a close-up. As Catherine describes her seduction in *Suddenly Last Summer*, for example, Williams called for these directions: "The lights have changed, the surrounding area has dimmed out and a hot white spot is focused" on her.[16] A spotlight was used similarly in *Cat on a Hot Tin Roof*: to follow and focus attention on Maggie, the lead character.

A final link between film and theater—one we might regard as a true mix of the forms—is the combination of live action and film action within the same production. Williams used such a mixture in his play *Sweet Bird of Youth* during a scene in which Chance Wayne, trapped in a building, abruptly encounters his foe. As Williams described the moment: "Chance walks slowly downstage, his head . . . in the narrow flickering beam of light. As he walks downstage, there suddenly appears on the big TV screen, which is the whole back of the stage, the image of Boss Finley."[17] Such mixed or multimedia approaches remain more of an occasional experiment, however, than an accepted form of expression. The intermedia experience is part of the theory of expanded cinema but for now is relegated largely to special showcases, such as cultural festivals and expositions found in world's fairs and Walt Disney's Epcot Center, and the occasional experimental happening.

NOTES

[1]André Levison, "The Nature of Cinema," *Theatre Arts Monthly* XIII, 9, (September 1929), p. 689.

[2]In his *Theory of Film*, Siegfried Kracauer noted that "any genuinely photographic portrait tends to sustain the impression of unstaged reality" (p. 93).

[3]Susan Sontag, "Film and Theatre," in *Film Theory and Criticism: Introductory Readings,* 2nd ed., eds. Gerald Mast and Marshall Cohen (New York: Oxford University Press, 1979), p. 361.

[4]Kracauer, *Theory of Film,* p. 96.

[5]Sontag, "Film and Theatre," p. 360.

[6]Wilfred Sheed, "A Grim Pursuit," in *Film 67/68,* eds. Richard Schickel and John Simon (New York: Simon & Schuster, 1968), p. 168.

[7]Tyrone Guthrie, *New York Times Magazine,* April 29, 1962, p. 46.

[8]Hollis Alpert, "Gorgeous Film-making," in *Film 67/68,* pp. 166–68.

[9]Sontag, "Film and Theatre," p. 364.

[10]J. Blumenthal, *Sight and Sound* 34:4 (Autumn 1965), p. 190.

[11]Stanley Kauffmann, *A World on Film* (New York: Harper & Row, 1966), p. 378.

[12]Alpert, "Gorgeous Film-making," p. 166.

[13]Pauline Kael, "Filmed Theatre," *The New Yorker,* Jan. 11, 1969, p. 60.

[14]Tennessee Williams, *The Glass Menagerie* (New York: ND, 1966), p. x.

[15]Gerald Weales, *Tennessee Williams,* University of Minnesota Pamphlets on American Writers, no. 53. (Minneapolis: University of Minnesota Press, 1965), p. 33.

[16]Tennessee Williams, *Suddenly Last Summer* (New York: ND, 1958), p. 81.

[17]Tennessee Williams, *Three Plays of Tennessee Williams: The Rose Tattoo, Camino Real, Sweet Bird of Youth* (New York: New Directions, 1964), p. 269.

9

FILM AND TELEVISION

THE MEDIA COMPARED

A study of film styles and functions today is incomplete without a survey of its chief competitor and primary consumer: television. The competition and commingling of the two media and the effect that the two industries have had on one another, on the nature of their product and on their audiences, are far-reaching, complex, and even today not completely understood. Even with the insight that over 25 years of association provides, remarkably little attention has been given to how the coming of television has influenced film form and function and how film and filmmaking have in turn affected the early growth of television.

Having set down a major theory of film, Rudolf Arnheim in 1935 made "A Forecast of Television" in which he suggested some of the potentials of "the new gadget," which he found "magical and mysterious." He saw television as an extension of radio in its ability to provide documentary information and "of making us witness immediately [to] what is going on in the wide world around us," and of giving the viewer the "feeling for the multiplicity of what is happening simultaneously in different places."[1] At the same time he was heralding television as a means of "cultural transportation," Arnheim was precluding any role for the medium beyond "a mere instrument of transmission, which does not offer new means for the artistic interpretation of reality—as radio and film did." Although Arnheim, the film theorist, failed to mention the potential links between film and television, he did recognize key qualities of the new medium that quickly set its course as a competitor with film as part of the cult of sensory stimulation, and its role as a direct experience which could, in Arnheim's words, either "enrich us" or "put our minds to sleep."[2]

At the time of Arnheim's forecast, television was moving from laboratory experiment to fledgling broadcast medium with limited but regular telecasting beginning in 1939. The moratorium on television growth during World War II coincided with film prosperity and box-office records. This situation changed quickly in the late forties and early fifties, however, with a rapid growth in the television industry reflected in the number of TV stations, number of hours of telecasting daily, and number of sets purchased. This boom coincided with a precipitous decline in both film viewing and the production schedules of the major studios. During this period television was establishing itself as a competitor to the film industry and an alternative form of entertainment. It was, in Kracauer's words "offering at least some of the satisfaction which make, or made so many people crave the movies."[3] It was also providing the immediacy in documentary reporting that Arnheim predicted. (The first glimpse of television for many Americans was the telecasting of the World Series in the mid-forties.) Television was also providing a more casual and intimate look at events, both staged and real, that had to this time been the domain of the motion picture. Central to the competition between film and television was the fact that home entertainment was more readily accessible, in greater variety of styles, in ever increasing blocks of time and, after the initial investment in the set, without cost. Although film still had its own unique qualities to offer audiences and ultimately the TV industry as well, it could no longer compete favorably with television as a form of mass entertainment. This failure is reflected in the statistics that mark the end of "Hollywood's Golden Era" and the establishment of the three commercial television networks as corporate giants by the mid-fifties.

At this point, through the early fifties, the relationship between the two media reached a critical stage. Unable to stem the tide of TV's popularity with conventional fare, the film industry sought ways to lure audiences back into theaters by providing what the home screen denied them. Intimacy and immediacy were qualities that TV provided, but it could not offer the scope, color, spectacle, and infinite variety of detail that movies occasionally displayed. The movie industry turned toward these production qualities and subject matter considered "too progressive" for home consumption during this critical period. Films had to be larger, more elaborate, and a bit daring to bring audiences, if only occasionally, back to the theaters. In the words of Stefan Kanfer in his article on "The Shock of Freedom in Film" for *Time* magazine, television had "all but taken over Hollywood's former function of providing placebo entertainment."[4] The Hollywood "B picture" had become as much of an anachronism as the short subject and movie newsreel. Feature films of the fifties were increasingly costly, elaborate in design, daring in subject, and fewer in number.

THE MEDIA COMBINED

Through the first decade of commercial broadcasting, television explored most of the basic program formats that have evolved as staples today. News, public affairs,

and documentary programming; musical variety, celebrity, and audience participation varieties; and the comic and dramatic narrative forms were all developing
a style and cultivating an audience. But television had an insatiable appetite for
material that could no longer be met through live programming. With video tape
still several years away, broadcasters turned to film to supplement programming
originating in the studio or from location pickups. Besides helping fill out the program schedule, film was able to surmount the technical limitations imposed by
the confines of the television studio and equipment, particularly in dramatic programming requiring a greater range in setting and flexibility in narrative design.
Scripts needing more expansive outdoor settings (westerns and sea adventures
come immediately to mind) could now be accommodated by filmed segments. Besides opening up the setting for the drama, the filming of parts or all of the drama
also allowed greater flexibility in narrative design, with film editing and principles
of montage proving their superiority in storytelling over the TV studio and electronic means of scene building. At the time, electronic wizardry could not compete
with film editing in providing dramatic impact through careful composition, sub-
tlety of shot relationship, and rhythm of cutting. Film also proved to be more
desirable for programming requiring a more sophisticated range and delineation
in lighting effects. Lighting in television, particularly in this period, was designed
for the set as a whole and concerned with adequate resolution for acceptably clear
transmission. There was little chance for the subtle forms of lighting to accommodate individual shots that have become routine in film composition. The use
of film that could be shot on the Hollywood sound stages or backlots also helped
free the television studio for rehearsal and telecasting of live programming.

By 1952 the formal marriage of film and television took place with Columbia Pictures forming the first of the television subsidiaries among the major
studios: Screen Gems. This was followed by the establishment of other TV units
on the Hollywood back lots and the merger of film and television units to produce
both program material and commercials for home consumption. Filmed program
material was expanded to include complete 30-, 60-, and 90-minute segments as
part of regular syndicated series. In this way film became the mainstay of much
of the on-going prime-time programming in a variety of series, particularly westerns and dramatic series requiring flexibility in setting and the exterior locations
that the western, crime drama, and adventure intrigues usually require. News and
public service programs, variety shows, quiz and other audience participation formats, and situation comedies continued to use the television studio set and the
live TV camera. With the arrival of video tape, they too joined the filmed programs
as a prerecorded mode that could be produced in segments, in multiple takes, be
edited (though less fluidly), and be stored on the shelf for future use. The advent
of video tape did not substantially affect the type of programming that had become
a staple for film. The prerecorded program replaced much of the live telecasting
originating in the studio. Exceptions include late-night comedy programs produced live, such as NBC's *Saturday Night Live* and ABC's *Fridays*, and the television news, documentary, sports, and special events fields, where new lightweight
and flexible "mini-cams" helped facilitate video recording of on-the-spot events
for either live or delayed telecasting.

By 1956 a further tie between film and television was established with the
release of more than 2,500 Hollywood films produced before 1948 for showing on

television. This accumulation of both major films and "B pictures" produced in the 20-year period since the arrival of sound (there has never been a significant market for silent features) initially provided schedule-filler material for local stations. "Late Shows," "Late Late Shows," "Matinee Movies," and "Milkman Matinees" flourished. By 1961 the networks joined the local stations to provide prime-time airing of major films that could now be seen in color by an ever increasing number of viewers. By the end of the decade, a new type of film had joined the filmed series and anthologies, commercial, and transplanted Hollywood feature films. It was the made-for-TV movie, which aspired originally not only to supplement the movies that had come from Hollywood studios but also to provide an initial showcase for films that would later be put into regular theatrical distribution. Although the made-for-TV movie has never gotten beyond home viewing in the American domestic market,[5] it continues to be a regular part of the television menu. Occasionally made-for-TV films are used as pilots for weekly TV series; such popular television fare as *Ironside*, *The Love Boat*, and *Fantasy Island* all began as TV movies.

More significantly, the "mini-series"—another made-for-TV format—has emerged in recent years. A mini-series can be as long as 12 to 16 hours in length and extend over several days or even weeks of programming. The mini-series is different from traditional continuing series (*Bonanza*, *I Love Lucy*, and *Charlie's Angels*, for example) in that it has a fixed termination; it does not go on indefinitely until low ratings force its cancellation. It differs from theatrical films and other made-for-TV movies because of its expanded length, which is much more conducive for adapting a novel. As it turns out, most mini-series are indeed adaptations of novels, since their increased lengths enable them to accommodate many more of the novels' narrative threads than can be done in conventional two-hour films. Television has enjoyed some of its greatest successes with the mini-series. Despite occasional potboilers such as *Aspen* and *Pearl*, the mini-series has enormously enhanced television's reputation as a purveyor of quality material. Spurred by such well-made British mini-series as *Edward the VII*, *I, Claudius*, and the pioneering *Forsythe Saga*, American television has produced high-quality, lavishly mounted mini-series such as *Roots*, *Roots II*, *Holocaust*, *Masada*, *Shogun*, and *The Winds of War*. These showcase productions, all of which have earned critical praise and exceedingly high ratings, rival Hollywood's best work, and they have gone a long way toward dispelling television's image as a medium of low-brow programming.

It has become increasingly difficult to distinguish between film and television today, for a variety of reasons. First is the relative amounts of production money set aside for films and television programs. The rule of thumb used to be that low-budgeted material was produced for television and high-budgeted for film. This is no longer true; we have seen a number of relatively low-budgeted efforts appear in theaters (for example, 1979's *Breaking Away* and *Going in Style*), while many television mini-series are extravagant, multimillion-dollar productions. A second reason for the difficulty of separating film and TV has to do with the fact that now many production companies—particularly the smaller, independent ones—make both films and television programs. An example is the Lorimar Company, which has produced not only television's *Eight Is Enough*, *The Waltons*, *Dallas*, and *Knot's Landing* but also such theatrical films as *Cruising* (1980), *The Postman Always Rings Twice* (1981), *S.O.B.* (1981) and *Victory* (1981). A third factor obscuring the division between the media is the fact that movies made for television in America are frequently shown as theatrical movies in other countries. A fourth factor is the rise of video cassettes, video discs, and pay-TV. It is possible for a viewer to purchase a prerecorded movie on cassette or disc, uncut and free of commercials, for viewing at home, just as it is possible to view relatively recent films, likewise uninterrupted and uncut, via various pay-TV services such as Home Box Office, Showcase, Preview, and Spotlight. Currently, movies shown on pay-TV are at least six months old, but it is likely that first-run films will eventually be presented by these services.[6] For these and other reasons, film and television are growing ever closer together. As suggested by industry-watcher James Monaco, discussing film and television separately will in the future make as much sense as discussing separately the hardback and paperback book publishing industries.[7] The most practical distinction between the media in the future will probably not be one of content or programming but of the fundamental modes of exhibition: in-home versus theatrical viewing.

VIEWING COMMERCIAL FEATURES ON TELEVISION

Of the many results of the competition and eventual cooperation between the film and television media, one of the more intriguing but least understood is the nature of the film-viewing experience when we see commercial features on the home screen. The physical effects of the move from theater to TV screen are fairly obvious. The average TV image is only 1/200 the size of the average movie screen. This reduction in size, coupled with the difference in resolution between the cinematographic and the electronic images (which is central to Marshall McLuhan's designation of TV as the cooler of the two media)[8] raises problems in composition. The television image can offer neither the scope of the big screen's broad vistas nor the complexity in design and concentration of visual detail that the image in the movie theater affords. The grandeur of the Monument Valley setting that served as a backdrop for several of John Ford's westerns and the exhilaration of space travel in *2001: A Space Odyssey* are largely sacrificed in the move from theater to TV screen. In *Citizen Kane*, Orson Welles revealed a lifetime's accumulation of possessions by tracking the camera over the contents of a Xanadu storeroom. This concentration of detail is largely lost when the film appears on television. Lost also is the detail of the outer edges of the film image by the "cropping" effect that takes place in the transposition. Film's greater facility for scope, spectacle, and detail prompted the film industry to compete with television by exploiting these affinities in the fifties. With the showing of these same films on television, particularly those produced in a wide-screen format such as CinemaScope, Todd-AO, and VistaVision, the differences are further amplified and much of the dramatic impact—to say nothing of the original compositions—is lost to the television viewer. What were assets in big-screen projection become liabilities when the movie reaches the TV picture tube. An audience watching a splashy wide-screen production such as *Seven Brides for Seven Brothers* or *Oklahoma* (1955) on television may be seeing as little as one-half of the original movie, with the other portion lost to cropping. While the portion that remains is ostensibly the most important part, it is obvious that such a televised wide-screen movie is not the same film as the original, since so much material has been lost and since the audience's freedom to choose what part of the frame to look at has been narrowed considerably. Since wide-screen films continue to be produced today, it is worth asking if filmmakers take television's standard 3 by 4 ratio into account when filming. They are undoubtedly aware that their works will eventually show up on the small screen, and it seems likely they would locate the most important elements of their compositions in the middle of the frame, to preserve the integrity of their films as much as possible when they make that inevitable transition to television.

Films made specifically for television are usually tailored to that medium's greater intimacy and more modest dimensions. With an eye to the eventual television airing of films, some producers of commercial features today try to have it both ways with a kind of intimate spectacle that they hope will work on both large and small screens. *The Godfather* (1972) and *The Godfather, Part II* (1974) illustrate a combination of spectacle and intimacy that allowed them to meet with reasonable success the dimensions and requirements of both media. (Indeed, the director of the *Godfather* films, Francis Ford Coppola, edited these movies together to form a three-part mini-series designed especially for TV, which included footage never shown in film theaters.) No such accommodation is evident in many other Hollywood films, however, particularly those designed to lure viewers away from the home screen. In fact, the exploitation of scope, spectacle, color, detail, and in general the larger as well as the more intricate features of cinematography, creates additional problems in the transfer to video. While some progress has been made in the development of large-screen television and the medium's resolution problems, the act of putting the expanses of *Lawrence of Arabia* and *Star Wars* or the detail in composition and decor of a *Barry Lyndon* or a *Citizen Kane* on TV continues to be a bit like using murals to adorn postage stamps.

Another of the more obvious differences in viewing films on television rather than at the theater is in the controls exercised by way of editing to expurgate material deemed unsuitable for home consumption, or simply to make the film fit an available time slot. Such physical modifications often have the effect of not only jeopardizing the continuity and flow of the work but also risking ambiguity and confusion in meaning. The deletion of both action and dialogue from films that have gone through the "adapted for television" process helps further separate the two viewing experiences and frequently puts the integrity of the work in doubt.

A far less noticeable factor that marks the move of films to television is the psychology and mental set of the viewer. Psychologists and film theorists have long recognized and described the isolation and absorption of the film viewer into the action on the screen when films are viewed in the theater setting. Hugo Mauerhofer, in his essay "Psychology of Film Experience," describes it this way:

> These psychological elements—namely, the boredom lurking continually on the brink of the *Cinema Situation*, the increased readiness of the *imagination*, the uncritical, voluntary *passivity*, and lastly, the anonymity which guides the spectator into his most private sphere—these are the mainstays of the "Psychology of Film Experience."[9]

Considerably less attention has been given to the differences between this experience and that of viewing films on TV. But we are learning that the differences in composition and resolution of images in film and on television already mentioned render the televised film the more casual, less absorbing experience. While the TV image is doing less to command our attention, there are usually a variety of other stimuli competing for attention when we watch a film on television in the home, neighborhood tavern, or other public gathering place. The room is usually lit, which results in less than total absorption in the "luminous rectangle." Added to this are the various sounds and sights that compete for our attention— conversation, telephone, and the general motion and din of household or public-room activity. Such potentially distracting external "noise" is compounded by internal intrusion when the film gives way to the commercial message. The careful attention given by a filmmaker to establishing mood and tempo and in providing for the most complete absorption in the screen drama can be neutralized in an instant by the break for a commercial, public-service announcement, or station identification. Getting the viewer back into the drama once the film resumes is a slow process and often fails to provide the same degree of involvement that preceded the break. This is particularly true when the commercial content itself fosters identification and lingering preoccupation with the sales message and its setting.

But what has probably come to be the most significant factor marking the psychology of viewing films at home is the more casual way we relate to TV generally. Going to see a film in a theater is still something of an event. It requires some planning, investment in time and money, and physical exertion to get to the theater. Viewing films on television requires no such commitment beyond the time it takes to watch the program or movie. We often come upon the film quite by chance, after it has already begun. Our attention is something less than undivided as we find ourselves engaged in a variety of other activities while keeping nominally in touch with basic exposition and progression. Subtleties of shot relationship, detail in design, composition, and a sense of *mise-en-scène* all become significantly diminished, partly the result of the physical limitations of telecasting and partly from our need to find activities to complement our viewing. Recognizing this "cool" relationship to the medium, creators of program material designed specifically for television will allow for the casual orientation and keep plot, dialogue, and visual design intimate, straightforward, and free of intricacies and subtleties. But the film fashioned primarily for large-screen viewing in the quiet dark of the theater is frequently put at a distinct disadvantage when competing with the traffic in household stimuli for our undivided attention.

Our casual attitude toward TV may also be due in part to cultural conditioning; we have heretofore always associated television with low-grade entertainment, and thus the medium is not worthy of our full attention. In other countries—most notably, Great Britain—television has long been considered a medium well above the level of mass-entertainment machine. In America, however, television enjoyed a "class" status only during its "Golden Age" of the early fifties, and it has again been striving for that status since the late seventies.

One way that film theater-owners have attempted to lure patrons into their movie houses is by providing them with a variety of viewing fare not unlike that offered by television. With the growth of multiplex theaters that feature usually two, four, or eight screens housed in the same facilities, it seems the exhibitors are trying to leave the impression that there is bound to be at least one film playing at these multiple-screen theaters that would attract a potential patron at any given moment. Concomitantly, it appears that these theater-owners are attempting to deemphasize the "event" nature of moviegoing in several ways: by scaling down the designs of theater interiors to their plainest and most functional levels, by offering discount admissions for twilight film showings, and by locating their theaters in or near large shopping malls. The implication is that the exhibitors want to make going to the movies an experience as casual and regular an event as going shopping, or, for that matter, watching television. As suggested previously, significant differences between the viewing experiences still remain. For example, once the theatrical-film viewers have committed themselves to a particular film, that's that; they do not have the luxury of moving back and forth between theaters as if they were watching television. Nevertheless, it seems clear that exhibitors have attempted to bring the theater and television-viewing experiences closer together, a situation that lends support to the assertion that the film and television industries as a whole are on the verge of becoming inseparable.

TV AND VISUAL PERCEPTION

In addition to being a carrier of film and a perpetuator of film stories and characters, television has become a conditioner of visual perception that has affected, and will doubtless continue to affect, the way we see images in both media. Two generations of film viewers have now been through a kind of basic training in visual perception by means of television. Such training has taught them to see and respond to images in a new way. Program material (along with commercials) has developed a style in visual design and pacing that is direct, streamlined, fast, and free of the encumbrances of transitional links and details in composition. It is worth noting that many of the older silent films—if viewed at their original filming speeds of 16 to 18 frames per second—seem very slowly paced by today's standards. Filmmakers back then believed that audiences could not apprehend visual information very quickly—a notion that seems rather quaint today. Partly to accommodate such conditioning today, particularly among younger viewers who have grown up with frenetically paced programs such as *Sesame Street*, and partly because they themselves have worked in television or are at least a part of the television age, film directors now are providing works with much of the frenetic speed and light of a television commercial. The trend began with films like Jean-Luc Godard's *Breathless* and Richard Lester's *Help!* and *A Hard Day's Night*, and it continues today with the momentum of rock music in films like *Saturday Night Fever, Heavy Traffic, Hair*, and *Grease*. The generation nurtured on the combination of television and rock music is prepared to experience film as sensory stimulus and environment rather than only as storytelling. Filmmakers have both the means and inclination to respond and show the way.

THE TELEVISION ADAPTATION

A chapter on film and television would not be complete without a discussion of the television adaptation. Just as the stage frequently provides a means for the dramatization of literary works, and film often becomes a showcase for adaptations from both literature and theater, so too does television become a medium by which works literary, dramatic, and cinematic are provided a new incarnation.

Early examples of stage and literary adaptations include such prestigious fare as the Hallmark Hall of Fame version of *Little Moon of Alban*, the NBC Opera Series, including *Amahl and the Night Visitors*, and the various productions of *Playhouse 90, Kraft Theater, Robert Montgomery Presents, Producer's Showcase*, and the *Philco Playhouse*. Most of these dramatic series drew from both established stage and literary works as well as those produced specifically for TV. The television mini-series, already discussed at some length in this chapter, depends heavily on literature in particular, as virtually all such productions are adaptations of blockbuster novels.

In addition to examining plays, novels, and short stories for inspiration and possible adaptation, American television producers have occasionally looked to TV programs produced in other countries. The Tandem Company's Bud Yorkin and Norman Lear successfully reworked a couple of British TV comedies titled *Til Death Do Us Part* and *Steptoe and Son* into the highly popular *All in the Family* and *Sanford and Son*, respectively. The Nicholl-Ross-West Company, formed by former Tandem executives, learned a lesson from Yorkin and Lear by likewise taking a British comedy hit, *Man About the House*, and creating the highly rated *Three's Company*.

A word needs to be said about television's affinity for the spoken word. It is easy to think of television as a visual medium, inasmuch as the TV camera has a hunger for physical reality like its motion-picture cousin. Yet the TV camera's appetite is not nearly as sharp. In terms of a faithful reproduction of physical reality, television's image-capturing and rendering abilities are comparatively inferior; subsequently, the medium depends a great deal more on verbal messages to sustain itself. Television would be severely handicapped if it lost its voice, much more so than cinema. In televison, especially American television, the verbal is constantly refining and interpreting the visual.[10] (The unremitting spiel of play-by-play sportscasters is a perfect example.) Visual and verbal work closely together, the verbal always explaining, filling in, and tying up any loose ends left by the visual. Because of TV's greater tolerance of language than film (indeed, the medium was first thought of as "radio with pictures"), plays and prose fiction that would easily become static and wordy in film have had successful television renderings and continue to provide a significant part of public television programming. The most ambitious project to date is the production of all Shakespeare's plays by the British Broadcasting Corporation and the Time-Life Corporation.

Television producers are less inclined to reproduce original screenplays for television, since the film itself—a known and often popular quantity—is usually available for airing. Between 1954 and 1957, NBC produced one-hour television versions of Hollywood movies on its *Lux Video Theatre*, but this is the exception rather than the rule. As is apparent to anyone who watches TV with any regularity, however, both film and television adaptations of stage and literary works appear frequently on TV schedules. More significant than the refurbishing of feature films for TV is the extent to which feature films have provided the inspiration, or perhaps more accurately, the visibility, for weekly television series. Series based on feature-length Hollywood motion pictures have included such durable properties as *Peyton Place, The Virginian, The Odd Couple,* and *M*A*S*H.* Interestingly, the last-mentioned program holds the distinction of eclipsing its motion-picture basis in popularity. It is safe to say that when most people hear the name "*M*A*S*H,*" they think of the TV program first and the movie second, with Alan Alda having superseded Donald Sutherland as Hawkeye Pierce in the public's eye (see Fig. 9–1).

The traffic in adaptation occasionally goes the other way, and we may find a final link between the film and television media in the television original becoming the basis for a subsequent feature film for theatrical release. One of the favorite topics of film historians is TV's influence on film form during the fifties and early sixties. They frequently discuss the growth of the big-budgeted, "blockbuster" film replete with Cinema, CinemaScope, or 3-D, vibrant color, extravagant musical numbers, and a cast of thousands, all designed to entice viewers away from their television sets. While historians have chronicled this phenomenon with regularity, there has been surprisingly little written on another, though considerably lesser, TV impact on the look of film: the growth of Hollywood films that had a distinctly "televisional" look. Film historian-critic Charles Higham is one of the exceedingly

Figure 9–1   *M*A*S*H* was one of the most popular series ever to appear on television. Its beginnings may be traced to a 1970 feature film starring Donald Sutherland and Elliott Gould as Hawkeye and Trapper John, a work which in turn was based on a novel. The TV version underwent many cast changes, but Alan Alda continued his dual role as star and writer for the series until its demise in early 1983.

few writers to recognize this small group of films: "Another way of combating the public obsession with TV was to provide them with something equivalent to that medium in the cinema theaters themselves, [in the form of the] low- or medium-budget black-and-white feature, dealing with ordinary people and situations."[11] Such films adapted from original television productions include Paddy Chayefsky's *Marty* (1955) and *The Bachelor Party*, (1957) both directed by Delbert Mann; Rod Serling's *Patterns* (1956) and *Requiem for a Heavyweight* (1962), directed by Fielder Cook and Ralph Nelson, respectively; and *Twelve Angry Men* (1957), directed by Sidney Lumet (see Fig. 9–2). Alfred Hitchcock's *Psycho* warrants special mention here, despite the fact that it was based not on a prior TV production but on a novel by Robert Bloch. It has a strong "televisional" look like these other films, a quality that is no doubt due to the fact that the film was produced by Hitchcock's television crew (the group responsible for *Alfred Hitchcock Presents*) instead of his regular film crew. There are a number of characteristics, both visual and thematic, that tend to unite these works. They include the extensive use of close-ups, the usual lack of outdoor and elaborate indoor sets, long runs of the camera (the *Psycho* shower scene is an obvious exception), gritty black-and-white cinematography, a

Figure 9-2 *Marty* (1955—American). The film version of *Marty* starring Oscar-winner Ernest Borgnine as a lonely Bronx butcher was based on a play that Paddy Chayefsky had originally written for television. Both versions reflect the intimacy of a drama written originally for the home screen.

brooding atmosphere, and an intense interest in the psychology of the characters, usually at the expense of action and spectacle. The fundamental differences between the basic film and television forms tend to work against the opening up of these closed, intimate dramas, and the prototypal films cited above have had few works following them to establish any kind of a tradition.

The most significant tie between television and film today is maintained through the countless segments from a broad range of program types that, together with video tape, form the foundation of documentary and dramatic programming on both commercial and educational television. The integration of film and video in these genres makes it difficult to keep what is film distinct from what is television. For example, Cinda Firestone's *Attica*—a documentary film on the 1971 Attica prison uprising—relies extensively on footage from television news and interview programs. Today the media continue to commingle and leave their mark on one another.

NOTES

[1]Rudolf Arnheim, "A Forecast of Television," in *Film as Art* (Berkeley: University of California Press, 1958), p. 193.

[2]Ibid., p. 195.

[3]Siegfried Kracauer, *Theory of Film: The Redemption of Physical Reality* (New York: Oxford University Press, 1960), p. 167.

[4]"The Shock of Freedom in Films," *Time*, Dec. 8, 1967, p. 67.

[5]American made-for-TV movies are, however, frequently distributed as theatrical films in other countries.

[6]As of this writing, the showing of first-run films via television is limited to the Los Angeles area during Academy Awards time, so that Academy members might be able to view nominated films at their leisure at home.

[7]James Monaco, "The Eighties," *American Film*, 5, no. 3 (December 1979), p. 32.

[8]McLuhan has used the term *cool* to describe the television image, which, because of the nature of electronic transmission is relatively low in resolution and detail. A cool image such as that offered by TV requires a more active participation on the part of the viewer to complete the image.

[9]Hugo Mauerhofer, "Psychology of Film Experience," in *Film: A Montage of Theories*, ed. Richard Dyer MacCann (New York: Dutton, 1966), p. 234.

[10]This may be more of a cultural factor than a technological one. For example, the American networks offered continuous commentary during the 1981 wedding of Britain's Prince Charles to Lady Diana Spencer, while the BBC provided an absolute minimum of narration, preferring instead to let the images speak for themselves whenever possible.

[11]Charles Higham, *The Art of the American Film* (Garden City, N.Y.: Anchor Books, 1974), p. 288.

10

DOCUMENTARY FORMS

PROBLEMS IN DEFINITION

The more careful and specific one tries to be in pinning down a definition for the term *documentary film*, the more problematic the task becomes. Theorists and practitioners generally agree that the term describes that class of film which, together with the experimental form (see Chapter 11), makes up the bulk of what we might call *nonfiction, nonnarrative,* or *nonfeature* films. These are all terms that set documentary and experimental film apart from the popular and familiar story form but say nothing of what they *are*. The term documentary was first used by one pioneer of the form to describe the work of another; John Grierson, the British filmmaker who shares with the American Robert Flaherty the distinction of "fathering" the movement, first used the term to describe Flaherty's early study of life on the island of Samoa: *Moana* (1926). Since then it has been applied to a range of cinematic works from news clips, teaching and training films, and travelogues to elaborate "feature-length" studies of real-world people, places, and events. It has included works designed for a variety of audiences, with a range of functions, and designed to be shown in both theaters and on the television screen. Film theorist Siegfried Kracauer gives some idea of the range when he suggests that "documentaries elaborate on natural material for a variety of purposes . . . from detached pictorial reports to glowing social messages."[1]

Although the range in function is considerable, the one characteristic that all so-called documentaries have in common is their concentration on actual physical existence. This focus on the real world and actual people being observed by the camera in actual activities is central to the definition and serves as the single common denominator in this form found in such diverse styles and functions. The Academy of Motion Picture Arts and Sciences describes documentaries as "those films dealing with significant historical, social, scientific, or economic subjects, either photographed in actual occurrence or reenacted, and where the emphasis is more on factual content than on entertainment."

The factual emphasis and even the social responsibility of the documentary were cornerstones of the British movement that helped mold the form and set its direction through its early development. Theorist and director Paul Rotha spoke of "creative treatment of actuality and expression of social analysis" in describing documentary function.[2] Ernest Lindgren, another director and theorist from the British school, similarly defined documentary as "a type of nonfiction film utilizing material either actual or reconstructed, drawn from real life and based on a sociological theme or having a sociological reference."[3] Like others of the British school, he emphasized the social function but allowed for "reconstruction" when necessary. Such reconstruction or simulation of actual events may raise problems in definition, depending on the extent of its use. Many early newsreels produced by the Edison and Biograph companies, particularly those covering the Spanish-American war, had to make do with studio reenactment of events inaccessible to the motion-picture camera. The legitimacy of these films as documentaries has been and will continue to be debated; nevertheless, these reconstructions of newsworthy happenings, along with the recordings of actual events, formed the beginnings of a newsreel tradition at the turn of the century that was to blossom into a broad and varied range of nonfiction forms.

Although its affinity for the real article is central to the definition of the documentary, Paul Rotha was probably right when he said that it would be "a grave mistake to assume that the documentary method differs from the story film merely in its preference for natural material."[4] Narrative or feature filmmaking has its own realist tradition, represented by the American gangster films of the 1930s, the neorealist studies of Roberto Rossellini and Vittorio de Sica, and the impromptu styles of the films of the French New Wave, among other works. It is a tradition that tends to blur the distinction between documentary and dramatic cinema. But part of what separates the commerical feature from the documentary film is the extent to which journalistic or dramatic intent determines structure. Documentarists turn their cameras on the world around them to explore, and frequently to interpret and judge. Film dramatists seek to take events from the real or imagined world and shape them into a story of some sort. According to these pursuits, the filmmakers' search for detail and inherent meaning motivates the progression in a documentary. In the fiction film, traditions in dramatic form and the demands of narrative construction determine such selection and progression. Despite its faithful representation of the actual event and authenticity in detail, Pudovkin's *End of St. Petersburg* (1927) is still a *dramatic rendering* of the historic occasion; and in spite of the occasional liberties that Robert Flaherty took with certain details of lifestyle and his need to rehearse and direct certain actions, *Nanook of the North* (1922) is still a *documentary record* of the life of the Itivimuit tribe of Eskimos.

Market and exhibition patterns also help define the documentary today via their emphasis on context. Commerical studios or independent producers create feature films for profit and have them shown in commerical theaters for the purpose of entertainment. The documentary, along with the experimental film, will usually be exhibited in schools or before community, social, religious, political, or industrial groups, or shown in small specialty theaters or via television, for public enlightenment. As there are legitimate claims concerning the aesthetic value of both the documentary and dramatic film, it is best not to make this a factor in distinguishing their functions. It is not even very fruitful to press the distinction between the entertainment and instructional or educational values because of their obvious overlap; but the *tendencies* toward the one or the other are usually apparent. Though it raises problems, the attempt at some definition of documentary styles and functions is still useful in both drawing attention to those characteristics peculiar to the form as well as the broad range of possible styles and uses, some shared with the fiction film. Given the range of the various definitions, it is still possible to distinguish the documentary as a medium in which filmmakers have used the camera to observe reality for the purpose of instruction, persuasion, or self-expression, and where storytelling, if it does occur, is incidental and instrumental to these ends.

EVOLUTION

Origins

Giving a new dimension to the practice of journalism was among the earliest uses of motion pictures. Among the earliest known films are those that set down a record of events both ordinary and extraordinary, a record now in pictures rather than words. While the Lumière Brothers in France were recording Auguste Lumière with his wife and child at the breakfast table as well as workers leaving the Lumière "factory" for their lunch break, Edison crews were filming street parades, military drills, and other routine happenings in the New York area. But at the same time they were recording the everyday happening, these and other pioneers began to turn their cameras on the more newsworthy current events, and a newsreel tradition was born. Observation became less random, and national and international personalities and events became the center of focus. The coronation of Czar Nicholas II in 1896, the funeral of Queen Victoria in 1901, and the inauguration of President McKinley all became part of the cinematic record.

The introduction of the newsreel as a regular part of a theater program began in 1911 with *Pathé's Weekly* (later, *Pathé News*). The crews of Charles Pathé filmed headline news in major cities around the world and compiled the footage for distribution to European and American theaters on various regular schedules (weekly, twice-weekly, even daily at one point). *Pathé's Weekly* was an instant success and spawned numerous foreign and domestic imitators, such as *Animated Weekly*, *Gaumont Weekly*, and *Mutual Weekly*, but it remained the standard to be matched. In early 1912, for example, Pathé's company had broken the world's record for filming current events in Europe and releasing copies of the completed newsreel in America. The intervening period was one month, incredibly slow compared to communication in today's age of the satellite, but which was at the time, according to the trade journal *Moving Picture World*, "an unparalleled feat in the history of motion pictures."[5] The newsreel form continued to grow in popularity in the rapidly expanding film industry, and by the early teens, filmmakers regularly documented major social and political events (such as the comings and goings of heads of state) as well as natural disasters.

Naturalist and Social Traditions

As long as the nonfeature film consisted of brief glimpses of immediate events, it remained within the realm of newsreels and contained a reasonable degree of impromptu reportage. In the next two decades, however, the nonnarrative film, like the story film, increased in length and began to allow for a more extended study of the event or personality, greater individual perspective and interpretation of the subject, and, in general, a greater range in styles and functions.

Robert Flaherty's *Nanook of the North*, the explorer's 1922 ethnographic study of Eskimo life and struggle for survival, moved the film of fact from the newsreel to more fully developed documentary design. Its greater length not only required attention to structure, progression, and other matters of form, but it also invited interpretation of the real world and a more creative rendering of actuality. Flaherty was not satisfied with simple description; he wanted to convey what he had learned while living with his subjects about the inner reality that his wife (and assistant) Frances Flaherty called "that high moment of seeing, that flash of penetration into the heart of the matter."[6] In both *Nanook* and *Moana*, Flaherty's camera became an instrument of his true profession as explorer (he had never made a film before) and examined in a curious and searching way the routine, the ritual, the high drama, and the humor of Eskimo and Samoan life. The films also revealed a good deal about the poet as filmmaker and his introspection and compassion for his subject (see Fig. 10–1).

Flaherty's move toward creative control of "actuality" was further developed by two of his contemporaries. In the new Soviet state, Dziga Vertov was concerned with the need to instruct the poorly educated workers—the foundation

Figure 10-1 *Nanook of the North* (1922—American). Robert Flaherty specialized in creating romanticized visions of remote and primitive societies, such as his treatment of a group of Eskimos living near Hudson's Bay which became his first and most famous documentary, *Nanook of the North*.

of the new proletariat—about the significance of their historic struggle and the ideals of the revolution. He saw the documentary camera as a "weapon" in that mission. Like Eisenstein and Pudovkin, who were celebrating the revolution and the end of the Czarist rule through feature-length dramatizations of events, Vertov saw the entire editing process as the means by which varied and apparently unrelated images could be fused to create a kind of cinematic mosaic not bound by linear, cause-and-effect continuity. His series of newsreels—*Kino Nedelya* (*Cinema Weekly*), which appeared in 1918 and 1919, and the more famous *Kino Pravda* (*Cinema Truth*), begun the same year as *Nanook*—resembled the Flaherty approach on a conceptual level by going beyond the simple recording of actuality to a creative rendering of factual detail. The critical difference between the Flaherty and Vertov approaches is one of politics and film form: Flaherty was the "innocent eye" creating visual poetry from exotic and primitive societies and establishing what was to be called the *romantic tradition* in documentary; Vertov, on the other hand, saw documentary film as having primarily a social function and frequently used highly expressive techniques in pursuit of that goal. In the interest of informing Soviet workers on events of the day and interpreting these events from a Marxist perspective, Vertov favored a proletarian cinema that caught life unawares and on the run, but always from the unusual and revealing vantage point, and by using the growing tradition of montage construction for the most meaningful arrangement of individual shots. Vertov used his camera, sometimes from concealed positions, to capture moments of everyday life of the Soviet worker—in the streets, shops, factories, and markets. He then skillfully arranged the seemingly unrelated shots into an orchestration designed to capture the spirit of the work ethic and the vitality of people on the move.

While working on his *Kino Pravda* newsreel, Vertov began attacking traditional, narrative forms of cinema and proposed the development of a new cinema concerned primarily with technology and poetry, subjects that intrigued Vertov well before his interest in film. By the mid-1920s, these various ideas had coalesced into a single set of principles, which Vertov called his *Kino Glaz* (Cinema Eye) theory. Elements of this theory, which eventually found their way into later Vertov documentaries, include (1) the superiority of technology to those things human, and (2) the importance of movement and energy, reflecting the nature of modern urban society. Though Vertov's ideas were not new (their roots may be found in an Italian-based artistic movement begun in 1909 called *Futurism*, which stressed such things as city life, furious movement, mechanization of humans, and humanization of machines), he nevertheless infused in them a unique spirit that was both cinematic and Soviet.

The best illustration of Vertov's *Kino Glaz* theory is his 1929 masterpiece, *The Man With the Movie Camera*. This feature-length documentary is a synthesis of his Futurist-based theory and related montage principles. On a surface level, *The Man With the Movie Camera* is a documentary of the city of Moscow, taking on the form popular with pre-Depression European documentarists known as the "city symphony." Like other city symphonies, such as Walter Ruttmann's 1927 *Berlin: Symphony of a Big City* and Alberto Cavalcanti's 1926 treatment of Paris entitled *Rien que les Heures,* Vertov's film follows a dawn-to-dusk progression of activities in a large city. Other city-symphony hallmarks include the use of various editing tempos designed to replicate the "rhythm" of a metropolis and an exploration of social themes; in Vertov's film, these include work, birth, death, marriage, and recreation.

But on another level, *The Man With the Movie Camera* is something completely different; it is not only a documentary about a typical "day in the life" of Moscow but also a documentary on the nature of film itself. *The Man With the Movie Camera* is a veritable grab bag of trick effects, including freeze frames, superimpositions, split screens, hand-held camera shots, slow-motion shots, fast-motion shots, some very rapid—almost subliminal—editing, and a continual rupturing of time and space. Virtually all of these effects are used in support of a major dictum of the *Kino Glaz* theory, which states that the camera eye is superior to the human eye. Vertov wanted to show that the camera eye could do much more than the human eye, since it could look at objects in different modes—it could look at things in slow motion, for example, or it could look at two separated things simultaneously—and from perspectives normally inaccessible to humans. Examples of the latter include views from under a train, alongside a building, and over a waterfall.

Reinforcing this notion of the supremacy of the camera eye is the observation that the camera, and not Moscow, is the real star of the film. We are forever seeing shots of various Moscow scenes intercut with shots of the cameraman filming the shots we have just seen. Unlike most documentaries of the time, which sought to downplay the presence of the camera, Vertov exploited his camera's presence for all it was worth. His obsession with making the audience aware of the camera manifests itself in *The Man With the Movie Camera* in a variety of ways: a human eye is superimposed over a camera lens; an animated camera on a tripod takes bows on stage before an appreciative audience; and a shot of a seminaked woman is followed by a close-up of a hand removing a small lens from the front of the camera and replacing it with a much-larger lens—a bit of whimsy that has both voyeuristic and phallic overtones.

Unsatisfied with presenting just the camera, Vertov even went to the extent of showing part of the editing process. For example, shots of children are followed by shots of the film editor examining these previous shots and hanging them up as strips of celluloid (which is, of course, exactly what they are) on the editing bench. Through these and other distancing devices, Vertov forces the audience to question what it has perceived in the film, and even to question the very natures of "truth" and "reality" as presented in film, documentary or otherwise.

The Scotsman John Grierson gave further support in both practice and proclamation to the social rather than the "aestheticky" function of the documentary. Grierson founded what was to become a major British movement in Realist cinema in 1930 with the formation of a film unit as part of the Empire Marketing Board, a government agency responsible for the control and promotion of British goods and services. Although an admirer of Flaherty, Grierson rejected the "self-conscious pursuit of beauty" and was drawn more to the philosophy of the Soviet filmmakers. He saw the true function of the nonnarrative cinema to be the interpretation of the real world through the arrangement and creative shaping of events, but always with a sense of social responsibility. This "creative dramatization of actuality and expression of social analysis" is described by Paul Rotha, who became

(A)

(B)

Figure 10-2 (A & B) *The Man With the Movie Camera* (1929—Russian). Throughout this landmark documentary, Dziga Vertov reminded his audiences that they were indeed looking at a film. One way he accomplished this task was to follow a "normal" shot with one depicting the camera and its operator filming the previous shot. For example, Fig. A shows two women riding in the back seat of a car traveling along a busy Moscow street. The shot which follows it in the film (Fig. B) shows the cameraman precariously perched on the edge of another car, filming the women.

a key spokesman for the movement as "a distinct kind of film, as an interpretation of social feeling and philosophic thought quite different in purpose and form from entertainment motives of the story film."[7] As with Grierson, he saw the mission of the documentary as a response to the sociological, political, and educational needs of the people.

Night Mail, produced by Grierson in 1936, has become something of a classic of the form; it effectively illustrates the blending of social analysis and aesthetic inspiration and discipline while serving an educational function. The film combines the talents of the two writer-directors, Basil Wright and Harry Watt, the composer Benjamin Britten, and the poet W.H. Auden. It turns the routine of the postal train that carries mail from London to Glasgow into high drama. Loading of mailbags, sorting of letters, drops and pickups along the route and the final delivery are among the regular functions that take on an urgency and through dramatic presentation impress the viewer with the importance, efficiency, and even the indomitability of the performed service. The film goes well beyond simple instruction to become a social and aesthetic document (see Fig. 10-3).

1

Figure 10-3 *Night Mail* (1936—British). Music and poetic verse combine with rhythmic editing and striking photography to uplift a mundane subject (the nightly London-to-Glasgow mail train) in *Night Mail*, directed by Basil Wright and Harry Watt, and produced under the auspices of John Grierson.

16 mm, TV, and Diversification

Sociological, political, educational, and aesthetic requirements have continued to influence the evolution of the documentary in the decades since Flaherty, Vertov, and Grierson were establishing traditions in the observation of real events and everyday happenings in the twenties and thirties. Worldwide depression, World War II, and the period of postwar readjustment became major arenas for documentary reportage and sociopolitical observation in the first two decades of sound. The cold war, Korea, Vietnam, and more recently the political strains of détente and the challenges of the environment and space have drawn particular focus and provided inspiration for the documentarist in the past thirty years. And aesthetic as well as social functions have been well established by poets, chroniclers, and persuaders who, with a sense of cinematic style, have made the viewing of a film of fact a pleasurable as well as an instructive experience.

But changes in production methods, exhibition patterns, and even changes in audiences have influenced the evolution of the form. Whether one comes to the defense of the aesthetic or social functions of the documentary, the fact remains that the genre lacks the broad popular appeal of the feature film. In addition to its inability to compete with the feature in star and story appeal, it has also been hampered by its awkward length, which has invariably relegated it to "added attraction" status even in its best form. While the documentary has remained a stepchild to the commercial cinema, it has found a more receptive audience in schools, among community groups, the business world, and even in the home. The development of economical, lightweight, and flexible 16 mm cameras and projection equipment gave the filmmaker greater mobility and access; it also opened up a whole new exhibition pattern whereby the classroom, executive boardroom, and community hall all became instant movie theaters. The arrival of television extended the exhibition of the documentary film to the lounge, recreation room, living room, and neighborhood bar as well. Though hardly in competition with the commercial feature, the documentary film is now more readily accessible to a virtually limitless audience because of television and the 16 mm film field. This access has been responsible for expansion and diversification in documentary forms. The newsreels, anthropological studies, social documents, and formalist exercises that made up the bulk of early documentary cinema have given way to films representing a wide variety of styles and functions but still drawing their substance from persons, places, events, and issues that are real and the object of direct cinematic treatment.

Generic distinctions are at least as problematic with the documentary as with the feature film. Kracauer, in his *Theory of Film*, attempted a breakdown that he based on the medium's degree of concern or indifference to material reality. Under the former he included both direct reporting and the imaginative interpretation of reality that marked the works of the pioneers Flaherty and Grierson. Under documentaries "indifferent to material reality," he included the impressionist studies that emphasize photographic values and transient impressions of the filmmakers—the so-called city symphonies of the late 1920s. Also representative are the contemporary short documentary studies of formal or ornamental relationships that provide a fresh, often abstract perspective from which to view the familiar and ordinary. Also included under films indifferent to material reality are those that carry some proposition of an ideological or intellectual nature—the so-called message picture or propaganda film.

Recognizing an even broader range of purposes to which the recording and rendering of reality on film may be put, Erik Barnouw, in his study of the form,[8] attempts to distinguish among the works of no less than 13 types of documentarists. These include: the explorer, reporter, painter, advocate, poet, chronicler, catalyst, and guerrilla. The more ambitious and extensive the system of classification becomes, the more likely questions of division and overlap will arise. The Barnouw labels do, nonetheless, give a better idea of the expanded role that the nonfiction film has come to play in contemporary art and communication.

We might draw the most generally useful breakdown of documentary genres from both the rhetorical functions suggested by Barnouw and the perspective on reality outlined by Kracauer. Such a division might include under one heading the *news documentary* and the field of *cinematic journalism* generally. Embracing a major portion of nonnarrative film shown on television, this type would include both the modern-day newsreel and the expanded investigative reporting represented by the works of Frederick Wiseman (*High School, Law and Order, Hospital*), the Maysles Brothers (*Showman, Salesman*), and the variety of television specials produced by Jacques-Yves Cousteau (*The Silent World, World Without Sun*) and David Wolper (*Biography*). The television documentary, both in individual special and series format, finds its roots in both radio reporting and the nonfiction film of earlier years.

A second reasonably distinct category would include those works specifically designed as *teaching* and *training films*, which make up the holdings of school film collections and the output of a substantial part of public-service programming on commercial television as well as the public television offerings in instructional film. These are equivalent to the "textbook" in the world of literature and are generally discounted in historical and critical surveys of film. Nonetheless, they represent a significant portion of the film to which we are all exposed, particularly through the years of formal education, and are to a large degree responsible for our conditioning to filmic instruction, or *cineliteracy*, as it is sometimes called.

A third category, which displays its aesthetic credentials most prominently and in fact is frequently labeled *art documentary*, is composed of the impressionistic studies, mood pieces, and in general the more interpretive works of the visual poets who stay generally within the realm of the real, as opposed to the imagined, world. Barnouw calls them the painters and poets of documentary cinema. The crossover with the experimental film is most apparent here, and earlier films of the genre such as Joris Iven's *Rain* or Willard Van Dyke's *The City* (see Fig. 10-4), as well as the more recent works of Shirley Clarke, Bert Haanstra, and Alexander Hammid, are as likely to be found in references to the experimental as to the documentary form.

Moreover, within the realm of the art documentary would go those biographical or topical studies that would seem to fall more logically within the category of instructional film except for the fact that their subject matter happens to be the art world. Biographies of major artists, which include a survey of the works themselves, tend to be placed within the art film category. The life, times, and works of Michelangelo, Rembrandt, and Alexander Calder have been documented on film by the poet-journalist.

The fourth type of documentary brings together the filmmaker that Barnouw identifies as the advocate, bugler, promoter, catalyst, and guerrilla. The common function here is the move beyond general enlightenment, specific instruction, or aesthetic indulgence to influence—that is, to either reinforce or to change—attitudes and beliefs of the viewer. *Film persuasion* began with the short advertising films described in Chapter 1 and has continued, through seven decades of peace and war, to sell ideas as well as products and to espouse some causes, to challenge others, and to prove again and again the special propensity of the motion picture as a friendly persuader. It is an important enough function to deserve special consideration later in this chapter.

Figure 10-4 *Berlin: Symphony of a Big City* (1927—German). For an example of a documentary film that relies heavily on experimental techniques, we need look no further than Walter Ruttmann's famous "city symphony," *Berlin*. In this scene, a Berlin storefront takes on expressionistic qualities.

INHERENT QUALITIES

Before turning to special styles in documentary and the particular persuasive traits of the medium, we need to look first at the inherent qualities of cinema that lend support to the general functions just outlined. Film works particularly well as a means of recording and interpreting the real world because it allows for direct, literal documentation of actuality with *detail* intact, while at the same time providing for such essential controls as *vantage point* and *selectivity* of that detail, both visual and aural. The fact that the motion picture can instantaneously record an impression of an action with all detail, sound, and motion intact is central to its documentary function. Before anyone thought much about creative or editorial possibilities, the camera's ability to provide visual documentation of actual occurrences, both mundane and extraordinary, attracted early filmmakers and audiences. The photographic process itself had put people in closer contact with the kind of literal, objective detail of a scene never before possible; as an outgrowth of that process, the motion-picture camera could provide greater detail by capturing natural movement. The arrival of synchronous sound rounded out the medium's recording capacities. Beyond the novelty of seeing the photograph in motion was the ability of the camera to satisfy our interest in historical detail, incidental as well as momentous. We see this modern historical consciousness not only in our attention to certain creative works but also in our more casual or incidental interest in keeping diaries, sinking and unearthing time capsules, and endorsing and embracing revivals of everything from art works to fads and fashions.

But what moved the nonfiction film beyond record-keeping and historical recall into the realm of creative interpretation and persuasion was the selection and control provided through the positioning of camera, the selection and arrangement of pieces of film, and the choice and juxtapositioning of sound with image. Vantage point is particularly important to the documentarist in affecting psychological response and in suggesting attitude toward filmic material. It is important in an even more basic way in putting the observer in the most advantageous position from which to view the action. The panoramic view of the "postal special" together with the close-up shots of the work of the mail handlers aboard give us instruction and also provide a sense of mission to the mundane in *Night Mail*. Countless instructional films have done their job better than any textbook because of the camera's ability to move in and, in Kracauer's words, "reveal things normally unseen"[9]—detail which would normally go unnoticed because it is too small, too fleeting, or too ordinary to command our attention.

When filmmakers combine perspective of the individual shot with selection and arrangement of groups of shots, they help realize fully the revealing function of the documentary. Pare Lorentz, head of the short-lived United States Film Service, was able to take his viewers the length of the Mississippi and several of its tributaries following the ravages of flooding, and then move as quickly to show how dam building and controlled land use is capable of taming *The River*. In *Night and Fog*, Alain Resnais moved the viewer through scenes of Nazi concentration camps as they appeared during their operation (through mostly still photographs) and cuts continually to shots of the camps as they appear today—peaceful, derelict, overgrown with wildflowers. Control of vantage point for Resnais (and Lorentz, too, for that matter) means control of time as well as space: moving the viewer as quickly from past to present as from the panoramic to close-up view.

The addition of sound gives the documentary an added dimension of realism and puts the filmmaker in even greater control of the subject. It is not by accident that the documentary as a genre did not mature until after the arrival of sound. Flaherty's *Nanook* and *Moana*, Vertov's *The Man With the Movie Camera*, Cavalcanti's *Rien que les Heures*, Ruttman's *Berlin*, and Grierson's *Drifters* (1929) have become classic formative works of the silent period, but not until film found its voice did these isolated beginnings in nonfiction reportage and interpretation become a recognized movement.

Voice, natural and invented sound effects, and music enabled Grierson to explore more fully the drama as well as the detail of food production, marketing, and communication in Great Britain in the 1930s. Flaherty used the sound of a raging storm to punctuate the power of the sea and fortitude of the islanders in *Man of Aran* (1934). Leni Riefenstahl edited together highlights of various Nazi speeches to powerful effect in *Triumph of the Will*, her ambitious documentary of the 1934 Nazi Party rally in Nuremberg. In this same film, she also interspersed the sights and sounds of firing cannons with images of Adolf Hitler shaking hands with his troops, presumably to underscore his forceful personality and strength. In Riefenstahl's documentary of the 1936 Olympics in Berlin, *Olympia* (1938), she combined the inspiring and "heroic" music of Herbert Windt with shots of male divers who seem to defy gravity to create a breathtaking aural-visual paean to the beauty of the human form in flight (see Fig. 10-5). By the time Frank Capra provided the "Why We Fight" film series for the United States War Department in 1942, filmmakers were exploring a full range of functions for sound in the documentary. The importance of sound in that series is suggested by the fact that Capra based the seven films directly on a series of troop lectures prepared by the Army's Bureau of Public Relations.

In the modern documentary, sound continues to add detail and dimension to film instruction, poetry, and persuasion. The immediacy of the on-the-spot coverage of events is supported largely by the spontaneous character of the sound track. In the age of television, sound often rivals the images for command of at-

Figure 10-5 *Olympia* (1938—German). Many producers of sports films and TV programming have borrowed ideas from Leni Riefenstahl's "Men's Diving Sequence" from *Olympia,* but few have matched her exquisite treatment of the human body in flight.

tention. It often provides the continuity for nonfiction programming and becomes the primary carrier of messages while the visuals are supportive and illustrative. The role of sound in recording and revealing the real world has become increasingly diverse and complex; with the television documentary, it has also become fundamental.

SPECIAL STYLES

The early 1960s saw the development of two major documentary styles, both of which had their roots in a short-lived, mid-1950s documentary movement termed *English Free Cinema*. *Direct cinema* and *cinéma vérité*, as these twin movements are called, shared with their British predecessor an interest in documenting the situation of the common person through impromptu, unrehearsed means, frequently using highly portable filmmaking equipment. The strongest bond between direct cinema and *cinéma vérité* today continues to be that of technology; both groups of filmmakers employ lightweight, hand-held cameras (or cameras mounted on body braces), synchronous sound, through-the-lens viewfinders, zoom lenses, fast (that is, highly light-sensitive) lenses and film stocks, and soundproof cameras. Through such modern filmmaking technologies, direct cinema and *cinéma vérité* filmmakers alike are able to capture unplanned, uncontrolled, ongoing events with maximum flexibility.

Because of the lack of preplanning and the difficulty in anticipating the complexion and direction of events, the films resulting from these two approaches are often marked by shaky camera work and ineptly composed, out of focus, poorly-lit shots. Sound is often characterized by occasionally inaudible dialogue, distracting noises, and long periods of silence. But such "raw" characteristics, considered flaws in other forms of filmmaking, have come to be heralded as the proofs of authenticity and spontaneity. They help preserve not only the details of actuality but also its unforeseen ambiguities, hazards, and contradictions.

The direct cinema and *cinéma vérité* approaches eventually part company over philosophic and stylistic issues, which we need to discuss at this juncture. There is inevitably some overlap among their qualities and concerns, but most documentaries made since the 1960s that do not rely extensively on archival material fall rather neatly into one category or the other.

Direct cinema is considered to be primarily an *observational* kind of cinema, in which its practitioners usually follow their subjects around with cameras and tape recorders, waiting for something significant to happen. Direct cinema filmmakers such as Richard Leacock, D.A. Pennebaker, Al and David Maysles, and Frederick Wiseman rarely if ever do the following things: (1) interview the people they are filming; (2) ask these people to repeat some action if that action was initially missed by the camera; (3) include material that does not originate directly from the people and events being filmed (such as narration, for example); or (4) indulge in cinematic trickery, a la Dziga Vertov. These filmmakers do not object if the subjects of the film ask questions of each other, but seldom do the filmmakers themselves conduct interviews. (Exceptions to this general principle may occur when the subjects insist on talking directly to the filmmakers, as did the two women who were the subjects of the Maysles Brothers' 1976 film, *Grey Gardens*.)

Direct cinema practitioners usually seek to downplay the presence of themselves and their filmmaking equipment, but they seldom if ever resort to the "candid camera" approach, in which the subjects are unaware they are being filmed. Instead, they may spend days or weeks with the subjects before any filming begins in order to acclimate the subjects to the presence of the filmmakers and their paraphernalia.

Subjects that lend themselves to the direct cinema approach include those with their own internal drama and structure. A key work in the direct cinema style is the intimate study of the 1960 Wisconsin Presidential primary involving Democratic candidates John F. Kennedy and Hubert H. Humphrey. In *Primary*, Richard Leacock, Al Maysles, D.A. Pennebaker, and Robert Drew followed the two candidates through a succession of telethons, parades, speeches, and on-the-road travels to the next engagement. With minimal intrusion on the events, the filmmakers captured the natural drama of the political maneuvering, the exhilaration, and the physical endurance that are a part of American national political campaigns.

In the decades following *Primary*, a significant part of direct cinema has been devoted to exploring the aspirations and tensions of the individual, both famous and unknown. These have included films such as the Maysles brothers' *Showman* (1962), a portrait of movie mogul Joseph E. Levine, and *Salesman* (1969), their chronicle of four door-to-door Bible salesmen, both on and off the job; *Don't Look Back* (1966), D.A. Pennebaker's study of the personality and lifestyle of Bob Dylan on tour; and Ricky Leacock's *Happy Mother's Day* (1963), which focuses on the birth and surrounding hoopla of the Fischer quintuplets in Aberdeen, South Dakota.

Social institutions have also been explored in direct cinema, primarily through the work of Frederick Wiseman. Among the organizations he has examined are a Philadelphia high school (*High School* [1968]), the Kansas City police department (*Law and Order* [1969]), a New York medical institution for indigent patients (*Hospital* [1970]), and a Massachusetts state facility for the criminally insane (*Titicut Follies* [1967], Wiseman's most famous and controversial film). In all cases, the direct cinema filmmakers have attempted to provide reasonably direct, immediate, and undistorted records of personalities and events in which the drama, though enhanced by the filmmaker through shot composition and editing, comes largely from within. The result is for the viewer, as it was for the filmmaker, what Lewis Jacobs has called "a direct encounter with uncontrolled life."[10]

Cinéma vérité represents a different philosophy and style in the documentarist's age-old quest of getting at the truth. While direct cinema filmmakers attempt to maintain a distance (however artificial) between themselves and their subjects, *cinéma vérité* practitioners become directly involved in the situation they are filming, often through interviewing their subjects. An assumption among *cinéma vérité* filmmakers borne out in their work is that the practice of merely following subjects around a la direct cinema will reveal to a large extent only a surface view of life. It is imperative, therefore, to probe beneath the surface to get at the essence of the situation being filmed, and this task is accomplished primarily through the question-and-answer process. One of the first filmmakers to introduce this approach was the Frenchman Jean Rouch, who in his *Chronicle of a Summer* (1961) asked Parisian passersby questions concerning their hopes, dreams, and fears.

The often startling replies that Rouch received would not have occurred had he opted for the more conservative direct cinema route. Rouch and others who have followed his lead have stressed the importance of letting the audience know that they are not attempting to be objective: that, instead, the filmmakers have become directly involved with the events being filmed and are working for social change. Erik Barnouw sums up the distinctions between direct cinema and *cinéma vérité* thus: "The direct cinema documentarist took his camera to a situation of tension and waited hopefully for a crisis; the Rouch version of *cinéma vérité* tried to precipitate one. The direct cinema artist aspired to invisibility; the Rouch *cinéma vérité* artist was often an avowed participant. The direct cinema artist played the role of uninvolved bystander; the *cinéma vérité* artist espoused that of provocateur."[11]

Because of *cinéma vérité*'s heavy reliance on interviews, a number of critics have argued that it suffers aesthetically due to its preponderance of "talking head" shots (that is, close-ups of people talking). Yet some of the most powerful, brilliant, and absorbing documentaries of all time have relied strongly on this supposed liability of *cinéma vérité*, including Barbara Koppel's *Harlan County U.S.A.*, Cinda Firestone's *Attica*, David Koff's *Blacks Britannica*, Peter Davis' *Hearts and Minds* (1974), and Marcel Ophuls' *The Sorrow and the Pity* (1970) and *The Memory of Justice* (1976). (Indeed, the two latter films run more than four hours each and consist primarily of interviews, yet they are moving and completely successful documentaries.)

Interviews are not the only means by which *cinéma vérité* filmmakers attempt to get at the "truth." They are continuously experimenting with various ways of bringing to the surface what they perceive as truth, including all sorts of cinematic devices. Michael Wadleigh's *Woodstock*, for example, employs everything from split screens to color filters to stop-motion photography to "follow-the-bouncing-ball" sing-a-longs, in addition to more conventional interviews. *Hearts and Minds*, Peter Davis' provocative examination of government, military, and domestic views on the Vietnam War, draws on several outside frames of reference, including a high-school football game and clips from a Hollywood World War II film. We seldom see such nonindigenous material in direct cinema films, but it is fairly common in *cinéma vérité* films.

If *cinéma vérité* seems to resemble the work of an earlier documentarist, it should; *cinéma vérité* is perhaps even more indebted to Dziga Vertov than to the English Free Cinema movement. It is no accident that the phrase *cinéma vérité* is the French translation of *Kino Pravda*, the title of Vertov's most famous newsreel series. By avoiding the pretense of objectivity and by incorporating a variety of cinematic devices, *cinéma vérité* practitioners have followed Vertov's lead en route to goals he would loudly applaud: getting at the truth as it exists below the surface, and working for social change.

If *cinéma vérité* and direct cinema are at one end of the spectrum of documentary styles, the *compilation film* is found at the other. As the name suggests, the compilation film is a welding together of film footage from various sources and times having some common link in subject or theme. Documentaries more expansive in scope that attempt an historical survey of personalities, works, and events are often created through archival research and the selection and organization of previously existing film pieces, rather than the positioning of the camera to capture the event as it unfolds.

The compilation documentary has its roots in the early newsreel and particularly in the works of Vertov, who in 1921 was already making a feature-length *History of the Civil War* from the thousands of feet of film that had been developed by Soviet cinematographers for the *Cinema Weekly* newsreel begun in 1918. A significant contribution to the form came with the "Why We Fight" series produced by Frank Capra for the United States War Department. This series of seven films, which traced the panorama of events and political posturing leading up to America's entry into World War II, was assembled from footage culled from a variety of sources, including the Office of Alien Property. In addition to newsreel footage of both Allied and Axis powers, the films contained clips from feature films and special animated sequences filmed at the Disney Studio (see Fig. 10–6).

With television taking on a documentary function, the compilation film has continued to make use of film material of the past to provide a chronicle of real events. Network television series such as NBC's *Victory at Sea* (1952–53) and CBS's *Twentieth Century* (1957–66) are among the early examples of the compilation film made for television. These have been joined in recent years by both series and individual specials produced for public television as well as the commercial stations. Though lacking the immediacy of direct cinema and *cinéma vérité*, the compilation documentary continues to provide an extraordinarily versatile means of collecting images of, and creatively shaping the perspective on, real people, places, and events.

DOCUMENTARY AND NARRATIVE DESIGN

By definition, the documentary finds its structure determined by real landscapes, designs, or chronologies of events. It resists the imposing of the traditional storytelling elements of conflict, crisis, climax, and resolution on its materials. In Kracauer's words, "The suppression of the story enables the camera to follow, without constraint, a course of its own and record otherwise inaccessible phenomena."[12]

Figure 10-6 *The Nazis Strike* (1942—American). The smiling visage of Adolf Hitler is from only one of many excerpts that Frank Capra borrowed from newsreels and Axis propaganda films to create the second in his "Why We Fight" series, *The Nazis Strike*. As with many of the "Why We Fight" films, *The Nazis Strike* combines such borrowed footage with animated sequences designed specifically for the series.

But frequently the recorded phenomena have their own story to tell. The documentarist, when concerned with human drama and real-life intrigues, will adopt a narrative framework and tend toward the dramatization of actuality. When relating real-life human drama, the narrator usually takes over the function of storyteller and provides a more emotionally involving experience for the viewer than the newsreel or straight expository or instructional film can offer.

In documenting both Nanook's struggle for survival and the wonder and excitement that a Cajun boy experiences with the arrival of an oil drilling rig in *Louisiana Story* (1948), Robert Flaherty's subject becomes the drama of human endeavor. Similarly, the French television documentary *Anderson Platoon* (1967) provides a dispassionate record of the routine of jungle warfare as the cameras follow the American fighting unit through not only days of anxiety and death but also the tedium that almost inevitably becomes a part of war. The film grows into both story and record, however, as individual members of the platoon become familiar and as we become aware of *their* sense of time, space, progression, and what the next bend in the river or the next day might offer.

Docu-drama and *true-life adventure* have become mainstays in the age of television documentary. The recording of real-life drama has now been extended in both commercial theaters and on both local and network broadcasts. Such prestige feature-length documentaries as *The Sky Above, The Mud Below, The Endless Summer, The Silent World of Jacques Cousteau,* and *Black and White in Color* have received both critical acclaim and a modest commercial market. The feature-length documentary has also led to a further blending of narrative and nonnarrative styles in television. In addition to the investigative reporting of the regular series such as *60 Minutes* and the specials of Jacques Cousteau and Frederick Wiseman, both commercial and public television have developed a form of semidocumentary or pseudodocumentary. Some go under the banner of historical fiction and weave fictional incidents into the fabric of real events. *Backstairs at the White House* and *Ike,* for example, use individual personalities and intimate drama as a means of embellishing and "dramatizing" the life and times of public figures. Others accommodate the personal drama, but more as a dramatization of real events than the documentation of fiction. In the case of both *Victory at Sea* and the more recent *Holocaust,* the focus is on the larger event but as told through the personal drama of the men and women who lived it.

DOCUMENTARY AS PERSUASION

A persuasive message in any medium draws its effectiveness from the combination of appeals that the Greek rhetoricians called *logos, ethos,* and *pathos.* Logos, or the logical appeal of a message, is built on the accumulation of evidence that a reasoning individual will judge supports a premise or proves a point. Ethos, or ethical appeal, depends on the credibility of the source of the message for its persuasibility—we tend to believe because of an inherent trust in the ability of the persuader or the medium to reflect things as they are. Pathos draws its appeal not from reasoned judgment based on the evidence or the source that provides it, but rather from the emotional impact that it has on us. Such a response requires some degree of identification, some link, either direct or indirect, between the message and the individual's personal existence and values. It is a response conditioned by such basic human motivations as physical well-being, security, sex, prestige, self-esteem, sense of belonging, and altruism.

Filmic messages and the changing or reinforcing of attitudes and beliefs are by no means limited to the documentary form. The narrative film has, as described elsewhere, long been accepted as a means whereby the filmmaker combines the role of storyteller with that of advocate or prosecutor to explore social issues and make judgments about them. What has also been recognized for most of film's history is the extent to which the "cinema situation," that is, the psychological conditioning that goes on while we sit in a darkened theater, affects viewer receptivity to filmic stimuli and therefore to messages, whether in the story or nonstory form.

In the nonnarrative film, and more specifically in the persuasive or propaganda documentary, we can observe the elements of logical, ethical, and emotional appeal most directly at work, and in ways unique to the medium. The inherent believability or ethos of the film image is probably the easiest to understand. We accept what is purported to be a record of an actual occurrence because we regard the motion-picture camera as a piece of technological apparatus that provides a direct and "objective" playback of what goes on in front of it. The ethos of the documentary recording is strong because we have been conditioned to understand that "seeing is believing," and that "pictures don't lie." The very term documentary suggests the authenticity of the material being presented.

The ethos of the documentary has been reinforced in recent years by the increased spontaneity of the filming process. High-speed film stock, which permits shooting with minimal lighting; and lightweight, portable sound recording and camera equipment have combined to make direct cinema an acceptable alternative to viewing the actual event. The apparent lack of any interruption or staging of the event or in any way affecting its development by the presence of the camera significantly raises its mark of authenticity. The few feet of 8-mm color film shot by a bystander that recorded the assassination of President Kennedy has been accepted as a true and unmanipulated document of the event by both the public and several investigative commissions.

In the hands of the filmmaker interested in the strategic planning and execution of a film message, the look of spontaneity and the style of *cinéma vérité* are no less important. The persuasibility of the film will be determined in part by the filmmaker's ability to make those choices in design and execution that will at the same time both represent the thesis or position to be supported, and also appear natural and uncontrived.

Hearts and Minds and Peter Gessner's *Time of the Locust* (1966) are both documentaries exploring the meaning of the war in Vietnam to those who were its architects and participants and also those who became its victims. Peter Davis, the producer-director of *Hearts and Minds,* has said the film is "my attempt to understand my own and other people's feelings about the Vietnamese war." Its combination of interviews, footage of combat, homecomings, football games, and old Hollywood war movies turns the film into an inquiry into human motivation and the final waste of war. The sense of inquiry and the filmmaker's own tentative position prove effective in building the film's ethos.

Time of the Locust, produced under the auspices of the Quakers' American Friends Service Committee, is clearly an indictment of the war and abandons any sense of investigative reporting. In place of interviews, speeches by American President Johnson and South Vietnam President Ky professing their love of peace are juxtaposed with bombings and burnings of villages. The entire film becomes a carefully contrived series of indictments against the war and warmongering by the irony Gessner fashioned through the counterpoint between two contrasting images or between image and sound.

If one escapes from, or remains immune to, the strong emotional shock of the film's juxtapositions, it fares less well than *Hearts and Minds* as a persuasive piece of filmmaking because of its often crudely manipulative linking of visual and aural detail that jeopardizes its believability. But *pathos*, or the emotional appeal that a film may have, will often distract the viewers from demanding truth in documentation or challenging the credibility of its source. The persuasion strategy that provides for the viewers' identification with character, situation, or detail and allows them to respond emotionally to them is hardly unique to film. What is unique is the cinema situation or the psychological conditioning of the film-viewing experience, which allows for the intensification of emotionally charged stimuli.

Sitting in a darkened theater (or even a classroom) isolates the viewers from the everyday world of stimuli that fight one another for attention. The viewers in a sense become willing slaves to the silver screen and its images, and become more receptive to the sights and sounds of a film world. Through this isolation and the intensified power of imagination it produces, viewers are able to accept the distortions in perspective, the manipulation in time and space, and even such embellishments as animation, narration, and music as being part of the world they know outside the theater. That faculty that discriminates between the world of fact and the world of fancy is numbed, and the persuader gains acceptance of the sounds and images that he or she orchestrates as a fair representation, if not a direct and inviolate recording, of real events.

Persuasion in any form involves the *interpretation* of reality to reinforce or modify beliefs or behavior. When that interpretation involves visual and aural stimuli tied to basic human drives and motivations, and when these are presented under the psychological conditions just described, the potential for strong emotional response to the "message" is greatly increased. In *The Battle of Britain*, (1943), Frank Capra documented the Christmas Eve bombing of London by juxtaposing shots of people huddled in underground railway stations with makeshift Christmas trees nearby with those of German bombers overhead. The scene is punctuated with the sounds of both bombs exploding and the strains of holiday carols. In *Time of the Locust*, Gessner established a similar kind of counterpoint, but it becomes even more emotionally charged when he linked shots of Vietnamese villages being destroyed by napalm to shots of the polished corridors and conference rooms of the Pentagon where smiling Defense Department bigwigs go about the business of war.

It has been argued that, in film persuasion, the viewer may reject an idea intellectually and still accept it emotionally. We become susceptible to unconscious drives strongly reinforceable by a variety of cinematic techniques. Filmmakers can establish comparisons, contrasts, and causal relationships through carefully calculated editing of both visuals and sound. Unusual camera angles, combined with editing, can give the viewer a feeling of omniscience that strengthens both the ethical and emotional appeal of the film. The voice of an authoritative but benevolent narrator can add support to both the pathos and ethos of the message. When the narration is itself laced with innuendoes and emotionally charged rhetoric (Capra's narrator speaks of the "Nazi henchmen" and "a new low in humanity" in *The Battle of Britain,* for example), the appeal is even stronger. The extent to which film persuasion goes beyond reasoned logical argument is suggested by John Grierson when he observed that "in documentary you do not shoot with your head only but with your stomach muscles."[13]

Putting aside the inherent believability (ethos) and emotional appeal (pathos) of the medium, film is an effective persuader in its potential for marshalling the evidence and presenting its case in sound logical terms (logos). Whether making one's argument through the inductive or deductive process, or by direct comparison or contrast, the filmmaker, through the judicious selection of factual detail and its orchestration in the finished film, is able to appeal to the viewers on rational, intellectual grounds. Aside from its ethical appeal, presenting evidence first hand is an efficient means of getting ideas across quickly and clearly.

Although film has these special facilities for persuasion, it is no easier to separate the three forms of appeal in the movies than in other communication media. Through shot selection, the juxtaposition of images, and the use of sound, filmmakers build their arguments through a combination of reason and passion while relying on the psychology of the viewing situation and the natural inclination of the viewers to accept what they see on the screen as a true reflection of the real world.

NOTES

[1]Siegfried Kracauer, *Theory of Film: The Redemption of Physical Reality,* New York: Oxford University Press, 1960), p. 194.

[2]Paul Rotha, "Some Principles of Documentary," in *Film: An Anthology,* ed. Daniel Talbot (Berkeley: University of California Press, 1966), p. 235.

[3]Ernest Lindgren, *The Art of the Film* (London: Allen & Unwin, 1963), p. 222.

[4]Rotha, "Some Principles of Documentary," p. 246.

[5]*Moving Picture World,* February 3, 1912, p. 402.

[6]Frances Flaherty, "Explorations," in *Film Book #1,* ed. Robert Hughes (New York: Grove Press, 1959), p. 63.

[7]Rotha, "Some Principles of Documentary," p. 234.

[8]Erik Barnouw, *Documentary: A History of the Non-Fiction Film* (New York: Oxford University Press, 1974).

[9]Kracauer, *Theory of Film,* p. 46.

[10]Lewis Jacobs, *The Documentary Tradition,* 2nd ed. (New York: W. W. Norton, 1979), p. 375.

[11]Barnouw, *Documentary,* pp. 254–55.

[12]Kracauer, *Theory of Film,* p. 212.

[13]John Grierson, *Grierson on Documentary,* ed. Forsyth Hardy (New York: Harcourt Brace Jovanovich, 1947), p. 16.

11

AVANT-GARDE FILMS

THE PROBLEM OF LABELS

Perhaps no type of cinema bears such a multiplicity of names as the *avant-garde film*. A wide range of titles have been used to subdivide this broad category of cinema, including *experimental film, underground film, independent film, art film, New American Cinema, expanded cinema,* and the term used primarily in this book, *avant-garde film*. While the relatively high number of labels underscores the diversity of these films, there is considerable overlap between some of the labels, and none is completely satisfactory when used as a generic label. Each term is either restricted to a select group of films, or has connotative problems, or both. For example, the term *underground* is largely restricted to American films made during the 1960s and is often considered synonymous with stag or pornographic films. *Avant-garde* is not a perfect choice either, since it is occasionally used in the context of the French cinema of the 1920s, but it seems the most flexible label to work with. As used in this book, it cuts across all countries and time periods, and it suggests that those engaging in this type of filmmaking are at the frontiers of the film medium; they are exploring film form, content, and function on new technological or conceptual levels, or both. While the term avant-garde is used for the sake of convenience here, it should be noted that this label in no way implies that the films it represents are marked by any uniformity beyond what will be discussed in the pages that follow. No other area of cinema has been so dominated by the individualistic, idiosyncratic spirit as the avant-garde film.

HISTORICAL OVERVIEW

It is exceedingly difficult to pinpoint the birth of the avant-garde film, primarily because the newness of the medium at the turn of the century tended to obscure the distinctions between various types of film. However, it is certainly demonstrable that *every* film produced during these earliest years was experimental or "avant-garde" to some degree. Attempting to break away from the heritages and conventions of drama, literature, music, dance, etc., the early shapers of the film medium were treading through *terra incognita*. Louis Lumière, Georges Méliès, Edwin Porter, D. W. Griffith, and countless others who plied their craft during the salad days of cinema can all rightly be regarded as experimentalists, since they were among the first to explore and develop various filmic techniques and concepts.

These and other innovators eventually discovered, however, that films require narrative structures to maintain a high mass-audience interest in the medium. Largely over this issue the narrative film and the avant-garde film developed in different directions. The most commercially successful films told stories, and various enterprises such as the gargantuan Pathé Frères organization were quick to pick up on this now commonplace observation in pursuit of profits, leaving behind the avant-garde film to fend for itself. The narrative film world never abandoned its relationship with avant-garde cinema; indeed, narrative filmmakers are not the least bit hesitant to incorporate a technique or concept that has been incubated in one or more avant-garde works. For example, the ancestry of many of the special effects in such famous science-fiction epics as *2001: A Space Odyssey* and *Star Wars* is traceable to John and James Whitney's computer films of the 1960s. Yet it is precisely this narrative-film tendency to exploit the ideas of the avant-garde for commercial gain that has created a tension between the two film worlds.

A partial explanation for the relative lack of harmony between commercial narrative film and avant-garde film may be found in the differing cultural contexts out of which they arose. As a truly "mass" medium, commercial narrative film has aimed largely at the lowest common denominator. During its first several decades, film was regarded as a working person's entertainment, a bastardized form of theater intended for the lower classes. (We find it noteworthy that theatrical performers wanted nothing to do with the new medium of film, thinking it was beneath them, just as forty years later, film performers—having reached the status of their stage counterparts—wanted nothing to do with the fledgling television medium, a situation that has of course changed.)

On the other hand, the first great wave of avant-garde cinema appeared in Europe during the post-World War I period, amid protests and cultural revolutions springing from a variety of causes: reactions to the war, growth of urban societies, the machine age, and the shortcomings of traditional art forms. As the photograph continued to supplant representational painting styles, new and radical forms of art developed through the first three decades of the century, many of which directly influenced what was to become the avant-garde cinema.

Among the most important were several conceptual descendants of the early twentieth-century art movement of *Cubism*. These offspring included *Futurism*, which focused on machine shapes, furious movement, and urban societies; *Precisionism*, which depicted barren city landscapes devoid of human activity; and *Suprematism*, which stressed simple monochrome geometric forms set off against neutral backgrounds. These movements exerted strong influences on a wide variety of avant-garde filmmakers.

Futurism was perhaps the most pervasive and influential of the movements. With its many close-ups of machine parts and kitchen utensils brought to life through rapid editing, Fernand Léger's *Ballet Mécanique* (1924) is heavily indebted to the Futurist movement, for example, as are many of the city symphony documentaries of the mid-1920s. Walter Ruttmann's *Berlin: Symphony of a Big City*, the most famous member of the symphony genre, works particularly well as an embodiment of Futurist concerns; in addition to showing the hectic pace of a typical "day in the life" of a large industrial city (accomplished in part through fast editing, shots of busy streets often filmed from moving vehicles, and shots of hyperactive businessmen), *Berlin* is laden with close-ups of moving machine parts—primarily those of telephones and typewriters—which Ruttmann occasionally presented in a fragmented, kaleidoscopic fashion.

The influences of Precisionism may be seen in such early avant-garde works as Charles Sheeler and Paul Strand's *Manhatta* (1921) and Robert Flaherty's *24 Dollar Island* (1924). The former film, which historian David Curtis has listed as the first American avant-garde film ever made,[1] is based on a Walt Whitman poem about New York City, with lines of Whitman verse intercut with beautifully composed but static shots of various Manhattan buildings. The latter film focuses on the architectural details of similar New York buildings. As with the classic Precisionist paintings, *Manhatta* and *24 Dollar Island* show no human beings; they are instead photographic essays comprised of geometric patterns formed by buildings.

As for early avant-garde films bearing the mark of Suprematism, we need look no further than Hans Richter's "Rhythmus" film series of the 1920s. For instance, *Rhythmus 21* (1921) consists primarily of animated white squares and rectangles against a black background. While the film's element of motion immediately distinguishes it from the Suprematist paintings, it nevertheless reflects strongly the Suprematist interest in goemetric purity and simplicity.

Along with these scions of Cubism, the early twentieth-century expressive movements of Dada and Surrealism helped give directions to the avant-garde cinema. Dada, an anti-art movement emphasizing the random juxtaposition of objects and the comic anarchy that frequently ensues, found expression in such playfully nihilistic films of the time as René Clair's *Entr'acte* (1924), the highlight of which is a group of erstwhile dignified people chasing after a camel-drawn hearse gone out of control; Hans Richter's *Ghosts Before Midday* (1927),[2] in which such normally inanimate objects as derbies, collars, guns, and coffee cups revolt against their human owners; and Man Ray's ironically titled *Return to Reason* (1923), which features bizarre juxtapositions of springs, buttons, nails, and tacks with a dancing naked woman.

As for Surrealism, an artistic movement concerned with depicting dream-states and other unconscious expressions and heavily influenced by the writings of Sigmund Freud, its most notable filmic representative is the famous eye-opening film by Luis Buñuel and Salvador Dali entitled *Un Chien Andalou*. With its grotesque and preposterous imagery (including a woman's underarm hair transplanting itself on a man's face, dead donkeys, ants emerging from a hole in a human hand, and, of course, the sliced eyeball), *Un Chien Andalou* still shocks and repels uninitiated audiences even today.

The avant-garde film experienced a hiatus during the 1930s as filmmakers largely shifted their attention from abstract artistry to deal directly with pressing social and economic issues. The form made a comeback during the 1940s, however, when such filmmakers as Maya Deren and Norman McLaren began plying their craft. Deren's films, the most notable of which is *Meshes of the Afternoon* (1943), frequently demonstrate her interest in dream, ritual, and dance. This dreamlike film, which concerns a woman (Deren herself) who contemplates suicide while in various states of wakefulness, consists entirely of representational images. Yet she and her cinematographer husband, Alexander Hammid, composed the images so unusually (an extremely tight close-up of an eye, an arm descending from the top of the frame to pick up a flower, a face reflected in a knife blade) and arranged them in such a dream-like way (a foot stepping on a series of completely different landscapes) that the resulting film became something strange, penetrating, and foreboding.

Norman McLaren's approach could not be further from Deren's. Beginning with his work at the National Film Board of Canada during the early 1940s, McLaren has investigated more kinds of movements, moods, and themes in animated films than anyone else in the history of cinema. He has animated paper cutouts, three-dimensional objects, even real people, but he is best known for his camera-less animated films, on which he has painted, scratched, tinted, and drawn directly, often without regard to frame lines.

The 1950s and 1960s have often been characterized as the era of the "underground film," when avant-garde filmmakers often explored taboo topics. Kenneth Anger's *Scorpio Rising* (1963), which examines the myth of motorcycle gangs, is one of the most famous and controversial examples of the avant-garde cinema of the time. *Scorpio Rising* contains so many offensive references to Jesus Christ, fascist politics, and sexuality that the Los Angeles police department seized the film during its premiere (mainly for its brief scenes of male nudity), while the American Nazi Party, outraged by Anger's treatment of the swastika and other fascist icons, brought Anger to court (see Fig. 11–1).

Since the 1950s and 1960s, avant-garde films have become more resistant to categorization. As a means of shedding some light on these elusive latter films, we turn our attention now to the basic nature of all avant-garde films, past and present. Despite their incredible diversity in form, content, and purpose, avant-garde films do tend to share several broad characteristics, which we offer herewith.

GENERAL CHARACTERISTICS

Perhaps the most distinctive feature of avant-garde films (and one considerably overworked by writers on the subject—including us, no doubt) is the usual lack of traditional narrative structure. A number of avant-garde films certainly have a basic

Figure 11-1 *Scorpio Rising* (1963–American). Images of death and James Dean are among the motifs of Kenneth Anger's provocative underground classic, *Scorpio Rising*. The American Nazi Party was among several groups incensed (if for widely varying reasons) by the film's content.

narrative thread running through them, including Norman McLaren's *Neighbours* (1952), in which two animated men fight to the death over a flower that springs up on the line dividing their properties, and George Kuchar's underground comedy *Hold Me While I'm Naked* (1966), which uses the most garish of Hollywood techniques and clichés with satiric glee to tell the story of a lonely and sexually frustrated young man. Most often, however, avant-garde filmmakers avoid entirely the linear progression inherent to traditional feature-length films or so obscure it as to make it virtually unrecognizable.

A second characteristic of avant-garde cinema is strongly related to the first: avant-garde films are usually highly personal expressions akin to poems, paintings, and sculptures. Unlike a typical commercial film, on which dozens or even hundreds of people may work, an avant-garde film is often the creation of an individual or at most a small group of people. In either of these situations, only one person makes all of the important decisions. And while the purpose of a commercial film is usually to offer escapism in the form of an easily understood story (accomplished in large measure through a highly familiar narrative structure) and to make money, the goals of avant-garde films are quite different: to evoke feelings or concepts not necessarily popular or commercial. Indeed, many avant-garde films are autobiographical and contain highly personalized symbolism that may be difficult to decipher on a mass-audience level, thus reducing their viability. Frank Mouris' Oscar-winning *Frank Film* (1973) is a case in point. This nine-minute short consists of a nonstop welling of images cut out of magazines that Mouris had collected for six years. Underneath *Frank Film's* mind-bending technical virtuosity is a film largely about the maker's own life (hence the title), with the images illustrating various phases, concerns, or influences while growing up in America. The sound track reinforces Mouris' preoccupation with himself; it consists of two overlapping voices—both belonging to Mouris. One voice recalls the major events in his life while the other recites a list of words beginning with "F"—the letter that not only begins both his first name and the name of the film but also seemingly provided endless fascination for the filmmaker. In short, Mouris saturated the film with aural and visual details about himself, and audiences exposed to the bombardment of its sounds and images cannot possibly hope to understand everything in it, even after several viewings (see Fig. 11–2).

Brevity is a third general characteristic of the avant-garde cinema. Though there are a handful of extremely lengthy films, such as Andy Warhol's six-hour *Sleep* and eight-hour *Empire*, the average running time of most avant-garde films is well under a half-hour. Samuel Beckett's sole venture into the film medium—the singularly titled *Film* (1965), starring Buster Keaton—is comparatively long at 22 minutes (see Fig. 11–3).

The final characteristic of avant-garde cinema consists of the various results that stem from an overriding concern on the part of many experimental filmmakers: a desire to forge a new relationship between the viewer and the medium. Viewing a film is generally a quasi-hypnotic experience, and commercial filmmakers usually make no effort to disrupt this mesmerizing quality of the medium. Indeed, viewers of traditional narrative films are strongly encouraged to "lose themselves" in the films, to be entertained, and to take what is offered in them at face value. The continuous stream of invisibly sutured imagery, the tight narrative logic, and the relatively lengthy duration of traditional narrative films strongly discourage the audience from subvocalizing, which might lead to a questioning of what one sees. Instead of risking such a potentially inharmonious response, the Hollywood filmmaker asks the audience to suspend its disbelief.

Just the opposite is true for avant-garde cinema. Instead of a smooth-flowing, easily understood narrative presented in an "invisible" form—that is, a mode of presentation that does not call attention to itself—a typical avant-garde film is usually complex and a challenge to one's expectations and understanding of the

Figure 11–2 *Frank Film* (1973—American). Frank Mouris' autobiographical film contains a flood of cut-out magazine images that the filmmaker had been collecting for several years. Mouris organized the images around several prominent themes, such as materialism, money, food, and religion.

Figure 11-3 *Film* (1965—Canadian). Samuel Beckett's single entry into the film field has only two characters: Buster Keaton and a camera. With a running time of 22 minutes, it's a bit longer than many avant-garde films.

nature of the film. It is usually presented in a highly visual form (rapid editing, out-of-focus shots, and grainy film stocks are common), and it occasionally employs "shock tactics" or features a taboo subject to jolt the audience. Stan Brakhage's extremely graphic meditations on birth (*Window Water Baby Moving* [1959]) and death (*Sirius Remembered* [1959], *The Act of Seeing With One's Own Eyes* [1972]), and the treatments of sexuality offered by Jack Smith and Kenneth Anger (*Flaming Creatures* [1963] and *Fireworks,* [1947] respectively) are excellent examples of these characteristics. Spawned in protest, the avant-garde film is frequently disturbing and unsettling—qualities that demand a deeper degree of involvement on the part of the viewer. Audiences weaned on traditional narrative Hollywood fare may find it easy to reject avant-garde films out of hand. But those intrepid souls who have the desire and courage to take on this more active viewing role—and it is indeed a courageous act to break away from the conventional—are often richly rewarded in that they will have likely been shown how to look at cinema, and life, in new and different ways.

THE POETRY CONNECTION

We can perhaps best appreciate the experience of viewing avant-garde films by comparing it with the experience of reading poetry. While narrative film and narrative literature have often been compared (as they are elsewhere in this book), the relationship between *nonnarrative* forms of film and literature has often been slighted. Even though film critics once widely applied the term *film poem* to avant-garde works, it would be misleading to revive the term as a label; as avant-garde critic Sheldon Renan has suggested, film poetry is an uneasy category because of a lack of a satisfactory definition of poetry *per se.* Yet Renan has also noted "that these films frequently instill in the viewer a sense of poetry,"[3] and this observation will serve as our rationale for examining the experience of viewing avant-garde films *vis-à-vis* the experience of reading or listening to poetry.

To help accomplish this task, we will use the characteristics of avant-garde cinema already outlined as a springboard for studying the responses engendered by these characteristics and the ways they correspond to our responses to poetry. At the same time, we will use the general form of poetry as a further means of comparison.

The usual lack of a narrative structure represents the first of several similarities between avant-garde cinema and poetry. It comes from an inclination of many poets and avant-garde filmmakers to eschew or downplay the traditional narrative function of film and literature in general. Many filmmakers and poets wish to express concepts, experiences, or emotions that are not stories, or do not lend themselves well to narration, or are items that their creators simply do not want to couch in a narrative structure. Consciously or not, avant-garde filmmakers and poets alike have frequently rejected traditional narrative structures (and, by implication, shown their displeasure with societies that created those structures)[4] in favor of what they perceive is a more fruitful means of expression.

A more specific version of this characteristic was offered years ago by avant-garde filmmaker, promoter, and theorist Maya Deren. She suggested that avant-garde films are similar to poems in that they are *vertical* studies of concepts or themes. In other words, avant-garde filmmakers and poets are concerned primarily with investigating the various layers of connotative meaning of a given moment, with minimal if any concern for that moment's place within a traditional narrative structure. Most novels and narrative films, on the other hand, feature *horizontal* developments, in which the action usually proceeds along a chronological cause-and-effect structure. Such a structure implies a certain kind of logic and rationality necessary to make the work easily understandable to the general public—qualities often absent in poems and avant-garde films.

What does this characteristic suggest about the respective experiencings of poetry and avant-garde cinema? Before we can arrive at a reasonable answer, we first need to examine a widely held notion related to the avant-garde filmmaker's characteristic quest to shape a new audience-medium relationship: the fundamental experiential qualities of literature and cinema *per se*.

It is a commonplace to observe that literature is a conceptual means of expression, while cinema is by and large a physical, concrete one. In other words, the general assumption holds that we literally see words in a sentence but apprehend them conceptually, while we literally see images in a film and apprehend them "as is." Thus, readers or listeners of literature partake of the interplay of words offered by the author and convert it into imagery or feelings, while film audiences merely have visual images thrust before their eyes that call for no conversion whatsoever. This rather specious argument is usually followed up by the misleading conclusion that the readers play a more active role of interpretation than their film-viewing counterparts.

This argument, frequently trotted out whenever comparisons are made between the acts of reading novels or short stories and watching narrative films, has some applicability to the issue of apprehending poems and avant-garde films. The acts of reading and viewing vary considerably on the level of *visual sensation*, or the most basic level of visual apprehension. In other words, the retinal images of all literary forms are words pure and simple, while the retinal images of cinema are visual images. The point that words and photographic images are strongly different from one another *as stimuli* is suggested by this observation: that they have markedly resisted efforts by filmmakers to be blended smoothly. Words and visual images had an uneasy alliance when narrative filmmakers attempted to yoke them in the silent cinema of yore, but the relationship breaks down even further when avant-garde filmmakers have attempted to fuse these stimuli in their works. Virtually all mixtures of visual images and evocative printed messages in avant-garde films show the strain of such a mix, including the combination of rotating concentric circles with wordplays in Marcel Duchamp's *Anemic Cinema* (1926), the mixture of such single words as "Scream" and "Crack" with highly expressionistic camera work in Melville Webber and James Watson's *The Fall of the House of Usher* (1928), the interlacing of Walt Whitman's verse with static images of Manhattan buildings in Sheeler and Strand's *Manhatta*, and the blending of a poem by Robert Desnos with such items as a starfish and a collapsing chimney in Man Ray's *Etoile de Mer* (1928).

If we go beyond the level of sensation, however, we find that the basic argument concerning literature and cinema (that is, that literature is conceptual while film is concrete) begins to erode when applied to the experiential natures of poetry and avant-garde cinema. In most avant-garde films, the images serve as points of departure for concepts. For example, the images from many such films are entirely nonobjective or nonrepresentational, such as the "Art Deco" curlicues of Viking Eggeling's *Symphonie Diagonale* (1920–22), the vibrant colors and shapes set to a big-band jazz score in Oskar Fischinger's *Allegretto* (1936), rapidly, almost subliminally edited patches of color in Robert Breer's *Blazes*, and alternating sections of pure black and pure white in Peter Kubelka's *Arnulf Rainer* (1957). In other words, the visual images in these films are not iconic, or objectively representative of people or things that exist in the physical world, as are those of traditional Hollywood films. Instead, these images are abstractions that eventually lead to concepts or emotions when placed in a given structure, just as words do. If the viewer is unwilling or unable to be led down a conceptual path, the resulting experience may be one of boredom or confusion, or the viewer may simply focus on the surface qualities of the images. The latter response would be the equivalent to enjoying the sounds of words for their own sake, such as listening to a person reading aloud a menu written in French. While such "sensorial" approaches may have their appeal (and no doubt some filmmakers cater to this approach), they seem limited and superficial.

What of avant-garde films that consist of representational photographic imagery? Are they to be taken at "face value," as traditonal narrative films supposedly are?

The answer lies in the ways that the images are arranged and presented. As noted previously, most avant-garde films do not feature the traditional cause-and-effect, linear structure common to narrative films. Thus, the thread that connects the images is based on some other structure, be it chronological and acausal (the whole of American history in three minutes in Charles Braverman's *American Time Capsule*), thematic (images of technology and violence from diverse Hollywood films and newsreels in Bruce Conner's 1958 *A Movie*), formal (geometric shapes and machine movements in Fernand Léger's *Ballet Mécanique*), random (Man Ray's Dadaist *Return to Reason*), or any other. The point is that a film based on a nonnarrative structure demands a different sensibility or *way of seeing* on the part of the viewer. Although the temptation may be great, one simply cannot look only on the face value of the images, for they are different from the simple surface illustrations for stories that require minimal conceptualization by the viewer. Instead, they frequently carry with them the qualities that allow for the creation of figurative and connotative meanings in the mind of the viewer, just as a figurative use of language may indicate truths that would be inexpressible through a literal use of language.

If, for example, we were to take an avant-garde film such as Maya Deren's *Meshes of the Afternoon*, which consists entirely of representational photographic imagery, and attempt to deal with it on a surface level only, our resulting experience would be extremely confusing and unrewarding. On the other hand, if we were to suppress temporarily our compulsion to analyze the film along rational, logical, narrative lines and instead allow the film to speak to the nonrational, intuitive, emotional side of ourselves, the resulting experience would be more powerful and portentous. Just as the evocative wordplay of a poem resonates within the reader in part because the reader is attuned to the special qualities of poetry, so also will the imagery of an avant-garde film resonate within the "attuned" viewer.

Of course, concept-arousing images are well represented in many feature-length narrative films, such as the dangling pince-nez of the ship's doctor in Sergei Eisenstein's *The Battleship Potemkin*, St. Peter's Basilica at the conclusion of Roberto Rossellini's *Rome: Open City* (1946), a young Abraham Lincoln performing "Dixie" on a jew's-harp in John Ford's *Young Mr. Lincoln* (1939), and the clumsy spider web and rabbits scenes in Charles Laughton's *The Night of the Hunter* (1955). The significant difference is that these moments are scattered and are subordinate to the story, and may thus be vitiated, while their avant-garde counterparts are often highly concentrated and may indeed be the very *raison d'etre* of the films of which they are a part.

Just as individual words and images may carry connotative meanings of their own, so also may the juxtaposition of words and images create other connotative meanings. Thus, the argument that film is strictly a physical, literal medium deteriorates even further, since it is perfectly possible for a viewer to draw a meaning not inherent in the individual shots or images themselves but from their juxtaposition. This is by no means a new argument, but it is one worth mentioning as it has direct bearing on the issue at hand. As we noted in Chapter 3, Sergei Eisenstein argued years ago that film can indeed be used as a conceptual medium by juxtaposing images (or sound and image) to create a new meaning. For example, if a shot of an imperiled person is immediately followed by a shot of a fly trapped in a spider's web, the meaning that arises from that juxtaposition would be clear for most viewers. Yet it is not present in the individual images but created in the minds of the viewers through the juxtaposition.

Such a potent quality of the medium is seldom used in commercial narrative films beyond the level of fleshing out an otherwise bare-boned narrative structure. Perhaps narrative filmmakers have learned from the films of Eisenstein and others who have used this approach extensively that an excessive use of such juxtapositions may add weight to the story and impede its progress by going off on conceptual tangents. Observed from this point of view, such films do not flow smoothly but instead move in fits and starts. Regardless of medium, the blending of complex horizontal and vertical structures within a single work has seldom been successfully realized (the works of William Shakespeare and Orson Welles are among the few exceptions). As a possible explanation, we return to the point that different structures require different ways of seeing; in other words, the incoming information of a strongly horizontal work touches a person's consciousness in a different way from that of a strongly vertical work. It may boil down simply to whether a film or literary work speaks to the rational, logical, linear side of the person or the nonrational, intuitive, holistic side. Poems and avant-garde films are almost always in the latter category.

As noted previously, avant-garde films are often highly personalized expressions. This "personal" characteristic underscores the similarity of experiencing such films and poetry. Since the brevity of most poems allows them to be read aloud, attending a poetry reading is akin to attending the presentation of an avant-garde film or a grouping of such films, in that the expression of a single person touches the consciousnesses of others. Indeed, a number of avant-garde filmmakers have adopted the strategy of presenting lectures and showing some of their films (primarily to recoup costs since avant-garde filmmaking is seldom a financially profitable undertaking). These presentations are generally quite similar to typical poetry readings: The artists from both groups present creative works, discuss them with their audience, and then move on to the next work.

Not all poems are meant to be read aloud to others, however; some poems are written for the eye, not the ear. What comparisons may be drawn from this observation? Or to put it in more specific terms, how does the experience of reading a poem silently to oneself, with its strong sense of one-to-one communing, compare with viewing an avant-garde film?

The experience of watching a film is usually described in these terms: It begins as a collective, communal experience (one almost always sees a film in the presence of other people), yet the experience invariably becomes a highly personalized one. The usual procedure is to "bracket out" mentally the other people in the audience as the film unfolds, yet they remain on the threshold of a viewer's consciousness. One is never entirely free of the feeling that he or she is with other viewers, the presence and actions of whom may impinge upon the experiencing of the film.

This situation holds true for viewers of all types of films, and it remains a significant difference between reading and viewing. A new tradition of sorts is underway, however, that may help individualize, or "de-mass," the mass medium of film on the experimental level. This tradition is the growing trend of buying or renting one's own copies of films in a variety of formats: 16 mm film, 8 mm film, Super-8 film, video cassette, and video disc. Avant-garde films hold a special advantage here over traditional narrative cinema. While the cost of buying or renting most narrative films remains relatively high—particularly in the 16 mm format—avant-garde films are available at significantly lower costs because of their usual brevity and lower consumer demand. Thus, a viewer may build up a collection of favorite avant-garde films, and while it would still be more expensive than obtaining a collection of cherished poems, it would be considerably less expensive than building up a collection of a like number of narrative films. As more and more noncommercial distributorships such as schools, libraries, and archives continue to increase their holdings of avant-garde films, the opportunities for viewing avant-garde works come ever closer to those opportunities for reading poems to oneself.

The brevity of most avant-garde films is another link between the viewing of such films and the reading of poems by allowing for reflection on what one has just viewed or read. The short lengths of avant-garde films correspond to those of most poems, where adequate opportunity is given to viewers and readers to reflect on, or let "sink in," what they have just apprehended. And in narrative literature, natural breaks in the form of chapter divisions are likewise offered, or the reader may simply pause anywhere to reflect on what has just been read before picking up the narrative thread once again.

Narrative film audiences, on the other hand, lack this kind of freedom. Under normal viewing conditions, they are discouraged from subvocalizing (or "subimaging," perhaps) by the continuous stream of images that flow into their senses for periods of from one to three hours. Indeed, it has been argued frequently by political film critics that the thinking has already been done for the audiences who watch typical Hollywood films.

The relatively short running times of avant-garde films offer the perfect opportunity for introspection, and thus this film genre bears another similarity to poetry. Even Andy Warhol's multiple-hour films offer such opportunities, as they seldom contain much activity, and Warhol himself has stated he expects his audiences to come and go during the presentations of these works. Instead of having to recall and deal logically with all of the various threads that run through a feature-length narrative film, the viewer of an avant-garde film typically deals with a single concept, experience, or emotion presented in a format that strongly encourages reflection. Some avant-garde filmmakers appear to have gone out of their way to provide time for this activity. For example, Bruce Conner inserted numerous blank passages in his A Movie, presumably to allow the audience to reflect on what it has just seen, while Bruce Baillie's Quick Billy (1967–70) carries with it the filmmaker's instructions to show the film's four reels on a single projector, since he intended the pauses between reels to be a part of the presentation.

MODERN DIRECTIONS

In a 1979 article entitled "Where Is the Avant-Garde Going?"[5] J. Hoberman suggests that there are several types of avant-garde films currently being produced with regularity. These include: (1) *the autobiographical/diary film* (a film dealing with some aspect or aspects of the filmmaker's life, ranging from a single moment, such as a birthday celebration, to a lifetime's worth of material; (2) *the assemblage film* (a film made up from fragments of other films); and (3) *the "absolute" film* (a film concerned almost exclusively with purely filmic elements, such as flicker, zoom shots, rapid editing, etc.). While the interest in these "subgenres" indicates that the avant-garde film is alive and healthy, it may also suggest that it has reached a level of stagnation in that all of these subcategories were developed many years ago. For instance, the roots of the autobiographical film may be found in the works of Maya Deren and Stan Brakhage (undertaken in the forties and fifties), since these filmmakers frequently played the lead characters in their respective films. Similarly, the ancestry of the assemblage film is traceable to the fifties and sixties films of Bruce Conner, and conceptually to the theories of Sergei Eisenstein. The antecedents of the absolute film are found even further back in film history, in the highly formalistic works of Viking Eggeling and Hans Richter, done in the twenties. Yet in refining these early tendencies, modern avant-garde filmmakers have created works that are often far removed from the originals. For example, Hoberman states that the new autobiographical films are "complicated by the politics of feminism" and "owe far less to surrealism [as Deren's works do] than they do to the films of Jean-Luc Godard or the novels of Marguerite Duras."[6]

Moreover, Hoberman neglects to mention what may well be the most exciting development in the avant-garde film in years: the fusion of film and video. Spurred by the efforts of such pioneers in this field as Scott Bartlett and Jordan Belson, many avant-garde filmmakers have crossed over into the video realm to borrow techniques and concepts for application to film.[7] The resulting film-video productions, along with the refinements in the autobiographical, assemblage, and absolute films—not to mention the possible crossovers between these subgenres—indicate that the avant-garde film continues to show signs not of stagnation but of growth and maturity.

NOTES

[1]David Curtis, *Experimental Cinema* (New York: Dell, 1971), p. 51.

[2]We offer this title as a more accurate translation of Richter's *Vormittagsspuk* than the usually cited *Ghosts Before Breakfast*.

[3]Sheldon Renan, *An Introduction to the American Underground Film* (New York: Dutton, 1967), p. 34.

[4]As any structuralist would argue, narrative structures represent the transmissions of a society, not of any one individual. Since avant-garde filmmakers tend to be highly individualistic and idiosyncratic, it is not surprising that many of them reject traditional narrative structures. See the following chapter for a further discussion of structuralism.

[5]J. Hoberman, "Where Is the Avant-Garde Going?," *American Film*, 5, no. 2. (November 1979), 36–40.

[6]Ibid., p. 37.

[7]This observation ties in neatly with the argument developed in Chapter 9 that the film and television media are growing even closer.

12

FILM THEORIES
AND CRITICAL METHODS

FOUNDATION OF MAJOR FILM THEORIES

For as long as motion picture cameras have been turning, professional observers and the general public have tried to describe and better understand in some ordered fashion the nature of the medium and how it functions. The development of theories of film construction likely began with the day-to-day perceptions and decisions of the early filmmakers long before anyone thought to set down such observations in writing, or to give some ordered and undivided attention to film expression and what methods might be used to accomplish what ends.

With a film technology coming under control, an industry on the rise, and the prospects of a significant mode of communication or entertainment in the offing, interest in film as more than a penny arcade or theater novelty led to more directed attention by those who began to take the medium seriously. With an increasing body of film work from which to draw, as well as a history of production and exhibition, film theorists and practitioners were able to make observations concerning film form and function that moved from the speculative to the more assertive. An ever increasing range in styles and functions followed, some suggesting that the motion picture might have some validity as an art form. The developing theory of film that paralleled the growth of the medium and the industry and technology that produced it gradually became a foundation for critical methodologies that provided a systematic and logical way of looking at movies (see Fig. 12–1). It gave the more than casual observer the means whereby a work could be better understood, more meaningfully described, and, finally, judged according to prevailing social, aesthetic, and technological values.

The Formalist Tradition

Early writings on the nature and function of film tended to follow a *formalist* or more overtly creative approach, drawing from both the world of art and psychology. In 1916, the American poet and theorist Vachel Lindsay published *The Art of the Moving Picture,* in which he set down an "Unchallenged Outline of Photoplay Critical Method." Containing an almost mystical approach to the high art of visual imagery and montage, the work today is considered a romantic and indulgent bit of dogma in which Lindsay enthusiastically provides models for "Photoplay Criticism in America." The same year witnessed observations on film from a theorist whose ideas foreshadowed the Gestalt school of psychology. Hugo Münsterberg, in *The Photoplay: A Psychological Study,* discussed the mental process involved in film viewing, and he focused in particular on the ways that the perception, memory, imagination, and emotions of the film spectator are engaged by the medium to create the filmic illusion.

The more substantial and enduring writings on which formalist film theory rests also embraced both aesthetic and psychological precepts and observations. Rudolf Arnheim, a Gestalt psychologist interested in a variety of media, established an aesthetic base or "art of visual perception" in his 1932 book, *Film as Art.* Arnheim combined the psychology of perception with aesthetic considerations in an attempt to "organize the sensory raw material creatively according to principles of simplicity, regularity, and balance."[1] Arnheim built his aesthetics of film on the *limitations* of the medium at the time and on the differences between the appearance of physical reality and the expression of reality through cinematic means. Film of the 1920s was an art form for Arnheim precisely because film could not faithfully reproduce physical reality in a number of areas. Arnheim argued that the lack of such basic information as color and synchronous sound in film forced the minds of the audience to become more active to compensate for, or mentally fill in, the missing information. As might be expected, Arnheim opposed the naturalistic use of such emerging film technologies as color, synchronous sound, and the wide screen. From his perspective, the addition of each new technology meant that cinema would move one step further from its status as an art form and another step toward becoming a mere recording device, the very thought of which apparently appalled Arnheim. He saw the role of the filmmaker as an *interpreter* and indeed as a *transformer* of physical reality through a conscious ordering of the details of composition, lighting, camera angle, etc., rather than as a simple recorder of the physical world.

The creative arrangement of sensory raw material was also the concern of Soviet theorists and filmmakers Sergei Eisenstein and V. I. Pudovkin. In *The Film Sense* (1942) and *Film Form* (1949), Eisenstein used his own earlier films as well as those of D. W. Griffith to develop a theory of film construction in which montage—the selection and arrangement of individual shots—was at the heart of the creative process. Through the control of the various cinematic elements, but particularly through montage, Eisenstein saw the means to creative control of the

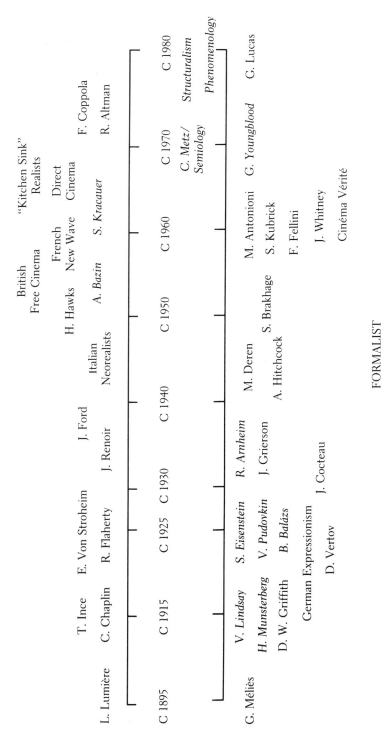

Figure 12-1 The various film theories did not develop in a vacuum but were intimately related to developments in film history and world thought. This diagram is primarily a historical overview of the realistic and formalistic tendencies in cinema as demonstrated in both theory and practice. The italicized names are those of the most prominent film theorists and schools of thought; the others reflect representative filmmakers and film groups. Several modern theories have downplayed and/or gone beyond the traditional formalist-realist division: hence their placement between the axes on this chart.

medium and the means to inspire in viewers a "pathos" for socialist ideology. Unlike Arnheim, he welcomed the coming of the new film technologies because they represented for him new elements for the director to control, or "new colors on the artist's palette." Individual shots for Eisenstein provided the mere raw material from which not only physical detail and action but also abstract concepts and "nondepictable" ideas could be conveyed through a range of associative values, including the shock value of linking opposite or contrasting images. He has in fact used the Odessa Steps sequence from his own *Potemkin*—perhaps the most famous sequence in all of film history—as a model for this montage theory of film construction. He argued that the individual shots, by themselves, are essentially meaningless; through juxtaposition with other shots, however, they become inflected with meaning.

Pudovkin, using a relatively simpler theory of *relational editing*, developed through his films and writings a means of constructing scenes by using individual shots as building blocks, allowing the meaning of each scene to come from both the content and juxtaposition of shots. While Pudovkin was certainly not above the idea of using rapid editing occasionally to accentuate a given scene, his style of editing remains more conservative than Eisenstein's. Like Eisenstein, he felt the responsibility of the filmmaker was to direct the audience's attention, but unlike Eisenstein he suggested it should be done rather subtly, through an *invisible editing* process, quite different from Eisenstein's shock editing. In other words, Pudovkin generally believed the filmmaker should guide the spectator into accepting the filmmaker's perspective during a given scene, accomplished largely through a process of editing that does not call undue attention to itself. Pudovkin occasionally turned to a more "Eisenstinian" montage to express an abstract idea, as he did in *Mother*, in which shots of spring floods are intermingled with shots of revolutionaries on the march, signifying the indomitable spirit and inevitable nature of the revolution. Pudovkin remained the champion of invisible editing, however, and most conventional narrative films bear his mark. Most television commercials, on the other hand, exhibit the stamp of Eisenstein's editing methods, even if their purpose—to sell commercial products—is far removed from the socialist goals of Eisenstein's cinema.

Formalist film theory was the first relatively homogeneous bloc of film theory to appear, holding sway from about 1915 through the silent cinema of the 1920s. One might well ask why so many individuals were concerned with raising cinema to the status of an art form so early in the history of the medium. Indeed, many of these early theorists centered their efforts on comparing cinema with the other media and art forms (for example, literature, theater, photography, painting), to accomplish several things: to differentiate film from the other forms from which it developed, and to show that film had comparable plasticity with the other arts. As a result of this obsession, these theorists deemphasized the realistic, mechanical recording qualities of the medium, and it is worth speculating why this school of thought developed first and with such fervor. A brief examination of the cultural context that surrounded and informed this bloc of theory may shed some light on the reasons for the growth of this way of thinking.

From the mid-nineteenth century through the first several decades of the twentieth, the Western world experienced incredible industrial growth. Tremendous strides were made in science and technology, resulting in the development and eventual mass-production of everything from automobiles to photographic equipment, phonographs, sewing machines, clothespins, light bulbs, and innumerable other items. In short, we had entered the "age of the machine," and with the tremendous interest in those things mechanical came a kind of "machine cult." Concomitantly, there was a strong interest in realism in the arts—an interest perhaps sparked by the new scientific discoveries and technologies, such as photography and cinema.

But what of traditional artistic sensibilities during this time, with their emphasis on formal properties? While some voices sang the praises of "machine art," most notably the Futurists, there were many who railed against realism, logic, technology, and machinery. The earliest fruits of this dissent appeared in the form of various twentieth-century expressive movements, such as Cubism, Dada, and Surrealism. (These and other such movements are discussed more fully in Chapter 11). Ironically, the medium of cinema—clearly a child of the scientific/technological revolution—was embraced by a number of theorists whose ideas constitute formalist film theory. They might have been inclined to reject cinema out of hand as a medium too technologically oriented, but instead these early theorists had the foresight to realize that cinema did not have to be used merely as a simple recording device for real events, or, in general, to travel a realistic path. They no doubt interpreted the realistic, mainstream cinema of their day as a "diamond in the rough": rather crude, but with enormous artistic potential. In brief, the formalist film theorists had the best of both worlds. They took this new mechanical recording device, which normally would have represented the "Machine Age" that they repudiated, and subverted it with missionary zeal to their own artistic ends. Spawned in the fertile European bed of post-WWI discontent and expressive thought, a formalist film theory began to emerge, tied to German Expressionism, the French Avant-Garde, and Soviet Formalism. Because of the newness of the medium, this body of film theory is often interpreted today as *prescriptive* or *predictive* ("This is how film should be used, or probably will be used").

The Realist Tradition

The theorists and practitioners of the formalist approach dedicated their efforts to finding the means, through cinematic invention, of rendering in visual terms worlds not directly observable in real life. But then a second major movement in film theory emerged (and in classic dialectical fashion), consisting of filmmakers and theorists who were more interested in photographic reality than in interior states of meaning. Chief among the proponents of a *realist* film theory were the German Siegfried Kracauer and the Frenchman André Bazin, both of whose writings appeared well after those of the formalists. Bazin and Kracauer were not filmmakers, but as theorists they gave careful attention to the sizable body of available film works and propounded theories based on actual practice rather than on hypothetical example. Unlike the formalist theorists, Bazin and Kracauer had a long tradition of extant films on which to draw. This fact led their theories to become more *descriptive* and *data-based* than those of their formalist counterparts. And, as Bazin has pointed out, the history of cinema has been characterized by a striving to make films resemble as much as possible the physical reality from which their imagery was taken. The earliest films were black and white, without sound, two-dimensional, and consisted of very short shots and narrow-screen photography. Gradually, however, the film medium became more realistic-appearing through the following additions: long camera-runs, color, synchronous sound, the wide screen, occasional probings into three-dimensionality (the "3-D" films of the 1950s and the holographic experiments of today), and even touch and smell (Emergo, Smellavision, and Odorama processes). As editor of the prestigious and influential film journal *Cahiers du Cinéma*, Bazin expressed a theory that challenged many of the expressive and formalist tenets set down by Arnheim, Eisenstein, and Pudovkin, and concerned himself with the unmanipulated surface of film experience and the dependence of the medium on physical reality. He saw montage as only one possible means of providing a simulation of reality and that this, like all other expressive techniques, must be kept carefully in check lest they intrude on the medium's ability to provide an empirical view of the world. In *What Is Cinema?* (1958), he described the "art of reality" and the power of the mechanically recorded image to explore physical reality automatically with little or no contrivance by the filmmaker. He accepted technological developments as synchronous sound and natural color as means of bringing the film experience in closer proximity to the directly observable world.

Bazin had a respect for the complexities of the real world that he felt could be easily distorted or violated by formalist devices such as montage. While recognizing the possibilities of creative control, he believed the filmmaker should employ a neutral, unobtrusive style, thereby yielding to the nature of film and its special affinity for photographic recording. While permitting the camera to seek out reality, Bazin's theory also supported freedom of perception on the part of the viewer. He believed film viewers, like theatergoers, should *discover* the reality of a situation through their own selection and focus, rather than have their perceptions controlled more rigidly by the filmmaker who uses the variables of composition, editing, movement, color, etc., to guide viewers closely in their interpretation of the scene, á la Pudovkin. Bazin's theory has important implications for the relationship of film to the other arts and media as well. In dealing with the screen adaptation of stage works, for example, he said the task of the realist director was to preserve the artificiality of the play. "The major heresy of filmed theatre," he argued, was in "the urge 'to make cinema.' "[2] He stipulated that the reality of the play was better preserved by "staging a play by means of cinema" rather than adapting or translating the play to conform to cinematic means of expression.[3]

Siegfried Kracauer, like Bazin, treated film as an extension of photography and emphasized the affinity of the medium for the recording of the visible world. Like Bazin, he also recognized the formalist or expressive possibilities of film, which he called "formative tendencies," but as a theorist in the realist school he saw the true function of film resting in the imitation of nature in the literal sense of the phrase. In his *Theory of Film: The Redemption of Physical Reality* (1960), he emphasized the special ability of the medium to record both movement and inanimate objects as they are found in nature. But the redemptive powers go even further, he suggested, to uncover and display those elements of the real world that normally go unnoticed because they are too large, too small, too fleeting, too mundane, or too overwhelming for us to cope with as they appear in life. The panoramic view of a vast landscape and the single drop of rain were for Kracauer equally cinematic material. In this rediscovery of the real world, he found film was able to bring "things normally unseen" within our consciousnesses.[4] The rediscovery or redemption he found was most effective when filmmakers turned their cameras on unstaged events, caught life seemingly unawares, and centered on what Kracauer called the "haphazard contingencies of life" or "nature in the raw."[5] Ironically, he repudiated most documentaries, insisting they presented only surface views of life; in other words, they had no human drama at their cores. (Kracauer likely would have rethought his position here had he the opportunity to view direct cinema and *cinéma vérité* films, which were in an embryonic state at the time *Theory of Film* appeared.) He insisted the best use of the medium was in presenting "found stories" (stories that seem to arise naturally out of their environments), which featured one or more forms of human conflict. Only then could film reach its fullest potential, Kracauer postulated.

Countering the earlier formalist film theorists, Kracauer maintained that cinema was not an art, or was at most an art very different from the other arts. This was so, he insisted, because of the medium's technological base (its heavy reliance on optics, physics, chemistry, mechanics, etc.), and because film is much more dependent on physical reality than the other arts. For example, the only concrete items a painter needs to create art are a brush, canvas, and paint. Similarly, the only such items that novelists, playwrights, and poets need are paper and writing implements. Filmmakers, on the other hand, need more than just a camera, raw film stock, and an editing bench to create films; filmmakers have to photograph *something*, and this something is some aspect of physical reality.

Like Bazin, Kracauer could not reject entirely the expressive possibilities of the medium and its function in conjuring appearances that are part of our imagined world as well as the literal one. "Film is better equipped than any other representational media to render visible things that have been imagined," he suggested.[6] He spoke little of the emerging "realistic" technologies of the medium, however, and his systemization of a realist aesthetic is finally less accommodating of the various dimensions of realism that Bazin seemed to have intuitively discovered. Although they do not form a single cohesive theory, the writings of these two men serve as a foundation for a realist school of film theory that evolved through the medium's revolutionary years following World War II.

EVOLVING THEORIES

The major film theories that have been developed through the long history of the medium have not been set down as immutable law. They have been varied, frequently conflicting, but always growing, shifting in emphasis, and articulating new ideas on the nature of film expression and those cinematic methods that might be used to accomplish various ends. This evolution of a theory of film has been strongly influenced by the ever increasing body of films available for study, and also by the gradually increasing interest in the very nature of the film-viewing experience and the ways that films may be interpreted.

The growth and change of theory based on the observation of a body of work rather than on hypothetical principle is illustrated at several key stages of development. Eisenstein and Pudovkin's montage theories were based heavily on an intensive study of the films of D. W. Griffith. Exercises in scene-building, comparison and contrast editing, and parallel construction, which were to be found in the early one- and two-reel films as well as features, became primers and models for the Soviet filmmakers. Griffith's *Intolerance* is said to have been screened so often that the print actually fell to pieces. Eisenstein best described the influence of Griffith on the Soviet pioneers when he said, "I wish to recall what David Wark Griffith himself represented to us, the young Soviet filmmakers of the twenties. To say it simply and without equivocation: a revelation."[7]

Much of the realist theory that has evolved since the 1950s has a direct link with the films that formed the core of the Italian neorealist movement. Although it has built on, modified, and sometimes even challenged the precepts on which the original movement was based, realist film theory of the past 25 years has continued to follow the underlying tenets of the neorealists—"to use the most direct language to say something in the most direct way."[8]

Semiology and *structuralism* are two interrelated theory-methodologies that have only recently been applied to film. These methodologies have attempted to bring systematic and scientific methods of analysis to uncover intrinsic meaning in film, and they have come from diverse sources, including the writings of the American philosopher Charles Sanders Peirce and the French anthropologist Claude Lévi-Strauss. They have been rooted particularly in structural linguistics and the work of Ferdinand de Saussure. As adapted to film study, the methods apply the linguistic theories of signs and symbols, and set about analyzing, but not necessarily judging, the means by which film codification and structure communicate meaning.

Semiology

The French semiotician Christian Metz has been at the forefront of attempts to formalize a system indicating *how* films convey meaning through signs and symbols (that is, a system of signification). As a "film grammarian," Metz has based his system on the dichotomy endemic to all language systems: the symbol and its referent, or, in semiological terms, the *signifier* and the *signified*. In verbal languages, it is the word and its meaning as narrowed by its usage (that is, its cultural significance and its juxtaposition with other words). The same definition holds for cinema, if we substitute "image" for "word." Metz has argued in his *Film Language* (1974) that cinema is not a true language. For example, individual words may be inflected by various suffixes and prefixes, of which there are no counterparts in cinema. It is, nevertheless, *like* a language and can be studied like a language, particularly its syntactical arrangements. While he has developed a system of signification according to the denotative and connotative meanings of signs in cinema, Metz has clearly been more interested in the *narrative* function of the medium and has largely restricted his inquiries into the meaning of individual shots and scenes to their surface level (their basic realism) and their place within the story of the film: in short their denotative—or to use the semiological term, *syntagmatic*—meaning. The exploration of connotative, or *paradigmatic*, meaning is perhaps best left to film humanists since they are experienced at grappling with the ambiguity of the associative or latent content of cinema, and since paradigmatic meaning often borders on the nebulous areas of art and judgment—subjects with which scientific-minded semiologists seem uncomfortable.

Several examples may help clarify the distinctions between signifiers and signifieds, and between syntagmatic and paradigmatic levels of meaning. The filmic image of John Wayne (a signifier) from *The Searchers* (1956) may signify, or refer to, one or more things (signifieds), offered here on a scale of increasing abstraction: the "real" or physical John Wayne; Ethan Edwards, the character he is portraying; the general Wayne persona; embodiments of machismo, goodness, perseverance, racism, or whatever (see Fig. 12-2). Semioticians are most at home dealing with the first two types of "signifieds" listed here, which together constitute *syntagmatic* meanings: the physical characteristics of the action (for example, his six-foot height, craggy face, commanding presence) and the place of the character within the story of the film. The remaining levels of meaning might be described as *paradigmatic* and would probably be shunned by semiology in its pure form, in part because they entail making judgments and speculation—areas that, as suggested above, are not terribly amenable to the scientific precision of the semiological method.

Orson Welles' *Citizen Kane* is another case in point. A recent semiological

Figure 12-2 *The Searchers* (1956—American). A photographic image can signify a variety of meanings simultaneously. In John Ford's *The Searchers*, for example, an image of John Wayne may signify any number of things: the physical appearance of the actor; Ethan Edwards, the character Wayne portrays in the film; and embodiments of such abstractions as perseverance, goodness, and/or racism.

study of this film (and an exhaustive one, rare among such studies) has established a comprehensive model by which the messages of the work might be better understood. This syntagmatic analysis is divided into those codes (signification "subsystems") that relate to narrative structure, time, the camera, patterns of sound, and the use of music.[9] The design for the analysis of music is divided among the major musical motifs of the film: the Xanadu theme, Emily's waltz, Susan's aria, the Charlie Kane tribute, and the *Inquirer* theme. The model for patterns of sound outlines a study of spoken language according to texture, rhythm, intonation, pitch, resonance, volume, idiosyncracies of speech, and register. The study also provides an analysis of semantics and verbal syntax, including the way that the biographical "News on the March" serves as a parody of the film newsreels of the period. As these elements of the *Citizen Kane* study suggest, semiology attempts to define in considerable detail the design of a work by showing the relationship between structure, content, and techniques, and it concerns itself with signification but without any preconceptions about how "reality" is to be represented.

Structuralism

Originally, the semioticians wished to develop an objective, neutral, scientific film analysis—a method free from the "taint" of philosophic belief. They wanted to deal with cinema on a *material basis* only, an approach reminiscent of the Aristotelian tradition in criticism: setting aside all external factors—historical, psychological, sociological, economic, etc.—and evaluating a work on the basis of its internal arrangement. In blunter terms, their original concern rested solely with the information that had been recorded and arranged on celluloid, nothing more. Eventually, however, the semioticians realized that there is no such thing as a neutral scientific method—and, by implication, a neutral science—and they quickly embraced the idea that a system of signification such as cinema cannot be studied in a vacuum but must be examined within the context of the social and psychological systems that formed it, and continue to form it. Thus, semiology in its pure form—a quasi-objective, quasi-empirical close analysis of data on celluloid—began giving way to *structuralism* as a means of film analysis. Like semiology, structuralism is a scientific, language-based approach to film concerned primarily with the ways that the medium communicates. It differs from semiology in that it emphasizes more strongly the fact that film is a product of human culture, and that it reflects that culture. In specific terms, it explicitly takes into account the role of a society's mythic structures in the formation of individual films. The structuralists are not nearly as interested as the semioticians in performing close analyses of individual shots and scenes in a film. Instead, their primary concern is to uncover and decipher societal codes—the so-called *deep structures*, or a society's deeply ingrained ways of thinking—and determine their effect on *surface structures*, such as languages and films. The deep structures find expression in a society's myths: those stories, rules, laws, etc., that have been handed down from generation to generation in a society, and which are considered truly *societal* expressions because they are free from individual authorship. The structuralists have frequently turned to the writings of Sigmund Freud and Karl Marx, along with those of their various disciples (Jacques Lacan, Louis Althusser, Roland Barthes, among others) for insight into the psychological and social factors that influence, and are a part of, a society's deep structures.

Let's take an example of the structuralist philosophy in action. One of the most durable of mythic structures is the story of Christ; it has been a part of our world for almost 2,000 years, and there is no question that its most fundamental premise—a "good" outsider interceding in the wayward affairs of others—has found its way into cinema. In addition to forming the backbone of films based specifically on the life of Christ, both traditional (*King of Kings, The Greatest Story Ever Told*) and updated (*Jesus Christ Superstar, Godspell*), this basic premise has also helped structure films that have seemingly little to do with the Christ story: a western (*Shane*), a domestic psychodrama (*Knife in the Water*), and science fiction (*The Day the Earth Stood Still, Superman*), to name a few. A structuralist would analyze and discuss in specific terms how various elements of the Christ myth have structured, or formed the framework, for these films.

Structuralism is largely indebted to the work of Claude Lévi-Strauss, a structural anthropologist who insisted on the complete priority of the collective over the individual—an idea that goes all the way back to Socrates, who argued that the collective enterprise forms the individual. Much of Lévi-Strauss' work is based on examining a society's underlying, unconscious patterns of thought—its deep structures—that mark the individual as a collective being. In short, the fountainhead of fundamental human nature is the *collective unconscious*. According to Lévi-Strauss, we as individuals owe our identities solely to our expressions of our society's deep structures.

This structuralist philosophy is quite different from *existentialism*, which stresses the primacy of the individual and the individual's freedom to forge his or her own identity and destiny. Instead of being at the center of his or her understanding of the world, the individual, according to Lévi-Strauss, is on an equal basis with the rest of nature: an object among other objects. Even human thought is regarded simply as one object amid many in the world.

Lévi-Strauss' articulations on the nature of human thought warrant further examination. He argued that human minds innately structure the world into polar opposites called *binary oppositions*, which is reflected in cultural expressions such as myths, folktales, and films. ("Good versus bad" is perhaps the most common and fundamental of such oppositions.) Thus, the secret to unlocking or decoding the meaning in a given film (or any other cultural expression, for that matter) is to isolate and identify as many binary oppositions as possible and then analyze the ways they are specifically handled in the work.

An example may help. In his review of Michael Cimino's *Heaven's Gate* (1979), critic Michael Blowen offers the following observation: "A litany of the film's themes seems eternal—landowners vs. immigrants; rich vs. poor; religion vs. atheism; order vs. chaos; hate vs. love; man vs. nature, intellect vs. emotion; capitalism vs. socialism; the individual vs. the group; fascism vs. democracy—ad infinitum."[10] Though he pursues it no further, Blowen has taken the first step in a Lévi-Strauss structural methodology by identifying some of the many polar opposites in this film. A person following up on this method—and it is by no means the only method employed by structuralists—would then take each pairing of opposites and discuss in specific terms how each one is dealt with (or reconciled, perhaps) in *Heaven's Gate*, but without attempting to judge or evaluate the film.

In general, structuralism and its blood relative semiology provide a blueprint for ordered and systematic analyses of the various levels and methods by which meaning may be conveyed in films. When these methods are applied to either individual or grouped film texts, they provide a way of sorting out and explaining the many codes that make up the messages conveyed by sound and image.

Phenomenology

In the late 1970s, a challenge to the linguistic and largely antihumanistic systems of structuralism and semiology was raised by theorists and critics concerned with the total experience—perceptual, imaginative, and aesthetic—of cinema. *Phenomenology*, as this philosophical perspective is called, has in general existed throughout this century and is manifested in the writings of Edmund Husserl, Jean-Paul Sartre, Martin Heidegger, and Maurice Merleau-Ponty. It is the philosophical study of human consciousness and of the appearances of things experienced, as opposed to the "objective qualities" of the things themselves.

Thus, as adapted to cinema, phenomenology is a viewer-oriented theory-method that emphasizes the spectator's reaction to film, not the film itself. Its recent application to cinema may be interpreted as a conservative backlash to the materialism and scientific slant of semiology and structuralism, whose investigations into the nature of cinema seldom discuss or even acknowledge the role of the spectator and are demonstrably too reductionistic. The phenomenologists are clearly distrustful of pure reason, which they consider only one type of consciousness, and of rationality, which they consider only one form of behavior. They have little faith in these and other approaches of the "grammarians of cinema" because of the incompatibility of scientific tools and creative processes. Using a scientific method to study the art form of cinema, they might well claim, makes as much sense as evaluating a Picasso by measuring it with a ruler. A more holistic approach is necessary because, as the phenomenologists argue, cinema goes beyond what one sees and hears to what one *feels*. Instead of analyzing a film's images from the outside by interpreting them in the light of societal codes, spectators should immerse themselves in the images en route to interpreting them from a highly personal and idiosyncratic perspective.

Phenomenology makes room for the broader experiences available through film, including the relationship of a work to its creator, to other films, to its audience, and the conditions under which it is seen. It invites the most eclectic approach to film criticism, allowing for the broadest interpretations of the film experience, which might be sensory stimuli for one viewer, storytelling for a second, and total psychic absorption for a third. For example, a Mel Brooks movie might be quite funny and satisfying to one person and in appallingly bad taste to another; similarly, a Michelangelo Antonioni film might invite a response of rigorous intellectual game-playing from one viewer and consummate boredom from another. Yet all responses would be legitimate.

Theories of film such as phenomenology, which are based on the nature of the film experience and the psychology of the viewer, also had their grounding in the writings of psychologist-theorists Hugo Münsterberg and Rudolf Arnheim. They have been given added dimension through the continued studies of both behavioral psychologists and mass-media specialists who study the broader range of media stimuli and effects as well as audience conditioning. In "Psychology of Film Experience," Hugo Mauerhofer tied the nature of film form and function to the conditioning factors peculiar to film that renders the viewer more receptive to the magic of the luminous rectangle. Marshall McLuhan, like Mauerhofer, saw the nature of film and its capacity to convey messages—be they cultural, aesthetic, or simply mechanical—in terms of the way the individual relates to the medium itself. His focus is on the process by which modern electronic media, particulary television, influence human sensory awareness. Although met by considerable challenge and refutation, McLuhan's ideas on the modern media as an extension of human senses have, along with other contemporary theories of communication, ultimately become an extension of film theory and its effects.

In recent years, films have been examined in relation to other media, and film theory of the 1970s has featured a new awareness of film as part of mixed media and our response to it as "intermedia kinetic experience." This has taken it out of the realm of behavioral psychology and into that of metaphysics. Gene Youngblood, in *Expanded Cinema* (1970), turned to the contemporary experimental film and what he calls "synaesthetics" and "cybernetic cinema" to describe the modern media in terms of total phenomena and a new dimension of awareness through technology. It is, according to Youngblood, a kind of "cosmic consciousness [in which] what we 'know' conceptually has far outstripped what we experience empirically."[11]

Phenomenology, for several reasons, provides a fitting conclusion to our discussion of film theory. With it, we have come full circle in the historical development of film theory to the psychological issues raised by the earliest theorists such as Münsterberg and Arnheim. And it also makes for a smooth transition to our discussions of film criticism since most mainstream, popular-press film critics are practicing phenomenologists, though they might not label themselves as such.

FILM CRITICISM

The Function

The role of the critic, in film as in other art forms, is to seek ways of better understanding and responding to a creative work. The critic asks questions and makes judgments about the source, the process, or structure of the work, and finally about its function. If the questions are the right ones (those dealing with the film's theme, technical quality, validity of ideas, and individual contributions such as acting, music, script, etc.) and the judgments based on informed and insightful observations, the critic can, if also blessed with a command of language, make the work more accessible and stimulating to others. Besides conveying the design and intentions of new works, the critic is also capable of helping others see familiar works with fresh insight and an increased level of awareness. Good criticism will not only render the exposure to art more meaningful but also give added dimension to subsequent reflection and contact with the same work or other works with which it shares common features or background. Our understanding and appreciation of what Alain Resnais was trying to do in *Hiroshima, Mon Amour* (1960) and *Last Year at Marienbad* (1962), for example, may be enhanced by exposure to a good piece of critical writing on his more recent film, *Providence* (1977). Good criticism will help noncritics better understand their own responses to a work and to describe with more precision their feelings about it to others. Theater and film critic John Simon has succinctly stated the critical process:

> With cogency, suasion, passion, charm, [the critic] induces us to think, to widen our horizons, to open yet another book, to reconsider a snap judgment, to see something from a loftier vantage point. . . . Good criticism of any kind—of movies, ballet, architecture, or whatever—makes us think, feel, respond; if we then agree or disagree is less important than the fact that our faculties have been engaged or stretched.[12]

Any but the most cursory and superficial attention to films will involve one in observations and judgments about the process and function of the medium and of individual works and groups of works. Film criticism developed as a discipline alongside the budding art the industry of film, and has evolved as a series of methods of interpreting form and function and establishing the various bases for sound judgment.

Early "reflections" on film fell into the category of reviewing—or perhaps even more basically, journalistic reporting—on the exhibition of early film programs. The first film reviewers or reporters were concerned mainly with identifying the film's genre, providing a basic synopsis of the action once the narrative had developed, and making general observations about the entertainment value of the work.

But in 1914, editors of *The Independent,* a literary journal of the period, announced the beginning of a regular film department devoted to "independent and conscientious criticism."[13] Noting the need for guidance by reputable periodicals in introducing readers to works of value in the infant art of moving pictures, the editors went on to pledge that "since this is a new field in which freedom of criticism has not yet been established, it may be necessary to state that our criticism of motion films will be as careful and unbiased as our criticism of books and plays has been."[14]

Ever since the recognition of the aesthetic potential of film in the teens, criticism, though not necessarily unbiased, has developed as a complementary discipline (some would say art) to the evolution of the medium. At times it has ventured little beyond reporting on the release of a film, giving its production details and credits, and providing a brief plot synopsis. In its more creative and rigorous form, it has gotten beyond such basic reportage and has helped reveal validity and meaning in individual works by formulating criteria on which judgments of value can be based and has stimulated an aesthetic consciousness about the medium as a whole. Along the way, film criticism has helped discover and promote previously unheralded films and the talents of those associated with them. It has drawn attention to changing trends, styles in filmmaking, the evolution of genres, and the influence of political ideology. Occasionally it has also become the battleground where critics have waged war on one another, armed with opposing perspectives and methods.

Most critical pieces fall into one of two broad categories: *popular-press criticism* and *scholarly criticism.* While the separation of the two is ultimately an academic activity, and while the terms themselves present connotative problems, we find it worth noting the number of reasonably distinct differences between them. First, there is the question of intended audience. The popular-press critics commonly aim for as broad and heterogeneous an audience as possible, while the scholarly critics usually cater exclusively to a rather elite audience made up of like-minded *cinéastes.* Some may find this distinction between "film fans" and "serious students of the cinema" a bit condescending, but it nevertheless seems a factor that these critics take into account, consciously or not.

Coupled with this first distinction is the second: the media through which the audiences obtain access to the criticisms. In the case of the popular-press criticism, they are found, as the name implies, in newspapers, magazines, and on television. The writings of scholarly critics, on the other hand, usually find their way into books and cinema journals—publications devoted entirely to intensive film study.

A third distinction may be found in the types of film criticized: popular-press critics tend to focus on those films currently playing at first-run film theaters, while scholarly critics deal with any and all types of film. A critic of the latter camp would think nothing of criticizing a film from the thirties today, for example, if he or she had new insights to offer; on the other hand, it would be virtually unheard-of for a popular-press critic to do the same, unless the film was a "revival" receiving much public exposure, such as the recently reconstructed and rereleased 1927 epic, *Napoleon*.

The final difference is tied to the popular-press critic's main concern of examining new films: the ultimate purpose of the criticism. The central question the popular-press critic tries to answer is: Is the film worth seeing? In a sense, this critic is acting as a "consumer advocate," informing interested people *before they have seen the film* whether or not it is worth going out of their way to see. This type of criticism—which might be more accurately labeled *reviewing*—is quite different from that of the scholarly critic, who is more interested in engaging in what almost becomes a dialogue with the filmmaker, and whose writings are usually meant to be read *after* seeing the film. Subsequently, scholarly criticism tends to consist of detailed and comprehensive investigations into individual films or groups of related films following fairly rigorous applications of specific methodologies such as *auteur*, genre, feminist, etc. (all of which will be discussed shortly), while popular-press criticism, which often resembles a loose amalgam of issues related to literary criticism (plot, character, rising and falling action, climax, etc.), psychoanalytic criticism (the behavior and motivations of the characters), and entertainment value (quality of acting, special effects, etc.), may seem rather undisciplined in comparison. This apparent cursory quality is due to a number of factors: the deadline pressures of those critics who write for newspapers; the limitations of time and space imposed on film critics appearing on television and in print, respectively; and the simple fact that these critics cannot give too much of the film away without spoiling it for their audiences. (A scholarly critic, assuming the audience has already seen the film, would be unconcerned with the latter issue.) As suggested previously, the distinction between popular-press and scholarly criticism may finally become an academic or artificial one, and there is still the problem inherent in the terms themselves: one is pejorative, the other is snobbish, and together they imply that the popular-press critics have less intelligence, insight, and integrity than their "scholarly" counterparts. Nevertheless, the various qualities and concerns evident in these two broad types of film criticism seem sufficiently distinctive to justify their separation here.

The Methods

In defining the roles of critics, Rudolf Arnheim suggested that they apply "theoretical standards for the purpose of gauging the validity of the work."[15] He believed that although critics are concerned with particular works of art, they must, to deal effectively with them, initially turn their attention to those generalities that occupy the theorist. The critical methods examined here are derived from the application of theory that has evolved with regard to the form and function of the medium. The theory of film then would provide the methodologies for the systematic and/or formal critical analysis of individual works.

Not all critics subscribe to a formal methodology in the analysis of films. Pauline Kael—perhaps the best-known film critic in America—has argued that a rigid methodology can never replace the refined sensitivity of the individual critic. Her own work, consisting largely of subjective responses to films based on her own experiences (an approach in the phenomenological tradition), bears out this philosophy. Even Andrew Sarris, Kael's longtime rival and chief spokesperson for the Americanized version of the *auteur* critical method, has said, "My response to my role as a critic has generally been intuitive, and nothing is to be gained by institutionalizing my intuitions."[16] Sarris believes that each critic needs to find both an individual approach and role according to his or her own personality and outlook. Whether or not one is willing to accept Sarris' intuitive methodology, it is clear that the expansiveness, diversity, and newness of film make the promotion of any single critical method an untenable proposition. This does not preclude the application of traditional approaches; it simply means that one should select the most appropriate method, or combination of methods, depending on one's own interests and the specific films to be studied.

The critical methods that form the foundation for the scholarly analysis of film today are largely derived from the theories related to the realist, formalist, and structuralist perspectives. These include *auteur*, genre, *mise-en-scène*, political, feminist, and sociocultural criticism.

Auteur Criticism

The method that puts the individual film artist and stylist in the forefront of the analysis of form and function is called *auteur* criticism. As a theoretical precept, it had its beginnings in France directly after World War II in such writings as Alexandre Astruc's "Le Camera Stylo" (the camera pen), and in the pages of *Cahiers du Cinéma*. *Cahiers* was at the forefront of promoting what became known as "La Politique des Auteurs," largely through the writings of André Bazin and his disciples, most notably François Truffaut, Jean-Luc Godard, and Claude Chabrol. In particular, a 1954 Truffaut-authored article entitled "A Certain Tendency of the French Cinema" set the stage for the *auteur* polemic. In this article, Truffaut attacked the traditional French cinema by arguing that it was largely a cinema of scripts. Truffaut was not really proposing a new critical method; rather, he was responding to other postwar French critics who assumed that the authorship of a film belonged to the scriptwriter. He wanted to show that there was a special kind of director—the *auteur*—who was not nearly as script-bound as were many directors working in postwar France, but instead could convey ideas primarily through visual means.

As adapted in this country by Andrew Sarris, Truffaut's ideas have evolved and coalesced into a critical method following this fundamental premise: Despite the fact that a film is a collective enterprise—made up of actors, cinematographers, electricians, musicians, makeup people, costumers, and others—its creation strongly depends on a single controlling consciousness. This single dominant point of view, the *auteur* critics argue, is usually held by the director, not by the script-writer. Through the philosophic underpinnings of this method, the film director is elevated to the status of a novelist; hence the term *auteur*, which means "author."

The *auteur* critics originally focused on American directors who had worked within the studio system in Hollywood and who managed to function as film stylists, despite the production requirements and the curbs on individual expression. In other words, the *auteur* critics drew attention to the ability of the director, particularly those Hollywood directors working under studio controls and script requirements who still were able to leave their distinguishable trademarks on the films they directed. The career of Alfred Hitchcock serves as a case in point. His stature as an *auteur* came under particular strain when he worked for such studios as Selznick International, RKO, and Universal Pictures during the 1940s. But in spite of the need to conform to scripts, studio practices, and even prese-lected casts, he was able to make films that were undeniably "Hitchcockian" in their visual style (close-up of the ringing telephone), thematic preoccupation (the wrong-man theme), and ironic sense of humor (murder by a babbling brook).

In addition, the method was initially regarded by its formulators and sub-scribers as a critical device for recording the history of American cinema as rep-resented by its key directors. This list of directors includes both those reasonably well known today, such as Charles Chaplin, John Ford, Howard Hawks, Orson Welles, and Alfred Hitchcock, and those who even now are largely considered "cult figures" and have not received widespread recognition, such as Douglas Sirk and Samuel Fuller. In 1968, Andrew Sarris used the *auteur* philosophy to rank Amer-ican directors according to their technical competence (a basic requirement), and on two other levels: their identity as stylists, and their ability to convey their own interpretation of the material, reflecting some personal vision or outlook on the world. On the basis of these three criteria, which he had originally developed in 1962, Sarris then ranked the directors according to his estimate of their worth, placing them either in the highest category—his "Pantheon"—or in one of the lower categories, such as "The Far Side of Paradise," "Expressive Esoterica," and "Less Than Meets the Eye."[17] While other critics have roundly attacked this rank-ing system, Sarris's criteria are generally applicable to non-American directors as well. Indeed, other critics following the *auteur* philosophy have examined the work of such directors as Ingmar Bergman, Federico Fellini, and Luis Buñuel, taking into account their technical capabilities, stylistic signatures, and thematic incli-nations or preoccupations that have marked their entire filmic outputs, en route to forming judgments regarding the status of these directors as creative artists.

At its most basic level, *auteur* criticism provides a means of classification and analysis according to the characteristics common to many films directed by the same filmmaker. It is based on the assumption that any one film can be better understood and appreciated by considering it in relation to the qualities and con-cerns evident in the other films made by the same director.

But Sarris' elevation of the director over other creative talents—especially the scriptwriter—and his insistence that *auteur* criticism is not only an analytical but a *judgmental* approach have caused the method to come under fire from a variety of sources. During the early 1960s, Sarris and Pauline Kael were engaged in a running battle over the role of the director and the appropriateness of the *auteur* method as a means of ascertaining value. Typical is this Kael response to Sarris' assertion that the distinguishability of the director's personality is a criterion of value: "That the *distinguishability* of personality should in itself be a criterion of value completely confuses *normal* judgment. The smell of a skunk is more distinguishable than the perfume of a rose; does that make it better?"[18] Fellow critic Dwight Macdonald has likewise repudiated the auteur *method* and the Sarris classification system: "This kind of grading is appropriate to eggs but not to works of art."[19]

More recently, the structuralists have entered the fray, attacking the very heart of the *auteur* philosophy: the primacy of the director. In particular, they seriously question the notion that an individual director can somehow avoid or transcend the "deep structures" of society by virtue of his or her intense, creative "inner visions." Labeling *auteur* criticism with such epithets as "conservative" and "neo-Romantic," the structuralists have attempted to dethrone the director by insisting that this individual is primarily a *passive agent*, unconsciously passing along— and only superficially embellishing—the messages of society in his or her films.

Regardless of one's philosophical stance, the real benefit of *auteur* criticism is as a means of identifying and understanding the basic components of style and structure in a director's work. At its worst, *auteur* criticism becomes a cult of personalities in which the films are used to illuminate the personality of *auteurs* and in which poor films made by recognized *auteurs* are preferred to better films made by directors not afforded *auteur* status. At its best, it functions as a systematic but flexible means of placing a film within a class and some historical context. *Auteur* criticism can extend a film's meaning by drawing attention to the links between its creator's life and the evolution of that person's art. It can also suggest something about the relationship between the director and the industry that gives an individual the opportunity to make films while challenging that person's ability to function as an independent artist. Finally, it may be a cause for the reevaluation of both famous and forgotten films, and for the establishment of previously unknown or denigrated directors as major film artists.

Genre Criticism

Like *auteur* criticism, *genre* criticism is a means of classification and analysis of films according to the charactertistics common to several works. By definition, genre criticism must relate the individual work to others of its species and to the archetypal patterns that form a common bond among all within the group. It is worth noting that such archetypal patterns often extend beyond the medium itself. We find, for example, that the actions, settings, themes, and, above all, the heroes of such common film types as Westerns, crime melodramas, and adventure sagas have their counterparts in both classic and pulp fiction.

At its most basic, genre criticism provides a filing system that enables one to sort, classify, and deposit individual films with those of its kind. Such a coding system enables us, in the words of one theorist, "to fit [a film] into a class of films about which we presumably have some *general* knowledge."[20] Conversely, the reader or viewer is able to make certain assumptions about the nature of the individual work by its identification with a particular genre, and can use those characterTstics that identify the genre—the group as a whole—as a yardstick for measuring the specific work in question. Having identified *High Noon* or *A Fistful of Dollars* (1966) as a western, for example, the genre critic is then able to proceed to an analysis of the work according to how well it fits the traditional and "composite" model of the genre, and, perhaps more importantly, how the director of that work used the elements of the genre—its *conventions*—to make a statement unique to that film.

Such genre identification and analysis may be used as a means of making judgments about individual films; they may also be used as a means of exploring the history of the genre and the evolution of certain film styles associated with it.[21] Genre identification and classification is an evolving process with variations on traditional patterns producing new classes of film and certain genres running their course and being replaced by others. For example, the gangster film, which had its beginnings in D. W. Griffith's *The Musketeers of Pig Alley* (1912) and reached its peak in the early thirties with *Little Caesar, The Public Enemy,* and *Scarface,* was largely replaced in the middle of that decade by a new breed of crime drama. Public pressure dictated the replacement of the racketeer with the G-man as protagonist. The swashbuckler adventure film, established by Douglas Fairbanks, Sr., during the twenties, continued a viable form through the heroics of Douglas Fairbanks, Jr., Errol Flynn, and Tyrone Power until the end of World War II. German Expressionism and Italian neorealism were represented by a relatively small number of films produced over a period of only a few years, while the gangster, western, and horror genres have evolved from patterns established in some of the earliest silents and continue in a modified form today (see Fig. 12–3). Some genres grow old and die while others continue to be refurbished and redirected. The gangster genre, for example, has experienced several rebirths since the 1930s; in America, it figured prominently in the post-World War II cinema, in low-budgeted potboilers of the early 1970s, and in such famous films as *Bonnie and Clyde* (1967) and the *Godfather* epics.

On the other side of the Atlantic, New Wave filmmakers François Truffaut and Jean-Luc Godard gave the genre a distinctly Gallic touch in their respective tributes to the American gangster film, *Shoot the Piano Player* (1962) and *Breathless* (1959). (See Fig. 12–4.) As a critical tool, the study of genres provides a means of discovery of the ability of the industry and the individual filmmaker to recognize and satisfy the expectations of viewers according to the generic labels with which certain films have come to be identified.

Genre criticism also opens up a means whereby social and cultural functions of film may be reflected. The ethnographic film, the third-world film, and the Depression film are examples of the classifications of works according to some social, political, or cultural reference. Genre criticism in this way becomes an approach to the study of social conditions and political thought within a particular society. For instance, the British anti-establishment film of the 1960s is a part of the sociopolitical realities of the time and reflects the concern over the entrapment and exploitation of the working class by the conservative "ruling class" and by its traditions and institutions. Genre identification, as Andrew Tudor suggests, "seems best immediately employed in the analysis of the relation between groups of films, the cultures in which they are made, and the cultures in which they are exhibited."[22] There is a danger that the separation of films into groups for analytic purposes may become too reductionistic, particularly for those films that appear to transcend the limits of any one genre. For example, it would be unfair and misleading to label *Citizen Kane* simply as a "newspaper film" or even a "biographical

Figure 12-3 *Young Frankenstein* (1974—American). A genre critic might view a Mel Brooks film such as *Young Frankenstein* from several perspectives. From one vantage point, the critic may see *Young Frankenstein* as a spoof on a well-established genre. From another, he/she may interpret the film as a hybrid of two broad and durable genres: horror and comedy. The goal, however, is the same: to understand the ways that the director employed generic conventions, whether to say new things or merely to rehash old ideas.

film." While some films defy attempts at easy classification, there are many more that are quite amenable to the genre method. Beyond providing a convenient means of grouping films, genre criticism helps extend the study of film to include the social, political, and cultural context in which the film and its composite model have been spawned and nurtured.

Mise-en-scène Criticism

Another critical approach to film centers on the extent to which various cinematic elements have been combined to create a controlled and complete atmosphere for the screen action. The importance of such control was recognized by the Soviet filmmaker Pudovkin, when, in his writings on film technique, he

Figure 12-4 *Breathless* (1959-French). Small-time hoodlum Michel Poiccard (Jean-Paul Belmondo) pays homage to his role-model Humphrey Bogart in *Breathless,* Jean-Luc Godard's tribute to the American "B" gangster film. The poster for Bogart's last movie, *The Harder They Fall* (1956), is one of several film-related references in *Breathless.* Another is Poiccard's alias: "Laszlo Kovacs," the name of a famous Hollywood cinematographer.

wrote of the need to immerse all of the action in some environment that must then "constantly pervade the whole film." This surrounding environment of a film, created through the careful control of composition, lighting, decor, texture, movement, and any other details that make up the scene arranged in front of the camera, is known as *mise-en-scène.* Film analysis that centers on the control of these variables and on the expressive function of the individual shots is the basis of *mise-en-scène* criticism.

Because total visual composition is so central to the identifiable style of individual directors, *mise-en-scène* criticism has close ties with *auteur* criticism. Directors like F. W. Murnau of the silent cinema, and Welles and Bergman working in sound, have given particular attention to the art of the image and the effect of deep focus, lighting, and the design of the setting itself on the total atmosphere of the film. Although editing invariably affects the composition of the scene, the individual "long take" or single extended shot provides the basis for *mise-en-scène* analysis, rather than montage.

In its focus on distinctive and recurring visual style, *mise-en-scène* criticism is related to the development of national cinemas as well. For example, the post-World War I German film and the post-World War II Italian film each had their own distinctive atmospheric styles, as conveyed by their respective visual properties (brooding and claustrophobic in the former, alfresco and gritty in the latter). In the United States, films of crime and passion produced in the late 1940s and the 1950s were identifiable by their expressive use of light and shadows, clarity of focus, and frequently offbeat, unbalanced compositions. *Film noir,* as the style is called, became a label for films that were vaguely nihilistic but otherwise difficult to define in clear thematic terms. Their sense of foreboding rendered through environment—their *mise-en-scène*—gave these films their strongest identity, even though they represented such diverse genres as gangster movies, westerns, and domestic dramas.

The analysis of *mise-en-scène* as a critical method helps one to better understand the total film in relation to its basic ingredients. It also provides a link with *auteur* criticism and with the development of national cinemas by defining cinematic styles according to the works of an individual filmmaker (for example, the "Lubitsch touch") or to a particular group of national films (America's *film noir*). Finally, *mise-en-scène* criticism deals with those thematic patterns or visual motifs that run alongside, and subtly comment on, the basic narrative structure of the work.

Political Criticism

Another critical method, one based primarily on ideological and moral—as opposed to aesthetic—grounds, is *political* criticism. An aesthetician like Rudolf Arnheim might examine *Birth of a Nation* and conclude that it is a great work of art because of its epic scale, structure, and use of close-ups, long shots, editing, and black-and-white photography. A political critic examining the same film would probably overlook such factors and instead focus on the frequently cited contentions that the film is racist, narrow-minded, romanticized, and otherwise warped politically. The very nature of political criticism is to downplay artistic and technical aspects of the medium in favor of questioning its political stance. The following is a fundamental premise underlying most political film criticism: The political-economic structure of a given society at a given point in time determines to a large extent the form and content of that society's films. Every film—even one as innocuous as *Rebecca of Sunnybrook Farm* (1938)—may be interpreted as a political statement because it was determined by, and hence reflects, the dominant ideology of the society that produced it. Thus, it is unthinkable that films presenting individuals who triumph over considerable adversity and who otherwise shape their own destinies would be produced in a Marxist country, just as Hollywood-made films depicting and advocating the overthrow of democracy and capitalism by the masses is likewise inconceivable. The task facing the political critic, then, is to analyze the relationship between a given film, its society, and the ideology of that society, en route to determining the specific ways that the film either supports or attacks the dominant ideology of the society that produced it. As might be expected, examples of the latter are considerably rarer than those that support the status quo. Among the dissenting films are many of the works of Luis Buñuel, who has frequently pressed surrealistic imagery and techniques into service to lash out at the Catholic Church and the manners and morals of the upper class. The surrealistic approach has allowed Buñuel to express his point of view in vivid and concise ways. The singular concluding image of his *The Exterminating Angel*—a flock of sheep entering a cathedral—is only one of many such instances in his films. Ousmane Sembene's *Xala* (1974), which paints an extremely unflattering portrait of the postcolonial government of the filmmaker's native country of Senegal, provides another example, as do countless avant-garde films that, as we noted in the previous chapter, are often diametrically opposed in form, content, and philosophy to the commercial Hollywood cinema.

The most prominent variant of political analysis is Marxist criticism. Marxist critics have reserved their most vitriolic epithets for the traditional, commercial films of Hollywood, which they claim present an incredibly distorted view of the world masquerading as truth. Most Hollywood films, they assert, do not prompt the audience to question what it is perceiving, or even to think about it. Instead, the audience is encouraged to react passively and "lose itself" in the story of the film, while concomitantly accepting blindly the purveyed capitalist and conservative dogma. Marxist critics argue that Hollywood is not about to question the society of which it is a part because it is an industry that literally profits heavily from that society.

Other, less radical variations on political criticism have emerged in recent years. For example, Jeffrey Richards has laid down the basic tenets of a branch of capitalist ideology stressing middle-class values entitled *Populism*—individualism, self-help, good neighborliness, anti-big government, anti-big business, etc.—and has shown how they have manifested themselves with regularity in a host of Frank Capra's films, including *Mr. Smith Goes to Washington* (1939), *Mr. Deeds Goes to Town* (1936), and *Meet John Doe* (1941).[23] Similarly, Susan Sontag has examined the underpinnings of fascist ideology in the works of the German filmmaker Leni Riefenstahl.[24]

Feminist Criticism

Related to political criticism is *feminist criticism*, which stresses the observation that films, products of a sexist society, frequently present biased and stereotyped depictions of women's roles. It is different from political criticism in that it deals with personal issues as well as social ones. Feminist criticism is marked by an intense interest in uncovering and examining historical patterns regarding the images of women that have been previously obscured by cultural factors. Like so much of film criticism, it strongly seeks the *reevaluation* of films, both praised and neglected. In general, feminist critics are concerned primarily with three broad areas: (1) the ways women have been depicted and treated in film through the years; (2) the qualities and concerns of films made by women; and (3) the ways that women in society have been affected by the sex roles presented in film.

Feminist critics have pointed out that men are often presented in films as the people in and of history—the Robin Hoods, Napoleons, and Abraham Lincolns—who shape the destinies of both their own lives and the societies they inhabit. Women, on the other hand, are typically in supportive roles, and they are presented as eternal, unchanging, and without much historical significance. The woman washing a man's shirt during the Napoleonic wars was essentially the same in the eyes of most filmmakers as the woman washing a man's shirt during the Great Depression. Following this fundamental assumption, feminist critics have identified and discussed various stock categories that women have fallen into since the dawn of cinema.

For example, most women appearing in films produced in America from the medium's beginnings through the mid-1930s may be classified under one (or occasionally a mixture) of the following stock categories: (1) the *Mother*, whose nurturing, selfless image offends many feminist critics; (2) the *Ingénue*, or the virginal, unworldly woman; (3) the streetwise *Whore*, or *Vamp*; and (4) for lack of a better term, *Window Dressing*. This latter category is best illustrated by the large, homogeneous groups of women who appeared in the Busby Berkeley musicals of the 1930s. With their identical costuming, hair color, body types, and vacuous smiles, these women were often called on to do no more than be a part of a huge, intricate geometric design. Audiences were never asked to relate to them as individual human beings, but rather as mass-produced female automatons to be leered at.

Stronger, more developed roles for women began emerging in the 1930s, primarily through the emergence of the "screwball comedy" and "working woman" (née "working gal") films. The former type often featured women who were more quick-witted and conniving than their male counterparts, while the latter promoted the image of the independent woman fully capable of meeting the demands of her job, which was often an occupation dominated by men before World War II. The working woman film continued through the war years, but it quickly vanished when the war ended. Most women appearing in the immediate postwar period of American cinema could generally be classified as one of two types of characters: the male-hungry woman who desired nothing more than marriage, children, and a clean suburban home; and the strong-willed, independent woman who by the end of the film was shown to be neurotic, psychotic, or both. Donna Reed and Doris Day epitomize the former type, while Bette Davis, Joan Crawford, Barbara Stanwyck, and Gloria Swanson typify the latter. Barbara Stanwyck's portrayal of a bed-ridden woman suffering from a severe case of hypochondria in *Sorry, Wrong Number* and Gloria Swanson's tour-de-force performance as a crazy silent-movie queen in *Sunset Boulevard* are notable manifestations of the strong-willed, independent, but ultimately crazy woman. It is clear that Hollywood, along with many other postwar American institutions, sought to discourage women from acting in an independent fashion—such as holding down a job outside the home, which might otherwise go to a man returning from the war—by suggesting that such behavior was abnormal. Simultaneously, women were encouraged to become "happy homemakers," taking up such domestic duties as housecleaning, baking, and raising children.

Little had changed until the 1970s. Then the aggressive woman began reemerging in such films as *Bonnie and Clyde, Klute* (1971), *Network* (1976), *Gloria* (1980), *The China Syndrome, An Unmarried Woman*, and *Norma Rae* (1979) in the personages of such actresses as Jane Fonda, Faye Dunaway, Gena Rowlands, Jill Clayburgh, and Sally Field. At the same time, the images of men have begun to move out of their macho, heroic stereotypes to become more sensitive, emotional, and self-questioning. Noteworthy among these are the characters portrayed by Burt Reynolds in *Starting Over* (1979), Michael Murphy in *An Unmarried Woman*, and Donald Sutherland in *Ordinary People* (1980).

Feminist critics are also interested in the kinds of films made by women. Until only a few years ago, they had only a handful to choose from: Leni Riefenstahl, Lina Wertmüller, Elaine May, Mai Zetterling, Agnes Varda, and "lost" directors like Ida Lupino and Dorothy Arzner. Today there is a virtual "new wave" of women directors both in this country and abroad; unfortunately, many of their initial works have been both critical and financial misfires. Some of their films have been well received, such as Diane Kurys's *Peppermint Soda* (1977) and Claudia Weill's *Girlfriends* (1978), but a number of others have received scathing reviews, including Jane Wagner's *Moment by Moment* (1978), Anne Bancroft's *Fatso* (1980), Joan Rivers' *Rabbit Test* (1978), and Joan Tewkesbury's *Old Boyfriends* (1979). The relatively poor quality of these films is not so much a reflection of their makers' talent as it is of the fact that women have traditionally been denied access to resources and experience in the film industry.

In general, there are few guidelines for feminist criticism. It has leaned heavily on such diverse disciplines as literary criticism, psychology, structuralism, social history, anthropology, and *auteur* criticism. By fusing one or more of these areas with feminist criticism, a feminist critic might make an area of interest narrower and thus more manageable. For example, a feminist critic might take into account the *auteur* philosophy in attempting to analyze the roles of women in Alfred Hitchcock's films. Eventually the questions that the feminist critics raise lead to broader areas that transcend gender roles, such as: What brings people together? Why do men and women behave the way they do? It provides for the broad reevaluation of role-shaping and role-playing as they exist in a wide variety of films (see Fig. 12–5).

Sociocultural Criticism

A final critical method provides a means of using films to better understand the societies that produced them. This method, called *sociocultural criticism,* has a link with political criticism in that both methods are concerned with the ways that societies are reflected in their films. But while political criticism is also

Figure 12-5 *Jules and Jim* (1961-French). Numerous films are amenable to a variety of critical approaches. In examining François Truffaut's *Jules and Jim,* for example, a feminist critic might focus primarily on the unpredictable character of Catherine (Jeanne Moreau) and her changing relationships with the two men and the child in her life. An *auteur* critic, on the other hand, might concentrate on locating the themes and motifs of *Jules and Jim* within the context of Truffaut's overall body of work.

concerned with such extraneous matters as the production, distribution, and exhibition of films (that is, who is allowed to make films, how films are distributed and shown), sociocultural criticism is largely unconcerned with such matters. Rather, the critics heralding this approach are almost exclusively interested in the content of films and how films may be used as "cultural artifacts." They see themselves primarily as social historians and are not as dogmatically ideological as their political counterparts.

Sociocultural criticism likewise shares a connection with structuralism, since both are interested in the ways that the unconscious messages of a society find their way into films. In a sense, sociocultural criticism and structuralism are engaged in a reciprocal arrangement; the former uses films as tools to better understand the society that produced them, while the latter uses a society's mythic structures to unlock the meanings of films. Together with political criticism, they form a comprehensive system for dealing with cinema, society, and ideology.

The fundamental premise underlying this method is that films as well as other cultural expressions will reflect to a certain degree not only the political structure of a given society but also various conventions of that society. These conventions include such fundamental items as automobile designs, hair styles, styles of clothing, and manners of speech. For example, the dialogue of virtually any American film of the 1930s, regardless of genre or director, is bound to contain such phrasings as "Isn't he swell?," "That's just grand," and "Isn't he a panic?"—expressions common to the time but seldom heard today. More important than these surface items, however, is another convention: the ways people thought at the time. In other words, a sociocultural critic is interested in examining a society's hopes, dreams, and fears as revealed in its films. An obvious example would be America during World War II and its films. While only about a third of the movies produced in the United States during the war years dealt directly with the battles and campaigns of that conflict—films such as *Guadalcanal Diary* (1943) and *They Were Expendable* (1945)—virtually every film contained some reference, even if only in passing, to the war. Someone's nephew might be going off to war, for example, or someone might state the need to "band together against the common enemy." Another example would be films reflecting the postwar atomic age. A host of giant-bug movies sprang up during this time, including *Them!* (1954), *The Beginning of the End* (1957), and *The Deadly Mantis* (1957). The mutation of the insects inevitably turned out to be the result of nuclear fallout from atomic testing. As horror expert Stephen King suggests, "Taken together, the big-bug movies form an undeniable pattern, an uneasy gestalt of a whole country's terror of the new age that the Manhattan Project had rung in."[25]

Unfortunately, only a handful of critics have undertaken the task of implementing the sociocultural method. One of the first to do so was Siegfried Kracauer, who examined Germany between the world wars and its films in *From Caligari to Hitler*.[26] Andrew Bergman has used the method to examine Depression-era America and its films in *We're in the Money*,[27] and Robert Sklar has studied the whole of American cinema from this perspective in *Movie-Made America*.[28] However, beyond these and other scattered works, not much has been done with the method.

A partial explanation for the relative dearth of sociocultural studies is the fact that such a critic should ideally examine dozens and perhaps hundreds of films en route to determining those things weighing heavily on a society's collective consciousness. Little will be gained by studying only a handful of films with this approach. The high number of films would ideally carry with it a broad cross-section of works, and it would tend to deemphasize the contributions of individual artists.

Another problem is that of cause and effect. It would be misleading for a sociocultural critic to state flatly that the conditions of a society directly influenced the form and content of the films that emerged from that society at any given time. Such a critic may fairly claim that societal conditions and films are associated, and may testify as to the reasonableness of his or her assertions, but it would be nearly impossible to prove that any set of conditions caused these particular films to be made.

Another problem centers around this question: Do films truly represent the norms and values of their societies? There are those who will argue that a filmmaking community such as Hollywood can in no way be considered a representative slice of American society. Hence, the resulting films, the argument might go, are more reflective of Hollywood and its obsession with profits than of America as a whole.

One means of circumventing this problem has been offered by Andrew Bergman. He has suggested that the sociocultural method is best used when examining a society and its films during a period of national stress. Under such conditions—for example, during a war or immediately following one, or during an economic depression—films represent more than just the views of the film producers. As suggested by Bergman, the films may be looked on as symptomatic of the conditions of the entire nation: "There are certain tensions [in any period of national stress] which permeate a society and affect the majority of its functioning members, artists and moviemakers included. . . . The premise is not that moviemakers intuited the yearnings of a national unconscious, but rather that they felt the same tensions everyone else did and wanted to represent them in various ways."[29] Seen in this light, films may be interpreted as cultural artifacts that offer insights into those subjects weighing heavily on a society's collective consciousness during a given time frame.

Challenges

New styles and functions of film have broadened the theoretical and critical base on which the medium rests and have in recent years changed substantially the implications of film for filmmakers, for students and scholars of cinema, for professional critics, and indeed for the viewing public. For any of these groups, the evolution of the medium has provided new challenges to understanding film and finding methods appropriate to the many ways in which film meets various needs and expectations. For filmmakers, it is the challenge of creating something original in style, message, or both. For students of film, it is the challenge of seeing more clearly and being able to understand and articulate the historical, structural, sociopolitical, psychological, and aesthetic elements of a work. For professional critics, it is the challenge of opening up the work, giving it added perspective, and revealing the range and diversity of the medium and the imagination as well as the discipline and control of its practitioners.

Film critics, whatever their methodologies, must themselves finally be judged by their intelligence, wit, passion, and understanding of the medium. Like the *auteur* filmmakers, they must have a basic technical competence, a style of their own, and a mission. They are involved in both an intuitive and analytic process. It is a process that sharpens our awareness, guides us in rational analysis, and invites us to enjoy more fully and understand why we enjoy.

It is neither possible nor desirable for critics to be completely objective in fulfilling their mission. The value of their criticism is determined in part by the extent to which their own experiences influence their feelings, even passions, over film, but without distorting what is presented on the screen or dulling the critical perceptions of others. Finally, critics, like the filmmakers themselves, must be open to new patterns and functions that continue to emerge, to meet the capacities and needs of a diverse readership and viewing audience, and to recognize their own mistakes and shifts in perspective as the medium and its related theories and methodologies continue to evolve.

NOTES

[1] Rudolf Arnheim, *Film as Art* (Berkeley: University of California Press, 1958), p. 3.

[2] André Bazin, *What Is Cinema?*, *Volume I*, trans. and ed. Hugh Gray (Berkeley: University of California Press, 1967), p. 86.

[3] Ibid., p. 93.

[4] Siegfried Kracauer, *Theory of Film: The Redemption of Physical Reality* (New York: Oxford University Press, 1960), p. 46.

[5] Ibid., pp. 62 and 68.

[6] Ibid., p. 83.

[7] Sergei Eisenstein, *Film Form* (New York: Harcourt Brace Jovanovich, 1949), p. 201.

[8] Spoken by Roberto Rossellini in the documentary film *Neorealism* (1972).

[9] The study appeared under the title "Semiotics and *Citizen Kane*" in *Film Reader*, published by Northwestern University in 1975.

[10] Michael Blowen, review of *Heaven's Gate*, Boston Globe, April 25, 1981, p. 8.

[11] Gene Youngblood, *Expanded Cinema* (New York: Dutton, 1970), p. 136.

[12] John Simon, *Private Screenings* (New York: Berkley Publishing Corp., 1971), pp. 10–11.

[13] *The Independent*, April 6, 1914, p. 8–9.

[14] Ibid.

[15] Rudolf Arnheim, "What Is a Critic?," *Saturday Review*, Aug. 28, 1965.

[16] Andrew Sarris, *Confessions of a Cultist* (New York: Simon & Schuster, 1971), p. 15.

[17] The eleven categories under which Sarris placed directors and five "nondirectorial auteurs" (comic stars) provide the chapter headings for his *The American Cinema* (New York: Dutton, 1968).

[18] Pauline Kael, "Circles and Squares," in *Film Theory and Criticism: Introductory Readings*, 2nd ed., eds. Gerald Mast and Marshall Cohen (New York: Oxford University Press, 1979), p. 671.

[19] Dwight Macdonald, *On Movies* (New York: Berkley Publishing Corp. 1971), p. 338.

[20] Andrew Tudor, *Theories of Film* (New York: Viking, 1974), p. 132.

[21] Several studies on *film noir* and on American silent-screen comedy provide good examples. See also Robert Warshow's celebrated essays on "The Gangster as Tragic Hero" and "The Westerner" in *The Immediate Experience* (New York: Doubleday, 1964).

[22] Tudor, *Theories of Film*, pp. 148–49.

[23] Jeffrey Richards, "Frank Capra and the Cinema of Populism," in *Movies and Methods*, ed. Bill Nichols (Berkeley: University of California Press, 1976), pp. 65–77.

[24]Susan Sontag, "Fascinating Fascism," in *Movies and Methods*, pp. 31–43.

[25]Stephen King, *Night Shift* (New York: Signet, 1979), p. xviii.

[26]Siegfried Kracauer, *From Caligari to Hitler: A Psychological History of the German Film* (Princeton, N.J.: Princeton University Press, 1947).

[27]Andrew Bergman, *We're in the Money: Depression America and Its Films* (New York: Harper Colophon Books, 1971).

[28]Robert Sklar, *Movie-Made America: A Cultural History of American Movies* (New York: Random House, 1975).

[29]Bergman, *We're in the Money*, p. xiv.

BIBLIOGRAPHY

CHAPTER 1

Bardèche, Maurice, and Robert Brasillach   *A History of the Motion Pictures*. Edited by Iris Barry. New York: W. W. Norton and the Museum of Modern Art, 1938.

Bohn, Thomas W., and Richard L. Stromgren   *Light and Shadows: A History of Motion Pictures*, 2nd ed. Sherman Oaks, Calif.: Alfred Publishing Co., 1978.

Brownlow, Kevin   *The Parade's Gone By*. New York: Ballantine Books, 1968.

Casty, Alan   *Development of the Film: An Interpretive History*. New York: Harcourt Brace Jovanovich, 1973.

Cook, David A.   *A History of Narrative Film*. New York: W. W. Norton, 1981.

Ellis, Jack C.   *A History of Film*. Englewood Cliffs, N.J.: Prentice-Hall, 1979.

Fell, John L.   *A History of Films*. New York: Holt, Rinehart & Winston, 1979.

Fulton, A. R.   *Motion Pictures: The Development of an Art from Silent Films to the Age of Television*. Norman, Okla.: University of Oklahoma Press, 1960.

Houston, Penelope   *The Contemporary Cinema*. Baltimore, Md.: Penguin Books, 1963.

Jacobs, Lewis   *The Emergence of Film Art*. New York: Hopkinson & Blake, 1969.

Knight, Arthur   *The Liveliest Art: A Panoramic History of the Movies*, rev. ed. New York: New American Library, 1979.

Macgowan, Kenneth   *Behind the Screen: The History and Techniques of the Motion Picture*. New York: Delacorte Press, 1965.

Mast, Gerald   *A Short History of the Movies*, 3rd ed. Indianapolis, Ind.: Bobbs-Merrill Educational Publishing, 1981.

Montagu, Ivor   *Film World: A Guide to Cinema*. Baltimore, Md.: Penguin Books, 1964.

Rhode, Eric   *A History of the Cinema from Its Origins to 1970*. New York: Hill & Wang, 1976.

ROBINSON, DAVID   *The History of World Cinema.* New York: Stein & Day, 1973.
SKLAR, ROBERT   *Movie-Made America: A Social History of the American Movies.* New York: Random House, 1975.

CHAPTER 2

ALTON, JOHN   *Painting with Light.* New York: Macmillan, 1949.
ARNHEIM, RUDOLF   *Art and Visual Perception: A Psychology of the Creative Eye.* Berkeley, Calif.: University of California Press, 1954.
BACHER, LUTZ   *The Mobile Mise en Scène.* New York: Arno Press, 1978.
CAMPBELL, RUSSELL, ed.,   *Photographic Theory for the Motion Picture Cameraman.* Cranbury, N.J.: A. S. Barnes, 1970.
CLARKE, CHARLES   *Professional Cinematography.* Los Angeles: American Society of Cinematographers, 1968.
HALAS, JOHN and ROGER MANVELL   *Design in Motion.* New York: Focal Press, 1962.
HIGHAM, CHARLES, ed.   *Hollywood Cameramen.* Bloomington, Ind.: Indiana University Press, 1970.
MacCANN, RICHARD DYER, ed.   *Film: A Montage of Theories.* New York: E. P. Dutton, 1966.
MALTIN, LEONARD, ed.   *Behind the Camera: The Cinematographer's Art.* New York: New American Library, 1971.
MILLERSON, GERALD   *The Technique of Lighting for Television and Motion Pictures,* 2nd ed. Woburn, Mass.: Focal Press, 1982.
NILSEN, VLADIMIR   *The Cinema as a Graphic Art.* New York: Hill & Wang, 1973.
SAMUELSON, DAVID   *Motion Picture Camera Techniques.* Woburn, Mass.: Focal Press, 1978.
SOUTO, H. MARIO   *The Technique of the Motion Picture Camera,* 4th ed. Woburn, Mass.: Focal Press, 1982.
WHEELER, LESLIE   *Principles of Cinematography,* 4th ed. New York: Fountain Press, 1971.

CHAPTER 3

ASH, RENÉ   *The Motion Picture Film Editor.* Metuchen, N.J.: Scarecrow Press, 1974.
BAZELON, IRWIN   *Knowing the Score: Notes on Film Music.* New York: Van Nostrand Reinhold, 1972.
CAMERON, EVAN W., ed.   *Sound and the Cinema: The Coming of Sound to American Film.* Pleasantville, N.Y.: Redgrave, 1979.
EISENSTEIN, SERGEI   *Film Form.* New York: Harcourt Brace & Co., 1949.
————   *The Film Sense.* New York: Harcourt Brace & Co., 1942.
EISLER, HANS   *Composing for the Films.* New York: Oxford University Press, 1947.
HAGEN, EARL   *Scoring for Films.* New York: Wehman, 1972.
HUNTLEY, JOHN, and ROGER MANVELL   *The Technique of Film Music.* New York: Focal Press, 1957.
LIMBACHER, JAMES L.   *Film Music from Violins to Video.* Metuchen, N.J.: Scarecrow Press, 1974.
McCARTHY, CLIFFORD   *Film Composers in America.* New York: Da Capo, 1972.
NISBETT, ALEC   *The Technique of the Sound Studio,* 4th ed. Woburn, Mass: Focal Press, 1979.
PRENDERGAST, ROY M.   *Film Music: A Neglected Art.* New York: W. W. Norton, 1977.
REISZ, KAREL, and GAVIN MILLAR   *The Technique of Film Editing,* 2nd ed. Woburn, Mass.: Focal Press, 1968.
ROSENBLUM, RALPH, and ROBERT KAREN   *When The Shooting Stops . . . the Cutting Begins: A Film Editor's Story.* New York: Penguin Books, 1980.
THOMAS, TONY   *Music for the Movies.* Cranbury, N.J.: A. S. Barnes, 1973.
————, ed.   *Film Score: The View from the Podium.* Cranbury, N.J.: A. S. Barnes, 1979.
WALTER, ERNEST   *The Technique of the Film Cutting Room,* 2nd ed. Woburn, Mass.: Focal Press, 1981.

CHAPTER 4

AFFRON, CHARLES   *Star Acting: Gish, Garbo, Davis.* New York: E. P. Dutton, 1977.
BARSACQ, LEON   *Caligari's Cabinet and Other Grand Illusions: A History of Film Design.* Boston: New York Graphic Society, 1976.

CARRICK, EDWARD *Designing for Moving Pictures.* London: Studio, 1947.
CHAPLIN, CHARLES *My Autobiography.* New York: Simon & Schuster, 1964.
GRIFFITH, RICHARD *The Movie Stars.* Garden City, N.Y.: Doubleday, 1970.
MARNER, TERENCE, ed. *Film Design.* Cranbury, N.J.: A. S. Barnes, 1972.
MUNK, ERIKA, ed. *Stanislavsky in America.* New York: Hill & Wang, 1966.
PUDOVKIN, V. I. *Film Technique and Film Acting.* London: Vision Press, 1954.

CHAPTER 5

ARISTOTLE *Aristotle's Politics and Poetics.* Translated by Benjamin Jowett and Thomas Twining. New York: Viking Press, 1957.
BUTCHER, S. H. *Aristotle's Theory of Poetry and Fine Art.* London: Macmillan, 1923.
FELL, JOHN L. *Film and the Narrative Tradition.* Norman, Okla.: University of Oklahoma Press, 1974.
LAWSON, JOHN HOWARD *Film: The Creative Process.* New York: Hill & Wang, 1964.
LUHR, WILLIAM, and PETER LEHMAN *Authorship and Narrative in the Cinema.* New York: Oxford University Press, 1977.
RICHIE, DONALD *The Films of Akira Kurosawa.* Berkeley, Calif.: University of California Press, 1965.
———— *Focus on Rashomon.* Englewood Cliffs, N.J.: Prentice-Hall, 1972.

CHAPTER 6

BAXTER, JOHN *The Gangster Film.* Cranbury, N.J.: A. S. Barnes, 1970.
———— *Science Fiction in the Cinema.* Cranbury, N.J.: A. S. Barnes, 1970.
BROSNAN, JOHN *Future Tense: The Cinema of Science Fiction.* New York: St. Martin's Press, 1978.
CLARENS, CARLOS *Crime Movies: From Griffith to the Godfather and Beyond.* New York: W. W. Norton, 1980.
———— *An Illustrated History of the Horror Film.* New York: Capricorn Books, 1967.
DAVIS, BRIAN *The Thriller.* New York: E. P. Dutton, 1973.
DILLARD, RICHARD *Horror Film.* New York: Monarch Press, 1976.
EVERSON, WILLIAM K. *The Detective in Film.* New York: Citadel Press, 1972.
EYLES, ALLEN *The Western.* Cranbury, N.J.: A. S. Barnes, 1975.
FENIN, GEORGE, and WILLIAM K. EVERSON *The Western: From Silents to the Seventies,* 2nd ed. New York: Grossman Publishers, 1973.
FOLSOM, JAMES K., ed. *The Western.* Englewood Cliffs, N.J.: Prentice-Hall, 1979.
FRAYLING, CHRISTOPHER *Spaghetti Westerns: Cowboys and Europeans from Karl May to Sergio Leone.* Boston: Routledge & Kegan Paul, 1980.
FRENCH, PHILIP *Westerns: Aspects of a Movie Genre.* New York: Viking Press, 1973.
GABREE, JOHN *Gangsters: From Little Caesar to the Godfather.* New York: Pyramid Publications, 1973.
GIFFORD, DENIS *Science Fiction Film.* London: Studio Vista, 1951.
GRANT, BARRY K., ed. *Film Genre: Theory and Criticism.* Metuchen, N.J.: Scarecrow Press, 1977.
HALAS, JOHN *Art in Movement: New Directions in Animation.* London: Studio Vista, 1970.
HUSS, ROY, ed. *Focus on the Horror Film.* Englewood Cliffs, N.J.: Prentice–Hall, 1972.
JOHNSON, WILLIAM, ed. *Focus on the Science Fiction Film.* Englewood Cliffs, N.J.: Prentice-Hall, 1972.
KAMINSKY, STUART M. *American Film Genres: Approaches to a Critical Theory.* New York: Dell Publishing Co., 1974.
KARPF, STEVEN *The Gangster Film: Emergence, Variation, and Decay of a Genre.* New York: Arno Press, 1973.
KITSES, JIM *Horizons West.* Bloomington, Ind.: Indiana University Press, 1970.
KOBAL, JOHN *Gotta Sing, Gotta Dance: A Pictorial History of Film Musicals.* London: Hamlyn, 1970.
LAHUE, KALTON C. *World of Laughter.* Norman, Okla.: University of Oklahoma Press, 1964.
MAST, GERALD *The Comic Mind.* Indianapolis, Ind.: Bobbs-Merrill Educational Publishing, 1973.
McVAY, DOUGLAS *The Musical Film.* Cranbury, N.J.: A. S. Barnes, 1967.
MENVILLE, DOUGLAS *A Historical and Critical Survey of the Science Fiction Film.* New York: Arno Press, 1975.
NACHBAR, JACK, ed. *Focus on the Western.* Englewood Cliffs, N.J.: Prentice-Hall, 1974.

NEALE, STEVEN *Genre.* New York: Zoetrope, 1980.

PILKINGTON, WILLIAM T., ed. *Western Movies.* Albuquerque, N.M.: University of New Mexico Press, 1979.

ROSOW, EUGENE *Born to Lose: The Gangster Film in America.* New York: Avon Books, 1978.

SCHATZ, THOMAS *Hollywood Genres: Formulas, Filmmaking, and the Studio System.* Philadelphia: Temple University Press, 1981.

SHADOIAN, JACK *Dreams and Dead Ends: The American Gangster Film.* Cambridge, Mass.: MIT Press, 1977.

SOLOMON, STANLEY J. *Beyond Formula: American Film Genres.* New York: Harcourt Brace Jovanovich, 1976.

STEPHENSON, RALPH *Animation in the Cinema.* Cranbury, N.J.: A. S. Barnes, 1966.

STERNE, LEE *The Movie Musical.* New York: Pyramid Publications, 1974.

TAYLOR, JOHN RUSSELL, and ARTHUR JACKSON *The Hollywood Musical.* New York: McGraw-Hill, 1971.

VALLANCE, TOM *The American Musical.* Cranbury, N.J.: A. S. Barnes, 1970.

WRIGHT, WILL *Sixguns and Society: A Structural Study of the Western.* Berkeley, Calif.: University of California Press, 1975.

CHAPTER 7

BEJA, MORRIS *Film and Literature.* New York: Longman, 1979.

BLUESTONE, GEORGE *Novels into Film.* Berkeley, Calif.: University of California Press, 1961.

CHATMAN, SEYMOUR *Story and Discourse: Narrative Structure in Fiction and Film.* Ithaca, N.Y.: Cornell University Press, 1978.

COHEN, KEITH *Film and Fiction.* New Haven, Ct.: Yale University Press, 1979.

GEDULD, HARRY M., ed. *Authors on Film.* Bloomington, Ind.: Indiana University Press, 1972.

HARRINGTON, JOHN *Film and/as Literature.* Englewood Cliffs, N.J.: Prentice-Hall, 1977.

HORTON, ANDREW, and JOAN MAGRETTA, eds. *Modern European Filmmakers and the Art of Adaptation.* New York: Ungar, 1980.

KITTREDGE, WILLIAM, and STEVEN M. KRAUZER, eds. *Stories Into Films.* New York: Harper Colophon Books, 1979.

KLEIN, MICHAEL, and GILLIAN PARKER, eds. *The English Novel and the Movies.* New York: Ungar, 1981.

PEARY, GERALD, and ROGER SHATZKIN, eds. *The Classic American Novel and the Movies.* New York: Ungar, 1977.

RICHARDSON, ROBERT *Literature and Film.* Bloomington, Ind.: Indiana University Press, 1969.

YACOWAR, MALCOLM *The Modern American Novel and the Movies.* New York: Ungar, 1978.

CHAPTER 8

HURT, JAMES, ed. *Focus on Film and Theatre.* Englewood Cliffs, N.J.: Prentice–Hall, 1974.

JORGENS, JACK J. *Shakespeare on Film.* Bloomington, Ind.: Indiana University Press, 1977.

MANVELL, ROGER *Shakespeare and the Film.* New York: Praeger Publishers, 1971.

MAST, GERALD, AND MARSHALL COHEN, eds. *Film Theory and Criticism: Introductory Readings,* 2nd ed. New York: Oxford University Press, 1979.

MURRAY, EDWARD *The Cinematic Imagination.* New York: Ungar, 1972.

NICOLL, ALLARDYCE *Film and Theatre.* New York: Thomas Y. Crowell, 1936.

VARDAC, NICHOLAS *From Stage to Screen.* Cambridge, Mass.: Harvard University Press, 1949.

CHAPTER 9

BARNOUW, ERIK *Tube of Plenty: The Evolution of American Television.* New York: Oxford University Press, 1975.

BLUEM, A. WILLIAM *Documentary in American Television.* New York: Hastings House, 1965.

BROOKS, TIM, AND EARLE MARSH   *The Complete Directory to Prime Time Network TV Shows, 1946-Present.* New York: Ballantine, 1979.

BROWN, LES   *The New York Times Encyclopedia of Television.* New York: Times Books, 1977.

CASTLEMAN, HARRY, and WALTER J. PODRAZIK   *Watching TV: Four Decades of American Television.* New York: McGraw-Hill, 1982.

GOLDSEN, ROSE K.   *The Show and Tell Machine.* New York: Dell Pub. Co., 1977.

MAYER, MARTIN   *About Television.* New York: Harper & Row, 1974.

NEWCOMB, HORACE   *TV: The Most Popular Art.* Garden City, N.Y.: Anchor Press, 1974.

————, ed.   *Television: The Critical View.* New York: Oxford University Press, 1976.

TERRACE, VINCENT   *The Complete Encyclopedia of Television Programs.* Cranbury, N.J.: A. S. Barnes, 1976.

CHAPTER 10

BADDELEY, W. HUGH   *The Technique of Documentary Film Production,* 4th ed. Woburn, Mass.: Focal Press, 1975.

BARNOUW, ERIK   *Documentary: A History of the Non-Fiction Film,* revised ed. New York: Oxford University Press, 1983.

BARSAM, RICHARD MERAN   *Nonfiction Film: A Critical History.* New York: E. P. Dutton, 1973.

————, ed.   *Non-Fiction Film Theory and Criticism.* New York: E. P. Dutton, 1976.

BEVERIDGE, JAMES   *John Grierson: Film Master.* New York: Macmillan, 1978.

CALDER-MARSHALL, ARTHUR   *The Innocent Eye: The Life of Robert Flaherty.* New York: Penguin Books, 1970.

FELDMAN, SETH   *The Evolution of Style in the Early Works of Dziga Vertov.* New York: Arno Press, 1977.

FIELDING, RAYMOND   *The American Newsreel: 1911–1967.* Norman, Okla.: University of Oklahoma Press, 1972.

GRIERSON, JOHN   *Grierson on Documentary.* Edited and compiled by Forsyth Hardy. New York: Praeger, 1971.

GRIFFITH, RICHARD   *The World of Robert Flaherty.* New York: Duell, Sloan & Pearce, 1953.

ISSARI, M. ALI   *Cinéma Vérité.* East Lansing, Mich.: Michigan State University Press, 1971.

JACOBS, LEWIS, ed.   *The Documentary Tradition,* 2nd ed. New York: W. W. Norton, 1979.

LEVIN, G. ROY, ed.   *Documentary Explorations: 15 Interviews with Film-Makers.* Garden City, N.Y.: Doubleday, 1972.

LORENTZ, PARE   *Lorentz on Film.* New York: Harcourt Brace Jovanovich, 1975.

LOVELL, ALAN, and JIM HILLIER   *Studies in Documentary.* New York: Viking Press, 1972.

MAMBER, STEPHEN   *Cinéma Vérité in America: Studies in Uncontrolled Documentary.* Cambridge, Mass.: MIT Press, 1974.

MARCORELLES, LOUIS   *Living Cinema.* New York: Praeger, 1972.

ROSENTHAL, ALAN   *The New Documentary in Action.* Berkeley, Calif.: University of California Press, 1971.

ROTHA, PAUL, RICHARD GRIFFITH, and SINCLAIR ROAD   *Documentary Film.* London: Faber & Faber, 1952.

SNYDER, ROBERT   *Pare Lorentz and the Documentary Film.* Norman, Okla.: University of Oklahoma Press, 1968.

STOTT, WILLIAM   *Documentary Expression and Thirties America.* New York: Oxford University Press, 1973.

SUSSEX, ELIZABETH   *The Rise and Fall of British Documentary.* Berkeley, Calif.: University of California Press, 1976.

CHAPTER 11

BATTCOCK, GREGORY, ed.   *The New American Cinema.* New York: E. P. Dutton, 1967.

CURTIS, DAVID   *Experimental Cinema.* New York: Dell Pub. Co., 1971.

LAWDER, STANDISH D.   *The Cubist Cinema.* New York: NYU Press, 1975.

LE GRICE, MALCOLM   *Abstract Film and Beyond.* Cambridge, Mass.: MIT Press, 1977.

MANVELL, ROGER, ed.   *Experiment in the Film.* London: Gray Walls Press, 1949.

MEKAS, JONAS   *Movie Journal: The Rise of the New American Cinema, 1959–1971.* New York: Collier Books, 1972.

RENAN, SHELDON   *An Introduction to the American Underground Film.* New York: E. P. Dutton, 1967.

SITNEY, P. ADAMS, ed.   *Film Culture Reader.* New York: Praeger Publishers, 1970.

———————   *The Essential Cinema.* New York: NYU Press, 1975.

———————   *Visionary Film: The American Avant-Garde 1943–1978,* 2nd ed. New York: Oxford University Press, 1979.

TYLER, PARKER   *Underground Film: A Critical History.* New York: Grove Press, 1969.

VOGEL, AMOS   *Film as a Subversive Art.* New York: Random House, 1974.

YOUNGBLOOD, GENE   *Expanded Cinema.* New York: E. P. Dutton, 1970.

CHAPTER 12

ANDREW, J. DUDLEY   *The Major Film Theories: An Introduction.* New York: Oxford University Press, 1976.

ARNHEIM, RUDOLF   *Film as Art.* Berkeley, Calif.: University of California Press, 1957.

BALÁZS, BÉLA   *Theory of the Film: Character and Growth of a New Art.* Translated by Edith Bone. New York: Dover Books, 1970.

BARTHES, ROLAND   *Elements of Semiology.* Translated by Annette Lavers and Colin Smith. New York: Hill & Wang, 1967.

BAZIN, ANDRÉ   *What Is Cinema?* Selected and translated by Hugh Gray. Berkeley, Calif.: University of California Press, 1967.

———————   *What Is Cinema?* vol. II. Selected and translated by Hugh Gray. Berkeley, Calif.: University of California Press, 1971.

BERGER, ARTHUR ASA   *Media Analysis Techniques.* Beverly Hills, Calif.: Sage Publications, 1982.

BERGMAN, ANDREW   *We're in the Money: Depression America and Its Films.* New York: Harper Colophon Books, 1971.

BETTETTINI, GIANFRANCO   *The Language and Technique of Film.* Translated by David Osmond-Smith. The Hague: Mouton, 1974.

BURCH, NOEL   *The Theory of Film Practice.* New York: Praeger, 1973.

CAVELL, STANLEY   *The World Viewed: Reflections on the Ontology of Film.* Cambridge, Mass.: Harvard University Press, 1979.

EBERWEIN, ROBERT T.   *A Viewer's Guide to Film Theory and Criticism.* Metuchen, N.J.: Scarecrow Press, 1979.

ECO, UMBERTO   *The Semiotic Threshold.* The Hague: Mouton, 1973.

———————   *A Theory of Semiotics.* Bloomington, Ind.: Indiana University Press, 1976.

HASKELL, MOLLY   *From Reverence to Rape: The Treatment of Women in the Movies.* New York: Holt, Rinehart & Winston, 1974.

HEATH, STEPHEN   *Questions of Cinema.* Bloomington, Ind.: Indiana University Press, 1981.

HENDERSON, BRIAN   *A Critique of Film Theory.* New York: E. P. Dutton, 1980.

KRACAUER, SIEGFRIED   *From Caligari to Hitler: A Psychological History of the German Film.* Princeton, N.J.: Princeton University Press, 1947.

———————   *Theory of Film: The Redemption of Physical Reality.* New York: Oxford University Press, 1960.

LACAN, JACQUES   *Ecrits: A Selection.* New York: W. W. Norton, 1977.

MACDONALD, DWIGHT   *On Movies.* New York: Berkley Publishing Corp., 1971.

MAST, GERALD   *Film/Cinema/Movie.* New York: Harper & Row, 1977.

METZ, CHRISTIAN   *Film Language: A Semiotics of the Cinema.* Translated by Michael Taylor. New York: Oxford University Press, 1974.

———————   *Language and Cinema.* Translated by Donna Jean Umiker-Sebeok. The Hague: Mouton, 1974.

———————   *The Imaginary Signifier: Psychoanalysis and the Cinema.* Translated by Ben Brewster, Alfred Guzzetti, Celia Britton, and Annwyl Williams. Bloomington, Ind.: Indiana University Press, 1981.

MURRAY, EDWARD   *Nine American Film Critics: A Study of Theory and Practice.* New York: Ungar, 1975.

NICHOLS, BILL *Ideology and the Image.* Bloomington, Ind.: Indiana University Press, 1981.

_____, ed. *Movies and Methods.* Berkeley, Calif.: University of California Press, 1976.

PERKINS, V. F. *Film as Film.* New York: Penguin Books, 1972.

ROSEN, MARJORIE *Popcorn Venus: Women, Movies, and the American Dream.* New York: Coward, McCann & Geoghegan, 1973.

RUSSO, VITO *The Celluloid Closet: Homosexuality in the Movies.* New York: Harper & Row, 1981.

SARRIS, ANDREW *The American Cinema: Directors and Directions, 1929–1968.* New York: E. P. Dutton, 1968.

_____ *Confessions of a Cultist.* New York: Simon & Schuster, 1971.

SIMON, JOHN *Private Screenings.* New York: Berkley Publishing Corp., 1971.

TUDOR, ANDREW *Theories of Film.* London: Secker & Warburg, 1974.

WARSHOW, ROBERT *The Immediate Experience.* New York: Doubleday, 1964.

WOLLEN, PETER *Signs and Meaning in the Cinema.* Bloomington, Ind.: Indiana University Press, 1972.

WORKS OF GENERAL INTEREST

BORDWELL, DAVID, and KRISTIN THOMPSON *Film Art: An Introduction.* Reading, Mass.: Addison-Wesley, 1979.

DICK, BERNARD F. *Anatomy of Film.* New York: St. Martin's Press, 1978.

EIDSVIK, CHARLES *Cineliteracy: Film Among the Arts.* New York: Random House, 1978.

FELL, JOHN L. *Film: An Introduction.* New York: Praeger, 1975.

GIANNETTI, LOUIS *Understanding Movies,* 3rd ed. Englewood Cliffs, N.J.: Prentice-Hall, 1982.

LINDGREN, ERNEST *The Arts of the Film.* New York: Macmillan, 1948.

MONACO, JAMES *How to Read a Film: The Art, Technology, Language, History, and Theory of Film and Media,* rev. ed. New York: Oxford University Press, 1981.

SHARFF, STEFAN *The Elements of Cinema: Toward a Theory of Cinesthetic Impact.* New York: Columbia University Press, 1982.

SOBCHACK, THOMAS, and VIVIAN C. SOBCHACK *An Introduction to Film.* Boston: Little, Brown & Co., 1980.

TALBOT, DANIEL, ed. *Film: An Anthology.* New York: Simon & Schuster, 1959.

WEAD, GEORGE, AND GEORGE LELLIS *Film: Form and Function.* Boston: Houghton Mifflin Co., 1981.

REFERENCES

ACETO, VINCENT J., JANE GRAVES, and FRED SILVA *Film Literature Index.* Albany, N.Y.: Filmdex.

BATTY, LINDA *Retrospective Guide to Film Periodicals, 1930–1971.* New York: R. R. Bowker, 1971.

BAWDEN, LIZ-ANNE, ed. *The Oxford Companion to Film.* New York: Oxford University Press, 1976.

BEAVER, FRANK E. *Dictionary of Film Terms.* New York: McGraw-Hill, 1983.

BOWLES, STEPHEN, ed. *Index to Critical Film Reviews in British and American Film Periodicals, 1930–1972.* New York: Burt Franklin, 1975.

BUKALSKI, PETER J. *Film Research: A Critical Bibliography with Annotations and Essays.* Boston: G. K. Hall, 1972.

CAWKWELL, TIM, and JOHN SMITH, eds. *The World Encyclopedia of Film.* New York: A&W Visual Library, 1972.

ELLIS, JACK C., CHARLES DERRY, and SHARON KERN, eds. *The Film Book Bibliography, 1940–1975.* Metuchen, N.J.: Scarecrow Press, 1979.

ENSER, A. G. S., ed. *Filmed Books and Plays: 1928–1974.* New York: Academic Press, 1974.

FEINBERG, COBBETT *Reel Facts: The Movie Book of Records.* New York: Vintage Books, 1978.

GERLACH, JOHN C., and LANA GERLACH, eds. *The Critical Index: A Bibliography of Articles on Film in English, 1946–1973.* New York: Teachers College Press, 1974.

GIFFORD, DENIS *The British Film Catalogue, 1895–1970: A Reference Guide,* 2 vols. New York: McGraw-Hill, 1973.

GOTTESMAN, RONALD, and HARRY M. GEDULD *Guidebook to Film: An Eleven-in-One Reference.* New York: Holt, Rinehart & Winston, 1972.

GRAHAM, PETER, ed. *Dictionary of the Cinema.* London: Tantivy Press, 1964.

HALLIWELL, LESLIE *The Filmgoer's Companion,* 7th ed. New York: Avon Books, 1978.

———— *Halliwell's Film Guide: A Survey of 8,000 English-Language Movies.* London: Granada Publishing, 1977.

International Index to Film Periodicals (FIAF). New York: R. R. Bowker, 1972–.

KATZ, EPHRAIM   *The Film Encyclopedia.* New York: Thomas Y. Crowell, 1979.

KRAFSUR, RICHARD, ed.   *The American Film Institute Catalogue of Motion Pictures Produced in the U.S.: Feature Films 1961–1970.* New York: R. R. Bowker, 1976.

LEONARD, HAROLD, ed.   *The Film Index: A Bibliography,* Vol. 1: *The Film as Art.* New York: Arno Press, 1966.

MacCANN, RICHARD DYER, and EDWARD PERRY, eds.   *The New Film Index: A Bibliography of Magazine Articles in English, 1930–1970.* New York: E. P. Dutton, 1975.

MANCHEL, FRANK   *Film Study: A Resource Guide.* Rutherford, N.J.: Fairleigh Dickinson University Press, 1973.

MANVELL, ROGER, and LEWIS JACOBS, eds.   *International Encyclopedia of Film.* New York: Crown Publishers, 1972.

MERCER, JOHN   *Glossary of Film Terms.* University Film Association Monograph No. 2, Summer 1978.

MICHAEL, PAUL, ed.   *The American Movies Reference Book: The Sound Era.* Englewood Cliffs, N.J.: Prentice-Hall, 1969.

MONACO, JAMES, and SUSAN SCHENKER, eds.   *Books About Film: A Bibliographical Checklist,* 3rd ed. New York: Zoetrope, 1976.

MUNDEN, KENNETH W., ed.   *The American Film Institute Catalogue of Motion Pictures Produced in the U.S.: Feature Films 1921–1930,* 2 vols. New York: R. R. Bowker, 1971.

New York Times Film Reviews 1913–1968, 6 vols. New York: New York Times and Arno Press, 1970.

REHRAUER, GEORGE   *The Macmillan Film Bibliography: A Critical Guide to the Literature of the Motion Picture.* New York: Macmillan, 1982.

ROUD, RICHARD, ed.   *A Critical Dictionary of the Cinema.* New York: Viking Press, 1972.

SADOUL, GEORGES   *Dictionary of Film Makers.* Translated and edited by Peter Morris. Berkeley, Calif.: University of California Press, 1972.

————   *Dictionary of Films.* Translated and edited by Peter Morris. Berkeley, Calif.: University of California Press, 1972.

SCHUSTER, MEL   *Motion Picture Directors: A Bibliography of Magazine and Periodical Articles, 1900–1969.* Metuchen, N.J.: Scarecrow Press, 1973.

THOMSON, DAVID   *A Biographical Dictionary of Film.* New York: Morrow, 1976.

INDEX

FILM

GENERAL

French New Wave, 96–97, 111–12, 118, 121, 172, 213, 247, 263
Freud, Sigmund, 254
Freund, Karl, 56
Fridays (TV program), 202
Friedkin, William, 51, 150, 184
Fuller, Samuel, 261
Futurism, 216, 234, 249

Gance, Abel, 16, 31, 45, 47, 53 (*see also* French avant-garde cinema)
Gangster genre, 7, 116, 139–46 *passim*, 157, 160, 164–65, 213, 263, 265
Garbo, Greta, 76
Garfunkel, Art, 81
Garland, Judy, 151
Garnett, Tay, 171
Gazzo, M. V., 185
Genet, Jean, 184
German expressionism, 36–37, 92–93, 121, 149, 247, 249, 263, 265
Gershe, Leonard, 184
Gessner, Peter, 229–30
Gestalt psychology, 246
Gibson, William, 185
"Gift of the Magi, The." (short story), 169
Gish, Dorothy and Lillian, 198
Glass Menagerie, The (play), 197–98
Glenville, Peter, 46, 133, 184
Godard, Jean-Luc, 96, 119, 144, 244 (*see also* French New Wave)
  and actors, 111–12
  and *Alphaville*, 38, 144
  and *Breathless*, 97, 140, 207, 263, 265
  as *Cahiers du Cinema* critic, 96, 260
  and *Weekend*, 54
Goethe, Johann Wolfgang von, 169, 171
Gould, Elliott, 209
Grant, Cary, 70
Gratuitous social commentary in film, 159–60
Great Expectations (novel), 11
Green, F. L., 171
Greene, Graham, 83
Grey, Joel, 152
Grieg, Edvard, 82
Grierson, John, 212, 217–19, 220, 223, 231, 247
Griffith, David Wark, 5, 8, 47, 116, 173, 233, 246, 247
  and actors, 110
  and *The Adventures of Dollie*, 121
  and *America*, 134, 148, 162
  and Billy Bitzer, 33
  and Biograph Co., 60–61
  and *The Birth of a Nation*, 5, 53, 63–64, 66, 134, 148, 162
  and *Broken Blossoms*, 141
  camera movement in films, 53
  close-ups in films, 20
  color in films, 42–43, 44
  and *A Corner in Wheat*, 158, 169
  editing in films, 61, 63–64, 66, 124–25, 179, 246, 252
  frame experiments, 16, 31, 36
  and "historical facsimiles," 5
  influence on Russian filmmakers, 61, 66, 173, 246, 251–52
  and *Intolerance*, 42–43, 116, 124–25, 126, 127, 129, 148, 186, 252
  and *Leatherstocking*, 169
  lighting in films, 98
  and *Lonely Villa*, 66
  and *The Musketeers of Pig Alley*, 161, 263
  and *The Necklace*, 169
  and *Orphans of the Storm*, 148

and *Pippa Passes*, 169
and *The Resurrection*, 169
and *The Sacrifice*, 169
Grimm Brothers, 169
Grubb, Davis, 171
Guazzoni, Enrico, 94
Gulf & Western, 168
Guthrie, Tyrone, 193

Haanstra, Bert, 221
Hall, Juanita, 150
Hallmark Hall of Fame, 208
Hamer, Robert, 170
Hammer Studios, 149
Hammid, Alexander, 221, 235
Hanna-Barbera, 153 (*see also* Animation)
Hardison, O. B., 156
Harris, Elmer, 185
Harris, Richard, 154
Hart, Moss, 185, 186
Hawks, Howard, 170, 247, 261
Hawthorne, Nathaniel, 169
Haycox, Ernest, 171
Hayden, Sterling, 27
Hecht, Ben, 171
Hedren, Tippi, 45
Hegel, Georg, 61
Heidegger, Martin, 256
Hellman, Lillian, 184, 186
Hemmings, David, 88
Henry, O., 169
Henry (Prince of Prussia), 2
Hepburn, Audrey, 40
Hepworth, Cecil, 60
Herrmann, Bernard, 85–86
Higham, Charles, 209–10
Hill, George Roy, 44, 52, 69, 140, 171
Hill, Walter, 103–04
Hiller, Arthur, 185
Hitchcock, Alfred, 49, 74, 107, 117, 120, 138, 155, 156–57, 189, 247, 261, 269
  and *Blackmail*, 87, 184
  camera angles in films, 22, 27, 29–30, 32
  color in films, 45
  and *Dial M for Murder*, 184
  editing in films, 19, 70–71, 125
  and *Family Plot*, 27, 107
  and *Frenzy*, 22, 29–30, 55, 56, 84, 86, 107, 155, 156, 179
  and *The Lady Vanishes*, 86, 156
  lighting in films, 39, 40–41
  "MacGuffin," 86, 118
  and *Marnie*, 45, 156
  metaphors in films, 179
  mobile camerawork, 19, 22, 55, 56
  and *North by Northwest*, 70–71, 107, 117, 155, 156
  and *Notorious*, 22
  and *Number Seventeen*, 117
  and *Psycho*, 40–41, 171, 210
  and *Rear Window*, 125
  and *Rebecca*, 171
  and *Rope*, 19
  settings in films, 56, 107, 117, 155
  sound in films, 76, 84, 86, 87, 89, 156
  and *Spellbound*, 156, 163, 171
  and *Strangers on a Train*, 32, 39, 179
  and suspense, 29–30, 32, 56, 66, 117, 125
  and *The 39 Steps*, 32, 86, 156–57
  and *The Wrong Man*, 156
  and *To Catch a Thief*, 156
  "Wrong Man" theme, 156

Hitler, Adolf, 27–28, 140, 152, 223, 227, 270
Hoberman, Jim, 243–244
Hoffman, Dustin, 26, 84, 111
Hollander, Alex, 169
Holocaust (TV program), 203, 228
Home Box Office, 204
Homer, 117
Hope, Anthony, 169
Hopper, Dennis, 54, 73, 163
Horniman, Roy, 170
Horror genre, 7, 120, 146–50 *passim*, 180, 263, 264
House of Dr. Edwards, The (novel), 171
Houston, Penelope, 163
Howard, Leslie, 70, 185
Howe, James Wong, 33, 35
How Green Was My Valley (novel), 176
Hugo, Victor, 169–72 *passim*
Humphrey, Hubert H., 225
Hunchback of Notre Dame, The (novel), 171
Hurt, William, 40, 149
Huston, John, 169, 171, 185

"Icebox," definition, 75
I, Claudius (TV program), 203
Ike (TV program), 228
I Love Lucy (TV program), 203
"In a Grove" (short story), 172
Ince, Thomas, 5, 7, 98, 161, 169, 247
Incidental music, definition, 82
Incidental social commentary in film, 159
Independent, The, 258
Ionesco, Eugene, 184, 196
Iris, definition, 61
Ironside (TV program), 203
Irving, Washington, 183
Irwin, May, 183
"Israel Rank" (literary work), 170
Italian neorealism, 37, 95–96, 102, 110, 118, 121, 130–31, 158, 213, 247, 252, 263, 265
Ivens, Joris, 52, 221

Jackson, Charles, 170
Jacobs, Lewis, 225
Jancsó, Miklós, 19, 190
Jannings, Emil, 110
Jefferson, Joseph, 183
Jesus Christ, 124, 235, 255
Johnson, Lyndon B., 230
Johnson, Nunnally, 170
Jones, James, 170
Joyce, James, 67, 179

Kael, Pauline, 194, 260–62
Kafka, Franz, 164
Kanfer, Stefan, 201
Kanin, Fay, 172
Kanin, Garson, 184
Kanin, Michael, 172
Karas, Anton, 83
Karloff, Boris, 141
Kasdan, Lawrence, 40
Katselas, Milton, 184
Kauffmann, Stanley, 193
Kaufman, George S., 185, 186
Kazan, Elia, 111, 171, 185
Keaton, Buster, 76, 109, 237–38
Keighley, William, 185
Keller, Helen, 86
Kelly, Gene, 82, 151
Kennedy, John F., 225, 229

Kenward, A. R., 184
Kerensky, Alexander, 68
Keystone Kops, 5–6, 51, 92, 101
King, Henry, 185
King, Stephen, 270
Kingsley, Sidney, 184
"Kino-Glaz" theory (Vertov), 216–17
Kinugasa, Teinosuke, 44
"Kitchen Sink" realism, 96, 247
Knot's Landing (TV program), 203
Knott, Frederick, 184, 185
Koff, David, 226 (*see also Cinéma vérité*)
Koppel, Barbara, 226 (*see also Cinéma vérité*)
Korean War on film, 219
Koster, Henry, 185
Kovacs, Laszlo, 35, 265
Kracauer, Siegfried:
    on actors, 192
    on *The Cabinet of Dr. Caligari*, 39, 140, 270
    on chases, 127, 139
    on close-ups, 21, 222
    on dance, 139
    on documentaries, 212, 220, 227, 251
    on film stories, 122, 227, 251
    on Germany and its films, 140, 270
    on movement, 47, 52, 250
    on the musical genre, 152
    as realist theorist, 247, 249–51
    on "redemption of physical reality," 129, 148, 250, 251
    on sleuthing, 154
    on "special modes of reality," 132, 148
    on television, 201
Kraft Theater (TV program), 208
Kramer, Stanley, 84–85, 189
Kubelka, Peter, 240
Kubrick, Stanley, 247
    and *Barry Lyndon*, 170, 192
    camera angles in films, 27
    and *A Clockwork Orange*, 44, 51, 85, 132
    color in films, 44
    and *Dr. Strangelove*, 27, 57, 85, 161, 162, 189
    editing in films, 69
    handheld camerawork, 57
    and *Lolita*, 170
    music in films, 51, 85
    and *Paths in Glory*, 69
    settings in films, 192
    and *The Shining*, 163
    and *2001: A Space Odyssey*, 62, 144, 168, 171
Kuchar, George, 236
Kurosawa, Akira:
    and *Dersu Uzala, the Hunter*, 135
    mobile camerawork, 54
    and *Rashomon*, 54, 118, 133, 172
    on sound, 83–84
    and *Throne of Blood*, 193–94
Kurys, Diane, 268

Lacan, Jacques, 254
Ladd, Alan, 113
Lagerlof, Selma, 107
Lang, Fritz (*see also* German expressionism):
    and *M*, 82, 86, 87, 155, 156
    and *Metropolis*, 93, 98, 144, 145
    sound in films, 76, 82, 86, 87, 156
    and Ufa, 93
Langley, Noel, 185
Laszlo, Andrew, 104
Laughton, Charles, 171, 241
Lawson, John Howard, 123, 176, 181–82